A Dictionary of World Mythology

A DICTIONARY OF
WORLD
MYTHOLOGY

ARTHUR COTTERELL

G. P. Putnam's Sons, New York

First American Edition 1980

© Arthur Cotterell 1979

Designed by Harold Bartram

Frontispiece: A manuscript illustration of Merlin and Arthur with Guinevere looking on

Cotterell, Arthur.
  A dictionary of World Mythology.

  Bibliography: p.
  Includes index.
  1. Mythology—Dictionaries. I. Title.
BL303.C66   291.1'3   79-65889
ISBN 0-399-12464-0

Printed in the United States of America

Contents

In memory of my father
Percy Cotterell
who in his own way knew

INTRODUCTION

The Meaning of Myth

'I am Nature,' declared the great goddess, 'the universal Mother, mistress of all the elements, primordial child of time, sovereign of all things spiritual, queen of the dead, queen also of the immortals, the single manifestation of all gods and goddesses that are. My nod governs the shining heights of Heaven, the wholesome sea-breezes, the lamentable silences of the world below. Though I am worshipped in many aspects, known by countless names, and propitiated with all manner of different rites, yet the whole round earth venerates me.' In these terms Isis reveals herself to Lucius Apuleius, her devotee, at the end of the ordeal described allegorically in his novel, *The Golden Ass*, which was written during the second century. Her pity was aroused and she had come to his aid, just as she might intervene on behalf of those who gave her worship in Phrygia, Greece, Ethiopia, or the Orient. It was insignificant that only 'the Egyptians, who excel in all kind of ancient learning . . . call me by my correct name, Queen Isis'.

The great goddess claimed to be universal. The truth of her revelation was the same for each and all, everywhere. No matter the specific form it might take at Pessinus or Eleusis, the recipient was afforded a glimpse in unspeakable intimacy into hidden depths. The agony of the quest had been superseded by the joy of vision. This notion of striking disclosure, as expressed here in the doctrine of a Greco-Roman mystery religion, can well stand as a description of the supreme quality of myth. For the greatest mythical tales make a direct appeal to the unconscious; they work through intuition. Their power is the flash of insight that illuminates the narrowness of matter-of-fact explanation and compels the intellect to acknowledge the need for a more adequate understanding. Myths possess an intensity of meaning that is akin to poetry.

The Origin of Myths

Recent interest in mythology indicates a general recognition of the power of these poetical tales. But there is still a fair measure of disagreement as to what is the strength of myths. For Plato, the first known user of the term, *mythologia* meant no more than the telling of stories which usually contained legendary figures. The main characters were not always gods, since the Greeks had an impressive number of heroes: Hercules, Jason, and Theseus, to name the most famous. Hercules may have undertaken his twelve labours because of goddess Hera's animosity, but his superhuman exploits fall short of true divinity. He remains the archetype of the indomitable man. Moreover, the theory that myths derived from rituals, which is the corollary of the idea that myths are about gods, is open to question even in West Asian tradition, the main source of the supposed evidence. Gilgamesh, the semi-divine king of the Babylonian epic, is obsessed with his own mortality. Like Hercules, the son of a deity and a mortal, he was certainly treated for the most part as a man and not a god.

Another theory of origin is that folklore and mythology are almost indistinguish-

The mother goddess Isis suckling her son Horus

able. An Eskimo said: 'Our tales are men's experiences, and the things one hears of are not always lovely things. . . . When I narrate legends, it is not I who speak, it is the wisdom of our forefathers, speaking through me.' Myths are seen as popular tales reworked by poets so as to absorb elements of religious belief. Yet it would be surprising if a sacred legend contained no features drawn from life; the annoyance of the Babylonian gods at the noise made by men 'below stairs' was even cited as the cause of the flood. Although the inhabitants of heaven were pleased that mankind had relieved them of the burden of work, they could not endure the noise and din. So they sent cosmic disaster in the form of water. The difference between a folktale and a myth lies in such an emphasis on the supernatural: it also reflects a preoccupation with the ultimate problems of existence, as opposed to an interest in narrative. The antithesis is Coyote, the trickster-god of North American Indian mythology, and his European cousin of medieval folklore, Reynard the Fox.

Experience of life among the Trobriand islanders of Melanesia led Bronislaw Malinowski (1884–1942) to the view that myth was neither primarily symbolic nor aetiological. He wrote: 'The myth in a primitive society, that is in its original living form, is not a mere tale told but a reality lived . . . the assertion of an original, greater, more important reality through which the present life, fate and work of mankind are governed. . . .' It was the recognition of the link between past and present established by myth in daily life. It was also a rejection of the absolute argument of the psychoanalysts, who contended that the creative images within the psyche were to be attributed to sexual repression. Sigmund Freud's (1856–1939) theory of the Oedipus complex as the 'primordial source . . . the *fons et origo* of everything', wrote Malinowski, 'I cannot conceive of . . . as the unique source of culture, of organization and belief.' Carl Jung (1876–1961), the other colossus of psychoanalysis, broke with Freud over this theory, too. He became convinced that the individual possessed both a personal unconscious and a collective unconscious; the former was filled with material peculiar to the individual, whereas the latter housed the common mental inheritance of mankind—the archetypes, or primordial images, which 'bring into our ephemeral consciousness an unknown psychic life belonging to a remote past. This psychic life,' Jung suggested, 'is the mind of our ancient ancestors, the way in which they conceived of life and the world, of gods and human beings.'

The Problem of Prehistory
Since the fantasies of the collective unconscious stem from the actual experiences of our remote ancestors, the men who lived at least a million years ago, the development of prehistory as a serious field of study is of considerable importance to the mythologer; but there are real dangers of projecting on to the sparse data available the ideas we have formed from known mythologies. Certain facts exist. The precursor of the mother goddess in West Asia and Europe was surely the incarnation of fertility represented by the so-called 'Venus' figurines. These statuettes often show a woman with ballooning breasts, thighs, and buttocks. Their import is plain: the overriding need of a primitive band of hunters and food-gatherers for the repeated fertility of its women. Prehistoric rock-painting gives us another figure, the animal-master. The antlered spirit or sorcerer of the hunt appears on the walls of caves, just as in the ceremonies of present-day aboriginals in Australia his horned counterpart enacts the tribal myths of 'dream

time', the remote period in which the ancestral spirits walked the earth. Lacking in prehistoric art, however, is the emphasis on human sacrifice found in early agricultural societies. The primitive hunters do not seem to have identified human destiny with the vegetable cycle of growth, maturity, decay, death, and resurrection.

No doubt the creative period of myth is set in prehistoric times. But in the civilizations of the first planters—the cities of the Nile, the Euphrates-Tigris valley, and the Indus—there evolved mythologies connected with a priesthood. The Sumerians even looked upon themselves as the property of their gods; they were workers on the divine estate. Here the earliest myths known today were shaped and recorded. Only in the living tradition of Indian mythology can we trace a direct link with this formulative time, since the displacement of the Vedic deities worshipped by the Aryan invaders may have been caused by the resurgence of older beliefs dating from the Indus valley civilization.

The Great Traditions

In the arrangement of this book can be discerned the seven great traditions of world mythology: namely, West Asia, South and Central Asia, East Asia, Europe, America, Africa, and Oceania. Within each of these traditions exist distinct and outstanding mythologies and myths—in West Asia there is Sumerian cosmology and *The Gilgamesh Epic*; in Europe the Greek myths and the cult of Odin; in Oceania Polynesian mythology and the exploits of Maui—but for historical and geographical reasons there is also a degree of internal coherence that can often be ascribed to mutual influence. The impact of Zoroastrian duality on the Judaism, Christianity, and Islam is a case in point. However, two traditions have been particularly seminal: West Asia had a profound influence on Europe, while South and Central Asia penetrated East Asia by means of the Hindu and Buddhist faiths.

In the contemporary situation of India it is possible to appreciate the value of an analogical way of knowing. As Heinrich Zimmer perceptively remarked: 'By an eloquence rather of incident than of word, the mythology of India serves its function as the popular vehicle of the esoteric wisdom of yoga experience and of orthodox religion. An immediate effect is assured, because the tales are not the products of individual experiences and reactions. They are produced, treasured, and controlled by the collective working and thinking of the religious community. They thrive on the ever-renewed assent of successive generations. They are re-fashioned, re-shaped, laden with new meaning, through an anonymous creative process and a collective, intuitive acceptance. They are effective primarily on a subconscious level, touching intuition, feeling, and imagination. Their details impress themselves on the memory, soak down, and shape the deeper stratifications of the psyche. When brooded upon, their significant episodes are capable of revealing various shades of meaning, according to the experiences and life-needs of the individual.'

A fundamental divergence in attitude towards time between Hindu thought and our-selves is evident in the notion of renewable myth. Whereas the Westerner adheres to a linear view of time, with events conceived of as unique phenomena, the Hindu holds that the history of the universe is a natural process in which everything recurs in periodic circles. A far off termination is expected, but this passing away of creation is an astronomical number of years away. Most extreme in their sense of timelessness are the

Odysseus, the endless wayfarer, bound to the mast of his ship so that he could listen to the fatal song of the Sirens; from a fifth-century BC Greek vase

Jains, whose ancient Indian belief has room for neither the creation nor the destruction of the universe. The Greeks, of course, shared the notion of cyclic time, though never on the vast scale of India.

A certain spaciousness seems to be the mental outlook best suited to the development of mythology. Yet there must always arise individuals with poetic gifts capable of enhancing myths, and to their inspiration we probably owe the fullest expression of mythical themes. Like the trickster hero Maui fishing up islands from the depths of the Pacific Ocean, these poets in a 'fine frenzy' would have dangled their own hooks into the creative recesses of the unconscious, where repose the archetypes. Drugs were used to stimulate the visionary faculty and arouse visions which had earlier been obtained unaided. In the history of mythology the use of stimulants usually occurs when the simpler methods no longer suffice. Among the North American Indian tribes fasting gave way to peyotl.

Modern Myths

Around historical figures legends have often collected. Where the accretion has been of an intense character, like the tales of the Trojan War, the legendary people were absorbed into the archetypal forms of myth. Odysseus became the endless wayfarer, a dangerous captain to serve. Prophets were soon endowed with miraculous associations. The founder of Sikhism, Nanak Chand (1469–1538), was the marvellous boy who consorted with holy men and angels. He was carried by the latter to the supreme being in order to receive his mission on earth: the proclamation of the unity of god. But the life of this reasonable reformer has nothing of the mythical power enjoyed by the antagonist of St Peter, Simon Magus. Only the earnest prayer of the great evangelist was enough to persuade the Lord to cut short the flying display of the Canaanite sorcerer above the temples of Rome and let Simon fall to the ground so as to 'break his leg in three places'.

This age-old tendency to invest important persons with mythical significance is by no means dead in the modern world. It is interesting to note the so-called 'cult of the individual' in Communist countries. The destruction of Stalin's statue in the Hungarian Uprising of 1956 was a symbolic act; the enraged people of Budapest were rebelling against the archetype of the tyrannical father. In an opposite direction the sorrow felt at the assassination of President Kennedy seven years later passed beyond a sense of either political or personal loss. The cultural-founder hero of a brave new world had disappeared. Mass media of course plays a crucial role in the propagation of legendary events. It exalts and lays low. Yet the images of its own creation are singularly weak: there is a synthetic quality about Superman. Where an individual pop star or an entertainer achieves recognition, the audience is often most conscious of the evanescence of such a career. They pass like comets across an electronic sky. Roland Barthes has pointed out the 'what-goes-without-saying' aspects of modern spectacles, whether it is the alchemical quality of plastic, the cult of foam in detergents, or the mask of the cinema heroine, but this study of contemporary signs is rather an investigation of ritual than of myth. In individual societies the mythical faculty is almost a thing of the past. This book represents an attempt to recover what our ancestors have rated so highly and what our psychoanalysts argue may still be within the unconscious. Even now, as Professor Kerényi has put it: 'Mythology, like the severed head of Orpheus, goes on singing even in death and from afar.'

WEST ASIA

Egypt Sumer Babylon Canaan Asia Minor Persia Arabia

Antiquity belonged to Egypt even in the Ancient World. Visitors to the immense temple of Karnak did not need to calculate the country's past from the number of statues there of high priests, though the Greek traveller and historian Herodotus used this method in the fifth century BC. They could observe everywhere the relics of a once mighty empire—colossal statues, temples, shrines, tombs, pyramids, and cities. They could also sense their intrusion into a religious and social system that stretched back time out of mind to the first settlers of the Nile valley. 'As the Egyptians have a climate peculiar to themselves, and their river is different in its nature from all other rivers,' Herodotus remarked, 'so have they made all their laws and customs of a kind contrary for the most part to those of all other men. Among them, the women buy and sell, the men stay at home and weave; and alone the Egyptians push the woof downwards. Men carry loads on their heads, women on their shoulders. Women relieve themselves standing, men sitting. This they do indoors, and take their food in the streets, giving the reason, that unpleasant things should be hidden from sight, but pleasant things open to the view of all. Whereas no woman is dedicated to the service of any god or goddess, men serve all deities, male or female. Sons are not obliged to support parents but daughters must always do so.'

For many centuries the Egyptians remained undisturbed in their river valley, since the surrounding deserts presented barriers formidable enough to deter foreign invaders. The perception of this natural security is apparent in the distinction they drew between 'the black land and the red land'. Egypt was the black land; other countries were the mountainous, red-earth lands. From the annual inundation of the Nile came the dark silt upon which their agricultural prosperity was founded. 'When the river overflows the countryside,' noted Herodotus, 'the whole of Egypt becomes a sea, and only the towns stick out above the surface of the water, rather like the islands of the Aegean. When this happens, people take boats across the land and not just along the waterways. . . . No men anywhere else gain so much from the soil with so little labour: farmers escape the toil of breaking up the soil with a plough or a hoe; the river rises unaided, irrigates the fields, and then drains away; seeds are broadcast and trodden in by pigs; these animals even thresh the harvested grain.' The Nile dominated the way of life as much as it determined the configuration of the land. The Egyptians thought of the world as being a bank of earth divided in the middle by the Nile and surrounded by water, the Great Circular Ocean. This water was personified by Nun, the first of the gods, the source of the river and rain. Above the earth was the sky, held aloft by four pillars at the corners of the world.

Differences between Upper and Lower Egypt—the narrow valley running nearly 600 miles from the first cataract to Cairo, the site of ancient Memphis, as opposed to the braided streams of the delta, 400 miles wide at the Mediterranean—found expression

Pharaoh Amenophis IV (Akhenaton); the champion of solar worship

in the mythological struggle of Osiris and Horus against Seth as well as the constitution of the state. The pharaoh *was* the god who united the two crowns of Upper and Lower Egypt: while he lived he was Horus, and when dead he was Osiris, king of the departed. Mummification and the cult of the dead were entwined with the Horus-Osiris myths. Unusual, too, in West Asia was the Egyptian preoccupation with the sun. Re, the sun god, according to one tradition, was the first pharaoh, and as Atum was creator of the world. It was said that Atum, either a self-created deity or the child of Nun, emerged from the primeval waters in the form of a hill. Solar worship reached its apotheosis during the short reign of Amenophis IV (1387–1366 BC). This pharaoh, better known as Akhenaton, seems to have rejected the innumerable deities which had been invoked by previous rulers, and concentrated his piety to one god, Aton, or the solar disc.

The divinity of the king was not professed in Mesopotamia, whose river valleys formed the other ancient cradle of civilization in West Asia. The Sumerian monarchs received their authority from the gods, a formula accepted equally by the later Babylonian and Assyrian kings. Kingship 'came down from heaven' and inscriptions maintain that the assembly of the gods chose and invested a monarch. In the third millennium BC, the age of Sumer, the city deity was conceived of as the actual owner of the city, and the temple possessed and worked most of the irrigated land, so that the temporal ruler was rather like a steward managing the god's estates. The temple was the house in which the deity lived, was fed and clothed, and received worshippers. The religious basis of the Sumerian institution of kingship was made explicit at the time of New Year Festival when the people celebrated a holy marriage between the king and the goddess of the city, represented by a priestess. The hymns which accompanied this sacral coupling bear an amazing resemblance to the poetry of the biblical *Song of Songs*. It appears that the king impersonated Dumuzi, the god of fertility, and the priestess became the goddess Inanna: for the city their union ensured prosperity, strength, and concord. During the ascendency of Babylon under an Amorite dynasty, the most famous ruler of which was the great legislator Hammurabi (1728–1686 BC), a change took place in the relationship of temple and throne. Although kingship was still regarded as a divine institution and the person of the ruler different from ordinary mortals, the earlier domination of the temple cult in city life began to diminish sharply, a curtailment of the priesthood that led to the unchallenged terrestrial authority of the Assyrian kings.

The origin of the 'black-headed', as the Sumerians called themselves, is uncertain. Arriving possibly from the East, they settled immediately before 3000 BC a flat desert area, with marshes, adjacent to the Persian Gulf. Their non-Semitic tongue was at first recorded in primitive pictographs, from which using clay as a writing material and a reed stylus to impress wedge-shaped signs they developed cuneiform, thereafter the script of both Sumerian and Semitic languages. In time the 'black-headed' people were swamped by Semites, who moved down the Euphrates valley in successive waves, but their contribution to ancient Mesopotamian culture was profound, especially in mythology and religion. Even after the rise of Babylon the transmission of ideas was uninterrupted as it was the practice to have Sumerian religious texts with an interlinear Akkadian translation that would be understood by the Semitic conquerors.

The cosmology of Sumer reflected the independence of this urban civilization from rainfall. Agriculture flourished on river water, spread by irrigation, and this sweet

The ziggurat at Ur, built around 2000 BC

water was believed to come from a huge subterranean reservoir named Abzu. This environmental factor may have been responsible for the largely chthonic character of Sumerian religion, which placed emphasis on the natural forces of the earth rather than the celestial powers of heaven, the sky, moon, and stars, so evident in Semitic belief. The land was the domain of Enlil, city god of Nippur, and the most powerful deity of the Sumerian pantheon. In striking contrast to Egyptian mythology, the creation of mankind was seen as a deliberate act of the gods, harassed by the necessity of obtaining their daily bread. Likewise the foundation of cities was the result of divine decree: they were built round the ziggurrats, gigantic artificial mounds of sun-dried bricks, on whose terraces dwelt the resident deities. The Babylonian creation epic, known from its first words 'When on high' as *Enuma Elish*, made service of the gods the reason for the appearance of mankind, too. In return the gods ensured the renewal of the world each day. As in Egypt, where the goddess Maat personified the correct balance of equilibrium of the universe, the early settlers of Mesopotamia were preoccupied with the ordering of the world. Another theme, however, darkens the mythology of Sumer and Babylon, and this is the notion of a titanic struggle against evil powers. Inanna has to struggle against the mountain god Ebeh, Gilgamesh was pitted against the monster Huwawa in the cedar wood, and Marduk made the universe out of the body of Tiamat, the appalling she-dragon of the watery chaos.

In the Assyrio-Babylonian pantheon the Sumerian god Enlil, known either by the same name or as Ellil, underwent a rather sinister transformation. The terrifying aspect of this god's authority over the atmosphere received emphasis; he was 'the wild ox', the hurricane, and the author of the flood sent to destroy mankind. Unlike the isolated Nile civilization, the historical experience of the inhabitants of Tigris-Euphrates valley was stormy and full of changes. Foreign invasions and internal conflicts combined with the uneven flow of its great rivers to mould a mythological outlook that found significance in·cosmic struggle as much as the divine ordering of the universe. Yet the conception of a cosmic battle against maleficent forces or monstrous beings in Assyrio-Babylonian legend paled before the contemporary Persian belief in the strict dualism of good and evil, light and dark, angels and devils. In the Iranian uplands the prophet Zarathustra, or Zoroaster (c. 628–551 BC), was casting aside the more usual mythological interpretation of good and evil as effects proceeding from a unique source of being that transcends and reconciles all opposites. This singular rethinking of myth affected not only the Persians, but also the inhabitants of Mesopotamia and Canaan. When in 539 BC Babylon fell to Cyrus, West Asia was incorporated into the Persian Empire.

Zoroaster's doctrine of rewards and punishments, of heavenly bliss and infernal woe allotted to good and evil men in another life beyond the grave had a direct influence on Judeo-Christian eschatology. The exiled Hebrews in Babylon found a kindred monotheistic creed in Persian religion, and one of their own prophets, Isaiah, declared openly that Cyrus as their liberator was Yahweh's anointed. The old idea of the nether world, Sheol, a shadowy abode for all the dead, gave place to a system of dividing the sheep from the goats. 'Many of them that sleep in the dust of the earth,' said Daniel, 'shall awake, some to everlasting life, and some to shame and everlasting contempt.' Of the Zoroastrian struggle between good and evil, personified by the twin-spirits Spenta Mainya and Angra Mainya, later transformed into Ormuzd and Ahriman, an exact parallel has been discovered in the Dead Sea scrolls too. According to the *Manual of Discipline*, Yahweh 'created man to have dominion over the world and made for him two spirits, that he might walk by them until the appointed time of his visitation; they are spirits of truth and of error.'

Persia was the name used by the Greeks. The followers of Zoroaster were Aryans, and the word Iran, formed from an earlier root, simply means 'the home of the Aryans'. The Persians, therefore, had much in common with the Aryan invaders of India—close linguistic ties as well as a similar pantheon—but history took them into the Euphrates valley and the teachings of their prophet, who probably lived in Chorasmia, were destined to impact upon West Asian mythology. The Zoroastrian faith hardly exists today. Its last period of ascendancy in Persia occurred during the Sassanian Empire (226–652), which went down before Moslem arms. Only the Parsees, a tiny group of exiles living around Bombay, preserve what was once a great religious tradition.

About the mythology of Canaan, the land situated between the civilizations of Egypt and Mesopotamia, there were only a few references in classical authors to eke out the

partisan account given in the *Old Testament* prior to the discovery of clay tablets in 1929 at Ras Shamra, the ancient city of Ugarit. The Arab peasant who stumbled upon its necropolis indirectly caused a revolution in our thinking about the West Semites. The tablets subsequently unearthed by archaeologists were impressed with a previously unknown cuneiform script of an archaic Canaanite language, and when deciphered they gave a picture of the religion of prosperous Ugarit about 1400 BC. Although this represents a very important addition to our knowledge of ancient Canaan, much more than a mere background to the better recorded Hebrew tradition, it remains the case that we have little detail of the myths belonging to the Aramaean peoples of Syria and the Nabataeans to the east of the Dead Sea.

The name Canaan derived from a shellfish famous for the dye it produced. The Phoenicians living in the coastal cities of Tyre, Sidon, and Byblos, or in their colonies dotted around the eastern Mediterranean, called themselves Canaanites. It was the Romans who introduced Poeni to distinguish the colonists at Carthage from the inhabitants of the motherland. Few sharp cultural divisions existed in Canaan. Even Israel, the supremely religious nation of West Asia, had a composite population, and the Hebrews were certainly not the only ones in the exodus from Egypt. Those who followed Joshua in his conquest of Palestine sometime after 1300 BC were assorted tribesmen bound together by their wanderings in Sinai—the strong influence of the Arabian desert could be discerned in their social solidarity.

The Canaanite myths, known through the Ras Shamra tablets, are characterized by their interest in fertility and the theme of the disappearing fertility god. But they also reveal in the nature of the highest deity, El, a close parallel to Yahweh, the god of Israel. El was the god before all others. He ruled as king 'at the source of the rivers,' which recalls the biblical Eden where a river went out 'to water the garden; and from thence it was parted, and became into four heads', the rivers that watered the world. El had decisive authority regarding both men and gods; he exercised a kind of detached omnipotence. According to one text, he 'is great and wise, and his grey hairs instruct him'. It was the singular achievement of the Hebrews to perfect the West Asian tendency towards monotheism. 'The Lord our God, the Lord is one.' While various arguments have been put forward to explain this development, the different stages of Hebrew consciousness are hard to distinguish. Was Abraham a monotheist? He hailed from Ur, whose city god Sin was credited with the determination of destiny. Was the experience of Moses crucial? In Egypt he would have been aware of Akhenaton's attempt at religious reform. Or were the Prophets, faced by the brute force of Assyria, the inventors of a divine plan for Israel? Whatever the answer, and a consensus is hardly to be expected, there is no doubt that we encounter a distinct mode of thought when the Hebrews address themselves to the question of divine omnipotence and omniscience. Take the complaint of Jonah. Having travelled to Nineveh at divine behest, via the stomach of a whale, and bravely raised his voice against the evil done there, Jonah was angered that the repentant were to be forgiven. Thus spoke Yahweh: 'And should I not spare Nineveh, that great city, wherein are more than sixscore thousand persons that cannot discern between their right hand from their left hand; and also much cattle?' Though Israel had a special relation with Yahweh, notice was being given that the chosen people could neither monopolize him as a national deity nor could they expect to comprehend how he swung the scythe of destiny. After all, it was but part of his plan for all mankind.

Yahweh, awful in holiness, terrible in righteousness, was an exclusive figure, his cult unconducive to epic stories including other gods. The edict outlawing graven images was a specific rejection of the temple ceremonies of other West Asian religions. 'For the Lord thy God is a jealous God.' While the Hebrews absorbed elements from the mythology of their neighbours, they used the symbols for their own vision. The strong perception of a single deity, an intimation doubtless strengthened in the centuries they wandered the northern borders of the Arabian desert, withstood settlement in Canaan, where an evolved urban civilization already flourished. Out of this tradition came Christianity and Islam, the other great monotheistic religions of the world.

In *Revelation* and the apocryphal gospels there is evident a continuity with the non-canonical books of late Hebrew writers, the pseudonymous Enoch or Baruch. Apocalypse for Christian converts was encouraged by the idea of the Second Coming, while the disastrous revolts against Roman authority in Palestine seemed to confirm the running down of the world. Exasperated beyond measure, the Emperor Hadrian in 135 built on the site of ruined Jerusalem the Roman colony Aelia Capitolina, in which only non-Jews were allowed to live. Yet the heroes of early Christian legend are the saints or their personal antagonists: St Antony ousted the Devil from his desert abode, and St Peter cut short the aerial acrobatics of Simon Magus, 'the father of heretics'. The elaboration of hagiography was to be a phenomenon of the Middle Ages and belonged to the European tradition of mythology, which after the conversion of the Emperor Constantine in 312 became progressively Christian.

'The temptation of St Antony' by Hieronymous Bosch

Three centuries later the belief of Jews and Christians in a Last Judgement struck a chord in Mohammed, the prophet of Islam. About 610 this Arab merchant began to see visions during his walks among the forbidding hill-tops north of Mecca. He was visited by Gabriel, 'the spirit of holiness', and commanded to proclaim that 'there is no God but Allah'. Legend also tells us that on a certain night the Prophet was conducted through the air, riding on the back of the winged steed Burak, first to Jerusalem and then up through the seven heavens, in which he met the patriarchs, Adam and Jesus, to the throne of Allah, where the mysteries of the divinity were revealed to him. Although Mohammed drew on other West Asian traditions, the god upon whom he called was unmistakably an Arabian one, whose scriptures were both direct and straightforward. They sought to replace divisive tribal loyalties with inclusive membership of a universal way of life. There was little room for myth. Within twenty years, Mohammed established himself as the leading chieftain of Arabia, but to his followers was given the task of world conquest. Not only did the peoples of West Asia pass under Islamic control, thereby ending a cultural heritage reaching back to the ancient Sumerians, but even more it seemed that Arab armies pushed outwards in every direction. While Europe gained in 732 a respite through the victory of Frankish cavalry at the Battle of Tours, an engagement with soldiers of the powerful T'ang Empire on the Talas river in 751 wrestled Central Asia from the Chinese sphere of influence. The region ceased to be Buddhist and was added to the Moslem world.

Finally, a word needs to be said about Asia Minor. The Hittites, a people of Indo-European descent, settled on the high tableland north of the Taurus mountains before the eighteenth century BC. Magnetized by the affluent civilizations to the south, their kings pushed expeditionary forces over this formidable range, with mixed success in the field. At Kadesh in 1300 BC Hittite chariotry under the direction of King Muwatallis almost routed the Egyptian army of Ramesses II. The Pharaoh claimed a victory, but the Hittite ascendancy in Syria was maintained. The result of southern expansion was the import of religious ideas, though the Hurrian state of Mitanni probably acted as an intermediary. To the weather god of 'the Land of Hatti', the name for the Hittite homeland, were added Hurrian deities so that a distinct pantheon evolved. Related to the inhabitants of the Caucasus mountains, the Hurrians had adopted Mesopotamian beliefs and exercised a powerful, if short-lived, influence over Syria and the upper reaches of the Euphrates. In 1370 BC the Hittites sacked Wassukkani, the capital of Mitanni, but King Suppilulimas, who led this successful campaign, may have been himself part Hurrian. The mythology of Asia Minor, whether Hurrian, Hittite, or Phrygian, turned on the missing fertility god.

Adapa

Son of Ea and Sumerian king of Eridu. He was regarded as the first man, sage but not immortal. Whereas Adam only named the beasts and fowl, the Akkadian myth credits Adapa with the invention of speech. On a fishing expedition in the Persian Gulf he was buffeted by the south wind, but his curse was powerful enough to break its wings. When Anu summoned the culprit to heaven, Ea dressed his son in sackcloth and told him to partake of no food offered to him there. Greeted by Tammuz, Adapa informed the dying god that he mourned his absence from earth, a sentiment which was well received. His frank admission of guilt also appeased Anu, who offered him the 'food of life' and the 'water of life'. Adapa declined and went back to Eridu.

Another legend relates his wrath at Ea: he

discovered that his father's advice was intended to deny him immortality. Like the fallen Adam, he learned that henceforth disease and death must be the lot of mankind.

Adonis

Derived from the Canaanite title, *adon* meaning lord. The Greeks adopted the fertility cult associated with Adonis, who was killed by a wild boar—for the Syrians a sacred animal. His most important temples were at Byblos and Paphos. According to the Greeks the god was loved by Aphrodite and Persephone, the goddess of the land of the dead. In Byblos the temple of Astarte celebrated the annual death and resurrection of Adonis. His reappearance on earth was marked by the blooming of the red anemone.

Ahriman

The principle of evil in Persian mythology. As Angra Mainya, 'the destructive spirit', who first introduced death into the world, he led the forces of evil against the host of Spenta Mainya, 'the holy spirit', who assisted Ahura Mazdah, 'the wise lord'—the final victor of the cosmic struggle. 'In the beginning,' said Zoroaster, 'the twin spirits were known as the one good and the other evil, in thought, word, and deed. Between them the wise chose rightly, not so the fools. And when these spirits met

A seventh-century BC silver plaque from Iran showing Ahriman and Ahura Mazdah

they established life and death so that in the end the followers of deceit should meet with the worst existence, but the followers of truth with the wise lord.'

Ahura Mazdah told Zoroaster that Angra Mainya had upset his plans for making Persia into a terrestrial paradise. All the creatures of 'the wise lord' were created with free-will: both spiritual beings and men. Angra Mainya, the twin brother of 'the holy spirit', simply took pleasure in 'choosing to do the worst things'. To thwart Ahura Mazdah he introduced frost in winter, heat in summer, all manner of diseases, and the other ills that men have to endure. His creation, too, was the dragon Azhi Dahaka, who brought ruin to the earth. When Ahura Mazdah fashioned the stars in heaven, he 'sprang into the sky like a snake' and in opposition to those luminaries formed the planets, whose baleful influence then fell across the world. Throughout creation there was a cleavage and antagonism so deep that under the Sassanians (226–652) there arose a myth to soften the dualism. The twin spirits became the offspring of a single pre-existing primeval being, Zurvan Akarana, 'infinite time'. Because Zurvan had vowed that the firstborn should rule as king and Ahriman 'ripped the womb open' in order to claim the title, the evil one was given the kingdom of the world for a *limited* period. 'After nine thousand years,' Zurvan insisted, 'Ohrmazd will reign and will do everything according to his good pleasure.'

The chief weapon of Ahriman was *az*, concupiscence, Zurvan's gift. 'By means of this power,' the donor remarked, 'all that is yours will be devoured, even your own creation.' Ahriman accepted because it was 'as his very essence'. The demonic Az, a female principle, included more than sexual desire: equally it was doubt, a weakening of the intellect. Possibly the idea represents a borrowing from Buddhism, which saw in *avidya*, 'ignorance', and its manifestation, desire, the reason for the endless round of conditioned being. Az was also connected with the Manichaean demon of the same name, 'the mother of all evil spirits'. In Zoroastrianism, however, the role of woman is by no means clear. Man was almost holy, a creation designed to play the foremost part in the destruction of evil. When Ahriman beheld 'the righteous man, he swooned away. For three thousand years he lay in a swoon . . . till the accursed whore' roused him. Jeh, the whore, coveted man and 'defiled herself with the destructive spirit' to obtain her desire. But this idea only found expression in late texts and it was generally accepted that woman's role was the propagation of the race.

Ahura Mazdah
Originally Ahura, 'the lord', may have been connected with Mithra, the ruler of the day, before he was elevated to the position of the supreme being in Persian religion by the prophet Zoroaster, and he acquired the epithet Mazdah, 'wise'. Although the Indo-European pastoralists settled on the Iranian plateau derived their gods from the same pantheon as the Aryan conquerors of India, the course of their religious development was entirely different. While the Indian mind sought a unifying principle within a multiplicity of gods, in Persia this monistic tendency moved in the direction of a universal monotheism under the inspiration of Zoroaster.

Fire was conceived of as the symbol of truth which Ahura Mazdah bestowed on his followers. Light was opposed to darkness and associated with truth and righteousness, *asha*. In the myth of Atar, the fire of the sky and Ahura Mazdah's son, there is a struggle with Azhi Dahaka, the three-headed dragon, who had usurped the earthly throne. His rule brought 'need and misery, hunger and thirst, old age and death, mourning and lamentation, excessive heat and cold, and the intermingling

of demons and men'. Atar overcame the dragon, who was either consigned 'to the bottom of the deep ocean' or chained on a high mountain. But Azhi Dahaka was destined to escape at the end of world and destroy a third of mankind, before he was slain. The divine fire, the spark indwelling in mankind, was the symbol of Ahura Mazdah, and in fire-temples the flame burning perpetually indicated his presence.

Ahura Mazdah is the god of prophetic revelation, the sole deity revealing himself to a traditionally polytheistic society not yet ready to receive the totality of his message. The Zoroastrianism of the Persian kings accommodated existing religious practices, not least because it was controlled by a priestly caste, the *magi*, with which it previously had nothing to do. Once the followers of the prophet realized that the establishment on earth of a righteous kingdom was not possible in the present cycle of world ages, the way was open for Persian mythology to evolve a thorough dualism, with the source of evil increasingly personified. At last two absolute rivals emerged: Ahriman, the master of deceit, challenged Ormuzd, a contraction of Ahuramazdah, and in the ranks of their hostile hosts room was made for the ancient gods whom Zoroaster attempted to abolish.

Alilat
The Arabian mother goddess, a deity under considerable Assyrio-Babylonian influence. At Petra, the capital of the Nabataean kingdom, the cult turned upon worship of Dusura, her dying son. He was either a mountain god or an astral deity; statues portray him as genius of the vine. An Arabic historian records that the Nabataeans revered a four-sided stone, known as Allat or Alilat. Veneration of stones and pillars was a feature of the nomadic peoples of West Asia. The Hebrews were attracted to rocks as natural altars during their wanderings in the desert, while the ascetic movement in Christian Syria reached its spectacular climax in the pillar saints, the chief exponent being St Simeon.

Although the ritual of early Arabian religions was a particular target of the prophet Mohammed, today Mecca affords the most conspicuous instance of veneration given to a stone—that proffered to 'the black stone which fell from heaven in the days of Adam'. The rock, probably an aerolite, is built into a corner of the Ka'ba, 'the house of God' and the place of pilgrimage for Moslems. Near by, legend says, is the tombstone of Ishmeal, the son of Adam and father of the northern Arabs.

Amun

An Egyptian ram-headed god, often shown as a bearded man wearing a cap with two tall plumes. The era of this Theban sky god's greatest ascendancy occurred in the sixteenth century BC when the Egyptians expelled the Hyksos invaders and extended the imperial frontiers into Canaan. Rivalry with Re was eliminated by the association of Amun with Re as Amon-Re, except during the reign of Akhenaton. As a dynastic guardian, Amon-Re was 'king of the gods', incarnate in the ruling pharaoh, and out of the tribute of Asia great temples were built for his worship at Luxor and Karnak.

Amun was looked upon as one of the creators of the universe and in prayers devotees besought his known generosity. To the Greeks he was Ammon, identified with Zeus, and famous for his oracle at Siwa in Libya. Herodotus was told by 'the priests of Thebes that two of their priestesses had been abducted by Phoenicians, who sold one in Libya, and the other in Greece. These women, they said, were the founders of divination in those two countries, setting up there the original oracles.'

An

In Sumerian mythology the personification of heaven. Unlike the Egyptian conception of their deities, who are frequently represented under theriomorphic forms, the Meso-potamian gods are always shown in human form, though they are often accompanied by their sacred beasts. It appears that Sumer did not pass through a totemistic stage of religious development, as the Egyptians clearly did. An early god like ·An simply remained a shadowy figure, the survivor of a creation myth. He was the father of Enlil. Though the Assyrio-Babylonian pantheon found a place for him as Anu, the god of kingship as well as of heaven, he retired very much into the background before the active gods, especially Marduk and Ashur. His symbol was the star.

Ark

When in 63 BC Pompey stormed Jerusalem and forced his way into the Holy of Holies, to see what was there, he found an empty room. Idols, images, the paraphernalia of the temple cult in West Asian religions were noticeably absent from Judaism. Worship took place on high places and under every green tree, yet the dwelling-place of Yahweh was 'Mount Zion, on the sides of the north, the city of the great Lord'. Here *saphon*, 'north', is an allusion to Mount Saphon near Ugarit—the Olympus of the Canaanite gods. At Sinai Moses went up the mountain, and Yahweh talked to him. But after the making of the golden calf and the breaking of the first tablets of the law, Moses was told by Yahweh to fashion a wooden ark or chest in which to store the second tablets. The 'Ark of the covenant of God', the symbol of Hebrew belief in a special relationship with heaven, was on one occasion captured by the Philistines, but they were obliged to return it, accompanied by a trespass-offering, since the inhabitants of every city where the Ark appeared were smitten with plagues.

Ashur

In Assyria, Ashur took over the roles of Marduk and Enlil, and was also, as might be expected in this military civilization, the god of war. It was usual practice to parade through the capital, known as Ashur too, the chained captives vouchsafed by the warrior god. He was portrayed as a winged disc enclosing a stretched bow ready to let fly an arrow. His consort was Ishtar, who responded to the warlike temperament of her mate by sprouting a beard which reached to her breasts.

Astarte

The mother goddess in the Ras Shamra texts appears as Anat, Athirat, and Athtart, or Astarte. The consort and sister of Baal, the most active Canaanite god, Anat was called the 'lady of the mountain', and it was through her flattery of El that Baal was allowed to build a house on Saphon, a mountain situated in 'the sides of the north'. In spite of titles like 'the maiden' and 'the virgin', Anat was an aggressive goddess: she slew Baal's enemies, waded in the blood of her human victims, and desired to possess Aqhat's bow. She was portrayed with helmet, battle-axe, and spear. In Egypt, where she was introduced by the Hyksos invaders, the cow's horns of Hathor became a part of her iconography.

Athirat, 'the lady of the sea', appears to be

the consort of El, an equivalent of the Hebrew god Yahweh. Her role was restricted to fertility. Less remote than Athirat and almost as fierce as Anat was Astarte, 'the queen of heaven'. The Hebrews knew her as the goddess of the Sidonians, and gave her worship. Yahweh told the prophet Jeremiah that 'the children gather wood, and the fathers kindle the fire, and the women knead their dough, to make cakes to the queen of heaven, and to pour out drink offerings unto other gods, that they may provoke me to anger'. At Mizpah temples to Yahweh and Astarte were actually erected side by side, while in Upper Egypt the Hebrew community still regarded the moon goddess as a divine consort in the fifth century BC. As in the cases of Ishtar and Inanna, the sacred marriage and temple prostitution were prominent features of the cult. 'When I fed them to the full,' Yahweh complained, 'they then committed adultery, and assembled themselves by troops in the harlots' houses.'

Astarte was dangerous as well as beautiful. She wore the horns of the bull: hers was victory in the fray as 'mistress of horses and chariots'. An Arabian variant could have been the god Athtar, also known as the 'terrible' lord who unsuccessfully tried to oust Baal.

Attis

In Phrygia the spring festival was held in honour of the self-mutilated and resurrected god Attis, the son of the mother goddess Cybele. According to one legend, Attis was so harassed by an affectionate monster that he castrated himself. Another recounts that he was put to death because of his love for Cybele, daughter of the King of Phrygia and Lydia. The sanctuary of the mother goddess was at Pessinus, hard by the River Sangarius, in the reeds of which she discovered her youthful lover. Cybele equates with Inanna, Attis with Tammuz. She was attended by lions, and the castration, death, and rebirth of her consort, usually shown as an effeminate youth, was recalled in an annual ceremony full of blood-letting. Rams were sacrificed, their blood used for baptism; initiates unmanned themselves, and her eunuch priests cut their own flesh in a frenzy. At Rome, where the 'mystery' cult was introduced in 205 BC, we

The god Baal; a Hittite bronze of fourteenth century BC

know that the pine was connected with Attis, whose effigy wore grave linen. Just as the god died and was restored to life again, so the initiate, in union with him, entered a state of blessedness which was thought to endure beyond the grave. Union was achieved through either self-mutilation or a sacred marriage: to all devotees was open what had once been the prerogative of West Asian kingship.

Baal

Literal meaning: 'lord'. In Canaan the old title of local fertility gods. Baal did not emerge as a distinct rain god till comparatively late times, when he appears to have assumed the special functions of each. Although there is no equivalent in Canaan of the sterile, scorching summer drought found in Mesopotamia, the cycle of seasons is marked enough to have caused a concentration on the disappearing fertility god, who trailed after him to the nether world the autumn rain clouds.

Having defeated the sea god Yam, built a house on Mount Saphon, and seized possession of numerous cities, Baal announced that he would no longer acknowledge the authority of Mot, 'death'. Excluded from Baal's hospitality and friendship, Mot was told to visit on earth only the deserts. In response to this challenge, Mot invited Baal to his abode in order to taste his own fare, mud. Terrified and unable to avoid the dreadful summons to the land of the dead, Baal coupled with a calf in order to strengthen himself for the impending ordeal, and then set out. El and the other gods donned funeral garments, poured ashes on their heads, and mutilated their limbs, while Anat, aided by the sun goddess Shapash, brought back the corpse for burial. El placed on the vacant throne of Baal the irrigation god Athtar, but Anat sorely missed her dead husband and brother. Without avail she beseeched Mot to restore Baal to life, and her attempts to interest the other deities in the question were met with cautious indifference. Thus, Anat had to assault Mot, ripping him to pieces 'with a sharp knife', scattering his members 'with a winnowing fan', burning him 'in a fire', grinding him 'in a mill', and 'over the fields strewing his remains'. Meanwhile in a dream El beheld a return to fertility, which suggested that Baal was not really dead, and he instructed Shapash to keep an eye open for him on her daily travels. In due course Baal was discovered completely restored, and Athtar fled from his throne. Yet Mot was able to renew the attack and, though on this occasion all the gods supported Baal, neither combatant could gain the victory. At last, El intervened and dismissed Mot, leaving Baal in possession of the field.

This myth—fragments of which exist on the Ras Shamra tablets—relates to the alteration of the seasons. Baal is the god of rain, thunder, and lightning. 'At the touch of his right hand, even cedars wilt.' Yam, the owner of salt water, gave place to Baal as the genius of rainfall and vegetation, a displacement that left Mot as the sole contender beneath mighty El. Torrid heat, sterility, the arid desert, death, the nether world: these were Mot's irresistible realm till Anat threshed, winnowed, and ground the harvested corn, the fecundity of Baal's land, just as the siding of El with the resurrected rain god at the close ensured the continuation of the annual cycle. A parallel of the magical rites involved can be found in Psalms, where 'they that sow in tears shall reap in joy. He that goeth forth and weepeth, bearing precious seed, shall doubtless come again with rejoicing, bearing sheaves with him.' This is sympathetic magic: the tears shed were expected to induce drops of rain.

Baal was son of El, or Dagon, an obscure diety linked by the Hebrews with the Philistine city of Ashdod. Dagon may have been associated with the sea—a coin found in the vicinity portrays a god with a fishtail. Although Baal himself overcame Yam, it is uncertain whether or not he fought Lotan, the Leviathan of the Old Testament, but we know that Anat 'crushed the writhing serpent, the accused one of the seven heads'. Another echo of Mesopotamian thought patterns occurs in the reasons advanced by Baal for needing a 'house'. His food offerings were too meagre for a god 'that rides on the clouds'. As far apart as Carthage and Palmyra there were temples dedicated to Baal-Hammon, 'the lord of the altar of incense' whom the Greeks indentified with Kronos. On Mount Carmel it was the prophet Elijah who discredited King Ahab's belief in the power of Baal, when at his request 'the fire of the Lord fell, and consumed the burnt sacrifice, and the wood, and the stones, and the dust, and licked up the water that was in the trench'. Afterwards Elijah had the people slay 'the prophets of Baal', thereby assuring the survival of Yahweh-worship in Israel.

Bastet

The Egyptian cat goddess was probably at first associated with a lioness rather than the domesticated cat. The cat-headed goddess had her cult town at Bubastis, where a necropolis housed mummified cats. Other deities that either protected a species or took an animal form also had cities sacred to the particular creature. At Fayum, where the god Sebek assumed the shape of a crocodile, the incarnate deity splashed about in a temple pool, from which his worshippers partook holy draughts. Though the greatest animal cult was undoubtedly that of the Apis Bull, Herodotus was amazed to note that 'as they bury oxen, so they do with all other beasts at death'.

Cats were revered in the household. 'When a fire breaks out', the Greek traveller continues, 'very strange things happen to the cats. The Egyptians gather in a line, thinking more of the cats than of putting out the flames; but the cats dart through or leap over the men and spring into the fire. Then, there is great mourning. . . . Dwellers in a house where a cat has died a natural death shave their eyebrows; where a dog has died, the head and body are shaven.' During the festivals of Bastet it was impious to hunt lions, a favourite sport of the pharaohs.

Daniel

The Hebrew myths gathered round the sojourn of Daniel in Babylon were apocalyptic, a 'revelation' of what was going to happen in later times. The reversals of fortune experienced by Israel cast a shadow of doubt over Yahweh's plan for the chosen people, despite the warnings of the prophets Jeremiah and Ezekiel. Captivity in Babylon was a shock: Nebuchadnezzar had seized Jerusalem in 597 BC, when leading members of the community were taken away as prisoners, but the final sack of the city and mass deportation did not occur till 587 BC. Yahweh told the prophet Ezekiel that once the lesson of unrighteousness was learned, then as a shepherd he would gather together his exiled sheep and 'bring them to their own land, and feed them upon the mountains of Israel by the

A seventh-century ivory of Daniel in the lion's den

rivers, and in all the inhabited places of the country'. Prediction started to be worked out in history through Cyrus, King of the Persians, who captured the cities of Sippar and Babylon in 539 BC. As it was his policy to restore exiled peoples to their own lands and encourage them in their traditional worship, the Hebrews had their opportunity to return to Jerusalem. This they did, but tribulation recurred after the death of Alexander the Great, whose conquest of the Persian Empire left rich pickings for his generals, and 'they brought untold miseries upon the world'. In particular the Seleucid ruler Antiochus Epiphanes (175–163 BC) drove them into open revolt.

The Book of Daniel, the earliest example of apocalyptic literature, was propaganda written to comfort the Hebrews resisting the Hellenizing policy of the Seleucids. It concerns the discomfiture of Nebuchadnezzar, the symbol of all oppression, and the vindication of Daniel as the true adherent of Yahweh. When Shadrach, Meshach, and Abed-nego refused to bow down before the king's golden image, they were cast into the fiery furnace, but they suffered 'no hurt' through the presence of a companion 'like the Son of God'. When mysterious handwriting appeared upon the wall of the palace during a feast given by Belshazzar, possibly a tributary king, the only person able to interpret the meaning was Daniel, who announced correctly the imminent rise of the Persians. When the devout interpreter of signs failed to obey a *firman* and continued to offer prayers to his proscribed deity, Daniel was cast into a den of lions. But Yahweh 'sent his angel and . . . shut the lions' mouths' so that he came to no harm. Though the vision of the future described in the final chapters of *The Book of Daniel* contains amazing beasts with dreadful jaws filled with 'great iron teeth', the outstanding image is Nebuchadnezzar roaming the steppe as a wild animal. 'He was driven from men, and did eat grass as oxen, and his body was wet with the dew of heaven, till his hairs were grown like eagles' feathers, and his nails like birds' claws.'

In another apocryphal book, *Daniel, Bel, and the Snake*, we have two accounts of Daniel's success in unmasking priestly deceitfulness. To Cyrus he demonstrated with the aid of ashes sprinkled on the temple floor that the footprints of those who came secretly to eat the food set out for Bel belonged to 'the priests, with their wives and children'. He also disposed of a sacred serpent by feeding it with cakes made from boiled 'pitch and fat and hair': these burst asunder its huge belly.

El

On Mount Saphon dwelt El, the 'first' Canaanite god. The father of gods and men, he was remote, 'old', the 'master of time', the 'benevolent and merciful lord'. It was under his suzerainty that Baal married Anat, defeated the sea god Yam as well as the deadly Mot, and was installed as the divine bestower of life-giving rain. El represented omnipotence at one remove, so that he was always portrayed as a seated figure, wearing bull's horns, the symbol of strength. In the *Old Testament* there is mention of the supreme deity as El and Yahweh. About Melchizedek, King of Jerusalem, we hear that 'he brought forth bread and wine, and he was the priest of the most high God'. This was El Elyon. It is now thought that the *Old Testament* is a compilation of at least three main versions of Hebrew religious history, the Yahwist one being the dominant tradition.

Two epic cycles associated with El concern Keret and Aqhat. The first tells of the assistance given to Keret, the son of El and a righteous king. The god helped find a second wife, blessed him with 'seven sons, yea eight', and towards the end of his reign saved him from senility. The text breaks off at a point where Keret is accused of incompetence by one of his sons. In the second epic conflict takes place when the goddess Anat seized the wonderful bow of Aqhat, the son whom El had granted to King Daniel. Grateful for the hospitality shown to him by the King, the smith god Kothar gave Aqhat a bow, 'its horns . . . twisted like a serpent'. The prince

refused Anat; he said that her offer of immortality in exchange for the weapon was an illusion to a man destined to die: for such presumption the goddess had him killed with the consent of El. But the bow fell 'in the midst of the waters' and broke along with its precious arrows. Moreover, with the disappearance of Aqhat, the vegetation withered away and Baal sent down neither rain nor dew. The fragmentary text leaves Paghat, Daniel's daughter, bent on revenge—'to smite the smiter of my brother'. The parallel with Baal is striking, though it is by no means certain that Aqhat was an aspect of a 'dying and reviving' fertility deity.

Enki

The Sumerian water god of Eridu. Along with An the god of heaven, Enlil the air god, and Ninhursag the earth mother, Enki was a creator deity. Priests often clothed themselves in a garment in the form of a fish, when officiating at rituals of purification, symbolic of the cleansing power of Enki as the god of lustration. The fish may refer to a Babylonian legend about Ea, the god's Akkadian title meaning 'lord of the house of water', which was the sweet water beneath the ground named Abzu by the Sumerians. In remote times, according to this myth, when men lived in a lawless manner like beasts, Ea appeared from the sea. Part man and part fish, the double-headed god instructed men in handicrafts, farming, letters, laws, architecture, and magic. He softened the primitive rudeness and since that time nothing has been added to improve on his teaching. After a day of instruction Ea retired into the sea, whence the divine fish man made only three other appearances over a period of thousands of years.

Enki figures in a Sumerian myth which is a parallel to the Hebrew story of Adam and the Garden of Eden. In paradisal Dilmun, now identified with Bahrain in the Persian Gulf, the water god lived with Ninhursag; it was a happy place, where animals did not harm one another, and neither sickness nor old age was known. The only thing wanting had been sweet water, and this Enki provided—his union with the earth mother turned the island into a fruitful garden. A quarrel arose when Enki devoured eight plants grown by Ninhursag. She pronounced on him the curse of death. It was effective: sickness attacked

An Assyrian frieze showing a ritual being conducted in front of a sacred tree

eight parts of his body, to the dismay of the other gods. Enlil was powerless to arrest Enki's decline, the situation appeared hopeless. Then the fox spoke up. It offered to bring Ninhursag back to Dilmun, providing there was suitable reward. This happened and the earth mother created eight deities to heal her consort's afflictions.

There are obvious similarities between this myth and the biblical picture of paradise. In *Genesis* 'there went up a mist from the earth, and watered the whole ground', while the eating of forbidden plants is distinctly reminiscent of the tree of life in Eden. The very idea of a divine paradise, a garden of the gods, was of Sumerian origin. Eve, Adam's spouse, and 'the lady of the rib', Ninti, the goddess created to heal Enki's side, also have something in common. We know that there was 'planted upon Abzu' a sacred tree, *kiskanu*, which acted as the central point for rituals. Though the term 'tree of life' does not occur in

any surviving Mesopotamian text, it can be deduced from pictorial representations of ritual observances that the tree played a significant role.

A Sumerian legend concerning the creation of man begins with the gods lamenting how difficult it was for them to get food. Roused from his slumbers, Enki acceded to their request for servants, and fashioned 'out of clay' mankind. It was he who gave warning of the deluge to Ziusudra, the pious King of Sippar. The gods, having tired of their mortal helpers, decided to annihilate the inhabitants of the earth.

Enlil

The Sumerian god of the earth and the air. At the beginning the primeval waters generated a cosmic mountain, which consisted of heaven and earth. From this union of heaven, personified by the god An, and earth, as the goddess Ki, sprang Enlil, the air god, who separated his parents and united with his mother to beget mankind. His chief gift to men was the pickaxe, an implement designed to assist in the construction of cities including his own seat of Nippur. The primeval waters, Nammu, were called 'the mother' and may have been synonymous with Abzu, the sweet waters in the earth, or perhaps they represented the marshlands at the mouth of the Euphrates and of the Tigris, where new land was being constantly created by riverine deposits.

A myth concerned with the birth of the moon god tells how Enlil was banished to the nether world for raping the goddess Ninlil, but she decided to follow him in order to give birth in his presence. The banished god somehow managed the escape of their child, Nanna, the moon god, so that he could become the light of the night sky. Yet fragments surviving of a flood myth indicate an even more violent side to Enlil, since as the devastating wind god he was probably the author of the disaster. Only pious King Ziusudra escaped in a boat, which he built on the instruction of the water god Enki. To this ruler of Sippar, 'the seed of mankind', was granted 'the breath of eternal life'.

In Babylonian mythology Enlil kept his name, or was known as Ellil, though he acquired the Akkadian epithet of Bel, 'the lord'. Disturbed by the racket of mankind, he sent to earth a plague, then a drought, and at last a deluge. But Ea warned Atrahasis, 'the very wise one', who saved himself in the ship *Preserver of Life*. In *The Gilgamesh Epic*, the other Babylonian treatment of the flood, it was Utanapishtim that Ea warned and the decision to destroy life was taken by the gods, not Enlil alone. Other legends underscore his ambivalent attitude towards men, too. Enlil created the monster Labbu, or Lahmu, 'the raging one', to wreak havoc on earth: it descended from the primeval chaos, being the offspring of Abzu and Tiamat. On the positive side, he held the 'tablets of destiny', *tupsimati*, by whose authority he ordered the nature of things. In the second millennium BC on the pillar recording his own code of laws Hammurabi, King of Babylon, invoked wrathful Enlil against the disobedient.

Etana

King of Kish. A Babylonian fragment relates an attempt he made to ascend to heaven on the back of an eagle in order to obtain 'the plant of birth', since his queen was unable to bear a son. Shamash, the sun god, had advised Etana to seek an eagle caught in a pit. The bird was trapped there by a serpent after it took the young of the serpent. Etana released the eagle, which in gratitude carried its rescuer heavenward. Their fate is obscure. On one hand it seems that Etana became afraid, the eagle faltered, and they fell to earth and were killed; on the other hand, there is mention of a son of Etana as King of Kish.

Gayomart

Literally, 'dying life'. In Persian mythology he was the primeval man, the creation of Ahura Mazdah. For 3000 years Gayomart lived as a spirit before he assumed the corporeal form of a handsome youth. After a life lasting thirty years he was poisoned by Ahriman at the instigation of Jeh, 'the whore'. From his seed grew plant-like the father and mother of the human race, Mashye and Mashyane, who foresook Ahura Mazdah for Ahriman, and were damned to punishment in hell until the last days.

Gilgamesh

Semi-legendary King of Uruk and hero of the Akkadian *Gilgamesh Epic* which was based on myths that existed for centuries in Sumer. The fullest surviving text is the Assyrian one from the library of King Ashurbanipal at Nineveh, and therefore no older than the seventh century BC, at least a millennium later than composition.

Born of the union of a goddess and a man—possibly the sacral coupling of the ruler and the high priestess during the New Year Festival—Gilgamesh was said to be two-thirds divinity and one-third mortal. In the Sumerian fragment of the myth the haunting fear of death spurs the hero's exploits and one view holds that we have here an account of a funerary ritual connected with the death chamber excavated at Ur. The Akkadian epic portrays Gilgamesh as a tyrant, overbearing and prone to sexual misdemeanours. His people beseeched the gods for help, and on the steppe the mother goddess Aruru fashioned from spittle and clay a hairy, grass-eating, wild man called Enkidu. On hearing the news, Gilgamesh ordered a temple prostitute be sent to ensnare Enkidu who had never known sensual pleasures. She nurtured the wild man in civilized ways, then fired his ambition to topple Gilgamesh. But the fight ended with Enkidu's defeat and the start of a lifelong friendship between the heroes.

Together the friends began a series of adventures. They invaded the cedar forest of the fire-breathing giant Huwawa, or Humbaba, whom they killed with the assistance of fierce winds provided by the sun god Shamash. Next Ishtar offered her love to Gilgamesh, but was rejected with pointed remarks about her fickleness and inconstancy. The goddess, mad with rage, demanded of Anu that a bull of heaven ravage the earth. While great damage occurred, it was slain by the heroes. The wrath of the gods, however had been excited, and Enlil obtained the death of Enkidu in punishment for their arrogance.

Overwhelmed by grief and stricken to the heart with the realization of mortality, Gilgamesh roamed the steppe. To find a means of personal salvation he finally resolved to consult his ancestor Utanapishtim, who had become immortal. At the edge of the sea that surrounded the world, Gilgamesh was accosted by Siduri, a manifestation of Ishtar. When she urged the mortal joys of the wine jug, he replied that he would not give up Enkidu for burial, but mourned him for seven days and nights till a worm fell from the corpse's nose. 'The gods appointed death for man', said Siduri, 'and kept life for themselves.' Yet the persistence of the hero forced 'the celestial barmaid' to reveal that Utanapishtim dwelt across the waters of death, a voyage he could only undertake with aid from the ferryman Ursanapi.

The meeting of Gilgamesh with Utanapishtim in his ark. An Akkadian cylinder seal from about 2200 BC

Gilgamesh found the ferryman, built a special boat, crossed the lethal waters, and came to 'the mouth of the rivers', the place which the gods had assigned to Utanapishtim and his wife for their eternal dwelling. Utanapishtim, the survivor of the deluge which had 'returned all mankind to clay', reminded Gilgamesh of his mortal third. The quest was hopeless: he could not resist sleep, let alone death. The only chance was a magic plant, 'Never Grow Old', which grew at the bottom of the sea. At great risk Gilgamesh fetched it from the deep and happily turned his steps to Uruk, but on his way home, while he slept by a water-hole, a serpent smelled the wonderful perfume of the leaves, stole up, and swallowed the lot. Immediately the snake gained the power to slough its skin. Gilgamesh awoke, saw his own fate as death, and wept in utter grief.

Another text relates how Gilgamesh assisted Inanna in felling a tree, guarded by a snake, a wind, and an eagle. From the sacred timber they made a magic drum and drumstick, which Gilgamesh accidentally let fall into the nether world. When Enkidu tried to recover them, he forgot to observe the special instructions given for his protection, and was trapped forever. Out of a hole, opened in the ground by Ea, the spirit of the dead hero issued 'like a puff of wind', and described 'the house of dust', where princes were servants and earthly rank offered no protection at all.

Hadad

Literally, 'the crasher'. The foremost deity of the Aramaean peoples of Syria was Hadad,

synonymous with Baal-Hadad, who convulsed the earth, shook mountains, and blasted trees, The rulers of Damascus were known in biblical times as Bar-Hadad, 'the sons of Hadad'. A reference in *Zechariah* suggests that he fulfilled a fertility role like Baal: there is mention of a lament for the dead god.

Haoma

The Persian equivalent of the Hindu Soma, the elixir of life. As a celestial deity Haoma was 'correct in faith and the adversary of death',

A wall painting from Queen Nefertiti's tomb of the goddess Hathor receiving an offering

the intermediary between earth and heaven. The sacrament of ancient Persian religion, probably connected with the blood-offering, said to have been instituted by Yima, the *haoma* rite was condemned for its 'filthy drunkenness' by Zoroaster. However, the orgiastic character suitably modified, it became at last the central act of the Zoroastrian liturgy, while Herodotus tells us that Xerxes sacrificed bulls during his invasion of Greece (480BC).

Hapi
The Nile was worshipped as a deity, unlike the rivers of Mesopotamia. To the Egyptians the river was Hapi, a well-fed and plump god, who took pleasure in exchanging gifts. He was usually represented holding ears of corn and a cornucopia. In recompense for the fertilization of the soil during the annual inundation the river god was offered food, precious ornaments, and jewels.

Hathor
Cow goddesses were worshipped in several parts of Egypt, but they were early identified with Hathor of Denderah. She was represented as either a cow with the solar disc or a woman with cow's horns between which was the solar-disc. Occasionally she even appeared as a hippopotamus, though her epithet was always 'the golden'. A fertility goddess, Hathor attended at childbirth and was regarded as the tutelary deity of beauty, love, and marriage. Sometimes she was identified with Isis, the wife of Osiris.

According to one legend, the doting sun god Re used Hathor to slaughter mankind. Nervous and uncertain of his power, he was so convinced that men were plotting against him that he sent the Eye of Re, in the form of the goddess Hathor, to destroy the impious. But, unwilling to witness universal destruction, he flooded the fields with beer, dyed with red ochre to resemble blood. Entranced by the sight as well as her own reflection, Hathor forgot her grisly task and became intoxicated. Thus mankind was spared.

Horus
Isis, sister and wife of Osiris, conceived Horus of the slain god by magical means. According to Egyptian myth she took refuge in the delta marshes, gave birth to her son and raised him in the utmost secrecy. On reaching manhood Horus sought to avenge the death of his father and in single combat with Seth, the murderous uncle, he lost an eye. But Seth was either killed or emasculated and judged the loser by the assembled gods. Although the eye was restored by Seth, Horus gave it to Osiris, and replaced it with the divine serpent, which thenceforth acted as the emblem of royalty. Horus, the falcon-headed sky god, thus

succeeded the anthropomorphic god of vegetation, Osiris, as the king, the pharaoh of all Egypt.

Just as Isis is the archetype of the mourning wife, so Horus is that of the dutiful son. He originated in Upper Egypt as a solar deity and may have been identical with Re. On death the pharaoh was thought to become Osiris, and his successor Horus and Re.

Illuyankas
Comparable to the victory of the Babylonian Marduk over Tiamat is the Hittite myth of the weather god as the slayer of the dragon Illuyankas personifying the forces of evil. There are two versions of the legend. In the older tale, Illuyankas overcame the weather god, but the goddess Inaras prepared a trap for the dragon. She spread a feast—'wine by the barrel, fruit juice by the barrel, other drinks filling every barrel brim full'—and obtained the help of a man named Hupasiyas, who was her lover. Illuyankas and his children ate and drank until they were no longer able to return to their lair. Then Hupasiyas trussed them up with strong cord and the weather god slew them. For Hupasiyas the goddess built a special house, but instructed him not to look out of the window lest he see his wife and children. Hupasiyas disobeyed the command, saw his mortal family, and asked to return home: so Inaras killed him.

According to the later version, the dragon took away with him the heart and eyes of the weather god when he vanquished him. In order to recover them the weather god begot a son, whom he married to the daughter of Illuyankas. This young man asked his dragon bride for the missing organs and was able to give them back to his father. Restored, the weather god killed Illuyankas and, at his own request, his own son, who like the Egyptian Horus had revitalized him. Both stories relate to the West Asian theme of the dying and reviving fertility god. Echoes of this fundamental myth in Europe are plentiful and appear in the springtime processions of dragons. As late as this century at Ragusa, in Sicily, an enormous effigy of a dragon, complete with moveable tail and eyes, was paraded on St George's Day.

Inanna
Early sites excavated in Sumer indicate that temples were located in groups of two. The

pair of deities worshipped were probably the mother goddess and her consort, later called Inanna and Dumuzi. Inanna was the most important goddess in the Sumerian pantheon, a variant of her name being Ninanna, 'mistress of heaven'. Daughter of An or Enlil, she was identified with the planet Venus, and as a war goddess overcame the mountain god Ebeh, most likely a reference to a victory over the steadily encroaching Semites. Inanna was best known, however, as the goddess of fertility and love.

Fascinating is the account of Inanna's descent into 'the land without return', *kur-nu-gi-a*, a dry, dusty place, situated below the sweet waters of the earth. She decided to visit this dark realm, which belonged to her enemy and sister goddess, Ereshkigal, 'the mistress of death', and assert her own authority there. Having adorned herself with all her finery and left behind Ninshubur, her Vizier, with orders to rescue her should she not return, Inanna descended to *kur-nu-gi-a*. At each of its seven portals she was obliged to take off a garment or ornament, until at last she appeared naked before Ereshkigal and the seven judges of the dead. 'At their cruel command, the defenceless goddess was turned into a corpse, which was hung on a stake.' After three days and nights had passed, Ninshubur became worried and besought the aid of the gods, who said that nothing could be done against the decrees of the nether world. But the persistent vizier appealed to Enki, and the water god created two sexless beings, for whom admission to the land of infertility and death could not be refused. They obtained access to Inanna's corpse and resurrected it with the 'food of life' and the 'water of life'. Unhappily the restored goddess could not shake off a ghastly escort of demons, which accompanied her on her wanderings from city to city. They refused to depart unless a substitute was found. Thus Inanna returned home to Uruk and found at a feast her husband Dumuzi, who was king of near-by Kullab. Outraged, she selected him for *kur-nu-gi-a*, and in spite of two incredible escapes from the clutches of the eager demons thither he went.

The descent myth reveals two aspects of the mother goddess: Inanna and Ereshkigal, the two sisters, light and darkness respectively, represent the antithetical, paradoxical nature of divinity. Our misfortune is that we have only a portion of this 5000-year-old story,

which was certainly very close to the origin of symbols fundamental to thought in West Asia. In other metamorphoses Inanna was Ishtar, Astarte, Cybele, Aphrodite, and Venus. The significance of Dumuzi is uncertain. His final capture and death occurred in the sheepfold; he was Inanna's shepherd lover, whom she preferred over her other suitor, the farmer Enkimdu. Yet attributes of other deities absorbed by Dumuzi included the date and grain. He was said to return 'from the river', drawn forth by the lamentations of his devotees.

Ishtar

'The foulest Babylonian custom', Herodotus remarks, 'is that which compels every woman of the land once in her life to sit in the temple of Aphrodite and lay with some stranger. . . . When a woman has once taken her place there she cannot leave before a man has cast money into her lap and united with her outside the temple. On casting the coin, he has to say, "I demand you in the name of Mylitta", which is the Assyria name for Aphrodite. . . . After sexual union has made the woman holy in the goddess' sight, she returns home: thereafter no bribe would be large enough to win her favour again. Handsome women are of course soon free to depart, but it happens that the uncomely sometimes have to wait several years. There is a custom like this in some parts of Cyprus.'

Mylitta was the mother goddess Ishtar, who derived from the Sumerian Inanna, goddess of fertility and love. In Babylonian mythology Ishtar, the wife and sister of Tammuz, the Sumerian Dumuzi, descended to the nether world as a hostile and threatening figure, even Ereshkigal's face blanched on her approach. Yet she was overcome there by death, with the result on earth that the springs of fertility ran dry. Ea secured her release by means of a 'brilliant' eunuch, which captivated the heart of the mistress of infertility and death.

An Akkadian fragment describes the wailing of Ishtar for Tammuz, whose annual death, resurrection, and marriage strongly indicate a fertility ritual connected with the agricultural cycle. His worship spread into Canaan, where the prophet Ezekiel bitterly complained that even at 'the door of the gate of the Lord's house . . . there sat women weeping for Tammuz'.

As a war goddess Ishtar was specially

A West Asian mother goddess, either Ishtar or Astarte; ninth-century BC ivory from Nimrod

honoured in Assyria. She carried a bow and a quiver, her warlike aspect receiving emphasis with a beard similar to the god Ashur. Inscriptions state that Ishtar was party to the choosing of the king. Certain of his divine election was Ashur-natsir-pala II (884–860 BC), a monarch renowned for the severity of his treatment of rebels and intractable enemies. Skinning captives alive or cutting off their hands became settled policy.

Isis

Literal meaning: 'seat'. The mother goddess of Egypt; the daughter of Nut, the wife and sister of Osiris, and the mother of Horus. She was depicted as a woman, often suckling the child Horus on her lap. When represented with the solar-disc and cow's horns, she was identified with Hathor. A legend tells how Isis discovered the ineffable name of Re, the sun god. Weary of worldly affairs, she determined to become a goddess by using the name of the sun god, already in his dotage. She collected some of his spittle, mixed it with earth and so created a serpent, which she placed in Re's path. Bitten and poisoned, the sun god was advised by Isis to utter his own name since its divinity bestowed life on whoever spoke it. At last the working of the venom compelled Re to speak, and Isis appropriated a portion of his power. Thereafter she sparkled as the constellation Sirius, while her cult spread to Greece and Rome.

Leviathan

Literally, 'coiled'. The sea serpent of Hebrew myth, a restatement of the chaos-dragon Tiamat, is the same as the Ras Shamra Lotan, the seven-headed monster slain by Anat. The apocryphal *Book of Enoch* speaks of a companion beast. 'And in that day will two monsters be separated, a female named Leviathan to dwell in the abyss over the fountains of waters. But the male is called Behemoth which occupies with his breasts an immeasurable desert named Dendain.' The *Talmud*, a compendium of the teachings of later Rabbis, states that the fins of Leviathan radiate such brilliant light as to obscure the rays of the sun. Though the plaything of Yahweh, in the last days of the world the sea serpent will repulse attacks from angels, till Behemoth kills it. According to Islamic tradition, Allah used Behemoth not as a destroyer of dragons but a firm foundation for the world, a mighty back overarching the water and the darkness below the earth.

A vivid description of Leviathan occurs in the *Book of Job*. To underscore man's weakness and ignorance compared with divine greatness, Yahweh asked: 'Canst thou draw out Leviathan with an hook? . . . None is *so* fierce that dare stir him up: who then is able to stand before me? . . . He esteemeth iron as straw, and brass as rotten wood. . . . He maketh the deep to boil like a pot.' It is not surprising that in medieval Christianity Leviathan, 'king over all the children of pride', was identified with hell, whose entrance iconography depicted as a gigantic maw.

Maat

Daughter of Re and the Egyptian goddess of truth, who wore a single ostrich feather. As a personification of truth and justice her feather was placed in one pan of the balance used for weighing the soul of a dead man in the judgement before Osiris, King of the 'other land'.

Marduk

Literal meaning: 'bull calf of the sun'. The son of Ea, Marduk seems to have been a god of magic and incantation from early times. This double-headed sun god was given the epithet Bel, 'lord', and identified with Enlil, especially after he had assumed leadership of the Babylonian pantheon during the cosmic struggle with Tiamat, the she-dragon of the salt-water ocean. Marduk, appointed as the celestial champion, slew Tiamat, fastened the tablets of destiny on his own breast, and created a new world order which included mankind. It is a paradoxical creation myth: for the chaos-monster, though slain and dismembered, remained the body of the universe and was manifest in her children, the gods and goddess from whom Bel-Marduk received homage.

Marduk told the assembly of gods that the centre of the universe was Babylon, where he had built himself a 'luxurious house'. He owed his prominence in Mesopotamian religion and his wide influence on Canaanite mythology entirely to the political and economic importance of the city, which became dominant after Sumerian power declined.

There was a strong henotheistic tendency at work in the Assyrio-Babylonian pantheon, so that a large number of deities were treated as manifestations of Marduk: he had 'fifty names'. His consort was Sarpanitu, 'the shining one', the planet Venus. The great festival of the god at the spring equinox was called *zagmuk*, 'the beginning of the year', when his resurrection took place in Esagila, 'the house that lifts up its head'. Nonetheless, this famous shrine was robbed of the sacred image by King Mursilis I, who led his Hittite warriors in a successful raid on Babylon about 1590 BC.

Melqart

The Canaanite Hercules and city god of Tyre. At his temple, Herodotus tells us, there were two tall pillars, 'one of pure gold, the other of emerald, which shone brilliantly at night'. He was connected with the sea and with navigation: Cape Melqart exists in Sicily and it is not unlikely that the Pillars of Hercules were once called the Pillars of Melqart. He died by fire and his annual awakening was celebrated at a festival held in January.

Mithra

Of all the celestial beings ruling over the earth he was the most popular with the Persians, who represented him as the son of Ahura Mazdah. He was the light that preceded the sun when it rose, the one who dispelled darkness; and from his penetrating gaze could nothing be hidden. Mithra was aware of every happening, no matter how insignificant each might appear. In pre-Zoroastrian times Mithra and Ahura were most likely twin sky gods, looked upon as *payu-thworeshtara*, 'the two creator-preservers' of the cosmic order. Later theological adjustment to Zoroaster's elevation of Ahura Mazdah as the supreme being indicates how potent a divinity Mithra actually remained. 'When I created Mithra of wide pastures,' said Ahura Mazdah, 'I made him as worthy of veneration and of reverence as I am myself.'

As a terrible war god Mithra was the special protector of the warriors, the *rathaeshtar* or 'riders on chariots'. Though all-wise and knowing, his warlike aspect found expression in ruthlessness, the merciless and relentless pursuit of those who had the temerity to oppose him. His weapons were deadly arrows, a huge mace, incurable diseases, and the boar Verethraghna, 'sharp in tusk, unapproachable, a raging beast. . . . He smashes the backbone. At one fell blow he destroys everything: bones and hair, brains and blood of men who break their contracts he mashes up together with mud.' Even his own devotees stood in awe of such limitless fury. 'Mithra, evil you are yet most good to the nations. Mithra, evil you are yet most good to men. In the world you have power over peace and war.' This 'evil', however, was reserved for the false, those who broke faith with 'the wise lord', Ahura Mazdah, and chose the dishonesty of Ahriman, 'the destructive spirit'. Mithra means 'friend'. He extended friendship towards people who honoured the sacred obligations—between men and men as well as between men and heaven.

Mindful of his complaint that people were paying him little worship Ahura Mazdah invited Mithra to take part in the *haoma* rite, which was central to the Zoroastrian liturgy. The consumption of the fermented juice of this plant appears to have descended from ancient practices of ritual intoxication. Having been so incorporated in worship, he was firmly re-established in the Persian pantheon, and the situation ready for his final development as the 'mystery' deity, Mithras.

The Mithraic mysteries which swept through the Roman Empire came from the late Zoroastrian acceptance of Mithra as the 'mystery of the sorcerers'. In the second century Plutarch wrote that between Ohrmazd and Ahriman 'is Mithras, whom the Persians call the Mediator. From him they learnt how to sacrifice votive offerings and thank offerings to the one, but to the other offerings for averting evil, things of gloom.' The origin of the bull-sacrifice in the Roman cult of Mithras is obscure, not least for the reason that the slayer of the primeval ox was Ahriman. Its consequences were thought of as twofold: continued prosperity and fertility in the material world, but also the continued life of the soul in the spiritual world, after death. Appealing to soldiers, the cult spread along the frontiers of the Roman Empire from the Danube to Britain. In the twilight of the pagan gods it also offered refreshment to high-born traditionalists like the Emperor Julian. At his palace in Constantinople he installed in 362 a *mithraeum*, a cave-sanctuary, and celebrated there a *taurobolium*, in which he sat in a trench over which a bull was slaughtered, and so was bathed in its blood. There is a possibility that the rite was borrowed from the Phrygian cult of Attis.

Moloch

Moses said: 'Thou shalt not let any of thy seed pass through the fire to Molech.' It was formerly thought that Moloch, or Molech, could have been Melqart, the god worshipped in Tyre as well as Carthage, its colony. A Roman author records that in Carthage there was a bronze statue of a deity on the outstretched hands of which children were placed, so that they fell into the fire below. Because the Ras Shamra tablets do not

mention child-sacrifice, the present view is that Molech was not a god but simply the term used for this primitive Canaanite rite. When Yahweh tempted Abraham, he said: 'Take thou thy son, thine only son Isaac, whom thou lovest, and get thee to the land of Moriah; and offer him there for a burnt offering upon one of the mountains which I will tell thee of.' The patriarch was released from this gruesome obligation when Yahweh provided a ram instead. The ultimate sacrifice of the firstborn, for Christians, was the crucifixion of Jesus, 'the Lamb of God'. This mode of death, which the Roman authorities reserved for the lowest criminals, originated in Canaan.

Nergal

According to one Babylonian myth, it happened that Ereshkigal, 'the mistress of death', summoned Nergal to account for his refusal to stand up in the assembly of the gods before her envoy. The gods agreed that Nergal should depart from them, and Ea gave him an escort of fourteen demons who caused sickness. The exiled god used these horrible comrades to advantage in seizing the seven portals of the nether world. Once inside the throne room himself, Nergal seized Ereshkigal by the hair and cast her on the floor. His dagger was only stopped from slitting the goddess's throat through a successful appeal to his masculinity. 'Kill me not', cried out Ereshkigal. 'I shall be your wife and the kingdom of the dead acknowledge your sovereignty. In your hand I shall place the tablets of wisdom.' Nergal accepted the proposal and henceforth as her consort ruled. in death. A variant legend recounts his return to the assembly of the gods, whence a distraught Ereshkigal enticed him back to her bed. Her ultimatum to the gods was: Nergal, or the cessation of all fertility and life on earth. This fertility aspect of the chthonic goddess was a Sumerian inheritance.

Nergal was represented as wearing a crown and waited upon by fourteen gruesome attendants. His city was Cutha, whose name could have meant the land of the dead. Associated with him were the plague and the destructive power of the sun: he was Irra, the god of pestilence, fire, battle, and the desert; also he was the sun god Shamash who lent fierce winds to Gilgamesh and Enkidu in their fight with the giant Huwawa. Nergal was feared and zealously propitiated. The

Babylonians thought that to lose the favour of a god was the beginning of trouble. They believed the divine spirit inhabited the body of its servant. To show displeasure or wrath this protective presence had only to be withdrawn. 'Then the one without a god', a tablet explains, 'headache covers like a garment when he walks in the street.'

Nimrod

According to Hebrew tradition, the iniquity and godlessness of Nimrod, King of Shinar, reached their climax in the building of the Tower of Babel. This cunning ruler had acquired world dominion through possession of the garments worn by Adam and Eve; these clothes made of skins were Yahweh's gifts to the ancestors of mankind, and they had a wonderful property. Animals recognized the authority of the person wearing them and in battle they always secured victory. The success of Nimrod led to his deification, and the people gave him unstinted worship, but the King remained unsatisfied. Therefore, he ordered the construction of a tower capable of delivering an assault on heaven. To forestall this plan Yahweh confounded the speech of Shinar. One man asked for mortar, and another handed him a brick; such misunderstanding soon caused strife, and the people split into hostile factions. So Yahweh dealt with the descendants of Noah. He reserved Hebrew for Israel—the language he had used at the creation of the world—and gave a different tongue to each of the other seventy nations.

In *Genesis* the myth is introduced to account for the break-up of the original unity of the human race and its dispersal into different nations, speaking different tongues. The name of the tower means confusion. Nimrod receives no mention here, though the prophet Micah calls Assyria 'the land of Nimrod'. Moreover, there have come to light recently fragments of a Sumerian legend that attributes the end of the Golden Age to Ea's diversification of language.

Noah

The flood myth of West Asia is Mesopotamian in origin. There survives a Sumerian king list with the statement that following the reigns of the first eight monarchs, a legendary era of 241,200 years, 'the flood swept over the land'. These kings, reminiscent of the patriarchs before the biblical deluge, included Gilgamesh and Dumuzi. According to the fragments preserved, when the gods decided to drown mankind, the water god Enki warned the pious and god-fearing Ziusudra, King of Sippar, who built a boat in order to escape the seven-day flood. Later Ziusudra acquired 'life like a god'. In Akkadian literature there are two versions of the flood story. *The Gilgamesh Epic* makes Utanapishtim the hero, while in another myth the survivor of primordial famine and flood is Atrahasis. During the Assyrian ascendancy, in the seventh century BC, the Atrahasis myth was used as an incantation at childbirth. For Christian symbolism the deliverance from the flood came to signify baptism, and Noah's ark the Church.

In Hebrew tradition the survival of Adam's seed depends on the uprightness of Noah, Methuselah's grandson. Whereas the Mesopotamian gods had wearied of the service rendered by their human servants, not least the din they made, Yahweh sent the deluge because of the curse brought upon earth by the sin of Adam. The life and conduct of Noah was a standing rebuke to his contemporaries, then incited to wickedness by fallen angels. But the treatment of Noah in the *Old Testament* obscures his cultural role as a founder of agricultural technique. He introduced the vine. Apocryphal literature relates that his drunkenness was the result of a wine-making partnership with Satan, who poured on the roots of the vine the blood of a slaughtered lamb, lion, pig, and monkey. In this manner he conveyed to Noah what the qualities of wine are: before man tastes it, he is as innocent as a lamb; after imbibing moderately, he feels as strong as a lion; after swallowing too much, he resembles a pig; and drinking to the point of intoxication, he behaves like a monkey, talks gibberish, cavorts, and is obscene.

Nun

The primeval waters of Egyptian mythology. In rare illustrations Nun is portrayed as a man standing waist-deep in water, his arms raised to support the barque of the sun. The chaos of the primeval waters was deep, endless, murky, and unperceived: each of these four characteristics was personified by a pair of chthonic deities—Nun and Naunet, Huh and Hauhet, Kuk and Kakwet, Amun and Amaunet—all

of whom comprised the Ogdoad of Khmun, 'the town of Eight'. The watery element was thought to surround the world, but singularly lacking in Egyptian legend is a flood.

A papyrus of Nut, the sky goddess, arched over Geb, god of the earth

Nut

The Egyptian sky goddess. Atum arose from Nun, the primeval waters, and created Shu and Tefnut, air and moisture; from their union came Geb, the earth god, and Nut, whose offspring included Osiris, Seth, Isis, and Nepthys. The sky goddess was usually portrayed as a naked, giant woman whose arched back, supported by Shu, contained the heavens. Legend accounted for day and night in terms of solar rebirth. The sun was a child who entered the mouth of Nut in the evening, passed during the night through her body, and was born from her womb again in the morning.

Osiris

The Egyptian saviour: the chief deity of death, and the only god to rival the solar cult of Re. Sacred to him was Zedu, a town which took its name from his fetish—several sheaves placed one above the other. There along the luxuriant waterways of the delta Osiris was lord of flood and vegetation as well as the king and judge of the dead. From Anubis, the earlier dog-headed or jackal god of death, he acquired the

jackal symbol just as in Upper Egypt the recumbent dog connected with the dead, Khenti-Amentiu, was merged with him at Abydos, where it was believed that Osiris' head had been buried. In Egypt the gods had no special abode such as the Olympus of the Greeks; for the local residences of deities remained the same down the ages, with the exception of those gods absorbed by the greater members of the pantheon.

Osiris was depicted as a bearded man, either green or black in colour, wearing the Crown of Upper Egypt, and swathed like a mummy. In his hands were a flail and a crook, insignia of the chthonic power vested in this dying and rising god. Credited with the introduction of agriculture and several crafts, Osiris was also the initiator of religious rituals, especially the mysteries surrounding the process of embalmment and mummification. At Zedu the mummy of Osiris himself was to be seen. The preservation of the body was regarded as essential for eternal life. Without a body there could be no survival after death. In addition to the body the Egyptians acknowledged the existence of a *ba* and a *ka*. While the *ba* was the soul, and pictured as a bird with a human head, the *ka* acted as a kind of guardian double of the body which was born with it and stayed on as a companion in the world of the dead.

At first only the pharaohs became Osirises on death, being identified with the god of the dead as their successors were with Horus, the son of Osiris. From the third millennium BC onwards all men able to pass the judgement of good and evil might achieve such salvation. Before Osiris and his forty-two assessors stood the scales of judgement, attended by Anubis, who placed the soul in the balance against the feather of truth, while the record-keeper Thoth inscribed on his palette the result of the weighing. For the unfortunate waited a monster, part crocodile, part lion, and part hippopotamus: it was Am-mut, 'eater of the dead'. In Egyptian cosmology the 'other land' of the departed was situated on the western horizon, where daily the sun disappeared with its light and life-giving warmth, and from which point descended on the Nile valley not only darkness but the chill winds of the rapidly cooling deserts.

In myth Osiris is drowned, dismembered, and scattered over land and water. He was shut in a chest or sarcophagus and dumped in the Nile by his brother Seth. 'The drowned one' floated down the river through one of the mouths of the delta into the Mediterranean Sea, and was carried to the port of Byblos. There he was discovered by Isis, his wife and sister, and daughter of the earth god Geb. Out of envy for the happiness of Osiris and Isis arose the undying enmity of Seth, who soon seized the coffin containing the dead god, cut the corpse into more than fourteen pieces, and scattered them throughout the land of Egypt. Again Isis sought her husband and with the assistance of Nut, the mother of Osiris, she resurrected the body, all except his genitals; these had been consumed by fishes. The reborn god, however, did not stay on earth, but became the lord of the departed in the infertile 'other land'. Another legend suggests Isis buried each piece of Osiris where she found it, thus spreading the potency of the god everywhere. Horus, the son Isis miraculously conceived of the dead god, was to be the avenger.

As a prototype of the resurrected dead man, Osiris and his cult spread widely, and during the Roman Empire assumed the form of a major religious sect in many provinces. One view of the origin of the myth is that the god was an historical king who at a remote period reigned over Egypt from his capital in the delta. His violent death could have been the result of an insurrection by Ombos, the city sacred to Seth in Upper Egypt. The divided kingdom according to this version was reunited by the King's son, deified as Horus, who slew the rebellious Seth. An alternative explanation places emphasis on the death and resurrection of Osiris, the vegetation god reborn through the annual inundation of the Nile.

Ptah

A leading member of the Egyptian pantheon. His cult centre was at Memphis, where he had the lion goddess Sakhmet as wife and Nefertem as son. At the beginning of things Ptah existed as Nun, the primeval waters. By speech or by kneading mud Ptah-Nun created the world. In one text he is even credited with the birth of Atum, the form Re assumed in the Heliopolitan creation myth. Thus the priests of Ptah tried to incorporate the principal elements of rival doctrines in their own cosmology. A more local merger took place with a necropolis god so that the deity of Memphis was Ptah-Sokar.

Ptah was represented as a person, always holding the *ankh*, the symbol of life and the generative forces in the universe. He may have been regarded as a smith god, because the Greeks associated him with Hephaestus, their god of the crafts. In Memphis, too, was the popular cult of the Apis Bull. A large number of bulls and cows were held to be sacred, but the various cults were eclipsed by the veneration displayed for the bull of Memphis. One Apis Bull was alive at a time, the next inhabitant of the sacred enclosure not being chosen by a panel of divines till the mummified body, robed like a prince, had been laid to rest in a sarcophagus alongside those of its predecessors. The priests of several prominent Egyptian gods took part in ceremonies associated with the Apis Bull. The exact relation of Ptah to the animal is unclear, but on death it was said to have become an Osiris.

Rashnu

The 'just' judge in Persian mythology. Along with Mithra and Sraosha, he judges the souls of men according to their deeds. 'His spiritual scales favour no one; neither the good nor the bad, nor yet kings and princes. Not for a hair's breadth will he deviate, for he is no respecter of persons. He deals out impartial justice to the highest and the lowest.' The soul was thought to sit beside the corpse for three days and nights, a period in which Rashnu arrived at a verdict and its fate was determined. Then, the saved would be assisted in crossing 'the bridge of separation' by a fair maiden personifying the soul's good deeds, and led safely to heaven where all was light and joy. But the damned, 'the unjustified soul', would find the bridge was as thin as the edge of a razor and topple downwards to hell, where a hideous woman personifying its misdeeds was waiting. To the demons she passed on the condemned soul, thereafter imprisoned in the place of torment, Druj, which had 'jaws like the most frightful pit, descending into a very narrow and fearful place . . . so confined that existence there was unendurable'.

Re

Heliopolis was the cult centre for Re, or Ra, the sun god. Such was his authority that he appears in the myths of many cults and even in his dotage the Egyptians thought of him as retaining immense power. In the third millennium BC the Pharaoh Chephren first styled himself 'son of Re', but it was the reforming zeal of Amenophis IV (1387–1366 BC) that raised the worship of the sun god to unprecedented heights. As Akhenaton, 'the devotee of Aton', this unusual pharaoh sought to concentrate devotion on the purely material character of the sun god as a solar disc, Aton. He rejected the deities invoked by previous rulers and persecuted the priests of Amun, the ram-headed god of Thebes, whose influence in religious affairs had been unchallenged since the expulsion of the Hyksos. He decided to build a new residence for Re and himself: this city, called Akhetaton, 'the horizon of Aton', was situated about half-way between Thebes and Memphis. There Aton was worshipped as the creative principle of all life, the father of all men, who gave them different coloured skins, different languages, and different lands. To the Egyptians he gave the Nile, to others rain. Preoccupied with religious doctrine, Akhenaton remained in Akhetaton, isolated from the rest of the country and apparently unperturbed by the loss of Egypt's possessions in Canaan. Yet he did not succeed in establishing a faith which dispensed with

Egyptian mythology, for after his death Tutankhamen brought the court back to Thebes, and under the last pharaoh of the Eighteenth Dynasty, Haremheb (1353–1319 BC), all trace of Aton-worship disappeared.

In Heliopolitan myth, Re as Atum was the creator of the universe. Self-existent and alone, Atum brought forth—either through an act of masturbation or by means of spittle—the divine pair of Shu, air, and Tefnut, moisture. From their union sprang the earth god Geb and the sky goddess Nut. The arch-enemy of Atum was the serpent Apophis, the equivalent of the Babylonian she-dragon Tiamat, slain by the sun god Marduk. Shu, Atum's son, vanquished the host of Apophis or, according to another version, the conqueror of chaotic forces was Seth. However, Apophis never assumed the same importance in Egypt as the evil spirit did in other West Asian traditions. The Nile inundation was a regular event, not the incalculable floods of the Tigris-Euphrates valley. We find nothing akin to the conflict of hostile powers evident in Babylonian mythology, where the archetypal dragon of chaos and its engulfing element, the primeval waters, required the heroic intervention of the sun god.

At a temple in Thebes there occurred a ritual to aid Re in his daily struggle with Apophis. It was believed that after sunset the forces of the serpent assailed Re and the ensuing battle lasted throughout the night. Even after sunrise Apophis would sometimes dare to raise storm clouds in the sky in order to obscure the light and power of the sun. The Theban ceremony involved the destruction of a magical image. A figure of Apophis, represented as a crocodile or a serpent, was made of wax, and on it his name was inscribed in green ink. Along with effigies of his followers, also wrapped in papyrus, Apophis was insulted, hacked with a knife, and thrown to the ground. Meanwhile the priest recited a spell. The practice of the magic arts was interwoven inextricably with religious ritual in Egypt, where even the gods themselves could be said to have used spells. The deities created by Atum were manifestations of his *hike*, or 'magical power'.

The dotage of Re is the subject of several popular myths. To Isis the terrified old man of the heavens revealed his ineffable name. To the cow goddess Hathor a short-tempered, quarrelsome greybeard entrusted the slaughter of

A bronze head of Re, represented as a falcon

mankind. Another example of the intermingling of legend concerns the eye of Re and the eye lost by Horus in his combat with Seth. Originally separate myths, they were often linked together in late versions of divine events. The eye of Re, the morning star, was connected with Osiris after he had been brought back to life by his son Horus. In the form of Tefnut, the eye of the sun god actually vanished for a period of time and only returned after long entreaty and propitiation.

Re played as conspicuous a role in the care of the dead as he did in the shaping of human destiny. With Horus he set up in the royal tomb the ladder of escape for the dead pharaoh. Re, too, led his spirit into the palace of the gods. Worship of Re finally succumbed to competition from the Osiris cult, whose prime interest in death and resurrection satisfied a need unmet by the cosmological speculation of the solar myths.

Saoshyant

Literally, 'saviour'. In Persian mythology the one who will come to renew all life at the end of time. He will remove every trace of the evil wrought in the world by Ahriman, and usher in the 'second existence', uniting souls with their bodies. The resurrection of the dead was expected to include both the good and the wicked: the followers of Ahura Mazdah, who dwelt in the abode of light along with celestial beings, or 'shining ones'; and the inhabitants of Druj, the cold, foul place of darkness reserved for those who chose Ahriman as their master. A mighty conflagration would ensue, molten metal pouring forth on the earth and hell. All men will have to endure the burning torrent which will seem like 'warm milk' to the just and be exactly what it is to the wicked. But the sins of the damned should be purged away in this dreadful ordeal and all creation return to Ohrmuzd in joy. It was to be the *frashkart*, 'the final rehabilitation'. In this late eschatology the ultimate fate of Ahriman and his demons is obscure, though the searing of Druj suggests a complete annihilation of the evil principle.

Zoroaster may have anticipated a reformation on the earth as the immediate consequence of his own mission. When this did not happen, his disciples thought the prophet would be succeeded by three saviours, each appearing at intervals of a thousand years. 'At the last turning point of existence' they anticipated a judgement in which the evil would be allotted their final doom and the good their eternal reward. The idea of heaven and hell as irremediable states was superseded under the Sassanians (226–652) by the ultimate triumph of Ohrmuzd, who replaced Ahura Mazdah and Spenta Mainya as the source of goodness.

According to a late myth, 'time was for twelve thousand years' divided into four periods each of 3,000 years. The first, a spiritual epoch, contained the *fravashis*, pre-existent external souls, the guardian angels; the second period saw the creation of Gayomart, the primeval man, as well as the primeval ox; in the third evil overcame Gayomart and the ox, while the three-headed dragon Azhi Dahaka tyrannized mankind; the present age has enjoyed the teachings of Zoroaster and will terminate with the advent of Saoshyant.

Satan

Belief in malevolent beings which haunt the air and the secret places of the earth stemmed from early man's instinctive fear of the unknown, the strange and frightening. In West Asia this common superstition expressed itself potently in a variety of ways: the Egyptians struggled against Am-mut, the 'eater of the dead', and the serpent Apophis daily threatened the sun god Re; the Babylonians attributed sickness and misfortune to demonic attack, while at night men were endangered by Lilitu, a beautiful, winged succubus; the Hebrews had to cope with a host of fallen angels under the crafty leadership of Satan and Beelzebub; the Arabs fought off the assaults of countless *djinn*, 'hidden ones', inhabitants of the world before man; the Persians, the hardest pressed of all peoples, faced in the dreadful creations of Ahriman nothing less than absolute evil. It was the impact of Persian dualism on the Hebrews, after the Babylonian Exile, that led to the crystallization of the Devil in the form we recognize today.

In the *Old Testament* the word Satan originally meant 'adversary', the supernatural being that Yahweh allowed to test Job, 'a perfect and an upright man'. But the idea of a spirit of evil was developed in apocryphal literature, especially the *Book of Enoch*, written down after 200 BC. The fall of Satan was explained in terms of envy: he was jealous of Adam and refused as 'a son of god' to pay him reverence and homage. Michael said he should worship 'the image of God' or face the wrath of Yahweh, but Satan and his followers refused. They were flung out of heaven, down to earth, and from that moment started the enmity between Satan and mankind. Other angels, however, fell earthward because of the sensual charms of the daughters of men. Thus did Shemhazai and Azazel, who fathered 'the wicked demon Asmodaeus', the Zoroastrian Aeshma. On the Day of Atonement the priests had to sacrifice a second ram. One scapegoat was for the sins of Israel, the other for Azazel. From the union of angels and women sprang the titans mentioned in *Genesis*, the giants who were drowned along with the 'corrupt' descendants of Adam in the flood.

Christianity inherited this demonology, to which was added the belief that the pagan deities were devils. St Paul was firm on this theological issue. 'Ye cannot drink of the cup of the Lord, and the cup of devils.' Beelzebub, or Baalzebub, 'lord of the flies', was a distortion of a Canaanite god's name probably meaning 'lord of the house'. The idea also grew up that each soul had assigned to it a good and an evil angel. But in the apocalypse of *Revelation* the faithful knew of the final defeat of Satan, clearly identified as the 'dragon' of *Genesis*. According to the evangelist St Peter, Jesus Christ, having died, even 'went and preached to the spirits in prison'. A graphic account of his descent into hell occurs in the apocryphal *Gospel of Nicodemus*, which dates from the fourth century.

The Gnostic ascetic Saturninus, a contemporary of Simon Magus, wrote: 'Marriage and generation are of Satan.' Because the world was under his evil sway, abstinence was the only way for the 'spark of life' to escape. In Gnostic mythology the Devil was in league with the female principle, who 'is without foreknowledge, wrathful, double-minded, double-bodied, a virgin above and a viper below.'

Seth

Representations on gravestones in Upper Egypt, dating from the third millennium BC, attribute to Seth a donkey-like appearance, with long legs, long and broad ears, and a short upright tail. But over the centuries the god was transformed into a fabulous beast, not unlike a massive dog. Seth was 'lord of Upper Egypt', his sacred city being Ombos, and in that capacity he became a rival to his nephew Horus. Myth recounts the struggle between these adversaries, following the murder of Osiris by Seth, who temporarily seized power in Upper Egypt. By the Greeks Seth was identified with Typhon, a huge monster who fought with Zeus, was defeated and buried in Sicily under Mount Aetna, whose volcanic rumblings and eruptions were the monster's struggles. Nepthys, the wife of Seth and sister of Osiris, was associated with the rites of burial, since she and Isis acted as guardians of the head and feet of the coffin. Nepthys means 'the lady of the castle'.

During the Hyksos occupation of the delta Seth enjoyed a short supremacy, because the Semitic invaders adopted him as their own god but, unlike the pharaohs, regarded him as the only god and even attempted to impose his cult on the rest of Egypt which had retained its independence. The *hekaukhasut*, 'the rulers of foreign lands', or the Hyksos to us, found that Seth had much in common with their own Baals. Moreover, the city of Avaris, their capital, was an old cult centre of the god. After the expulsion of the Hyksos about 1570 BC the country was reunited by the Pharaoh Amosis and the other Egyptian gods restored. However, an indirect legacy of Seth's elevation may have been the attempt made by Amenophis IV to replace all the gods with Aton, the solar disc.

Sheba

The Queen of Sheba came to Jerusalem and tested the wisdom of King Solomon 'with hard questions'. Around the visit of this nameless Queen legend has woven a rich tapestry. Her gifts were magnificent because the wealth of her land, present-day Yemen, derived from a near-monopoly over the supply of frankincense and myrrh. In Hebrew mythology Solomon 'lay with the Queen of Sheba and from her went forth Nebuchadnezzar'. In Ethiopia the legend took on a political significance, for the 1955 Revised Constitution stated that the pedigree of Emperor Haile Selassie 'descends without interruption from the dynasty of Menelik I, son of the Queen of Ethiopia, Queen of Sheba, and King Solomon of Jerusalem'. Most surprising of all, however, are the embellishments found in Islamic tradition, where the visitor has become not the Queen, but Solomon. He travelled from Mecca to Sheba and expected to find its queen with 'legs like a donkey's because her mother was a *djinn*', a demon. To his relief the legs of the Queen of Sheba proved attractively human, though they were rather hairy. So they married—after she had used depilatories.

Simon Magus

The Gnostic teachings of this Canaanite sorcerer exercised the minds of Christian theologians. While in Jerusalem St Peter had to rebuke Simon the Samaritan for attempting to buy the magical powers which he supposed the apostles had received from the Holy Spirit, the legendary encounter between the two men took place in Rome, where the apocryphal *Acts of Peter* tell how the Samaritan tried to fly heavenwards. Perhaps Simon should have been called *magnus*, 'the great', rather than *magus*, 'the magician', since he told the Romans that he would forsake them, 'impious sinners, and fly up to God whose Power' he was. When he soared and 'was lifted up on high, and all beheld him flying above Rome and its temples and hills', the faithful turned to Peter, who was disturbed by the impression that the spectacle made on their minds. 'Hasten thy grace, O Lord,' implored the evangelist, 'and let him fall from the height and be injured. Let him not die but be discomforted, and break his leg in three places.' And so it happened that Simon fell to the ground and broke his leg in three places, whereupon he received the added insult of a shower of stones from the disappointed crowd.

For the Ebionites, 'the poor', a Jewish-Christian sect living near the Dead Sea, Simon Magus was a hostile disguise for St Paul in his bitter controversy with St Peter. The *Acts of Peter*, whose theme was the demise of Simon, may have been Ebionite in origin. The real opponents of St Paul were undoubtedly the leaders of the Jewish converts living in Jerusalem. They included the original disciples of Jesus and they seem to have rejected the version of the faith expounded to the Gentiles by St Paul, a Hellenistic Jew and the first saint not to have known the historical Messiah. He viewed conversion as the adoption of a new religion, Christianity, which had discarded the trappings of Hebrew belief, like circumcision and the payment of temple tithes. After the Roman destruction of Jerusalem in 70, the challenge to St Paul's theology ceased, and converts were freely accepted into the fold.

The germinal significance of Simon Magus was recognized. Bishop Irenaeus (130–200) wrote that from him 'all heresies originated.... He led about with him a certain Helen, after he had redeemed her from a life of prostitution in Tyre.... He said she was the first conception of his mind, the Mother of all, through whom in the beginning he had the idea of making angels and archangels. This Idea, leaping forth from him and knowing what her father had willed, descended and generated angels and archangels, by whom this world was created.' Angelic envy and ignorance led to her enslavement in a human body, so that her soul 'transmigrated' down the ages, once animating Helen of Troy, till finally Simon came 'to rescue her and free her from her bonds, before he offered men salvation through his knowledge'.

Gnosis, 'knowledge', was the principal claim of people like Simon Magus, who passed on to initiates an understanding of the cosmos, human nature, and destiny. The sharp dichotomy of body and soul in Gnosticism found a cosmological analogue in the opposition of the Demiurge and the supreme being, which Simon said he was. Although the Demiurge created the world, about AD 160 the Gnostic philosopher Ptolemaeus wrote that this being, 'who is impotent to know spiritual things, considered he was the only God and said through the prophets "There is no other one"'. The archetypal conjurer, Simon Magus is only remembered today in the sin of simony.

Sin

The moon god of Ur and son of Enlil, the Sumerian god of earth and air. As 'lord of the calendar', his cult exhibited monotheistic tendencies, since it was Sin 'who determines the destinies of distant days' and whose 'plans no god knows'. According to *Genesis*, Abraham hailed from Ur by way of Harran, both cities devoted to the moon god. In Arabia, Sin was also worshipped under various titles and it is likely that Mount Sinai, first mentioned in Hebrew texts about 1000 BC, was connected with moon-worship.

Sphinx

In Egyptian mythology the Sphinx was an image of the sun god, though it may have been no more than the peculiar shape of a limestone hillock on the Giza plateau that suggested the original notion of a recumbent lion with a human head wearing the headdress of the pharaohs. It was in the third millennium BC that Chephren had craftsmen shape the Great Sphinx at Giza. It is 240 feet long and faces the rising sun. Protector of the pyramids and scourge of the enemies of Re, the Sphinx was a popular motif in Egyptian art and architecture. According to legend, Tuthmosis IV (1425–1412 BC) was promised as a prince by the Sphinx that he would ascend the throne if he cleared away the sand which was submerging the paws of the Great Sphinx.

In Greek mythology the Sphinx was a monster with the face and breasts of a woman, the body of a lion, and wings. Sent by the earth goddess Hera as an affliction on the city of Thebes, she guarded a pass on a cliff by the sea and asked all who would pass a riddle. When Oedipus gave the correct answer, the Sphinx hurled herself over the cliff to her death in the sea below.

A Greek sarcophagus showing Oedipus confronting the Sphinx

Sraosha

Literal meaning: 'to hearken'. Originally the genius of hearing and obeying in Persian mythology, he survived the Arab conquest as Surush, the messenger of Allah sometimes identified with the Archangel Gabriel. In Zoroastrian times Sraosha was Ahura Mazdah's all-hearing ear which listened for the cries of men wronged on earth by the servants of Ahriman, 'the destructive spirit'. Because all wicked things were most active at night, he descended to earth after the sun had set and pursued Aeshma, the demon of anger and violence. His chief enemy was this evil spirit, who had been ordered to attack the primeval ox. Sraosha, like Mithra, was a mediator as well as the bond of obedience that united earth to heaven. In the heavenly court he alone was allowed to stand in front of Ahura Mazdah.

St Antony

Throughout the Middle Ages, St Antony was celebrated on account of his legendary temptations. He went into the Egyptian desert about 270, when he was twenty years old. The young man who 'blushed to eat', accepted as a personal command the saying of Jesus: 'Go, sell all ye have and give to the poor and follow me.' There the Devil assailed St Antony by various temptations, but nothing could disturb him, not even a monstrous hippocentaur, in Christian iconography the symbol of bestial sensuality. The eremite's aloofness remained intact. Satan even complained that the waste, for ages past in West Asia the acknowledged preserve of demons, was swarming with unkempt hermits. The solitary Saint died in 356, when he made it plain that he was to be buried. The art of the embalmer was at that time becoming popular with Christians. Of his body, St Antony said: 'In the day of resurrection I shall receive it incorruptible from the hands of Christ.'

St Christopher

The calendar of the Coptic Church recalls the martyrdom of St Christopher on 28 March. This Egyptian saint 'belonged to the land of those who eat men and dogs'. His father had been converted to Christianity and he himself brought up in the faith. At a time of border hostilities he was taken captive by the Romans, but his ignorance of their language left him speechless. In response to his earnest prayers God endowed him with the ability to converse with them, just as on another occasion by special grace he was able to supply miraculously the famished soldiers with food. On hearing of St Christopher the Emperor Decius ordered that he be brought to Antioch, where in 250 the anti-Christian ruler assayed his belief by means of temptation and torture. Having failed to win over the holy man, or boil, drown, and mutilate him, Decius had the palace guards chop off his head.

Coptic was the vernacular language of the native population of Egypt: in it survived the notions of the ancient Egyptians, albeit the sounds were written not in hieroglyphics but alphabetic signs, which the Greeks had first borrowed from the Phoenicians. Legend ascribes the foundation of the Egyptian Church to the preaching of the evangelist St Mark among the Greek settlers of Alexandria, but it was not too long before Christianity in Egypt became an entirely Coptic phenomenon. Upon the native heritage it seems likely that the stories gathered around St Christopher drew much of their strength. In the background lurks Anubis, the jackal-headed god of death, who played such an important part in the ancient funeral cult. The fine seventeenth-century icon of St Christopher the Dog-headed, preserved at the Byzantine Museum in Athens, may well be the martyr from 'the land of those who eat men and dogs'.

St Simeon Stylites

The ferocious individualism of the Syrian saints was unmatched in West Asia. They were 'men of fire', souls purged through fierce asceticism. Most idiosyncratic was Simeon (c. 390–459), archetype of the pillar saints and the inspiration of ascetics for a millennium. He lived for forty years at the top of a 60-foot column in the hills behind Antioch. Utter rejection of the body drove the Stylites, whose self-immolation took the form of hair shirts, spiked collars, burns, insect bites, flagellation, rotten food, induced constipation, and constant exposure to the elements. Legend recounts that St Simeon was feeding worms on self-inflicted wounds which he kept open for that purpose, when a maggot fell off. Putting it back, the Saint remarked testily: 'Eat what God has given you!' At least one pillar saint was killed by lightning and, though monastic authorities discountenanced ascetic excesses, these wild men amazed and disquieted the eastern Mediterranean. The fame of St Simeon Stylites was spread as far afield as Gaul and Persia.

Telipinu

The Hittite weather god was also a fertility god, and he disappeared like his son Telipinu, the deity of agriculture. A myth deals with the desolation on earth caused by the angry withdrawal of Telipinu, and with measures adopted to appease him and secure his return. When the god of agriculture left in a temper, 'in such haste that he put his right boot on his left foot and his left boot on his right foot', both gods and men were faced with ruin. Trees withered and fields and springs dried up; oxen, sheep, and women ceased to bear young; famine crept over the world, as 'off to corpses stalked Telipinu, and in a corpse buried himself'. When the eagle sent out by the sun god failed to locate the missing deity, the mother goddess Hannahanna implored the weather god himself to undertake a search. He broke into Telipinu's city, discovered no one there, 'and then sat down in despair'.

Thereupon, Hannahanna sent forth a bee, ordering it to sting Telipinu, when it found him, on his hands and feet so as to rouse him, then smear him with wax and bring him back home. But the stings only enraged Telipinu and he created floods which 'swept away houses, men and animals'. It was not until Kamrusepas, the goddess of spells, or perhaps of healing, removed his anger through a magical ceremony that he was persuaded to return to his temple on the back of an eagle, and take thought for the land. 'Then before Telipinu they set up an evergreen and from it hung a fleece', in which mutton fat was placed, and offerings of corn, wine, and oxen.

Thoth

The scribe of the Egyptian gods. The chief deity of Khmun, or Hermopolis, was conceived as having either the head of an ibis or of a bamboo. In early times Thoth had been a creator god, but from the second half of the third millennium BC he was credited with the foundation of law, the advancement of learning, and the invention of hieroglyphic writing. The modern pack of playing-cards, held by some to be an adaptation of hieroglyphics, is sometimes called 'the book of Thoth'.

From his studies Thoth acquired mastery of *hike*, 'magic'. The creation myth of Khmun tells how the god of wisdom, self-created, uttered words which sprang into life: 'they were clothed with being'. This myth had particular appeal to later magicians and thaumaturgists. An interesting variant of the Khmun cosmology was the lotus flower that arose from the primeval waters, opened, and revealed the beautiful child creator of the world, the infant sun.

Tiamat

The Babylonian she-dragon, the original of which was the Sumerian monster Labbu, begot and destroyed by Enlil. *Enuma Elish* contains an account of what the universe was like before the events took place which resulted in the creation by Marduk of a new world order. At first there were only the mingled waters of Abzu, the abyss of sweet water, Tiamat, the salt-water ocean, and

St Christopher with a dog's head; from a seventeenth-century Byzantine icon

Mammu, the mists hovering above their surfaces. Abzu and Tiamat were the parents of the first gods, Lahmu and Lahamu, whose own children were Anshar and Kishar, and grandchildren, Anu and Ea. The commotion introduced in the universe by these younger deities annoyed Abzu and Tiamat, who, on Mummu's advice, planned to destroy their progeny. When Ea knew of this he used his magical powers to thwart their attack and may have even killed Abzu. Final deliverance was achieved through Ea's son Marduk, who was born in the sweet water.

When news of the fearsome preparations Tiamat was making for war reached the gods, there was dismay and despair. Along with her second husband Kingu and an army of monstrous dragon and serpent forms, Tiamat, the mother of the gods, was bent on universal destruction. Chaos menaced the world. Then Anshar proposed that Marduk be appointed as the divine champion and armed 'with matchless weapons' for the terrible battle. This was agreed as well as Marduk's insistence that he be acknowledged as first among the gods. With bow and trident, club and net, and an armoury of winds, he rode his chariot into the fray. When Tiamat opened her jaws to swallow him, he launched a raging wind straight into her mouth, so that she could not close it, shot an arrow into her belly, and slew her. He took her followers captive, and fastened the tablets of destiny on his own breast—the wedding gift of Tiamat to Kingu. Then he split the carcass into two parts: one he pushed upwards to form the heavens, the other he used to make a floor above the deep. In the world between he created man out of the blood of Kingu, before retiring to his temple at Babylon.

Tiamat was imagined to be a composite creature, part animal, part serpent, part bird, revolting in appearance, and dreadful in anger. She was evil: a she-dragon. The beneficent aspect of the mother goddess has vanished entirely. The West Asian myth of the dragon, representing the chaos of original matter constantly at odds with the created order, found its fullest expression in the conflict between Marduk and Tiamat, who was probably the prototype for Satan.

The number of Christian saints who encountered dragons is endless, St George being the most famous. His victory happened in Libya, where he relieved the inhabitants of the daily sacrifice of a virgin to the beast's hunger. A less chivalric encounter with one of Tiamat's descendants is recorded in Georgian legend. St David of Garesja, a forerunner of the animal-loving St Francis, was a native of Assyria, and a hermit. When his deer were molested by 'a large and fearsome dragon with bloodshot eyes and a horn growing out of his forehead, and a great mane on his neck', St David threatened to rip open its stomach with his staff and turn it into food for mice, unless it quietly departed. But from the safety of its cave, the dragon exclaimed that it dared not venture forth because of its terror of thunderbolts. Only if the Saint promised not to take his eyes from it until the river was reached would it agree to leave. St David gave his word and together they set out—the Saint reciting Psalms and the dragon shaking the ground with his heavy tread. But close by the river the angel of the Lord spoke from behind and said 'David!' So he looked round, and as he turned the dragon was struck by a thunderbolt and completely burnt up. When the kind-hearted St David saw this he was sad and asked the reason for the trick. In reply the angel told him that if the dragon had entered the river waters, it would have passed on into the sea, where grown enormous on fish it could overturn ships and destroy many living souls. Perhaps at this point the ninth-century chronicler turned dragon into Leviathan.

Ullikummi

The *Song of Ullikummi* is a Hurrian myth, although as it happens we know of it only through Hittite tablets recovered from Hattusa. The song narrates a conflict between the generations of the gods. In the beginning Alalus was king of heaven, served by Anu, 'the first among the gods', until a conspiracy toppled him, sent the dethroned deity to 'the dark earth', and elevated Anu. In turn the successor was attacked by 'the father of the gods', Kumarbi, who emasculated Anu with a single bite and then spat out of his mouth three new deities—Teshub, the storm god, Tasmisus, that god's attendant, and a river god. It appears that Teshub displaced Kumarbi, but the tenacious father refused to accept this loss of dignity and plotted against his usurping son. He enlisted the support of the sea god, or, according to a variant, married the sea god's daughter and begot the giant named Ullikummi, which may mean 'de-

stroyer of Kummiya', the abode of Teshub. Ullikummi was made of diorite stone, and when he was taken down to earth and put on the right shoulder of Upelluri, an Atlas figure, he grew with such rapidity that the sun god fled in alarm to warn the storm god.

From the summit of a mountain, Teshub, Ishtar, his sister, and Tasmisus viewed the monstrous Ullikummi rising out of the sea. Amid tears the storm god decided to give battle, yet thunder and rain left the growing giant unmarked, and soon Ullikummi was tall enough to reach the heavens. Overshadowed by the immense form of Kumarbi's stone son, Teshub was forced to abdicate and quit Kummiya. Whereupon Teshub appealed to Ea, who summoned the gods in the sweetwater ocean of Abzu to see what could be done to meet the desperate situation. When the council broke up in dismay, Ea consulted Enlil and then went to Upelluri, self-absorbed and unaware of the struggle. 'When heaven and earth were placed on me,' Upelluri told Ea, 'I knew nothing of it. When they came and cut heaven and earth asunder with a copper saw, I also knew not. Now something is hurting my right shoulder, but I know not who the god is.' On hearing these words Ea looked at Upelluri's right shoulder and there were the feet of Ullikummi. He pondered. Then finding in an old store-house the cosmic cutter, the copper saw mentioned by Upelluri, Ea returned to sever the stone feet, and thereby destroyed the giant's power. Although the end of the story is lost, we can assume that in the subsequent fight the gods triumphed and Teshub was restored.

The Ullikummi myth of sacred combat was part of the ritual connected with the spring festival. The stone giant represented a threat to gods and men, as a power whose phenomenal growth threatened the very order of the universe. A Greek parallel is Typhon, a monster whose head reached to heaven and who challenged Zeus on behalf of Gaia, the earth goddess. Ouranos, the sky god, was also castrated by his son Kronos, the father of Zeus. Moreover, the divine pregnancy of Kumarbi finds a paler comparison in Kronos' swallowing of his children, and his eventual disgorging of them under threat from Zeus.

Vahagn

The national deity of the ancient Armenians, who seem to have entered Asia Minor from

Thrace during the seventh century BC. Vahagn, the god of war, was popular enough not to share the fate of lesser deities, whom the Persian gods replaced after Armenia was conquered by Cyrus. Vahagn was associated with the sun, lightning, and fire. At birth 'he had hair of fire, he had a beard of flame, and his eyes were suns'. His exploits in slaying dragons led to identification with Hercules, though he would have reminded Hannibal rather of Melqart when the Carthaginian general took refuge in Artaxata. In 190 BC Artaxias, the Seleucid commander of the province, declared his independence and Hannibal, a fugitive from the Romans after the disastrous invasion of Italy, assisted the rebel in founding a dynasty.

Yima

In Persian mythology Yima is schizoid. Like the Hindu Yama, he was regarded as the first man and progenitor of the human race. For Zoroaster, however, he was a sinner, 'who, to please his people, gave them the flesh of the ox to eat'. The price of this transgression was his own immortality and with it the immortality of his descendants. Yima's crime may have been not so much the toleration of meat-eating in his kingdom as that he had slaughtered cattle in sacrifices to gods other than Ahura Mazdah, 'the wise lord'.

Despite the attack of Zoroaster the myth of 'royal' Yima's golden age persisted till the Arab conquest of 652. During his 700-year reign Yima was credited with the subjugation of the demons, taking away their lands and riches, and on three occasions he extended his borders to make room for all the 'cattle, great and small, men and dogs, birds, and red, burning fires' that the conditions of peace and plenty had done so much to multiply. But the golden age could not last forever, and so Ahura Mazdah warned that in the future 'wicked' men on earth would suffer 'destructive winters'—lashing hail, deluging rain, and heavy snow. To escape this calamity Yima was told he must hollow out for his choicest possessions a *vara*, or subterranean sanctuary. 'Gather together', said Ahura Mazdah, 'the seed of all men and women that are the tallest, best, and most beautiful; gather together the seed of all kinds of animals that are the finest on this earth; gather together the seed of all plants and fruits that are the tallest and sweetest. In pairs bring them to your retreat.

But take with you nothing mis-shapen or diseased, nor any of the other afflictions laid upon the world by Ahriman.' At the end of time it was anticipated that Yima would return and refurbish the surface of the earth.

Zu

Throughout Mesopotamian mythology there persists a legend of the tablets of destiny, *tupsimati*, on which the universal laws were inscribed. Zu, the lion-headed Sumerian storm bird, took these tablets from Enlil and threatened the very existence of the gods, for whoever wore them on the breast was supreme ruler of the world. Abashed and frightened, the assembly of the gods could not find a champion, until the son of Enlil, Ninurta, god of war and the chase, found the nest of Zu on the fabulous mountain of Sabu and rescued the tablets.

The *tupsimati* originally belonged to the Babylonian she-dragon Tiamat, who existed prior to the creation of the earth. They were her wedding gift to her second husband Kingu, whom Marduk slew in order to make man from Kingu's blood.

SOUTH AND CENTRAL ASIA

India Sri Lanka Tibet

India thinks in images. Symbol and metaphor have been available to Indian thought in an intimacy unparalleled in any other advanced civilization. Unlike Greece, its mythology was never devalued by philosophers nor were the great legends transformed into allegories by poets. Hindu myth has remained archaic, the collective heritage of a religious community which even today continues to refashion and reshape what is the most complex living culture in the world. Just as the traditional Indian system of social organization, caste, has grown over the past three and a half millennia through incorporation, not abolishing the customs of newly assimilated peoples but assigning them to a low place in the hierarchy, so Indian mythology rejected few beliefs, but included them in its own developing form, even if they seemed incompatible at first sight. Thus Sri Ramakrishna could say of his devotions towards the end of the nineteenth century: 'I have practised all religions, Hinduism, Islam, Christianity, and I have also followed the paths of the different Hindu sects. I have found that it is the same God towards whom all are directing their steps, though along different paths. You must try all beliefs and traverse all the different ways once.' While Mahatma Gandhi may have been correct in describing Ramakrishna's life as 'a story of religion in practice', the Bengali holy man did not once waver in his allegiance to the Divine Mother, whose aspect as Kali, the Black One, derives from her satiation with the blood of her innumerable victims.

Such a monistic view of the universe, whose every part is seen as alive and a manifestation of the total divinity, is fundamental to Hinduism, despite the hosts of gods and superhuman beings with which its mythology teems. The multitudes of apparitions are only aspects of the eternal cycle of creation; duration, and dissolution. To escape the endless round of rebirth and to enter into the unconditioned reality beneath the surface of daily appearances is the quest of the sage, the ascetic. *Moksa*, 'release, liberation, freedom, rescue, deliverance': this was the inner, non-dual perception of Ramakrishna and those others who attain the ultimate vision in *samadhi*. The understanding of this unity is the goal of Hindu wisdom. Beyond aversion and desire lies the union and coincidence of all kinds of opposites in one, transcendent source. Birth, love, joy, friendship, beauty, anger, sickness, pain, terror, and death have their rightful place in the constant universal evolution of the basic reality.

The *Rig Veda*, a collection of hymns, contains the earliest details we have of the gods of the Aryan invaders who overthrew the ancient Indus valley civilization about 1700 BC. Their chief god was Indra, god of the storm, whose weapon was the thunderbolt, and he rode to battle in a golden chariot drawn by two ruddy horses. As *puramdara*, the 'fort-destroyer', he gave the nomadic Aryans victory over the sophisticated agriculturalists living in the cities of Harappa and Mohenjo-Daro. The Indus valley civilization extended over an area much larger than either Egypt or Sumer and appears

Pilgrims bathing in the sacred waters of the Ganges at Benares

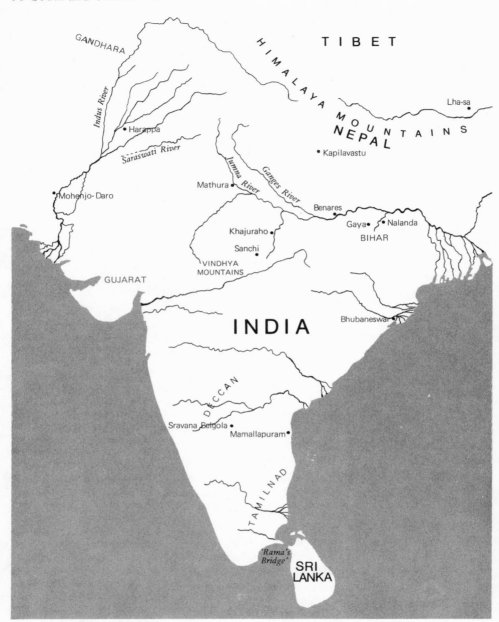

to have reached its zenith about 2500 BC. In spite of evidence suggesting trade links with Mesopotamia the Indus valley cities display a more highly developed architecture as well as a notable absence of temples. Conspicuous at Mohenjo-Daro was a public building housing a bathing-pool with chambers; it prefigures the holy bathing-places of later India, such as are found now along the sacred rivers and within temple compounds. 'In places without tanks', a more recent Hindu text declares, 'gods are not present.' The two main Indus valley cults were phallic worship and sacrifice to the mother goddess, the ancestress of Kali. In addition to the phallic *lingam*, fragments unearthed by archaeologists that anticipate other attributes of Shiva include the cosmic dancer and the three-faced yogi. These few remains indicate the tantalizing possibility of a continuous mythological tradition extending over no less than 4,000 years. There may have been a resurgence of old beliefs in the subsequent displacement of the Vedic deities worshipped by the Aryan invaders, and the triumph of Vishnu, Shiva, and Devi, the mother goddess, over Indra, Brahma, and their kin.

The history of the period after the collapse of the Indus valley civilization is still obscure, the archaeological record of the next phase of urban life dating only from 1000 BC. The scene has shifted to the Ganges valley, where settlements with ramparts appear on fertile riverside clearings amid the dense jungles then covering the northern plains. Artefacts discovered there reveal an evolved society and from 400 BC onwards are found the remains of Buddhist temples and stupas, funerary monuments usually containing a relic of the Buddha. Four castes existed: the *brahmins*, or priests; the *kshatriyas*, or warriors; the *vaisyas*, or peasant farmers; and the *sudras*, slaves and servants, probably formed of the non-Aryan, indigenous people. To this latter caste in time were added the untouchables in the same way that their southern neighbours were transformed into the demonology of Hinduism.

Indra has fallen into the second rank. He is inferior to the triad of Brahma the Creator, Vishnu the Preserver, and Shiva the Destroyer. Initially conceived as a personification of the *Brahman*, the transcendent and immanent absolute, Brahma always lacked a mythological roundness. He was the positive aspect of the life process in the universe, and was never represented as destroying what he had created. A spiritual concentration ignoring the enigmatic and disturbing side of creation, therefore, left scope for the rise of Vishnu and Shiva as deities comprehending birth, life, *and* death. But Brahma does provide the timescale of the universe and here it is that Indian mythology stands out in stark contrast with the rest of the world. For though the world cycles of Hinduism are subdivided in four *yugas* or ages, not unlike the Greco-Roman ages of gold, silver, brass and iron, they follow each other in the apparently endless stream of time. The wheel of birth and death, reincarnation, encompasses the individual, the species, the social structure, the planet, the gods, the universe: it is the timescale of Nature herself. Endless, irreversible, unquenchable are the processes of alteration and change. The cycle of emanation, fruition, dissolution, and re-emanation from the primeval substance, has a vastness incomprehensible to mankind. Even Indra finds it hard to grasp the truth when on one occasion Shiva and Vishnu tell him that there has already existed an army of Indras. These deities themselves recur in each slowly moving cycle to repeat their mythological actions. As the boar avatar, carrying the earth goddess whom he has rescued from the waters of the deep, Vishnu remarks: 'Every time I carry you this way . . .'

Indian computation of time is an exercise in adding noughts. A *kalpa*, a day and night of Brahma, is 8,640,000,000 years of human reckoning, and comprises 2,000 world cycles. At the end of one hundred Brahma years of Brahma days and nights there occurs a total dissolution, before a Brahma century of quiescence having elapsed, the universal cycle may start anew, or there may be a final passing away of creation. Anxiety over this cosmic uncertainty is somewhat allayed by the knowledge that it is approximately 31,000,000,000,000 years away. An entirely different perspective on the world was devised by the seventeenth-century Anglican divine James Ussher, Archbishop of Armagh, who calculated from evidence in the *Old Testament* that the date of the creation of the earth was 4004 BC. In 1642 Dr Lightfoot, Vice-Chancellor of Cambridge University, refined the dating and declared it was 23 October 4004 BC, at nine o'clock in the morning—an academic commencement if there ever was one. Although their calculation has long been disregarded, the underlying assumption informs present-day thinking in the West, which views events as unique, unrepeatable phenomena.

Related to the boundlessness of time in Indian mythology is the concept of *maya*, perhaps the most difficult and fundamental of all notions. Our word 'magic' has connections and carries something of its meaning. Maya can mean an illusion created by supernatural agency. In the ninth century Sankara, looked upon by some as an incarnation of Shiva, by others as the pre-eminent medieval teacher and saint, considered the visible cosmos was maya, an illusion imposed upon the adamantine soul, *jiva*, through the unpurged senses and the unilluminated mind. Yet at the same time maya is the generative force within the primeval substance: it gives shape to the myriad forms of creation, sustaining gods, saints, and men. A favourite metaphor is the snake and the rope. Ignorant of the character of a rope lying on the ground, a man believes he sees a snake. The chief aim of Hinduism is to unveil the oneness within the play of maya.

Buddha, 'the enlightened one', also literally awakened from the dream-like process of maya. He escaped the net of illusory experience, the continuous round of being, *samsara*, and his ministry was nothing more than a pointing of the way. Gautama Siddhartha (*c.* 563–479 BC), the North Indian prince who became the Buddha, lived during a period when men were turning their attention inward. According to a Sri Lankan tradition the Buddha realized his Enlightenment was ineffable but Brahma persuaded him to teach those few capable of following him. Another source recounts the setbacks he encountered when he tried to communicate his vision of *sunyata*, the universal void. Finding men frightened, he passed on his deeper message to the *nagas*, or serpent genii, who in the second century initiated Nagarjuna, the philosopher of Mayahana Buddhism. Though the Buddha, like Lao-tzu the founder of Chinese Taoism, knew that his experience could not be adequately explained in words, and deliberately restricted pictorial representations of his life and deeds, there developed an intricate mythology which in India eventually synthesized with Hinduism, but elsewhere has continued to develop and influence other traditions. The conversion of King Asoka to the Buddhist faith in the third century BC ranks, for Asia, with the conversion of the Emperor Constantine to Christianity six centuries afterwards for Europe. It inaugurated an unprecedented era of religious activity which spread Buddhism to Central Asia, then to China, Korea, and Japan; to South India and Sri Lanka, and to South-east Asia.

The Buddha, however, was not alone on his inward journey. In 526 BC died Mahavira, the last of the twenty-four Jain *tirthankaras*, 'makers of the river-crossing'. Today there are only about 2,000,000 Jains in India but they still support the astonishingly austere group of ascetics, both male and female, at the centre of this ancient belief, perhaps one surviving from the remote antiquity of pre-Aryan times. A tirthankara is superior to the gods and untouched by the endless changes of the eternal cosmic order. Dwelling near the crown of the universe, the tirthankaras are sublimely detached from celestial as well as terrestrial affairs. Since the Jains posit neither creator god nor creation, the sole function of these ascetic beings is to signify the ultimate destination, a supernal level where liberated souls float in infinite knowledge and bliss. The colossal statue of Gommatesvara, standing on its granite eminence at Sravana Belgola in Mysore, perfectly sums up the Jain attitude of dismissing the body, *kayotsarga*. Naked, *digambara*, 'sky-clad', ethereal, the saint's posture is of an ascetic superman whose consciousness is anchored on things above the concerns of men or gods.

Jainism pictures the universe as a giant human figure: either male or female. Indeed, cosmological diagrams have been always a matter of intense speculation. With time conceived as eternal, Jains even succeed in making the Hindu and Buddhist interest in cycles of events appear hasty. The pre-Aryan roots of Jainism are probably revealed in the dualistic nature of their universe, because matter itself holds *karma*, the sinful trigger of rebirth, and pollutes the immaterial soul. A Jain ascetic would carry a broom to sweep his path, lest his feet crush minute creatures and earn further disability. The rite of *sallekhana*, or fasting until death, is favoured as a way of final withdrawal by advanced ascetics. Kalanos, the holy man who burned himself on a pyre at Susa in front of the bewildered troops of Alexander's army, could have been a Jain.

Opposed to this drastic life renunciation was Tantric Buddhism and Hinduism, a movement culminating at the turn of the first millennium and finding its enduring monuments in the temples at Khajuraho and Bhubaneswar. Impressive for their erotic sculpture, whose loving figures exalt in *mithuna*, 'the state of being a couple', these were the places of worship for Hindus seeking oneness with the primeval substance through the biological impulses. Ritual was devised in order to contemplate the divine without any rejection of maya: in sexual union devotees experienced momentarily non-duality, the erasure of all distinctions. It was known in Tibetan Buddhism as *Yab-Yum*. The mystical marriage of opposites, the male and the female principles, antagonistic yet co-operating forces, like Shiva and his consort, his *sakti*, marked the return of the mother goddess, Devi, and the start of her present ascendancy. Yet the austere symbol of the stone phallus had hardly left the safety of its position in the earth womb. The most sacred image of the Hindu temple has remained the *lingam* within the *garbhagrha*, 'the womb house', a small chamber situated at the very centre of the building. In this man-made sanctuary, as dark as the cave in the mountain, the individual may be spiritually reborn through realization of the unconditioned character of the primeval substance. For in India congregational worship has only limited scope.

Ramakrishna went through the *tantrika-sadhana* with a nun in his worship of Devi, and travellers report that till the beginning of this century the vestiges of temple prostitution were still evident. Mother Kali, however, does not obscure her darker sides from her devotees. Like Shiva and Vishnu, she has the whole range of attributes—creation, preservation, and dissolution. When asked by a disciple why Mother Kali keeps the world as it is, Ramakrishna replied: 'That is Her Will. She wants to continue playing with Her created beings.'

India is the holy land for South, Central, and East Asia. Out of its spiritual wrestlings came not only the evangelism of the Buddhist faith but also the profound influence exerted by Hinduism on the peoples living in South-east Asia, whose most

The great rock-cut reclining Buddha at Galvihara in Sri Lanka

imposing monument, Ankor Wat in Cambodia, today stands witness. But the impact of Indian mythology was greatest upon the countries immediately adjacent to its borders, namely Sri Lanka and Tibet. Their later adaptation and development of Buddhism, a process of accommodation to two separate traditions of indigenous belief, could be said to have been delayed until the faith became extinct in India. With the revival of Hinduism at the beginning of the second millennium the followers of Buddha in Tibet and Sri Lanka found themselves free to interpret the scriptures in their own ways.

Legend credits Sri Lanka with three visits by the Buddha. Once he went to the top of Adam's Peak, and there left his footprint. Along with the relic of the tooth, a left eye-tooth of the Buddha imported in fifth century, the footprint remains a magnet for pilgrims, and is a potent symbol of popular belief that Sri Lanka is the *dhammadipa*, the island which acts as the guardian of the true doctrine. Even before King Asoka commended the Buddhist religion to Devanampiya Tissa, King of Tambapanni (Sri Lanka), there had appeared divisions among the *sangha*, the monk community. From these doctrinal differences, and changes in attitude towards the monastic life, a new movement within Buddhism emerged, which finally became known as the 'Greater Vehicle', Mahayana. Its emphasis on compassion and the ideal of the *bodhisattva*, or Buddha-to-be, a saviour-like figure reminiscent of Christianity, contrasts with the spiritual wisdom so prized in the older tradition, thereafter called Hinayana, the 'Lesser Vehicle'. Whereas the people of Sri Lanka came to adhere to the monastic goals of Hinayana, whose lineage is traced back directly to Ananda, one of the Buddha's principal disciples, the conversion of the Tibetans was to Mahayana doctrines.

Perhaps the more evolved iconography of the 'Greater Vehicle' accounts for the comparative vigour of Tibetan myth. Or the land itself may have been a contributory factor. Far removed from lush Sri Lanka are the snow-covered peaks of the Tibetan mountains, where icy winds and thunderstorms bring hailstones which are heavy enough to kill. Destruction has always been close to the Tibetans. They portray Yama as the epitome of annihilation, a monster who crushes the wheel of life in his deadly grasp. Though King Stron-btsan-sgam-po (died 650) is regarded as the original Buddhist ruler, not till the end of the first millennium did the imported religion oust Bon, the Tibetan form of that old animist-shamanist faith which at one time was widespread not only in Siberia but throughout the whole of Central and North-east Asia. The relative merits of Indian and Chinese forms of Buddhism were debated at Lha-sa in 792, to the advantage of the former, but not until 1042 did a leading Indian teacher visit Tibet. Then Atisa, who had previously even travelled to Sumatra at the invitation of its Buddhist rulers, arrived and expounded doctrine, before he moved on to Sri Lanka. During the Mongol conquest of China (1279–1368) the Tibetans converted the nomad invaders to their form of Buddhism, and such was the influence of the lamas in the Celestial Empire that in 1322 when copper for coins was becoming scarce, a 300-ton statue of the Buddha was cast for a temple near Peking. Shortly after this period they applied the notion of reincarnation to the succession of chief monks. It was believed that the bodhisattva Avalokitesvara was reborn in the person of each Dalai Lama: the fourteenth in the series now lives as an exile in India. By this century the idea had spread throughout the monasteries of Tibet so that numerous abbots are conceived of as the reincarnations of their predecessors.

Yet the significant figure in South and Central Asia remains the outsider, the saint. He is the one for whom everything is holy. According to a Hindu legend, an ascetic once slept with his feet resting on the lingam, Shiva's symbol. A brahmin saw this desecration and rebuked him fiercely. The ascetic said he was sorry and asked for his feet to be placed where there was no lingam. Angered, the brahmin seized the ankles of the ascetic, but wherever he swung them a lingam sprang from the ground. Thereupon the brahmin reverently bowed to the reposing saint and went his way.

Agni

One of the three chief gods in the *Rig Veda*, he personified fire and was at the centre of ancient worship. The fire altar was orientated towards the East, the direction of sunrise, the ever new beginning. As the bestower of immortality and the cleanser from sin after death, Agni acted as a mediator between gods and men.

Born from a lotus created by Brahma, the god of fire is pictured as red, with two faces and seven tongues to lick up the butter used in sacrifices. When in the *Mahabharata*, an epic dating from the beginning of the first millennium, Agni is depicted as having exhausted his vigour by consuming too many oblations, he renewed his strength in consuming the Khandava forest, with the assistance of Krishna and Arjuna and in defiance of Indra. No longer the object of a separate cult Agni is invoked by Hindu lovers and by men for virility.

Amitabha

The boddhisattva of 'infinite light', who represents the primordial, self-existent Buddha. A manifestation of the underlying essence of the six 'meditation Buddhas', he sprang from a lotus and he ceaselessly stretches out to aid the weak and faltering. Amitabha vowed that he would refuse personal salvation unless he should gain the power to cause any being who appealed to him to be reborn in the Pure Land, the Western Paradise, immediately after death. All that is asked of the would-be saint is worship or uttering the holy formula of his name. On the lips of the dying for countless generations, therefore, has been the name of bodhisattva of the 'immeasurable enlightening splendour'. It was a spiritual 'short cut' that appealed to Chinese Buddhists, who were first introduced to him as A-mi-t'o-fo by an Indo-Scythian, Chih Ch'ien, about AD 230. Chih Ch'ien made a considerable impression in China: he was appointed by the ruler of Wu as a scholar of wide learning, *po-shih*, and charged with the moral instruction of the Crown Prince. The archetype of compassion, Amitabha became in China and Japan the gentle, easy, and popular way of salvation for

Amitabha in the Western paradise; from an eighteenth-century Tibetan painting

Mahayana Buddhists. Solitary exertion, asceticism, even good works, vanish before the promise of boundless grace. Each being reborn in the Pure Land can confidently expect a lotus throne.

Amrita

Literal meaning: 'non-dead'. The water of life in Hindu mythology. It was recovered at the Churning of the Ocean, when Rahu, the demon, succeeded in obtaining a sip, forcing Vishnu to cut off his head in order to prevent him from gaining complete impregnability. This severed piece of immortality, hideous, horned, with bulging eyes and ravenous jaws, was adopted as a talisman, a protector from evil influences, and can be seen on Hindu temples serving a function similar to our gargoyle. Another legend of Kirttimukha, 'the face of glory', recounts that Shiva persuaded a lion-headed demon to feed on its own flesh, which it did until all was devoured to the lower lip.

Probably identical with *soma*, the favourite beverage of Indra, amrita is an echo of practices that must antedate the Aryan invasion. Soma, the juice of a milky climbing plant, was fermented as a drink for the gods and the brahmins. In India the terrible heat of the devouring sun has been looked upon as a deadly power, while Soma, the moon, the bringer of dew and the controller of waters, took on the role of the source of life. 'We have drunk soma,' the Vedas recall, 'we have become immortal, we have entered into the light, we have known the gods.' Its exhilarating qualities serve to remind us of the role of drugs in ancient religions.

Ananta

The World Serpent of Hindu mythology. During the quiescent period of the cosmos, the night of Brahma, Vishnu sleeps on coils of a prodigious snake, Sesha, known as Ananta, 'the endless', whose thousand heads rise as a canopy over the recumbent deity. The anthropomorphic god, the serpentine rings that form his couch, and the waters on which the infinite snake floats are, of course, all manifestations of the primeval essence.

As Balarama, the half-brother of Krishna, Ananta takes on human form, though towards the end of the legend, when he is sitting beneath a tree on the shore of the ocean, lost in thought, a serpent crawls out of his mouth,

leaving the hero disincarnate. Back in the watery deep, Ananta spews forth venomous fire that destroys creation at the end of each kalpa. The gods and the demons, once temporarily at peace, used the World Serpent as a rope, which they twisted round Mount Mandara, and so churned the ocean for the elixir of immortality, amrita.

Asuras

In the *Rig Veda* the word asura describes the supreme spirit and means 'spiritual, divine'. An equivalent was Ahura Mazdah, the ancient Persian deity. Afterwards the word ceased to denote a god and acquired an entirely opposite meaning, that of an anti-god or demon. Asuras descended from Prajapati, 'the progenitor', an aspect of Indra, Soma, and other early deities. Their dwelling-places are the caverns of Mount Sumeru and the depths of the ocean. Gods and asuras are complementary: these contenders, locked in a series of perpetual wars, never gain complete victory, since the elimination of either side would make the other redundant.

Avalokitesvara

The Buddhist epitome of mercy and compassion. When Avalokitesvara attained to supreme consciousness, he chose not to pass into nirvana, but vowed to stay behind as the succour of the afflicted. He was filled with compassion, *karuna*, for the sufferings of the living, whom he ever seeks to bring to enlightenment. This is the Mahayana ideal of the bodhisattva, as opposed to the Hinayana goal of the *arhat*, the monk who has gained supreme knowledge. Whereas Sri Lanka followed the monastic tradition of Hinayana—the hard and lonely path of the isolate—there grew up in India the complicated iconography of the Mahayana bodhisattvas. When about 400 the Chinese pilgrim Fa-hsien visited the main Buddhist shrines of the Ganges valley, he witnessed public celebrations in which Avalokitesvara and other saints were treated as demigods. Along with images of the Buddha, they were paraded through city streets on elaborately decorated ceremonial carriages, accompanied by singers, musicians, and monks. Like the temple cars of

Brahma the four-headed and four-armed god of wisdom and guardian of the Vedas

Hindu deities, these carriages rose to a height of five storeys, overtopping all but the chief buildings and the city gateways.

Avalokitesvara was represented as a handsome young man holding a lotus flower in his left hand. Often he wore in his hair the picture of Amitabha, the bodhisattva who in Mahayana Buddhism virtually replaced Sakyamuni, the historical Buddha. The Chinese transformed Avalokitesvara into the goddess of mercy some time before the tenth century. The female consort of Avalokitesvara was Tara, also known as *pandaravasini*, 'clad in white', an attribute echoed in Kuan-yin, the Chinese transformation.

In Tibet it was the fortune of Avalokitesvara to become the national deity, where he is still incarnated in the person of the Dalai Lama, the most senior monk. On the death of a Dalai Lama the spirit of the god passes to a new-born child, who is identified and brought up within the Tibetan Church. However, Avalokitesvara has the divine power of assuming forms at will; his manifestations include a figure with eleven heads and one thousand arms, a fabulous cloud, and all manner of animals and people.

Brahma

Though regarded as one of the Hindu triad, whose other members are Vishnu the Preserver and Shiva the Destroyer, Brahma has lost his creative powers to these deities as well as to the Divine Mother. Red in colour, he has four heads; originally there were five, but one was burned off by the fire of Shiva's third eye because he had spoken disrespectfully. In his four hands Brahma holds a sceptre, or a rosary, a bow, an alms-bowl, and the manuscript of the *Rig Veda*. A late myth shows him presenting to the Supreme Goddess the pot of the mendicant ascetic and the magic wisdom of the scriptures, alongside the rest of the Hindu pantheon gathered to do homage to the female principle.

A creation legend concerns Brahma. The primeval essence, or unconditioned, self-existent substance, *Brahman*, created the cosmic waters and deposited in them a seed, which became a golden egg, the *hiranyagarbha*, in which it was born itself as Brahma, the creator of the universe. This first being was Purusha, the Cosmic Man, one of the names of Brahma. According to another legend, Brahma emerged on a lotus flower from the navel of Vishnu, in the presence of that god's consort, Lakshmi, the lotus goddess, who personifies abundance and good fortune. His own passion for his slender and enchanting daughter was responsible for the birth of mankind. The incestuous relation of Brahma was with divine Vak, 'the uttered Word', 'the melodious cow who brings forth milk and water', or 'the mother of the Vedas'. Vak represents both speech and the natural forces: she is in a sense maya. A lioness, Vak appears in the company of a man as a symbolic decoration round the base of a Hindu temple. The gander, or *hamsa*, Brahma's vehicle, *vahana*, is an extension of this myth, because the bird's name is linked with the fundamental sound of the universe: breath. Inhalation is said to make the sound, *ham*, the exhalation, *sa*. It is the breathing exercises of the yogi and the breath of life. Again in temple architecture a recurrent motif is the hamsa, a pair of ganders often depicted each side of a lotus, the symbol of knowledge.

The myth of the origin of the lingam concludes with Shiva settling an argument between Brahma and Vishnu as to who is the creator of the universe. Their quarrel is interrupted by a towering lingam crowned with flame, rising from the depths of the cosmic ocean. Brahma, the gander, and Vishnu, the boar, decide to investigate. Flying upwards, the gander is startled to observe the cosmic phallus burst asunder, and in a cave-like sanctuary the hidden creator, Shiva, the supreme power of the universe.

Buddha

Gautama Siddhartha (*c.* 563–479 BC), the North Indian prince who became the Buddha, 'the Enlightened One', required his followers to isolate themselves from worldly life. The saffron robe worn by Buddhist monks was a badge which showed ordinary society that they had elected to leave its toils; the colour of this garment was the same as that used to dress condemned men on the day of execution. Being liable to rebirth because of the self, and knowing the sorrow of living, *dukkha*, 'world weariness', they sought the unborn, the final escape from karmic bondage—*nirvana*. What was demanded from the individual devotee was nothing less than the extinction of the ego, freedom from aversion and desire.

Although there are striking parallels in the stories of the lives of the Jaina saviour Parsva and the Buddha, connections possibly suggesting the continued existence of a pre-Aryan religious tradition, Siddhartha had begun as a Hindu, and his own quest for wisdom was essentially a new and invigorating approach to the classic problem of release, *moksa*. Where the Buddha encountered difficulties was in the communication of his new understanding of the bondage of individualized existence. These problems sprang from the paradoxical position in which he found himself as a teacher. He alone understood Enlightenment, because it was an internal experience, yet he wished to point others along the way to self-realization. It was ineffable. Perhaps this block in communication explains the reluctance of the Buddha to sanction pictorial representation of his life and deeds. Instead, an empty seat, a footprint, or a wheel, were supposed to indicate the way he had discovered and taught. In contrast with the other great teachers of the world—Zarathustra, Confucius, Jesus, Mohammed—the Buddha was known as Sakyamuni, 'the silent sage of the Sakya clan'. The role of the *sangha*, the monk community, was to act as a permanent spiritual signpost for lay folk, who were daily reminded of the true path by the mendicant monks, the *bhikkhus*. At the moment in Sri Lanka and Thailand it is still the custom for young people to adopt holy orders for a short period of time. But, as the Buddha is said to have foreseen, his teachings became an organized religion over the centuries, and evolved a distinct mythology, till in its final stage in India Buddhism was merged with Hinduism.

The Buddha had many earlier lives which are described in the *Jataka*. Here we are only concerned with the chief legends surrounding the life of the historical founder of the Buddhist faith. The Buddha never denied the Hindu pantheon. On the contrary, prior to his incarnation as Gautama Siddhartha he lived in the heavenly realm, where he taught the law to the gods. 'Truly, monks,' the Buddha once said. 'I have been Indra, the ruler of the gods, thirty-six times, and many hundred times was I a world-monarch.' As the moment approached for his birth as the Buddha, earthquakes and miracles occurred, those ancient harbingers of significant events. In the city of Kapilavastu, on what is the modern Indo-Nepalese border, his earthly mother, Queen Maya, experienced a miraculous conception. She dreamed that she saw the

A fifth-century limestone head of the Buddha from Gandhara in north-west Pakistan

future Buddha come down into her womb in the form of a white elephant. This dream and the corresponding natural signs were interpreted by sixty-four brahmins, who pre- dicted the birth of a son who would become either a world-monarch or a world-saviour. When the time approached, Queen Maya made her way to the near-by grove of Lumbini, where the wonderful child was born, emerging from her right side without causing her the slightest pain. Received by Brahma and the other gods, the young prince was found to be endowed with speech, and there appeared on the ground a lotus every time he took a step. Instantaneously were born Yasodhara Devi, his wife; Kantaka, the horse on which he fled from the palace to seek for supreme consciousness; Chandaka, his charioteer; Ananda, his chief disciple; and the Bo Tree, beneath whose spreading branches he received Enlightenment.

According to one legend, Queen Maya died seven days after giving birth to Prince Siddhartha, and out of filial piety the Buddha, having attained to supreme knowledge, ascended to the Trayastrimsa Heaven and remained there for three months, preaching the law to his mother. This particular *sutra*, or narrative scripture, became very popular in China, where Buddhist missionaries were confronted with a civilization that set great store by ancestor worship. A religion of individual salvation had to be made relevant to a society based on family and clan harmony, lest the saffron robe seem quite incongruous.

Mindful of the prophecy that the young prince would not become a great ruler, but a great sage, if he became aware of the sufferings of mankind, King Suddhodana, his father, did his utmost to prevent Siddhartha from having any contact with the outside world. A costly palace was built in which all possible pleasures were offered to beguile the youth's mind, and even the words 'death' and 'grief' were forbidden. King Suddhodana conceived the plan of forging an inseparable link between his son and the kingdom through the marriage of Siddhartha, who would be declared heir-apparent. The beautiful Yasodhara, the daughter of a minister, was chosen and, as a *kshatriya*, the prince had to win her hand by a display of prowess in fencing, swimming, and combat at a special tournament. Yet within Siddhartha the spirit was beginning to stir, for on hearing the news of the birth of their son, he pronounced the boy's name, Rahula, in such a way as to mean 'a bond'. Though King Suddhodana took every precaution, ordering that the streets of the capital be swept clean, decorated with flowers, and emptied of everything unpleasant, the visit of twenty-nine-year-old Siddhartha and Chandaka proved a shattering experience. The prince saw a tottering old man, bowed double over his walking stick, and later had view of an incurable invalid. These sights troubled him considerably, but it was an encounter with a corpse being carried to the cremation ground that jolted him into active discontent with his luxurious surroundings. The serene calm of a hermit suggested a course for him and, abandoning throne, family, and offspring, he became a wandering ascetic, bent on discovering the nature of things. Having tried the way of self-mortification for six years without success, the monk Gautama, as he was now called, travelled to Gaya and resolved to sit in meditation under a fig-tree till he completed his quest. His Enlightenment followed, whereby he became the Buddha, the One who was released from the overwhelming consciousness of suffering.

The demon Mara assaulted the contemplative monk, immobile beneath the Bo Tree, but nothing could disturb his single-mindedness. To no avail were the enticements of Mara's daughters, skilled in all the magic arts of desire and voluptuousness; unheeded went the threats of an army of hideous devils, grotesque in shape and powerfully armed; and the ultimate weapon of Mara, his fiery discus, turned into a canopy of flowers when hurled at the Buddha. For five weeks the possessor of perfect illumination, *bodhi*, stayed rapt in meditation, all his previous lives being revealed to him. It was during the final week that the world-shaking tempest happened, when Muchalinda, King of the Nagas, protected the Buddha with his serpentine body.

The Enlightened One was then faced with a choice. He could enter nirvana: literally, the cessation, *nir*, of mental turnings, *vritti*; the undisturbed condition of supreme consciousness. Or, renouncing personal deliverance for the moment, he could preach the law. Mara urged one course, Brahma the other, and it was to the great god's entreaties on behalf of all created things the Buddha yielded. He began to travel and teach, founding a monastic order as well as preparing the framework for the Buddhist era of Indian civilization. One day a little child wanted to make him an offering, but had no worldly possessions. Innocently the boy presented for blessing a pile of dust, which the Buddha accepted with a smile. This child is reputed to have been reborn as King Asoka, who reigned from 272 to 232 BC. Not only did this monarch establish throughout his realm countless monasteries and have constructed 80,000 *stupas*, or reliquary shrines, but his Buddhist

*Durga, the eighteen-armed warrior maid
manifestation of Devi, defeating Mahisha*

missionaries were dispatched even to Syria
and Egypt.

Devi

The great goddess of the Hindus: Mahadevi.
The consort of Shiva, she is worshipped in a
variety of forms corresponding to her two
aspects—benevolence and fierceness. She is
Uma, 'light'; Gauri, 'yellow or brilliant';
Parvati, 'the mountaineer'; and Jaganmata,
'the mother of the world' in her milder guise.
The terrible emanations are Durga, 'the
inaccessible'; Kali, 'the black'; Chandi, 'the
fierce'; and Bhairavi, 'the terrible'.

Shiva and Devi are regarded as the twofold
personalization of Brahman, the primeval
substance. Like Vishnu, Shiva has no direct
contact with the tangible elements in the
universe, and is obliged to emanate a manifestation, a putting forth of energy, *sakti*, which
myth has conceived as a wife or daughter. In
Hindu iconography the presence of the sakti

of a deity, the female companion, is important,
not least for the reason that she attracts and
helps the devotee. The height of worship for
Devi was the period of the Tantras, the
seventh century onwards, when release was
found possible through *mithuna*, 'the state of
being a couple'. But the earliest known
example of this close embrace of devotees is a
carving on one of the Buddhist monuments at
Sanchi, which dates from the second century
BC. Licentious rites performed for the fertilization of the ground are of course world-wide,
just as vestiges of the ritual utterance of
licentious language to stimulate the dormant
sexual energy of the living power can still be
found in the racy jokes and insinuations made
by guests at a wedding reception. In the *Golden
Bough* there is an interesting report of a
ceremony of rope-pulling, undertaken by
certain Indonesian peoples to produce rain
and assure the growth of their crops. Men and
women used to take opposite sides in the tug of
war, and in pulling against each other they
imitated by their movements the union of the
sexes. At the end of the Vedic era there were
apparently several goddesses acknowledged as

the wives of Shiva, or Rudra, while other goddesses were worshipped by different castes in different parts of India. These diverse deities eventually coalesced into one great goddess, Devi, whose ultimate origin may have been the mother goddess of the Indus valley civilization. Supreme, Devi holds 'the universe in Her womb': she 'lights the lamp of wisdom' and 'brings joy to the heart of Shiva, Her Lord'. Thus wrote Sankara in the ninth century, and today the Divine Mother remains the greatest power in Hinduism.

The first appearance of the great goddess was as Durga, a beautiful warrior maid of yellow hue, seated on a tiger. The circumstance of her miraculous arrival, a sort of potency welling up from the combined wraths of the gods, was the tyranny of a monster-demon named Mahisha, who through terrific austerities had acquired invincible strength. Of this colossal water-buffalo bull the gods were afraid, for neither Vishnu nor Shiva could prevail against it. Alone, the joint energy, sakti, of all celestial beings seemed capable of vanquishing Mahisha, and so it was that eighteen-armed Durga went out to give battle. After the titanic combat, she overcame both the bull and its weapon, an appalling mace. Thereafter the ascendency of Devi was guaranteed; the gods in time of need had surrendered to her every weapon and power; she became 'the All-comprehending One'.

Most shocking is the manifestation of the goddess as Kali. She is represented as standing upon the prostrate body of Shiva, who lies on a lotus bed. Dressed in fetching attire and decorated with precious ornaments, Kali also wears a girdle of severed arms and a necklace of skulls. Her tongue lolls from her mouth, probably savouring the taste of blood. She has four arms. One left hand grasps a bloody sword, the other dangles a head by the hair; one right hand confers blessing, the other bids her devotees to be without fear. She has absorbed the inexorability of Rudra, and Shiva as Bhairava. Yet there is both life and death in the attributes of this form of the Divine Mother. 'Your hands', Sankara said, 'hold delight and pain. The shadow of death and the elixir of immortal life are yours!'

Dharma

An ancient Hindu sage, a *rishi*, who married thirteen of Daksha's daughters. According to the *Mahabharata*, Daksha sprang from the

A popular nineteenth-century drawing of Devi in her most horrific manifestation as Kali

right thumb of Brahma, and his wife from that god's left thumb. Their numerous progeny, transparently personifications of virtues and religious rites, were married to Dharma, moral duty, to Kasyapa, another ancient sage and the grandfather of Manu, the progenitor of mankind, and to Soma, the king of the brahmins, the guardians of sacrifices. *Dharma* in Hindu religion is the doctrine of the duties and rights of each caste in the ideal society, and as such the mirror of all moral action.

Ganesa

The elephant-headed son of Shiva, who is the Hindu counterpart of Hermes, removes obstacles and vouchsafes wisdom. He is propitiated at the beginning of any important enterprise, and is invoked at the commencement of books. He often appears today on the covers of Indian students' notebooks.

Ganesa is represented as a short pot-bellied man of yellow colour, with four hands and a one-tusked elephant head, sometimes riding on a rat or attended by one. In one hand he holds a shell, in another a discus, in third a club, and the fourth a water-lily. His temples are plentiful on the Deccan and he is depicted in many Shivite shrines.

A legend explains his elephant head as the result of a dispute. Parvati went to her bath and told her son to guard the door, which Ganesa tried to do even against Shiva. So upset was the goddess at the decapitation of their son that to pacify her Shiva replaced the head with an elephant's, the first that came to hand. The loss of one tusk is accounted for by a tale which represents *parashu-rama*, 'Rama with the axe', visiting the sleeping Shiva. Again Ganesa opposed entrance and for his pains sustained injury, though he willingly received the blow on his tusk once he recognized the visitor wielded his father's axe, which Shiva had given to the avatar.

Gommatesvara

Jainism attained to a peak of prosperity in the fifth century and remained a potent force in Indian religious life till the Moslem invasions seven centuries later. Its irreversible decline and final disappearance has been forecast by Jaina seers for over a thousand years; the name of the last Jaina monk should be Dupasahasuri. During the medieval period there was a considerable following in South India, where in 983 at Sravana Belgola the 56½-foot-high statue of Gommatesvara was erected.

Bahubali, known as Gommatesvara, was the son of Rishabha, the first Jaina saviour, and the brother of Bharaba. Legend tells of a struggle for empire between the brothers, which resulted in Bahubali's disillusionment at the moment of victory, his handing over of the earthly kingdom to Bharata, and his retirement to the forest in order to do penance. This was supposed to have occurred at a place called Paudanapura in North India. There Bahubali stood unflinchingly for a year in *samadhi*. Vines crept up his legs and arms, anthills arose about his feet, and snakes kept the company of his solitary vigil. To commemorate this amazing feat, which was an imitation of their father's renunciation, Bharata is said to have raised an enormous

statue, over 500 bow-lengths in height. So famous was its renown that even Ravana, the demon king of Sri Lanka, made a pilgrimage to the site.

The colossal sculptured figure at Sravana Belgola may have been set up by Chamundaraya, a senior minister of King Rajamalla of the Ganga dynasty. Chamundaraya was staying at the monastic temples on the granite hillock of Chandragiri when his attention was drawn to the twin eminence of Vindhyagiri, on the opposite side of the town of Sravan Belgola. On climbing the 500 feet to its crest the minister was greeted by a female earth-divinity, Kusmandi, who revealed the sacred spot where the statue of Gommatesvara was hidden. The soil was cleared away and craftsmen were brought to restore the image. This story of miraculous discovery in 983 may have been intended to link the statue with Bharata's monument, or it may have been simply a poetical expression of the stupendous task of carving this free-standing sculpture, larger than any of the statues of the Egyptian Pharaoh Ramesses. According to another legend, Chamundaraya wanted to worship and anoint the newly carved statue, but found that no matter how many pots of milk and honey he had emptied from the scaffold about Gommatesvara's head not a single trickle reached to the feet. Thereupon Kusmandi appeared in the form of an old woman and with great devotion poured just a cup of milk over the head of the statue. This single act bathed the whole body of Gommatesvara. Today the surface of the statue still looks fresh and clean because it receives an anointment every twenty-five years, the last occasion being 30 March 1967.

Hanuman

In Hindu mythology, the monkey chief and son of Vayu, was an ally of Rama in his battle with Ravana. His divine nature was very versatile, permitting dramatic changes in shape and size as well as the power of flight. When Hanuman leapt across the sea to Sri Lanka, the stronghold of Ravana, a female demon named Surasa tried to swallow him bodily. To avoid this interception Hanuman distended his body, forcing Surasa to elongate her mouth enormously, then he suddenly shrank to the size of a thumb, shot through her head, and emerged from her right ear. Landed safely on the island, he dealt the forces of

Ravana mortal blows and burned down the capital. For his many services Rama rewarded Hunuman with the gift of perpetual life and youth.

In Buddhist mythology the story of the monkey deity is reproduced with many embellishments. The most celebrated account of his exploits is found in the Chinese novel *Pilgrimage to the West* by Wu Cheng-en (1505–80); it tells of Hanuman's assistance to Tripitaka on his long journey to India in order to obtain the Buddhist scriptures.

Hayagriva
Literally, 'horse-necked'. According to one legend, a demon who stole the scriptures from Brahma's mouth while he was asleep, and was killed by Vishnu as *matsya-avatara*, the fish incarnation. Another version relates that Vishnu himself assumed this form to recover the stolen Vedas from the demons.

In Tibetan Buddhism Hayagriva became the lord of wrath, the first of the eight dreadful gods, the *drag-gshhed*. The others also derive from Hindu mythology and include Yama, his sister Yami, and Devi. In these deities is evident the Tibetan genius for portraying the terrible aspect of the spiritual powers, a frightening perception that even clouds the usual benevolence of bodhisattvas.

Indra
King of the gods in the *Rig Veda*, the early collection of Hindu hymns, Indra has authority over the firmament, dispensing rain and thunderbolts at his pleasure. He won his position by slaying Vritra, or Ahi, the serpent of drought, who had swallowed the cosmic waters and lay in coils on the mountains. The decisive thunderbolt split the stomach of Ahi, releasing the waters, generating life, and liberating the dawn. This victory of a sky god over the snake, the embodiment of mother earth, is a very old myth. For the Greeks it was a zealous earth goddess, Hera, sister and consort of Zeus, the paternal sky god, who sent her snake attendants to kill Hercules, the child of a clandestine affair between Zeus and the mortal woman Alcmene.

Indra rescued the sacred cows of the gods from the *asuras*, or demons, and pitted his

The monkey god Hanuman who could fly and make dramatic changes in size and shape

strength against human foes on the battlefield, where his presence was signalled by a rainbow in the sky. Though he usually rides a golden chariot drawn by two ruddy steeds, an elephant is sometimes depicted as Indra's mount. This animal was the Vedic symbol of kingship and on occasions even the Buddha is called an elephant. The son of a god and a woman, or a cow, Indra exhibited a strong tendency towards wantonness. The *Mahabharata* records that one of the women he seduced was Ahalya, the wife of the sage Gotama, who was so incensed that his curse impressed on the king of the gods a thousand marks resembling the female organ. So Indra was known as Sa-yoni until fortunately they changed into eyes.

The defeat of Indra at the hands of demon Ravana, the Rakshasa king of Sri Lanka, and his release from captivity at the behest of Brahma was attributed to the seduction of Ahalya. But the tale of this humiliating punishment, as recounted in the *Ramayana*, may have been no more than recognition of the decline of Indra's celestial status, lowered perhaps by the brahmins as a means of reducing the influence of the divine patron of the warrior caste.

Jataka

The 'birth-stories'—of which there are 547—are tales told by the Buddha of his previous births as bird, animal, man. A number of the stories are pre-Buddhist in origin and are found in such Indian collections as the *Panchatantra*; others have a provenance outside South and Central Asia. They were remembered and recorded by the followers of the Buddha not long after he passed into nirvana. To a Buddhist they are of autobiographical and moral interest, since the characteristics or situation of those concerned are supposed to be at least partly explainable in terms of their conduct in previous existences as told in the *Jataka*.

Throughout the tales the thread of rebirth which ended in the Buddha's own life and mission is celebrated and analysed. Virtues and vices are treated equally. The story of the pariah dog is not untypical. It explains that the Buddha once took the form of a homeless dog and lived on refuse in a cemetery. Owing to his character he became leader of all the stray dogs and was called upon to defend them against the king's wrath. The harness used for

the royal chariot had been left lying in the palace courtyard and overnight rain making the leather parts soft and sodden, the king's own pack of hounds tore it to pieces and devoured it. Informed by the palace attendants that the guilt lay with stray dogs entering the courtyard through the sewers, the king ordered an extermination drive in the city. The Buddha-dog calmed his agitated followers and set out for the palace. By the simple expedient of calling upon the truth, the faultless pariah dog was able to reach the throne room unmolested. There, he persuaded the king to feed the royal pack with grass and butter-milk, whereupon the dogs vomited the pieces of leather and established proof of his followers' innocence. Impressed and delighted by this wisdom, the king ordered that the pariah dog should share his own food. He also granted the request that lives of all living things should be spared. Buddha was the chief dog; Ananda, his chief disciple, the king.

Kama

Like Eros, Kama arose at the creation of the universe, first-born of the gods. Desire was the primal germ of the universal mind. Yet the Hindu god of love is no Cupid; instead of the fleshly infant portrayed by Western artists, Kama is a brilliantly adroit youth, the husband of Rati, the goddess of sensual desire. His sugar-cane bow is stretched by a string of bees, and fires arrows tipped with flowers, whose scent announces the sweet, piercing, irresistible attack of love. The mysterious origin of Kama and the general influence of his power have given rise to an interesting variety of titles. He is Dipaka, 'the inflamer'; Gritsa, 'the sharp'; Mayi, 'the deluder'; Mara, 'the destroyer'; Ragavrinta, 'the stalk of passion'; and Titha, 'fire'.

Kama's assay on Shiva cost the deity his beautiful form. Commanded by Indra to fire at the divine yogi, in order to break his perfect meditation and enflame him with love for the goddess Parvati, Kama received the full impact of Shiva's third eye and was reduced to cinders. Hence, his description as *ananga*, 'bodiless'. In a later birth, however, Kama succeeded in piercing the heart of Shiva and filling it with love for Sati, an incarnation of the Divine Mother. The instigator of this second attack was Brahma, much concerned that Shiva's austerities would bring the universe to a standstill.

Lakshmi

The lotus goddess of Hindu mythology, wife of Vishnu and symbol of his creative energy; she is the goddess of agriculture, characterized by the lotus, the vegetable symbol beneath her and the lotus flower she carries in her left hand. Lakshmi, 'good fortune', is not only the universal mother of life in her benevolent life-increasing aspect, but more in her magnanimous wisdom-bestowing activities she is the entrance to transcendental life.

A myth recounts that at the beginning of every universal renewal, the cosmic waters grow a thousand-petalled lotus of pure gold, which in turn gives birth to Brahma the Creator. With this universal womb Lakshmi is associated as Loka-mata, 'the mother of the world', and Jaladhi-ja, 'ocean born'. Lotus-eyed, lotus-coloured, and decked with lotus garlands, she stands as the symbol of maternal benevolence, her full breasts the constant source of succour and delight.

Mahavira

The last Jaina saviour, he was a contemporary of the Buddha, and died about 500 BC. His childhood was distinguished by miracles. One day he overcame a serpent that threatened his friends, thus earning the title Mahavira, 'great hero'. During the lifetime of his parents Mahavira was an ordinary householder, married with a daughter, but as soon as his mother and father who wére devotees of Parsva committed the rite of *sallekhana*, fasting unto death, he decided that there was no longer any hindrance to his own ascetic inclinations. At the age of thirty-two he distributed his personal possessions to the needy and commenced his inner quest, a terrestrial event that brought an immediate response from the heavens;. the firmament glowed like a lake covered in lotus flowers, the air was filled with the sounds of celestial music, and gods descended to pay their respects to Mahavira.

For a time the names of Mahavira and Makkhali Gosala were linked together, possibly they inhabited the same religious community. The teachings of Gosala had the distinction of the Buddha's condemnation as the very worst of all contemporary erroneous doctrines. He likened them to an hempen garment—uncomfortable and giving no protection against the cold of winter or the heat of summer. Gosala argued that all beings, all

created things, attain perfection in the course of time. There was nothing that could be done to hasten this process spread over the span of countless rebirths. The split between the two hermits was caused by their different views on the freedom of the will. Asserting traditional Jaina belief, Mahavira taught that the individual soul, the transmigrating *jiva*, was free to make its own escape through a sustained act of self-renunciation. In contrast with the attitude of the Buddha, Mahavira regarded the soul as physically bound and fettered by karmic matter, so that the path to release, spiritual ascension to the top of the universe, involved complete disentanglement. Jaina monks wore a veil over the mouth and even lay folk were forbidden to drink water after sunset, lest some small insect be swallowed. Thus *ahisma*, 'non-violence', is carried to an extreme.

The utter renunciation of the tirthankara, the last of whom was Mahavira, is perhaps the most austere symbol ever devised. It stands at the impersonal end of the spectrum of ancient myth, far removed from the Occidental belief in the survival of the personality. In India there has never existed a Hades for the shadowy dead, nor an Elysium for the translated living. Reincarnation excludes individual personality.

Maitreya

Or Metteyya, is the name of the Buddha who is yet to come. This is in accord with the Buddhist notion that there is a series of Enlightened Ones, existing before and after the historical Buddha. Maitreya is regarded as living at the moment in a Tusita heaven at the apex of the sensual universe. In China as Mi-lo this aspect of his myth underwent considerable development, his abode becoming identified with a sanctuary from the endless round of birth. In Tibet and China there are rock-cut inscriptions which read, 'Come, Maitreya, come!'

Manjusri

A bodhisattva who like Avalokitesvara receives worship as a divinity in Mahayana Buddhism. In Nepal and Tibet the bodhisattva has been accorded the rank of a Buddha. He is a popular deity and looked upon as the bringer of civilization to the Himalayas. His concern is to lead suffering beings to enlightenment; the fetters of ignorance and desire break before his blow. In his terrific aspect he is 'the annihilator of Yama, the lord of death'. The archetype of wisdom, Manjusri holds in his hands a sword and a book. In China he became an important bodhisattva, texts about him being translated some time before 420. Just as the Dalai Lama is regarded by Tibetans as an incarnation of Avalokitesvara, so outstandingly wise rulers in East Asia have been regarded as incarnations of Manjusri.

Manu

He is the Hindu Noah. One day, in the water which was brought to Manu for washing his hands, he discovered a tiny fish which begged him to spare its life. 'Preserve me,' said the fish, 'and I will preserve you.' When Manu asked how the fish could save him, he was told of an imminent flood, which would carry away all living things. So Manu put the fish in a pot, but it grew so rapidly that he was obliged to move it to.a tank, a lake, and at last, the sea itself. Thereupon the fish predicted the flood and told Manu to prepare a ship against the danger, which he did. When the waters rose and Manu floated on their surface, the fish returned and towed the vessel by a cable fastened to its horn. Their journey was long and took them above the submerged peaks of the Himalayas. Lonely, Manu prayed for offspring and was granted a wife. From their union sprang the generations of Manu, progenitors of mankind.

In one myth the fish reveals its identity as Vishnu, in another as Brahma. There are, however, fourteen Manus in Hindu cosmology, since there are fourteen *manvantaras* or Manu-deluges, in every kalpa. The lawbook ascribed to Manu was compiled by one of them. The present era is the seventh of the kalpa and our particular deluge will be known in due course as that of 'Manu, the Son of the Radiant Sun'.

Mara

In Indian mythology Kama and Mara are the two sides of existence: the desire for life and the fear of death—the tasty bait and the keen hook. These two powers rule the world of the unawakened, those beguiled by maya. To escape from this non-enlightenment the Buddha preached his doctrine, which was called *yana*, a vehicle, a ferry to the other shore, where spiritual ignorance no longer held sway.

Mara, the master magician of illusion, became in Buddhist myth the Evil One. Because the Buddha delivers men from desire, birth, and death, Mara was his special enemy, and thus his tempter as well as those who would follow his law. Threatened by Enlightenment, the powerful démon committed his entire strength to the capture of the Gautama's mind, but below the outstretched branches of the Bo Tree the meditating sage sat unmoved. Assailed by the forces of Mara, the Buddha simply touched the earth with the tips of his fingers, whereupon there was a tremendous roar of approbation and the gods descended to pay their homage. Though defeated and shamed, Mara is said to linger in the world, hoping to seize the souls of the dying.

Milinda

The *Milindapanha*, (*Questions of Milinda*), records the conversation of Menander to Buddhism. This Greek general invaded the north of India from the Greco-Bactrian kingdom of Gandhara about 190 BC and set up a separate kingdom. Coins with bilingual inscriptions were struck: they used Greek and Indian languages, combining visual motifs from both cultural traditions.

Menander, as Milinda, acquired legendary stature for Buddhists. His ashes were entombed in a stupa and his name was connected with the origin of the statue of the Emerald Buddha, which Menander's teacher Nagasena made out of a magic emerald by supernatural power.

Muchalinda

A gigantic serpent-genie, who dwelt in the roots of the Bo Tree under which the Buddha attained to supreme consciousness. In a state of bliss, the meditating sage did not perceive the gathering of a frightful tempest, and so Muchalinda devoutly encircled the body of the Buddha seven times before spreading his broad hood above as an umbrella. Once the storm had passed, the *naga* monarch unwound his coils, changed into a young man, and with hands joined respectfully together he bowed low to the world-saviour. The myth is a classic statement of non-duality: Enlightenment encompasses all.

Nagas

The serpent-genii figures in the mythologies of

Hinduism, Jainism, and Buddhism. They are
serpent-like water gods, whose generally
friendly disposition contrasts with the saviour
versus serpent symbolism of West Asia. An
example was the protection afforded the
Buddha by Muchalinda, when in a seven-day
storm that prodigious cobra enveloped the
meditating sage with its coils and spread its
hood above as an umbrella.

A naga was pictured as having a human face
with the tail of a serpent, and the expanded
neck of the cobra. Nagas sprang from Kadru,
the daughter of Daksha, son of Brahma, and
the wife of Kasyapa, the ancient sage. They
inhabit subaquatic paradises, dwelling at the
bottoms of rivers, lakes, and seas, in
splendid, jewel-studded palaces ever alive with
dancing and song. Their girls are renowned for
good looks, cleverness, and charm; many
nagini feature among the ancestresses of
South Indian dynasties.

The protective function of nagas is apparent
in temple architecture, where they stand guard
at the portals of shrines. In South India

nagakals, stones decorated with a single
serpent or an entwined serpent-pair, are set up
as votive gifts by women desiring offspring.
After the carving is finished, the stone is left in
a pond for about six months, before its ritual
placement in a temple courtyard, near a
gateway, under a tree, or beside a pond.

Parsva

The twenty-third Jaina tirthankara, Parsva, or
Parsvanatha, is reputed to have lived in the
eighth century BC, some 84,000 years after the
death of his saintly predecessor, Neminatha.
According to legend, he dwelt on earth for a
century, having quit his family at the age of
thirty to become an ascetic. Parsva was an
incarnation of Indra, a handsome and noble
man whose relations accepted only as a last
resort his determination to take the vow of
world-renunciation known as sannyasa. His
father, King Asvasena of Benares, had been

*A detail of carvings at Mamallapuram
showing three nagas on the right*

informed through the pre-natal dreams of his queen that their son would be either a world monarch or a world-saviour.

The encounter between the eight-year-old Parsva and his maternal grandfather Mahipala appears to have been something of a turning point in his development. Parsva was riding an elephant in the jungle when he chanced upon Mahipala, an ascetic since the death of Parsva's grandmother over a decade before. The old hermit was beside himself with anger: had he not once been a king, had he not been disturbed in the midst of the severest penances, and had he not received from the young prince an improper salutation! Seizing an axe, he was about to split a log into two pieces, when Parsva told him that he would kill two serpents within the wood. 'And who are you? Brahma? Vishnu? Shiva? I perceive that you can see everything, no matter where', said Mahipala scornfully. Then he swung the axe, and did slice in half the serpents hidden inside. Grudgingly the recluse acknowledged his grandson's rank as a great sage, especially when the hymn-singing of Parsva was sufficient to ensure the reincarnation of the dying snakes as Ananta, the cosmic serpent, and Lakshmi, the spouse of Vishnu.

Tired of the imperfections of existence, Parsva turned to meditation, increasing so rapidly in his awareness that the gods in the heavens trembled, then descended as a host to beseech him to open the road to bliss for all living creatures. He divested himself of all attire, the last vestiges of earthly longing, and stood in a rigid posture, fasting without break, till he attained the supreme consciousness. Nothing could distract him, except the earnest prayers of the gods and his chief disciple, Svayambhu, who successfully requested that Parsva teach the way of escape from eternal rebirth.

Pushan

Frequently mentioned in the *Rig Veda* this Hindu deity acquired a distinctly defined character only in later times. 'The nourisher', the supplier of cattle and possessions, Pushan carries an ox-goad, and he is drawn by goats. Because of his toothlessness, worshippers offer gruel and cooked foods of ground materials. One account of this dental disaster relates that Pushan unhappily caught the full force of Shiva's fist in the celestial fracas at the sacrifice of the rishi Daksha.

Rishabha

Son of semi-divine parents—his father is sometimes regarded as one of the fourteen Manus—Rishabha was the first tirthankara, and founder of Jainism. He had one hundred sons. Relinquishing his kingdom to Bharata, the eldest son, he retired to a hermitage, where he led a life of such incredible austerity that he was no more than a bag of skin and bones on his death. Although the theme of abdication and retirement is a perennial one in India, the Jaina doctrine of the karmic bondage of the soul, a profound sense of contamination in daily experience, meant that those who sought spiritual release had to detach themselves utterly from ordinary existence. To Sravana Belgola, the granite eminence sacred to the Jains in Mysore, came the aged Chandragupta Maurya, having taken a similar vow of renunciation and travelled southwards with his *guru*, Bhadrabahu. This monarch had come to power in 322 BC, five years after the raid of Alexander the Great into the north-western plains of India, and under his energetic rule the states of the Ganges valley were amalgamated into a powerful empire. Like the Buddha, Chandragupta Maurya belonged to the pre-Aryan nobility, whose more vigorous sons were able to re-establish native dynasties once the invading Aryans showed signs of exhaustion. Out of this indigenous stock and its traditions Jainism probably sprang, though the historical date of Rishabha was always considered to be beyond computation.

The first of twenty-four tirthankaras, or 'makers of the crossing', Rishabha was the pristine example, whose ethereal form carved in rock would forever concentrate the devotee's mind upon the ultimate freedom of the spirit, nirvana. The only sign of individuality exhibited in the statues of this saint is a bull beneath his feet.

Rishis

Hindu seers. These divinely inspired sages composed the Vedic hymns, which in symbolic language convey the inner mysteries and deepest philosophy of Aryan belief. They were the forerunners and founders of the brahmins, their poetry extending the religious horizons of the invading pastoralists. In a state of samadhi, they experienced visions of the cosmic unity of the universe, an inward revelation that is indicated in the title of 'the seven rishis': people called them *prajapatis*, 'the mind-born sons' of Brahma. The oldest list includes the names of Gotama, Bharadwaja, Viswamitra, Jamad-agni, Vasishtha, Kasyapa, and Atri.

Of Bharadwaja it is said that 'he lived through three lives', after which 'he became immortal and ascended to the heavenly world, to union with the sun'. Jamad-agni had a more adventful span, his single life being that of a warrior brahmin. Having mastered all holy lore, he took as his spouse Renuka, a solar princess, who bore him five sons and shared in his ascetic life. One day she went to bathe and saw a loving couple in the shallows of the river, a sight that filled her with envious desire. Perceiving her 'fallen from perfection and shorn of the lustre of sanctity', Jamad-agni reproved her and commanded in turn her sons to kill her. Four of the boys refused and were cursed to idiocy by the enraged father, but the fifth, Parasurama, obeyed the order, striking off Renuka's head with a single blow of his axe. This act of obedience calmed Jamad-agni, and he asked his faithful son to make a request. Parasurama begged that his mother might be restored to her purity and that his brothers might regain their wits. All this the warrior brahmin granted. A second legend allots Parasurama a decisive role too. When the thousand-armed Kartavirya visited their hermitage during the absence of Jamad-agni and his sons, he abused Renuka's hospitality by tearing up the trees around the dwelling and stealing the calf of the sacred cow, Surabhi, which the warrior brahmin had earned through austerities. Parasurama went in pursuit and slew Kartavirya, but the sons of the thief staged a surprise counter attack that cruelly killed Jamad-agni. On finding his father's corpse, Parasurama swore that he would extirpate all the kshatriyas. Twenty-seven times did he carry out his oath.

The myths surrounding Vasishtha, 'most wealthy', and Viswamitra, the son of Gadhi, who was an incarnation of Indra, receive separate treatment elsewhere, but a word or two needs to be said about the other original rishis. Atri, 'the eater', was later held to have been the father of Soma, the moon, as well as the ascetic Dattatreya, in whom a portion of Brahma, Vishnu, and Shiva was incarnate. To Gotama is ascribed authorship of a book on law, while Kasyapa, 'tortoise', relates to Vishnu as an aspect of Time. As *vamana-avatara*, Vishnu was born as a dwarf, the son of Kasyapa and Aditi, 'the unbounded', a personification of visible heavens. The seven rishis are represented in the sky by the seven stars of the Great Bear constellation.

Bhrigu and Daksha were added to this illustrious company in the course of time. They were then called the nine brahma-rishis. Bhrigu, the son of Manu, was once asked by the other rishis to ascertain which deity was best entitled to the homage of a brahmin. Shiva's quarrel with his wife prevented Bhrigu from making any contact, so the sage obliged the god to assume the form of a lingam. With Brahma the questing seer had little more success because that deity's self-conceit ruled out a sensible conversation. Therefore, Bhrigu excluded Brahma from regular worship and hurried on to Vishnu, whom he found asleep. Indignant at this indifference to the world, the rishi stamped his foot and woke the reclining god, who instead of showing anger gently pressed Bhrigu's offending foot as a sign of respect. The deity and the rishi conversed, and satisfied with this encounter, the latter returned to his fellow sages with the report that only Vishnu deserved the worship of gods and men, which was unanimously accepted.

Daksha, 'intelligent, able,' was the son of Brahma, springing from the god's right thumb. Daksha and Aditi were conceived as interdependent; she was eternal, infinite, beyond limitation and bounds, while he was the spirit within, the generator of the gods in eternity. According to the *Mahabharata*, Daksha went through a rebirth as the result of a curse by his son-in-law Shiva. The tale of Daksha's sacrifice to Vishnu turns on another misunderstanding with Shiva, who violently interrupted the ritual and laid into the worshippers with devastating affect. Indra was knocked flat, Yama had his staff broken, the goddess Saraswati lost her nose, Mitra's eyes were gouged out, Pushan had his teeth punched down his throat, Bhrigu's beard was torn off, and other gods and rishis buffeted, stabbed, trampled, and pierced. The author of the catastrophe, Daksha, who had forgotten to invite Shiva to the ceremony, was decapitated and his head thrown into the sacrificial fire. After due apology and entreaty Shiva consented to restore his victims, though Daksha had to manage with the head of a ram since his own could not be found. A variant of this myth has Shiva's blazing trident destroy

Daksha's sacrifice and fall with an immense impact on the chest of Vishnu. The consequent fight between them only ceased on Brahma's intervention: he persuaded Shiva, as Rudra, to propitiate Vishnu, as Narayana, 'He who moves in the waters'.

Saraswati

The Ganges, Jumna, and Saraswati are the sacred rivers of Hindu mythology. The Saraswati river acted as the boundary of Brahmvartta, the homeland of the early Aryans, and was personified as a river goddess who blessed them with purifying waters. Later Saraswati added to her attributes sound—she became Vak, the goddess of river-like, streaming speech. A Bengali legend explains her marriage to Brahma. Finding three intelligent wives more than he could manage, Vishnu transferred Saraswati to Brahma and Ganga to Shiva, retaining for himself Lakshmi alone. The river Ganges, a goddess too, flowed from the toe of Vishnu and was assisted in her descent to the earth by Shiva, whose matted locks deflected and tamed the mighty surge of her waters.

Shiva

The name of Shiva is unknown in the ancient scriptures, but Rudra, 'the Howler or Roarer, the Terrible One', another name for this deity, and almost equally common, occurs frequently. Early in the evolution of the Hindu triad Shiva absorbed the Vedic Rudra, a personification of the implacable powers of destruction. Shiva was 'he who takes back or takes away'. In appearance Shiva is fair, has four arms, four faces, and three eyes. The third eye, situated in the centre of his forehead, possesses a fiery glance from which all created things shrink: it is sometimes represented by three horizontal lines, a mark worn today by his devotees. Shiva wears the skin of a tiger and has a snake twined round his neck, two items of attire he acquired in defeating these beasts when they were sent to destroy him by jealous rishis, or sages. He is the arch-ascetic, the Divine Yogi, who sits alone on Mount Kailasa, high in the Himalayas. At Indra's command, the god of love, Kama, fired an arrow of desire to arouse Shiva from his timeless contemplation and draw his attention to Parvati, 'the mountaineer', divine daughter of the mountain king Himalaya as well as an incarnation of the Supreme Goddess. But

Parvati, the wife of Shiva. A Chola bronze of the eleventh century

when the flower-shaft found its mark and Shiva was shaken from his perfect meditation, a lightning flash of anger broke from his middle eye so that Kama was scorched to cinders. Though Shiva agreed to let the god of love be reborn as Rukmini, the son of 'delusion' or maya, the beautiful body could not be restored, and Kama is now called *ananga*, 'bodiless'.

The destructive aspect, too, is clear in the title of Bhairava, 'the joyous devourer'. In this guise Shiva haunts cemeteries and places of cremation, wearing serpents round his head and skulls for a necklace, attended by hosts of demons and imps. Yet the opposite side of his character becomes equally apparent in his cosmic dance, when as Nataraja, 'king of the dancers', he performs before Parvati in order to relieve the sufferings of his followers. Here it

Left: Shiva, the Divine Dancer

Below: 'Descent of the Ganges' from the rock carvings at Mamallapuram

is that we encounter one of the resplendent symbols of world mythology, a profound conception realized in the beautiful bronzes of South India. That the trances induced through dance and yoga were viewed as the same can be observed in the provision made for ritual dancing before the holy image in a Hindu temple. Shiva Nataraja is encircled by a ring of flames, the vital processes of universal creation, and with one leg raised, he stands upon a tiny figure, crouching on a lotus. This dwarfish demon represents human ignorance, the conjurings of maya, whose conquest is the attainment of wisdom and release from the bondages of the world. In one hand the god holds a drum, the sign of speech, the source of revelation and tradition; his second hand offers blessing, sustenance; in the palm of the third hand a tongue of fire is a reminder of destruction; and the fourth hand points downward to the uplifted foot, already saved from the power of illusion. It signifies the refuge and salvation of the devotee.

At Mamallapuram, south of Madras, there is a famous rock-carving of the Descent of the Ganges. It celebrates an equally famous incident relating to the intervention of Shiva as Ganga-dhara, 'the upholder of the River

Ganges'. Once the earth was deprived of moisture and the life-maintaining waters of the Ganges flowed in heaven, washing only the sky. The land became so filled with the ashes of the dead that there seemed no possible way of cleansing it. To put an end to this terrible drought the sage, Bhagiratha, sought to bring the Ganges out of heaven. But such were the dimensions of the sacred river that its fall would have wrought destruction on earth had not Shiva intervened and let its full force pour over his head, where the waters were able to meander amid his matted locks and compose themselves into seven smoothly flowing tributaries. This legend as well as Indra's slaying of Vritra, the serpent of drought, appear to be an account not so much of creation as of some regularly recurring phenomenon. There are obvious connections with the torrential rain-storms of the monsoons and the rush of the great rivers charged with melted snow.

Shiva's vehicle is Nandi, a milk-white bull, which is conspicuous outside the front entrances of the god's temples. Nandi is the guardian of four-legged creatures.

Sumeru

Meru, or Sumeru, is the world mountain of Hindu mythology. The vertical axis of the universe, Mount Sumeru rises into the clouds like a gigantic Babylonian ziggurat, providing on its natural terraces delectable abodes for a host of gods, whose king is Indra. Around its majestic form the sun, moon, and stars revolve. Shiva's paradise is situated on Kailasa, a mountain in the Himalayas. Both the ranges of the Himalaya and the Vindhya Mountains have been long regarded as homes of the gods. The Vindhya range, which marks the northern extremity of the Deccan, was for the Aryans the place of sunrise, while the rivers flowing out of the folds of the Himalayas were the waters of life.

Surya

In the *Rig Veda* the god of the sun was one of the three chief deities: the others were Indra, god of the rain, and Agni, god of fire. The most distinct of several Hindu sun gods, Surya is described as short, with a burnished copper body, riding through the sky in a chariot drawn by seven ruddy horses and driven by Aruna, dawn, his wife or mother. He is credited with several parents, one of whom is

Brahma, while his own progeny includes Yama, the king of the dead, and Yamuna, the present River Jumna. These two, brother and sister, are by some looked upon as the first human beings, just as Yama was the first man to die and journey to the other realm. When Surya's wife Sanjna, overpowered by his radiance, fled as a mare to the shade of a forest and studied meditation, the sun god came to her as a stallion. Later her father, Visvakarma, reduced Surya's brilliant rays by cutting away one-eighth of his substance, the fiery trimmings falling to earth among other things as the disc of Vishnu and the trident of Shiva. Worship of Surya can be found in Bihar and Tamilnad, where his benevolence is invoked for the healing of the sick.

Tara

Avalokitesvara, in Tibetan Buddhism, is accompanied by a spouse, Tara. She is the sakti of the bodhisattva, the energy of his essence. It was she who aroused him to bring into existence on earth Gautama Siddhartha. The two wives, the Chinese and the Nepalese princesses, of Sron-btsan-sgam-po, the first Buddhist king of Tibet are held to have been incarnations of the white and green aspects of Tara.

Though the first record of her worship is a Javanese inscription of 778, there is reason to believe that the great Chinese pilgrim Hsuantsang, who travelled in India between 629 and 640, encountered Tara at a shrine near Nalanda. He reports that an image accompanying Avalokitesvara and known as *to-lo* was a 'popular object of worship'. On the other hand, a Bon myth relating to the origins of the Tibetan people claims that 'a devil and an ogress held sway, and that the country was called Land of the Two Ogres. As a result, redfaced flesh-eating creatures were born.' An adaptation of this legend to suit Buddhism says that the monkey Boddhisattra, an incarnation of Avalokitesvara, and the lustful rock ogress, an incarnation of Tara, sprang the Tibetan nation. Most likely the introduction of Tara's cult in Tibet occurred through the agency of Sron-btsan-sgam-po's Nepalese wife. She is known to have brought

A sixteenth-century Nepalese copper statuette of the Buddhist goddess Tara

with her a sandalwood statue of a goddess.

The worship of Tara is one of the most widespread of Tibetan cults: she transcends social distinctions and offers a personal relationship to her devotees unmatched by any other single deity. She is kind and loving, despite the gulf of being which necessarily separates her from ordinary people.

Vajrasattva

He is 'of the adamantine substance' and 'the wielder of the thunderbolt'. This Buddha is one of the six dhyani-buddhas, 'meditation Buddhas'. In Tibet he is regarded as the primeval Buddha, from whom all the others issued forth, and is invoked as the protector of the devotee in quest of enlightenment. Bronze statuary reveals this inwardness: the Yab-Yum, the eternal embrace of the male and female principles; the union of Vajrasattva with his sakti represents, as in the case of Shiva, the coincidence of opposites, the attainment of oneness. Nirvana and samsara, enlightened extinction and the endless round of rebirth, are thus seen as not fundamentally different from each other, but stand for contrary manifestations of the transcendent source, which is beyond both.

Yet there is a terrible side to the character of Vajrasattva. His violent fury is expressed in rain, hail, and snow—elemental forces he often uses to protect the nagas from the cruel talons of the giant garuda birds.

Varuna

He is one of the oldest Hindu deities. Unlike Indra, whose birth was described as the product of a union between 'a vigorous god' and 'a heroic female', Varuna is uncreate. He is the universal encompasser, a personification of the all-investing sky, the source and sustenance of created things. Associated with Mitra, the ruler of the day probably connected with the Persian Mithra, Varuna ruled the sky at night, whose star-like presence was the cause of wonder in early men everywhere. In later times he lost his position as the supreme deity and became a kind of Neptune, a god of the seas and rivers, who rides upon the Makara, a fabulous sea animal, part crocodile, part shark, and part dolphin.

Vasishtha

This Hindu sage was the possessor of a sacred cow, called Nandini, which had the power to give him anything he might desire. The rival rishi, Viswamitra, failed in his attempt to seize this wondrous animal, and the enmity between these two holy men is central to the themes of several texts. It has been suggested that their contentions reflect the struggle of their two castes for social superiority: Vasishtha the brahmin and Viswamitra the kshatriya.

Another legend sets forth a conflict involving the rishi Gotama. King Nimi of Mithila requested that Vasishtha officiate at a sacrifice which was to last for 1,000 years. The seer explained how an engagement to Indra for 500 years meant he could not undertake the ceremony immediately, but it seemed agreed by both parties that at a future date Vasishtha would be the priest. When Vasishtha discovered that the Nimi had engaged Gotama to perform the sacrifice, he cursed the King to lose his body. The latter returned the compliment and both departed their physical forms. At length Mitra and Varuna furnished Vasishtha with a new body, but Nimi was too distressed for rebirth and the gods agreed that he could become a part of the eyes of all living creatures. Hence, nimisha, the wink of an eye, became a general habit.

Vayu

Literally, 'air, wind'. In the Rig Veda he is often linked with Indra, whose chariot he shares. Hindu exegesis states: 'Agni dwells on earth, Vayu and Indra reside in the air, and the place of Surya is in the heavens.' Later scriptures involve Vayu in conflicts with Vishnu. When the sage Narada incited the wind to break down the summit of Mount Meru, Vishnu's bird, Garuda, shielded the mountain with his wings and blunted the force of the mighty blasts. But in Garuda's absence the scheme of Narada was ultimately successful, the top of the mountain being torn off and hurled into the sea, where it became the island of Sri Lanka.

Vishnu

As preserver and restorer, Vishnu is a very popular deity with Hindu worshippers. The root of his name, vish, means 'to pervade', and he is regarded as the all-pervading presence, whose power has been manifested to the world in a variety of forms called avataras, or 'descents', in which a part of his divine essence was incarnated in a human or supernatural form. An avatar has appeared whenever there was urgent need to correct some great evil influence in the world. 'When order, justice, and mortals are endangered', remarked Vishnu, 'I come down to earth.' Though the devotees of Shiva propose twenty-eight incarnations for their own deity, it is the ten principal avatars of Vishnu that hold the stage in Hindu mythology.

Vishnu is generally represented pictorially as a handsome youth of a dark blue colour, and dressed like an ancient king. In his four hands he holds a conch shell, a discus, a club, and a lotus flower. His vehicle is Garuda, the sun bird, enemy of all serpents. This antagonism is dramatically portrayed in Krishna's defeat of the water serpent Kaliya. Reminded of his divine nature by Balarama, Vishnu, lying as Krishna at the bottom of a pool bestirs himself and dances upon the threatening Kaliya's mighty head. Sparing the exhausted serpent king, Krishna said: 'You shall no longer reside in the Yamuna River, but in the vastness of the ocean. Go! Moreover, I tell you that Garuda, the golden sun bird, deadly foe of all serpents and my vehicle through infinities of space, forever shall spare you,

Vishnu, the World Saviour, as a boar rescuing earth from a flood

whom I have touched.' It has been suggested that this popular legend recounts the supplanting of the local nature divinity by an anthropomorphic god, Krishna, who in turn was merged with Vishnu. A parallel in Greek myth could be Apollo's conquest of the earthbound serpent of Delphi, whose oracle he arrogated to himself after killing the python. The importance of Garuda was not restricted to Indian lore, since in Cambodian architecture the whole temple rests on the back of the mythical bird.

Of Vishnu's chief avatars half are human and half are animal. The fish incarnation, *matsya-avatara*, was connected with the saving of Manu in the deluge; *kurma-avatara* occurred when as a tortoise the deity secretly assisted in the Churning of the Ocean; the boar incarnation, *varaha-avatara*, involved the rescue of the earth from the depths in another flood, whither it had been stolen by powerful demons; and through the *nrisimha-avatara*, 'man-lion', Vishnu dethroned Hiranyakasipu, a demon king who as a result of his austerities had gained enough strength from Brahma to push Indra out of the heavens. At the behest of the other gods Vishnu assumed the form of a dwarf, *vamana-avatara*, in order to reconquer the three worlds from the demon Bali. While

this usurper was engaged in offering a sacrifice on a riverbank, the Brahman dwarf approached and asked of him a boon. Respectful and conscious of his duty as a host, Bali consented to his request, though he knew that he was likely to be the loser for it. The dwarf said: 'I ask you only for a little patch of earth, as much as I can measure with three of my strides. Nothing more I require, since a wise man should be content to ask for no more than he needs.' Then, the tiny priest suddenly waxed into the cosmic giant, and with two strides crossed the universe, his third one resting on the head of the vanquished demon. More warlike was *parashu-rama*, 'Rama with the axe', the avatar who destroyed the thousand-armed King of the Himalayas, Kartavirya. This monarch had 'oppressed both gods and men'.

The hero of the oldest Sanskrit epic, the *Ramayana*, is Vishnu's incarnation as Rama, descendent of an ancient solar dynasty. The circumstance of his birth as son of King Dasaratha of Oudh was divine apprehension over the threats of demon Ravana, the Rakshana King of Sri Lanka, who had obtained extraordinary power through severe penances and austere devotion to Brahma. When the frightened gods appealed to Vishnu for deliverance, he appeared to Dasa-ratha within the sacrificial fire and gave him a pot of nectar for his wives to drink. The monarch passed half of the nectar to Kausalya, who gave birth to Rama with a half of the divine essence, a quarter to Kaikeyi, whose son Bharata possessed a quarter of the deity, and the remainder to Su-mitra, who gave birth to two sons, Lakshmana and Satru-ghna, each having an eighth part of the divine essence.

The sage Viswamitra sought out the young Rama for protection against the Rakshasas. Supplied with celestial arms and encouraged by Viswamitra, Rama overcame his reluctance to fight a woman and killed the female demon Taraka. Afterwards the sage took Rama along with his brothers to the court of Janaka, King of Videha. This ruler had a beautiful daughter named Sita, whom he offered in marriage to any one who could bend the wonderful bow which had once belonged to Shiva. Rama not only bent the bow but broke it: Sita became his

A seventeenth-century manuscript of the love of Krishna for Radha the milkmaid

wife, and his brothers also married her sister and cousins.

When the time came for Rama to be declared the successor to his father, Kaikeyi, the mother of Bharata, prevailed upon Dasaratha to install Bharata as king and to send Rama into exile for fourteen years. Rama, Sita, and Lakshmana departed, and travelling south, they took up residence in the Dandaka forest. Although Bharata declined the throne and asked his brother to return, Rama insisted on completing his exile and made Bharata act as regent. During this period Rama went to live in Panchavati, an area under Rakshasa control, and his indifference to the amorous advances of Surpanakha, sister of Ravana, led to a conflict with Sri Lanka. To be avenged Surpanakha inspired in her brother such a passion for Sita that the demon carried her off to his kingdom by force. In their pursuit Rama and Lakshmana slew Kabandha, a headless monster, whose spirit advised them to seek the aid of Sugriva, king of the monkeys. Supported by the monkey host, Sugriva and Hanuman, an agile monkey chief, the brothers crossed over to Sri Lanka on Rama-setu, 'Rama's bridge', a line of rocks in the channel between the continent and the island called in modern maps Adam's Bridge. Taking the demon capital they killed Ravana and freed Sita, though at first Rama regarded her with considerable suspicion. Her innocence was established by an act of truth, an ancient belief that the one who has enacted his dharma, duty or role, without a single fault throughout the whole of his life can work magic by the simple act of calling that fact to witness. This Sita, 'a furrow', did: Mother Earth was her witness, by opening up and receiving her. Unable to endure life without his wife, the disconsolate Rama followed her into eternity, walking into the waters of the Sarayu river. Vishnu, of course, is associated with the primordial waters as Narayana, 'moving on the waters'; he reclines on the coils of Ananta, the world snake.

As Krishna, the avatar of the *Mahabharata*, the Sanskrit epic containing the 'Bhagavad Gita', 'Song of the Blessed Lord', Vishnu is the exponent of a loftier view of events. Yet Krishna, the most popular deity in India today, also displays a number of very human weaknesses—deceit, dishonesty, and trickery. It is likely that this hero, around whom a vast mass of legend and fable has been gathered, lived during the period after the fall of the Indus valley civilization, when the Aryans had not advanced far beyond their first settlements in the North West. Later addition to the account of his heroic exploits has raised Krishna to divinity, and it is in the character of 'the Almighty Prince of Wisdom' that he 'shows Arjuna the Supreme Form of the Great God'. This cosmic vision occurs when Krishna acts as Arjuna's charioteer at the battle between the Pandavas and the Kauravas. Then 'there were countless eyes and mouths, and mystic forms innumerable, with shining ornaments and flaming celestial weapons. Crowned and resplendent stood the Marvellous, Boundless, Omnipresent One. Could a thousand suns blaze forth together it would not be a faint reflection of the radiance of the Supreme Lord.' Arjuna is overwhelmed and terrified by the revelation, which 'has never been seen by any other'. Reassured by Krishna, returned to his earthly shape, Arjuna expresses relief—'I am myself again!'—and possibly like Peter, James, and John, after the transfiguration of Jesus, he begins to forget the avatar's god-nature and accept his outward human appearance. However, the dangers of such exposure were always recognized. Swami Vivekananda, the chief disciple of Ramakrishna, who announced himself as the reincarnation of Vishnu, said about the year 1885: 'When people try to practise religion, eighty per cent of them turn into cheats, and about fifteen per cent go mad. 'It's only the remaining five per cent who get some direct knowledge of the Truth and so become blessed. So, beware!' Despite the accretion of folklore to the figure of Krishna, and especially his mischievous childhood among the cowherds, the vision of the 'Bhagavid Gita' has remained the sacred book of Hinduism.

Krishna, the Dark One, was the last of the Yadavas, an old pastoral nation. Vishnu plucked out two of his hairs, one black, the other white, which he placed in the wombs of Devaki and Rohini respectively. The black was born as Krishna and the white hair became Balarama. Kansa, the usurper of Mathura, learned from a sage that Devaki's son would destroy him, so the harassed mother had to exchange Krishna for the newborn daughter of the cowherd Nanda and his wife Yasoda. During this rural sojourn the young Krishna undertook numerous adventures: notable were his triumph over Kaliya;

the abduction of the daughter of the Gandharva king; the overthrow of Saubha, the flying city of the Daityas; and he obtained the discus from Agni, the fire god: such exploits must have encouraged the Greek settlers of north-west India, whose kingdoms flourished during the second century BC, in their identification of Krishna with Hercules. Yasoda was first made aware of Krishna's special powers when she chanced to look down his throat. She was stupefied to see the whole universe there. But it is the love of Krishna for Radha, the milkmaid, that comprises the focus of modern worship—as the perfect deification of life.

On reaching manhood, Krishna left the cowherds, and returned to Mathura, where he killed Kansa. In the war between the Pandavas and the Kauravas, to both of whom he was related, Krishna played a decisive role, not least in overcoming the hesitations of Arjuna over joining a battle which was destined to end as a senseless massacre of friends and relatives. Krishna reminded him that as a kshatriya it is his duty to fight and declared that 'the hero whose soul is unmoved by circumstance, who accepts pleasure and pain with equanimity, he alone is fit for immortality'. On the actual battlefield Arjuna was supported by Krishna, while the Kauravas had the assistance of his army. Some time after the cessation of hostilities there was at Dwzraka, 'the city of gates', in Gujarat, a drunken brawl that left Balarama for dead beneath a tree. Then Krishna himself was unwittingly killed with an arrow fired by the hunter Jaras, or 'old age'.

The next avatar of Vishnu will be Kalki, 'the white horse'; it will appear at a moment during the coming 428 centuries of Kali Yuga, the present age of the world. Meanwhile the devotees of the god regard him as supreme. Vishnu is the creator because from his navel emerged Brahma on a lotus; he is, as Krishna, the preserver; and, as Shiva, who according to the Mahabharata sprang from his forehead, he is the dissolver.

Viswamitra

One of the seven great rishis, he was of royal lineage, the son of a kshatriya with the qualities of a brahmin. The Rig Veda, the collection of ancient Hindu hymns, alludes to the rivalry between Viswamitra and Vasishtha a struggle for precedence that these seers were prepared to carry over into deeds of violence.

Once Viswamitra ordered the River Saraswati to bring Vasishtha to him for execution, but instead of doing so, the waters floated Vasishtha out of his reach. Thereupon, the enraged rishi turned the river into blood. In the *Ramayana*, however, Vasishtha humiliates his relentless enemy, a defeat that the kshatriya determines to overcome through his own elevation to the brahmin caste. Finally, the incredible austerities of Viswamitra—so alarmed did Indra become at the seer's gain in power that he sent a nymph to beguile his senses—won him the prerogatives he sought, and a reconciliation with Vasishtha took place.

Yama

The Hindu god of death. He is the 'restrainer', and was originally conceived as the king of the departed spirits who lived in the upper sky. He and his sister Yami, the first mortals, were the children of Surya, the sun god. Yama's role as friend of the dead gradually altered to that of a less beneficent deity; he became the terrible judge and punisher of human misdeeds, in appearance green, armed with a noose as well as a club, and seated on a buffalo. Two insatiable dogs with four eyes and broad nostrils guard the road to his abode. A soul when it quits the body hastens past these fierce beasts to the palace of death, where the recorder, Chitragupta, reads out its account so that Yama may reach a judgement. The sentence will dispatch the soul to either a heavenly dwelling-place, one of the twenty-one hells, or back to the world for rebirth. Reminiscent of the Greek underworld are Vaitarani, the river bordering the land of the dead, and the gnathic threat from the guardian dogs, whose reputation probably derived from observation of their scavenger relations on earth. Greek corpses were actually provided with honey-cakes to feed Cerberus.

Yuga

In Hindu cosmology, an age of the world. The four ages—Krita, Treta, Dwapara, and Kali—are preceded and followed by periods of twilight, whose duration is each one-tenth of a yuga. Krita Yuga, the first age of the world, lasts 4,000 divine years; Treta Yuga, the second age, 3,000; Dwapara Yuga, the third, 2,000 years; and Kali Yuga, the fourth, 1,000 years. The entire cycle of ages and intervals of twilight extends over 12,000 years, which equals, allowing for the fact that a year of the gods is reckoned at 360 years of men, a total of 4,320,000 years. This unit of cosmological time is known as a mahayuga, 2,000 of which constitute a kalpa, a day and night of Brahma, or 8,640,000,000 years. Though Brahma re-creates the universe at the beginning of each kalpa, this process lasts for not more than a *para*, a century of such days and nights. According to Hindu tradition, the life of Brahma and the universe lasts for a para. Our present kalpa is at the beginning of the second half of the para, making Brahma fifty years old. Only one Hindu school of philosophy has ever denied that the world is finite in time, and shared with Jainism the idea of an eternal, uncreated universe.

During the Krita Yuga righteousness is supreme. People are virtuous and fulfil their duties without malice, sadness, pride, or deceit; there is nothing to disturb the calmness of this age. In the Treta Yuga changes in relationships start to occur. Duties are no longer the spontaneous laws of human behaviour, but have to be learned. Sacrifices are needed; people follow truth and devote themselves to righteousness through ceremonies, which are regarded as a means of obtaining specific objects. Dwapara Yuga witnesses increased imbalance along with a steady decline in righteousness. The *Rig Veda* appears. Diseases, desires, and disasters harass the people, some of whom seek release in austerities or ritual practices. Finally, Kali Yuga, the dark age of today, is riven with quarrels, dissension, wars, and strife. Love and sex are separated. Few know truth. Possessions, not righteousness, confer rank and the outer trappings are confused with inner religion. Our period, which began in 3102 BC, has another 427 centuries to run.

EAST ASIA

Siberia Mongolia China Japan South-East Asia

Beyond the Great Wall of China a nomadic way of life has always prevailed. Across the endless wastes have roamed the herds belonging to the peoples of the north—the Mongols, the Turks, the Tartars, the Tungus, the Huns. A world apart, the steppe was until the beginning of the nineteenth century a constant source of anxiety for Asia and Europe, whose civilizations have always rested upon intensive agriculture and urban settlement. From the steppe mounted raiders had descended with such fury that the nomad terror was legendary. Most notorious was Genghis Khan (c. 1162–1227), who laid down the rule that any resistance to Mongol arms should be punished by total extermination. 'The greatest joy', he once said, 'is to conquer one's enemies, to pursue them, to seize their belongings, to see their families in tears, to ride their horses, and to possess their daughters and wives.' Although the Mongol onslaught of the thirteenth century failed to establish a world imperium, the devastation wrought in the numerous campaigns was immense, China bearing the brunt of the attack.

Yet the Mongol conquest of China (1279–1365) did result in the introduction of Buddhism to Mongolia and Siberia because the Tibetan form was adopted as the official religion of the nomad empire. The 'yellow faith' began to replace the old 'black faith', the original animist-shamanist religion of the north. Many old folk-customs were tolerated by giving them new meanings and the early myths were preserved by the art of the story-teller, but the authority of the shamans declined. No longer was the only custodian of the soul the *saman*, the 'medicine man'. Previously these spirit-possessed men were used to seek out and recover the lost or abducted souls of the sick. In trance and frenzy the shaman raised himself to the world of the spirits, where he gained control over certain incorporeal beings, especially those of disease and death, in order to exorcize them from people. The Buriat tribesmen living on the shores of Lake Baikal, for example, declare that Morgon-Kara, their first shaman, was able to bring back to earth even the souls of the dead. So perturbed was the lord of 'the land of beyond' that he complained to the high lord of heaven, who decided to put the shaman to a test. He got possession of the soul of one man and placed it in a bottle, stopping the opening with his thumb. When the man fell ill and his relatives asked Morgon-Kara to help, the shaman rode on his magical drum and searched every corner of the universe, till at last he observed where the missing soul was held. Then the wily shaman changed himself into a wasp, and flew to the deity's forehead, which he stung hard enough for the thumb to jerk away from the mouth of the bottle. The king of heaven, however, was not prepared to allow Morgon-Kara a complete triumph. The shaman's flight with the recovered soul almost became a headlong fall as the angered god split his drum in two. Afterwards, Buriat tradition explains, magical drums were only fitted with a single head of skin in token of the diminished power of the shaman.

An eighteenth-century Japanese print of the Buddha Sakyamuni entering Nirvana. He lies in the centre with animals and disciples around him

Within the Great Wall the sorcery of the North Asian peoples found a place in Taoism, the Chinese religion of individual salvation. Taoism had two origins. First there were the philosophers of the Warring States period (481–221 BC) who withdrew from the courts of feudal princes and spent their lives in the forests or on mountains meditating upon Nature. Lao-tzu, 'the Old Philosopher', had simply quit civilization: the absence of a tomb for this 'hidden wise man' is a notable omission in an age that placed immense store by the rites of ancestor worship. 'Confucius walks within society', wrote Chuang-tzu (350–275 BC), the most distinguished follower of Lao-tzu, 'whilst I walk outside it.' Taoists felt wisdom 'in their bones', and rejected the elaboration of social duties so favoured by Confucianism. Instead of emphasizing the family and the clan, they sought after a feminine and receptive knowledge that could only arise as the fruit of a passive and yielding attitude in the observation of natural phenomena. This philosophical outlook was important for the early development of science in China, since Taoist observation and experiments in alchemy represent the dim beginnings of scientific method. What these adepts tried to discover was the elixir of life, the chemical means of immortality. There was a persistent belief in such a possibility, as the following incident of the ninth century shows. The chance excavation of a long-buried stone box filled with silk disturbed a grey-haired man of dignified mien who arose, adjusted his clothing, and then disappeared.

The other root of Taoism was the magic of the *wu*—female and male thaumaturges. Their sympathetic magic eased the lot of the hard-pressed peasants by placating malignant spirits and invoking those more kindly disposed. Details of a ceremony of exposure survive; it suggests that the drops of sweat shed by the sorcerer, dancing within a circle under the blazing sun, were expected to induce drops of rain. The psychic powers of the wu also enabled contact to be made with departed spirits, though their abilities in this direction were unappreciated by the nobility. The wu magicians, with the whole tradition of peasant belief, remained beyond the pale, utterly divorced from respectable worship. Not for nothing did Taoism, in opposition to Confucian orthodoxy, draw upon the primitive strength of the wu, whose shamanism was continually reinforced by fresh waves of invaders from the north.

In AD 165, there was an increase in the prestige of Taoism at the court, the Chinese emperor offering sacrifices to Lao-tzu for the first time, but this ceremony did not really endanger the Confucian supremacy. Only Mahayana Buddhism made a sustained challenge to become the national religion, though competition with this foreign faith transformed Taoism into an organized church. At every level in Chinese society the teachings of Buddha have had a profound effect. Until the modern period, only India, the Holy Land for East Asia, has influenced China. Yet that singular Chinese capacity to absorb alien peoples, whether Tartar, Mongol, or Manchu conquerors, was active in the development of Buddhism, too. At last the imported faith was modified to suit Chinese society, rather than China modified by the new religion. The Buddhist church adjusted to the Confucian state.

According to legend, when Confucius was born in 551 BC, a *ch'i-lin* (unicorn) appeared and spat out a piece of jade on which it was written that the philosopher would be 'an uncrowned emperor'. The prophecy of the unicorn proved correct. Although Confucius remained an obscure and neglected teacher throughout his life, the impact of his thought upon the subsequent history of China has been immense. He

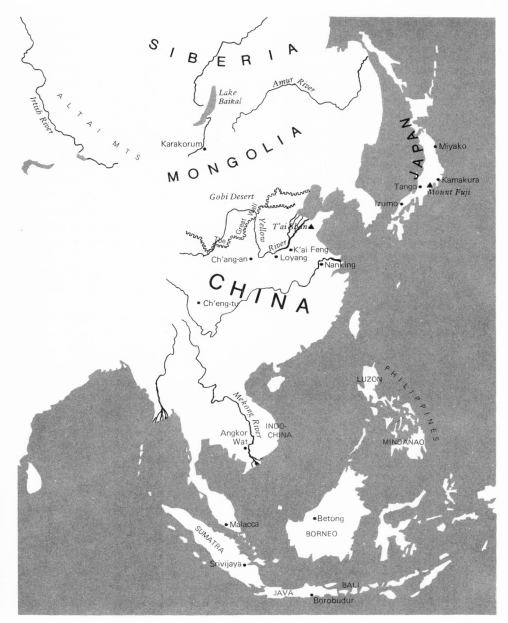

was a moral philosopher, his this-worldly doctrine being a feudal ethic, which expected the prince to rule with benevolence and sincerity. The ruler was the Son of Heaven, whose harmonious relation with the spiritual realm ensured the welfare of the people. The unworthiness of a monarch would be reflected in the attitude of heaven, *Shang Ti,* just as 'the earth shook' and 'rivers were dried up' during the bad years of a tyrant, an unfilial son. The primitive rites of ancestor worship, thus elevated into a moral code by Confucian philosophy, were the ceremonial meeting of two worlds, the spiritual and the temporal. They underpinned authority—throne, clan, and family.

The attitude of Confucius to religion was entirely practical. 'I stand in awe of the spirits,' he told his students, 'but keep them at a distance.' He did not disbelieve, he simply had too much to consider in the temporal world. He was rather sceptical of man's powers of comprehension; the celestial realm could not be readily plumbed by divination or star-gazing. This reluctance of Confucius to pronounce on religion introduced a sense of balance in the spiritual world as well as on the earthly plane. It came to the aid of traditionalists opposed to the fervour generated by Buddhism. When Emperor T'ang Hui-ch'ang decided that the religious establishment had grown too large in AD 845, his course of action was straightforward enough. All monks and nuns in China, numbering 260,500, were laicized; thereafter, strong control was exercised over the affairs of religious orders, extending to the recruitment of personnel and ownership of property. While such scepticism meant that Chinese history has been unblemished by religious wars, it has taken its toll of imaginative speculation. Mythology tended to remain the preserve of Taoism and Buddhism, especially after the latter had succumbed to the Chinese political tradition of a strong central authority and accepted its role as a popular, not state, religion. The Chinese mind added to Buddhist cosmology, initiating several advanced schools of thought, but to Japan was left the final development of the faith in East Asia. In the twelfth century Chu Hs'i, the pre-eminent Neo-Confucian scholar, boldly said: 'There is no man in heaven judging sin.'

The Constantine of Japan, Prince Shotoku (572–621), compared the three ethical systems of his country to the root, the stem and branches, and the fruit and flowers of a tree. Shinto was the tap-root embedded in the rich soil of folk tradition; Confucianism served as the sturdy stem and branches of the social order and learning; Buddhism engendered the blossoming of religious sentiment, the mature fruit of spiritual development. The three ways were seen as mutually co-operative, a view that lasted till the political upheavals of the fourteenth century, when religious strife raged side by side with feudal wars.

Shinto, 'the way of the gods', the indigenous belief of the Japanese people as distinguished from Butsudo, 'the way of the Buddha', always remained the focus of national aspirations for the reason that reverence for the ruling family is inseparably linked with the worship of Amaterasu, the sun goddess. As the ancestress of the Royal House, she is the chief divinity of the numerous folk pantheon, yet herself only the highest manifestation of the unseen spirit of the universe, Kunitokotachi. Though Shinto was supported by the government, having shrines throughout the country, it never achieved the organization of a national church. Rather, it is a means of showing respect to local spirits, ancestral powers, the throne, and the family. This moral emphasis received strength from Confucian ethics, which after the third century penetrated Japan through the agency of the Koreans. Chinese names were even adopted for the various relationships and the virtues necessary in the conduct of social life. The first direct official contact, however, occurred in 607 when Prince Shotoku sent an envoy to China. Soon monks and students followed in the wake of the ambassadors with the result that Chinese culture had a tremendous influence on Japan.

Most potent of the imports were the new schools of Buddhism then arising, such as the Ch'an Tsung, or 'inner-light school', which reached its culmination in Japan as

The Temple of Heaven in Peking

Zen. In mythology the new faith introduced a great deal of the Indian imagination, its vastness of scale and its myriad forms, along with the subtle additions of the Chinese mind. Not only did the elaborate iconography of the 'Greater Vehicle' stimulate the evolution of Japanese myth, but more the arrival of Buddhist literature had a remarkable effect on Japanese folklore. Open to outside influences, just as it was open to immigration from the peoples inhabiting the continent to the west and the islands to the south, 'the land that faces the sun' has had few inhibitions about taking over the development of foreign ideas. Japan is the Sicily of East Asia.

Indo-China, the antiquated name for the countries nearest to the southern border of China, did have in its coinage an insight into the historical experience of Cambodia, Laos, and Vietnam. Here it was that the two hoary traditions of India and China met, though only in Vietnam were the political and religious ideas of Confucianism firmly rooted. Beyond the area of direct control the Chinese did not succeed in exporting their culture; they were content with the acceptance of a vague suzerainty by more distant kings. Representative of overseas policy would be the treatment of the Sultan of Malacca, near whose city the famous Chinese admiral Cheng Ho established a temporary naval base in 1406. The Chinese were welcomed at Malacca, a state which had only recently gained its independence, the ruler travelling to Peking three times to offer homage. That he began his reign as a Buddhist and then converted to Islam caused the tolerant Son of Heaven no anxiety at all.

Cambodia and Laos, along with Thailand, Burma, Malaysia, and the western part of Indonesia, Sumatra, Java, and Bali, were originally under Hindu influence, although never conquered by any Indian power. There is no exact record of how this came about, but it is likely that at first traders from South India came for spices, their ships taking advantage of the monsoon winds. They were followed by brahmins who converted the ruling tribal chiefs to the worship of the Hindu pantheon, and also set up kingdoms modelled on the ancient Indian system of kingship. According to a Cambodian legend, an Indian brahmin named Kaundinya landed with a merchant vessel in the first century, married a local princess, and so became the ruler of the coastal country. The princess-bride is said to have been a *nagini*, snake girl, many of whom feature among the ancestresses of South Indian dynasties. The influence of these immigrants was strong and continued for several centuries, later strengthened by the arrival of Buddhist monks, who left India when resurgent Hinduism threatened to extinguish their faith. Brought by the monk-missionaries was the older of the two Buddhist traditions, the Hinayana or 'Lesser Vehicle', which was dedicated to the ideal of individual salvation and represented the way to this end as monastic self-discipline. The Sailendra kings of Srivijaya welcomed the new religion, an inscription of 778 registering the construction of a shrine in their territories on Java. The most magnificent Sailendra monument immediately followed, likewise in the central part of this island; namely, the vast stupa of Borobudur. Its erection at the beginning of the ninth century is evidence of the wealth belonging to Srivijaya, the dominant state in South-east Asia, while the stupa's iconography reveals the eclipse of the 'Lesser Vehicle', overtaken as it was at this time by the more vigorous 'Greater Vehicle', or Mahayana tradition, which proposed the ideal of salvation for all and developed disciplines of popular devotion and universal secular service. Today Hinayana survives chiefly in Burma and Thailand.

The decline of Hindu-Buddhist states in the Indonesian archipelago resulted from volcanic eruption, famine, internecine war, and the steady progress of a gradual Moslem infiltration. For Islam had been establishing itself among the islands since gaining its first foothold on the north-western coast of Sumatra at the end of the thirteenth century. Soon Malacca became Moslem, and thereafter most of the immigrants from India also professed the faith. The conversion of the local peoples was largely a peaceful event; but it was none the less decisive. With the exception of the tiny island of Bali, which stubbornly clung to its Hindu culture, the mythology and arts of this overseas India withered and disappeared under the iconoclasm of Islam. On the East Asian continent alone did Hinduism or Buddhism persist as national religions, even though conflict with the Thais forced the Cambodians to abandon their immense temple complex of Ankor Wat in 1450 and to withdraw to the lower reaches of the Mekong River.

The remainder of South-east Asia is that area which received neither Chinese nor Indian civilization, and which derives its present culture principally from the more recent arrival of Islam and Christianity. This includes the Philippines, annexed by the Spaniards in 1521, a considerable portion of the extensive island of Borneo, and the eastern part of Indonesia, the Celebes, and Amboina. Indigenous belief was a primitive animism, and where it still exists, as in the notable oral traditions of the Borneo tribesmen, we find a mythology full of ghosts and spirits connected with natural phenomena. Of the mythological world this is the far shore, located just outside the currents of the major traditions: Indian and Chinese ideas never reached it, and West Asian thought came through the intermediary of either Christian Europe or Arab Islam. As the Dayak people of Sarawak call the jungled interior, this portion of South-east Asia is *ulu*, the end of the world.

Ajysyt

Literally, 'birthgiver'. The mother goddess of the Yakuts, a Turkic people living near the Lena River in Siberia. 'The mother of the cradles' was believed to be present whenever one of her devotees gave birth. She was *Ajysyt-ijaksit-khotan*, 'birthgiving nourishing mother'. From heaven she brought the soul of the baby so that a complete human being could come into existence. Other Siberian tribesmen thought that the mother goddess dwelt in heaven on a mountain with seven storeys, where she determined the fate of all, by writing at the birth of each child in a golden book.

The Altai Tartars acknowledged a goddess called the 'milk lake mother', but the Yakuts themselves possess a strange myth about the white youth who encountered a calm 'lake of milk' near the cosmic tree, the world pillar of *Yryn-al-tojon*, the 'white creator lord'. Having besought the blessing of the tree, the white youth felt a warm breeze, heard the tree creak, and observed a female divinity arise from the roots. She proffered him milk from her full breasts, and having satisfied his thirst, he felt how his strength had increased a hundredfold. The milk-breasted mother goddess and the tree of life are thus combined. The importance of the cosmic tree, whether conceived as a sky-pillar or a source of fecundity, can be seen in the notion of its other job—the tethering-post of the stars wandering in the heavens.

Amaterasu

The Japanese sun goddess. Her myths are the most important of the indigenous faith, Shinto, 'the way of the gods'. This folk tradition is fundamentally not so much a religion as a set of ancient beliefs and observances which have remained comparatively unchanged over the past millennium, despite the importation of Confucianism and Buddhism. Amaterasu is the East Asian sister of Inanna, the Sumerian goddess of fertility and love.

The chief legend is that of the drawing forth of the radiant goddess from a heavenly rock-dwelling during a critical moment for the world. Her retreat had been brought about by the misbehaviour of her brother Susanowo, the storm god. Although his realm was the sea, the 'swift, impetuous deity' neglected his duties there and caused every sort of disturbance and tumult on land, previously ruled by Amaterasu with benevolence and wisdom. In spite of his sister's entreaties Susanowo destroyed rice-fields, uprooted trees, and even tore down sacred buildings. As a final provocation, he broke a hole in the roof of her weaving-hall, frightened to death her ladies, and drove the sun goddess herself into a cave. It was only after Amaterasu had closed the entrance of her sanctuary, making the door fast and immovable, that the gods realized the enormity of Susanowo's arrogance. He was responsible for the permanent disappearance of the sun—without its benign rays the universe was finished. Darkness covered the world, evil spirits ran riot, and panic seized the heavenly host.

On the bed of the tranquil river of heaven, *ama-no-yasu-gawara*, a conference of the gods decided that they must induce Amaterasu to return. Many things of divine efficacy were produced, such as a mirror, a sword, and cloth

Amaterasu, the Shinto sun goddess, emerging from the cave

offerings. A great tree was set up and decorated with jewels; cocks were placed near the entrance of the cave that they might keep up a perpetual crowing; bonfires were lighted and a dance was performed, with loud musical accompaniment. So amusing and spirited was the dancer, a goddess named Uzume, that 'the eight million divinities' present laughed and laughed, till the air was filled with their noise and the great plain of heaven shook.

The sun goddess in the cave heard the merriment and was curious to know what was going on outside. Slightly opening the door of her sanctuary, she asked how it was that the gods could find the heart to laugh in the darkness. With subtle cunning Uzume replied: 'We rejoice and are glad because there is a more illustrious deity than the sun goddess.'

While she was speaking, two gods carried forward the mirror and respectfully showed it to Amaterasu, who was immediately astonished by her own reflection. As she gazed, a powerful god widened the opening, took her hand, and drew her out. Whereupon another stretched a rope of straw, called the *shimenawa*, across the cave's entrance, saying: 'Never shall you enter again.' So Amaterasu reappeared. The universe was once more brightly illuminated, evil forces shrank away, and order and peace returned to earth. Thereafter the sun was only absent at night, as the shimenawa prevented Amaterasu from disappearing forever.

This triumph of the sun goddess over the storm god secured her rule of the world, and the belief in her as the foremost deity was associated with the tradition that the ruling family descended from the sun goddess. She was the highest manifestation of Kunitokotachi, the unseen, transcendent yet immanent, spirit of the universe. The idea of the sun as a goddess, instead of as a god, is rare and it may be a survival from the most archaic stage of world mythology. In the timidity of Amaterasu, her distress at the depredations of Susanowo, and her flight from his unyielding hostility, we can discern something of the tenderness felt by the original Japanese towards the gift of light. Amaterasu was the beautiful goddess, benign, compassionate, meek; the deity who delighted to pour down on her favourite islands the life-giving rays of the sun.

Amida-nyorai
Of all the deities in the Japanese Buddhist pantheon 'the Buddha of Infinite Light' approaches closest to the West Asian and European idea of an exalted yet personal god. Amida-nyorai, the Japanese Amitabha, is the great refuge that the devotee thinks of at the moment of death.

Strictly speaking, Buddhism denies a permanent resting-place to the soul and teaches a perpetual process of change in an individual's moral character. But this continuity, the endless round of rebirth caused by *karma*, sin, has come to encompass in Mahayana tradition numerous realms of existence, from highest heavens to nethermost hells. Japanese mythology is full of details about the pilgrimage of the soul to and from these realms, and the spirits of those who hover between them, perhaps as Tengus. Most popular are the legends clustered round the Paradise of the Pure Land, Gokuraku Jodo, the realm of Amida-nyorai. This celestial abode has a lotus pond brimming with ambrosia, groves of jewel-studded trees, on the branches of which perch marvellous birds and hang melodious bells, and above the Buddha and his saints circle angels, scattering petals on the gentle breeze.

The Jodo, or 'pure land', sect was founded by Genku, better known under the name of Honen (1133–1212). It arose to meet the spiritual needs of a period of social and economic crisis. Previously the followers of Amida-nyorai had put their trust in his compassion as the sole means of salvation, believing that the end of the world was nigh. With the teachings of Honen there emerged a distinct doctrine of piety, based on a simple faith in the kindness and merciful will of the Buddha to save all men. According to Honen,

whoever invokes with a sincere heart the sacred name of Amida-nyorai will obtain at the end of his days access to the Western Paradise of the Pure Land. Upon the consciousness of the monk a deep and lasting impression had been made by the violent death of his father at the hands of bandits. The dying man had asked his young son to forgive his attackers and 'strive to lead men into the way of eternal salvation'. Honen's method was the complete removal of mystical elements and monastic rigour from the worship of Amida-nyorai: it was the openness of the trusting child. There were dangers in such an easy approach, not least because the invocation of the sacred name could degenerate into a mechanical, empty formula.

Benten
In Japanese folklore Saraswati, the Hindu river goddess, was transformed as Benten into the genius of music, the guardian of eloquence, and the giver of wealth. As a deity of good fortune she has been popular since the twelfth century, many local legends collecting about her and her shrines. In the vicinity of Kamakura, on a small island, there is a temple built to celebrate the marriage of the goddess with a serpent king. According to legend, the serpentine appearance of her lover distressed Benten, who yielded herself to his embrace with great reluctance. Belief in the existence of serpent peoples in the seas around Japan is long-standing.

Bishamon-tenno
One of the celestial guardians of the world, he was successfully invoked by Prince Shotoku in 587 during the campaign against the anti-Buddhist clans of Japan. Bishamon-tenno appears in iconography as a powerful monarch, wearing armour and holding a lance.

Bodhidharma
Ta-mo of China, Daruma of Japan—the founder of the Ch'an Tsung, or 'inner-light school' of Buddhism. This sect was one of the most distinctive and original products of the Chinese mind, while its culmination as Zen in Japan has had a profound influence not only on East Asia, but even on the West.

Bodhidharma reached Nanking from South India about 520. Legend has been thickly woven around this enigmatic man, who soon acquired an outstanding fame. An inkling of the strength of his personality can still be gauged from the following account of his interview with the Chinese Emperor. The audience was brief and abrupt, for when the Emperor described all that he had done to promote the faith, such as founding monasteries, supporting translators, and undertaking charitable deeds, and asked what merit he had obtained in so doing, a reasonable question in terms of gradualist Mahayana doctrine, Bodhidharma replied, 'No merit whatever!' Amazed, the Emperor asked the visitor about the first principle of Buddhism. 'There isn't one,' was the answer, 'since where all is emptiness, nothing can be called holy.' 'Who, then, are you?' the Emperor asked. 'I don't know,' replied Bodhidharma. Leaving Nanking, he went northwards and settled in a monastery where he spent the rest of his life in meditation—'gazing at a wall'.

Another legend is an account of the transfer of awareness from Bodhidharma to his successor Hui-k'o, the Second Patriarch. Hui-k'o again and again asked the Indian sage for instruction, but was always refused. Yet the Chinese disciple remained in meditation outside Bodhidharma's sanctuary, waiting patiently in the snow in the hope that he would at last relent. One day he could bear the suspense no longer, so he cut off his left hand and sent it in. At this Bodhidharma asked Hui-k'o what he wanted. The Chinese monk requested peace of mind, but could not find his mind when Bodhidharma told him to bring it out. Thereupon, the Indian sage said: 'You see. I've pacified your mind!'

Hui-k'o experienced a single flash of insight: a sudden awakening—in Ch'an terms *tun wu*, in Zen *satori*. Bodhidharma inaugurated in East Asia a spiritual tradition that eschewed scripture and managed without words. It was a method of 'direct pointing to the soul of man', which perceived the inner Buddhahood of all. Every tie of human society, whether expressed in secular or monastic regulations, vanished like dust in such a moment. Without detriment to the contribution of Bodhidharma, there are obvious parallels with Taoist quietism, particularly in the lack of formal organization thought necessary for the pursuit of wisdom. Han-shan, the famous ninth-century Chinese monk poet, was very like a Taoist hermit, keeping the clouds company on his rocky hillside, where he read the works of Lao-tzu and the Buddhist scriptures.

Yet it is the legendary life of Bodhidharma that retains something of the shock wave he caused. Once he fell asleep in meditation and was so furious that he cut off his eyelids. From them grew the first tea plant, thereafter used as a beverage for monks.

Buga
Literally, 'god'. The supreme deity of the Tungus peoples of Siberia. Buga created the first two people out of iron, fire, water, and earth. Out of the earth he fashioned the flesh and bones, out of the iron the heart, out of the water blood, and out of the fire warmth.

Dainichi-nyorai
The Buddha Mahavairocana, the 'great illuminator', was the special form of the Enlightened One for the Shingon sect. This sect, whose name means 'true word', was founded in Japan by Kukai (774–835), better known under his posthumous title of Kobo-Daishi, 'propagator of the law'. In 804 Kobo-Daishi went to China, where he was initiated into the esoteric doctrine of the Chen Yen, or 'true word school'. Returning to Japan in 806 he established a monastery on Mount Koya and propagated the mysterious teachings of Shingon. Kobo-Daishi attained national prominence, in 823, by his appointment as abbot of the great temple complex at Miyako. When a decade or so later he considered that his earthly mission was finished, the contemplative monk had himself buried alive, in *samadhi*, at a secluded spot on Mount Kayo. His body is believed never to have rotted, but awaits resurrection at the advent of Miroku-bosatsu, the Buddha who is yet to come.

Legend recounts that nothing could disturb him. Once sea serpents strove to trouble his meditations, but Kobo-Daishi dispersed them with magic, projecting upon them the rays of the evening star. Another time, as he was praying in a temple, he used a magic circle to baffle the demonic Oni. Kobo-Daishi maintained that deities and demons of the various religions were manifestations of Dainichi-nyorai, whose body comprises the whole cosmos. He was present even in a speck of dust. Such a point of view represents an attempt to unify pantheons, to find unity within increasing theological diversity.

Dainichi-nyorai is depicted as seated in deep, serene contemplation on a white lotus; around him are ranged his emanations, stretching outward through bodhisattvas and saints to the myriad beings which comprise the universal order. These emanations are, as it were, the ideal forms, industructible potentialities destined to manifest themselves in the dynamic aspect of the universe. They are *kongo-kai*, 'elements of diamonds', and their manifestations occur in the *tai-zo-kai*, the unrefined, 'primitive element'. By means of elaborate ritual, according to the Shingon sect, it is possible to evoke magical powers that allow Dainichi-nyorai to realize his presence on earth.

Erlanga

The only Balinese prince to govern the islands of Bali and Java. His eventful life encouraged the accretion of legend, so that his death image was made in the shape of Vishnu seated on Garuda, the golden sun bird.

Born in 991, Erlanga left his native island as a young man for the Javanese court, where he married a princess and became a *yuvaraja*, a 'young king' charged with the government of a province. In 1006 the kingdom succumbed to foreign invasion, the royal house was decimated, petty chiefs embroiled the population in civil war, and the yuvaraja had to roam the forests and mountains—the haunt of hermits. Thirty years of hard fighting were needed to restore national unity, but after the completion of this gigantic task and a brief reign, Erlanga divided the kingdom between his two sons, and retired to the solitude of a hermitage, where he died about 1050. Erlanga was the great restorer, the sustainer, an incarnation of Vishnu: it was an honour he shared with the Khmer kings of Cambodia.

Erlik

In Siberian mythology the spirit of evil, who was sometimes thought of as the primeval man fallen from grace. In Lapp mythology he was always 'lord of the underworld', a monstrous guardian of departed souls.

The Altaic Tartars have a story of Erlik's genesis. Once Ulgan saw a piece of mud with human features floating on the ocean. The high god gave a spirit to it, naming the creature Erlik. But the friendship of Ulgan and Erlik did not last long, for the pride of the latter obliged his banishment to the depths, where he became the king of the dead. Despite this acquisition of terror, an aspect doubtless owing something to the Tibetan development

of Yama as the epitome of annihilation, the Altai Tartars never overlooked Erlik's parentage of mankind. He was still 'the father'. A parallel myth of choosing evil is the Persian account of the father and mother of the human race, Mashye and Mashyane, who foresook the wise lord for Ahriman, the evil one. Interestingly, the Tungus near the Amur River thought that the first human pair, Khadau and Mamaldi, were shamans who used their magical powers to become masters of 'the land of beyond'.

Erlik claimed the dead as his own, leaving to Ulgan 'those with breath'. This indifference towards the dead on the part of Ulgan was typical of creator gods in North Asia. One myth relates that the creator's son was the first to open the way to 'the land of beyond': he was the archetypal corpse, the final state for all 'those with breath'. According to the Altai Tartars, the unpleasant, boggy places were formed by Erlik. When the primeval man was commanded by Ulgan to bring up from the depths of the primordial ocean a piece of earth, Erlik hid a portion in his mouth, thereby hoping to create a world of his own. When it started to expand, like the piece Ulgan threw upon the surface of the waters, Erlik nearly choked to death. Seeing the entire scheme, Ulgan told Erlik to spit out the earth, which he did, the disgorged mud becoming marshlands.

The spittle of Erlik, the Black Tartars maintained, was responsible for the present appearance of mankind. When a demiurge fashioned the first human beings, he discovered that he could not give them life-giving souls. So he had to ascend to heaven and beseech the aid of Kudai, the supreme deity. During his absence, a 'naked' dog was left to guard the unfinished people. Erlik approached the dog and offered to give it a coat of golden hair in return for 'the soulless ones'. Tempted, the dog agreed. Erlik defiled them by spitting on them, and departed. When the demiurge returned with the souls and perceived the situation, he turned the human bodies inside out. That is why we have spittle in our intestines.

Fu Hsi

Legendary Chinese emperor, thought to have ruled at the beginning of the third millennium BC. Though attributed to Fu Hsi, the *pa kua*, 'eight trigrams', used for divination were not invented till about 1000 BC. These three-lined figures, in their sixty-four combinations, form the basis of Chinese cosmological speculation, whose classical handbook is the *I Ching* (*Book of Changes*). Some representations of Fu Hsi show the ancient ruler as possessing a fish-like tail.

Fudo-myoo

The guardian of wisdom, 'the unshakable spirit'. One of several forces or formulae personified in Japanese Buddhism. Another is Aizen-myoo, who represents love transformed into desire for illumination. Terrible figures to behold, the wrath of the myoo is only directed against things liable to distract the pilgrim from the true path. Fudo-myo, an intense saver of souls, is the patron of ascetics.

Fugen-bosatsu

In Japan the bodhisattva Samantabhadra, who will be the final Buddha and at present out of his 'divine compassion', *bhadra*, is spreading around 'enlightening wisdom', *samanta*. He is pictured as a young man seated on an elephant, which is usually white and has six tusks, and either he carries a lotus flower, like the bodhisattva Avalokitesvara, or he has his hands joined together. Of particular appeal to women in medieval Japan was Fugen-bosatsu, who in the thirteenth century appeared to a monk as a courtesan, thereby revealing that Buddhahood was potential in all beings. Today the bodhisattva is little worshipped.

It was Samantabhadra who initiated Sudhana to full and perfect enlightenment. This young Indian ascetic had visited all the places and people connected with the Buddha, shortly after Sakyamuni passed into nirvana. His was the first spiritual quest in a world lacking the living, physical Buddha; hence the link with the heavenly bodhisattva. Sudhana is the archetypal pilgrim, and remains the pattern for Buddhists living in the present age. Having learned of the Buddha's life and work from Manjusri, the vanquisher of death, Sudhana wandered from place to place, practising ever greater austerities, till he came finally into the presence of Maitreya, the future Buddha. Passed on to Samantabhadra at last the earnest pilgrim achieved illumination. The quest of Sudhana appears prominently in the reliefs of the vast stupa of Borobudur in Java. This monument, dating

from the eighth and ninth centuries, was erected at a time when Mahayana replaced Hinayana as the form of Buddhism on the island. Borobudur may mean simply 'many Buddhas'.

Fujiyama

The troubles of medieval Japan were the prime cause of a revival in Shinto belief. Amid civil strife there was little room for the old tolerances of Ryobu, 'the twofold way of the gods', in which indigenous Shinto had merged with imported Buddhism. In the sixteenth and seventeenth centuries new, patriotic sects arose, teaching that Japan was the chief of all nations and the centre of the world, and that Mount Fuji was the abode of the supreme deity, Kunitokotachi. So Fujiyama, the sacred spirit mountain, became the guardian of the nation, only to be ascended after ritual purification. Each July thousands of pilgrims still climb to the summit of the mountain.

A Shinto legend accounts for the appearance of Mount Fuji. Long ago an old man who cultivated bamboo trees on its slopes found an infant called Kaguya-hime. The old man brought up the child until she was recognized as the most beautiful girl in the country, becoming a princess consort of the Emperor. Seven years after the marriage Princess Kaguya-hime announced that she was not a mortal and must return to her celestial home. To ease her husband's sadness, she gave him a magic mirror, in which he could always see her image. Then she disappeared. So upset was the Emperor that he determined to follow her to heaven, and carrying the mirror in his hands, he ascended Mount Fuji. Yet on the summit he could see no trace of the lost princess, nor could he by any means climb higher. His love burst out of his breast, its fiery passion setting the mirror ablaze. From that day smoke has always risen from the top of the volcano.

Gimokodan

The nether world of the Bagobo tribes of Mindanao in the Philippines. At the dark river surrounding this land resides a giant female whose body is covered with nipples and who suckles the spirits of infants before they pass on. Gimokodan itself has two parts: the red is reserved for those killed in combat; the white is like the world above except that everything is reversed. Spirits go about at nights, in the daytime they turn into dew and rest in cupped leaves. Large animals and human beings are said to have several souls, or *gimokod*.

Hachiman
The Shinto war god, a popular deity in Japan. While the favourite of soldiers, Hachiman is also worshipped as a protector of life, especially children, as god of agriculture, and as guardian deity of the archipelago. In 783 he was styled a boddhisattva, a Buddha-to-be, and identified with the eightfold path of Buddhist morality. At this period the indigenous Shinto faith was nearly absorbed by the imported Butsudo, 'the way of the Buddha'. It was known as Ryobu, 'the twofold way of the gods'.

Hari-Hara
Literal meaning: 'grower-remover'. *Hari*, a popular name for Vishnu, implies the renewal and growth of plants, while *Hara*, 'he who takes away', is a common epithet for Shiva. Together, they symbolize the great opposites, creation-destruction, life-death: the intimate harmony of the two supreme, antagonistic divine principles. Visual form is given to this mysterious concept in the figure of Hari-Hara, where the right side is Shiva and the left is Vishnu. Fine examples are found in the temple ruins of Cambodia, once a renowned Hindu-Buddhist kingdom.

Near their capital of Angkor Thom, in the middle Mekong valley, the Khmers under the leadership of King Suryavarman II began to build the immense temple of Ankor Wat in 1112. A palatial temple-residence, with walls and moats measuring some 300 yards along each side, Ankor Wat celebrated the mythical exploits of Vishnu, whose incarnation the Khmer monarch was supposed to be. Within the king's body reposed a portion of the deity, a formula which explains the Cambodian practice of fashioning statues of royalty in the attitudes of the highest gods. Others celebrated in the magnificent architecture are Shiva and the Buddha: the name 'palace monastery', *ankor wat*, seems to have been adopted during the reign of King Jayavarman VII (1181–1201), an ardent Buddhist. The famous

The vast temple of Ankor Wat seen from across a moat

mukha-lingams, 'face lingams', sculptured on the numerous towers of the Bayon temple, situated close to Ankor Wat, are the four faces of Shiva, deep in meditation. In late mythology the four-faced Shiva chopped off the fifth head of Brahma, which the latter had grown to prove his superiority. As a penance, Shiva was obliged to carry the severed head on a long pilgrimage, from which he was eventually released by the holy waters of the Ganges at Benares.

According to an Indian legend, the union of Vishnu and Shiva occurred as a joint response to the threat posed by Guha, 'he who conceals', a fierce demon of unlimited strength. Through appalling self-inflicted sufferings Guha had forced Brahma to make him invulnerable even to Vishnu and Shiva. Against the cosmic encroachment of the demon, first Vishnu, then Shiva, battled in vain. As a final resort, they combined as Hari-Hara, confronted the universal tyrant, and overthrew him. The underlying notion is the equality of Vishnu and Shiva: respectively, the maintaining and destroying aspects of divinity. Vishnu becomes Shiva when a life has reached its term, while Shiva becomes Vishnu when be bestows wisdom and peace. A parallel myth is the androgynous Shiva—*ardhanari*, 'half woman'—where the god and his consort are merged to form an hermaphrodite; again Shiva is on the right side, the female on the left. In Tibetan Buddhism this late formulation of the coincidence of opposites mutually supporting each other takes the form of Yab-Yum, the sexual union of the bodhisattva and his sakti, 'female aspect'. Explained in terms of meditation the female form, *yum*, is regarded as time and the male, *yab*, as eternity: as one, they stand for nirvana, transcendent repose.

Hou T'u

The agricultural character of Chinese civilization is mirrored in the worship accorded to Hou T'u, or She, 'prince of the earth'. Every village possessed a shrine, usually a mound of earth symbolizing the fertility of the soil, and in important towns there were larger mounds for the public celebration of the cult. In Peking, near the Yung Ting Men or South Gate, stands the Altar of Agriculture, on whose terraces the emperor used to conduct the sacrifices associated with the spring ploughing, the *keng chi*. This annual rite of Confucian orthodoxy, when the emperor with his own hands turned the first furrow, exercised a strange fascination on the eighteenth-century *philosophes* of Europe, to whom it appeared a perfect token of the solicitude of the ruler for his people; a paternal benevolence. So much so that in 1756, Louis XV, at the suggestion of the encyclopaedist Quesnay made through Madame de Pompadour, followed the example of the Chinese emperors, and incidentally honoured Hou T'u.

Hsien

Literally, 'an immortal', living on or above the earth, but within natural things, a material immortality in which the body was still needed, however preserved in a 'lightened' form. Hsien were Taoist immortals, supposed to have partaken the elixir of life, and in early illustrations they often appear as feathered men. The ancient Chinese believed in the existence of drugs which could be taken for this purpose. During the fourth century BC the elixir notion arose, perhaps encouraged by a rumour from India, Persia, or Mesopotamia about a drug plant, and an unprecedented wave of alchemical experimentation occurred. The absence of a sharp dichotomy between good and evil in Chinese thought had hindered the development of an ethical eschatology, which separated the sheep from the goats, and left the way open to the conviction that there were technical means whereby men could enlarge the length of their days so much as to be virtually immortal, not in the underworld of the Yellow Springs, but among the mountains and forests of this world.

Man was envisaged as a body joining together two souls. The *hun* soul came from the sky and returned to it, while the *pho* soul derived from the earth and fell back into it after death. Their vital balance in the body corresponded to the universal theory of the Yin-Yang. Ko Hung, the eminent alchemical writer of the third century, mentions two varieties of elixirs: one restrained the flight of the pho, the other recalled the hun. For Ko Hung, the change from mortal to immortal state was only one aspect of those changes and transformations of which all Nature was full. Metals altered, landscape changed, people turned into animals, snakes became dragons, caterpillars grew into moths—everywhere was natural spontaneity. Likewise, he wrote, 'the masters of the highest category are able to

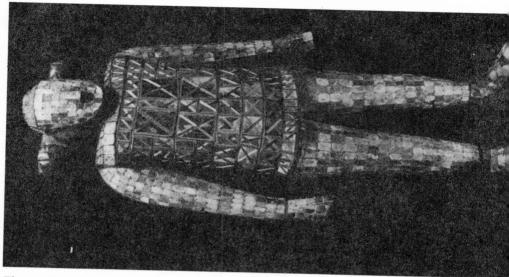

The jade funeral suit of Princess Tou Wan, discovered in 1968

raise themselves, their souls and their bodies, high up into the airy void. These are called celestial immortals, *t'ien hsien*. Those of the second category resort to the famous mountains and forests and are called terrestrial immortals, *ti hsien*. As for those of the third category they simply slough off the body after death and are called corpse-free immortals, *shih chieh hsien*.' Quite where the third group reside is unexplained, but presumably it is somewhere more agreeable than the Yellow Springs.

According to legend, Ko Hung succeeded in preparing pills of immortality. He gave one to a dog which dropped dead; he then took one himself with the same result. Yet in the midst of preparations of the funeral, both Ko Hung and the dead dog came to life. Most dramatic was the exit of Chang Tao-ling, reputed to have lived from 34 till 156, a span of 122 years. The first *t'ien shih*, or 'heavenly teacher', of the Taoist church, he is said to have left behind only his empty clothes. Beside the consumption of elixir, Taoist adepts practised five techniques, namely breath control, 'wearing the sun rays', gymnastics, 'the arts of the bedchamber', and diet.

'Aged but not dying', the hsien have roamed the universe at will, their actions and 'miracles' generating a bizarre mythology. San Ch'ing, 'the Three Purities', compose the Taoist trinity, the chief divinities of highest class, the t'ien hsien. The first, Yuan-shih, is son of P'an-ku, primeval man, and T'ai-yuan, the holy woman. At birth Yuan-shih was able to walk and talk, while a cloud of five colours surrounded his body. The second immortal is associated with Wu-wang, a noble who in 1027 BC overturned the unjust and repressive rule of Chou Hsin, the last of the Shang kings. The vices of the tyrant and his consort—licentious games, excessive drunkenness, and torture—may be no more than garbled and unfriendly accounts of a religious festival to the fertility gods, but as Wu-wang, the hsien Ta-chun is credited with the establishment of rational government. The third of the trinity is Lao-tzu, the original Taoist philosopher..

Other notable hsien are the genius of literature, Wen Ch'ang, a brilliant sixth-century scholar, who rose to high office and disappeared suddenly; the adept Li T'ieh-kuai, a strict ascetic and disciple of Lao-tzu; the magistrate Lu Tung-pin, the rewarder of honesty; and Ho Hsien-ku, a girl who attained immortality after eating the powder of mother-of-pearl.

Raising oneself to hsien-ship required elaborate preparation. In funerary rites we know now that the well-to-do expended vast sums on jade, long regarded as a preserver from physical corruption. Ko Hung had noted the preservative effects of small pieces situated 'in the nine orifices', but the 1968 discovery of

Princess Tou Wan's tomb confirmed that people were buried in 'jade clothes sewn with gold thread'. Her funeral suit comprises more than 2,000 pieces of jade knitted together with gold and silk-covered iron wire. Interestingly, the jade as well as the idea of its inhibition of bodily decay may have been imported from Siberia, the nearest source of supply for the stone in ancient times.

Huang-ti
Literally, 'yellow emperor'. Patron saint of all Taoists. Though the most ancient of the legendary emperors, Huang-ti was in fact among the last to be invented, not appearing in Chinese mythology till the fourth century BC. He is invariably associated with Lao-tzu.

In the *Book of Lieh-tzu*, the composition of which may be later than 100 BC, there is a large section devoted to Huang-ti, whose reign was troubled after fifteen years. While his subjects rejoiced in his benevolence, the Yellow Emperor 'amused his eyes and ears, pampered his nostrils and mouth, till his complexion became sallow and his dulled senses were stupefied'. Another fifteen years on the throne, amid growing disorder, and 'his face was haggard and pale, and his dulled senses more stupefied'. Whereupon, he decided to leave decisions of state to his ministers, dismissed his attendants, simplified his daily routine, and took up residence 'in a hut in his main courtyard, where he fasted to discipline body and mind'. One day he fell asleep and dreamed of the kingdom of Hua-hsu, mother of the mythical ruler Fu-hsi. The kingdom 'was beyond the reach of ship or chariot or any mortal foot. Only the soul could travel so far.' It was an ideal state, 'without head or ruler; it simply went on of itself. Its people were without desires or cravings; they simply followed their natural instincts. They felt neither joy in life nor abhorrence in death, so none of them died before his time. They felt neither attachment to self nor indifference to others; thus they were exempt from love and hatred alike. . . . They rode space as though walking the solid earth, and slept on the air as though on their beds. Clouds and mists did not hinder their sight, thunder did not stun their ears, beauty and ugliness did not disturb their hearts, mountains and valleys did not trip their feet—for they made only journeys of the spirit.'

On waking Huang-ti assembled his ministers and said that The Way, *Tao*, 'cannot be sought through the senses. I know it, I have found it, but I cannot tell it to you.' After another twenty-eight years on the throne, when there was orderliness in his kingdom almost equalling that in Hua-hsu's, Huang-ti rose into the sky as a hsien, an immortal. The people bewailed him for 200 years without intermission.

This legend of the wonderful emperor, whose long reign was a veritable golden age, is used here an an illustration of wisdom. Huang-ti attained to perfection, within and without. He is also the cultural founder hero. Apart from subduing rebels—once represented as a monster with an iron head, bronze brow, hair bristling like swords and spears, and the body of an ox, with six arms, each having eight fingers—the Yellow Emperor introduced governmental institutions. Some traditions credit him with the invention of the compass and coined money, which replaced cowrie shells as the medium of exchange, while his wife excelled in sericulture and the domestic arts. When his chief minister first devised written signs, 'all the spirits cried out in agony, as the innermost secrets of Nature were thus revealed'.

Inari
In Shinto mythology the god of rice, sometimes called the 'food god', and identified with Uke-mochi, the 'food genius'. When the latter received the moon god Tsuki-yomi, she furnished for his entertainment the land with 'boiled' rice, the sea with fishes, and the mountains with game. But the moon god was displeased because these gifts had come forth from her mouth, and therefore he killed his unfortunate hostess. From the corpse, however, other things grew: plants, cattle, and silkworms.

The origin myth lacks a certain historical validity for sericulture, the Chinese monopoly only being ended in the second century when silkworm eggs were smuggled to Korea. In the idea of universal fertility it does emphasize the fundamental importance of replenishment, of the dying-into-life of the soil.

Every Japanese village contains a shrine dedicated to Inari, as the giver of agricultural prosperity, and in many houses he also receives worship as the bringer of wealth and friendship.

Izanami

The primeval mother of Shinto. She was the sister spouse of Izanagi, who unsuccessfully descended to the nether world after her.

At the beginning, according to ancient Japanese records, there was only an ocean of chaos. Out of the mire in the form of a reed grew Kunitokotatchi, 'eternal land ruler', and two subordinate deities, who seem to have symbolized the female and male principles, not unlike the interacting Yin-Yang forces of Chinese cosmology. Izanami, 'the female who invites', and Izanagi, 'the male who invites', were the descendants of these subordinate powers. Together they created the terrestrial world as well as its divine rulers, Amaterasu the sun goddess, Tsuki-yomi the moon god, and Susanowo the storm god.

Strangely, the female principle was later transformed into the genius of decay, after she had died on giving birth to fire and gone to a subterranean place where darkness prevailed. To *yomotsu-kuni*, 'the land of gloom', journeyed Izanagi in the hope of bringing back Izanami, since the work of creation was 'not yet finished'. Meeting him at the entrance, Izanami requested that he wait there while she arranged for her release with the deities of death, and she warned him not to look at her closely. When she had been gone for a long time, he broke off one of the end teeth of the comb that was stuck in his hair, and, lighting it as a torch, he entered yomotsu-kuni and looked. What he saw was shattering: maggots swarmed everywhere, and Izanami was rotting.

Overwhelmed at the vision of dissolution, Izanami fled, pursued by a hag. To escape this hideous creature he threw down his head-dress, which turned into a bunch of grapes, and, as his pursuer paused to devour them, he sped on his way. Then he broke a comb and threw it down to the ground, where it turned into succulent bamboo sprouts, and while she stopped to gobble them up, he rushed on. Knowing of these deceptions, Izanami sent after her brother spouse eight thunder gods with an army of ghastly warriors. But Izanagi reached the frontier pass between the abode of the living and the abode of the dead, and when the force rushed against him, he hurled three peaches and routed his pursuers.

Finally, Izanami came in person to find that Izanagi had shut the pass with a huge rock, beyond the strength of 1,000 men to shift. So the divine couple exchanged leave-takings. She threatened to 'kill a thousand people in his

kingdom every day', while he retorted that he 'would cause every day one thousand and five hundred women to give birth'.

While the myth ends on the question of population, the balance between births and deaths so critical for the survival of an ancient society, the real import of the story would appear to be the grave itself. Izanagi's action shut out the grisly prospect of death, his mighty rock allowing his subjects a brief, untroubled span of life.

Jizo-bosatsu

Ti-tsang of China, Jizo of Japan—the bodhisattva Ksitigarbha—wanders eternally through the realms of hell, comforting tortured souls and rescuing them from darkness by his very presence. Ksitigarbha, 'he whose womb was the earth', does not seem to have been a popular bodhisattva in India, where he appeared at a comparatively late date, but his association with the judgement of the dead greatly attracted Chinese Buddhists. Ti-tsang, and later Jizo, became the counsel for the dead and their consoler. He is usually depicted as a gentle-faced monk with a shaven head, dressed in a long robe and holding a staff with clattering rings on one end. The staff—originally called a khakkhara in India, on account of the khak sound it made—announces the otherwise silent mendicant as he walks along the street or comes with his begging-bowl for his daily meal. The Buddhist monk never asks for alms, nor does he acknowledge them. The only sound comes from the staff, which in the hands of Jizo-bosatsu is potent enough to disperse the powers of evil.

The Jodo, or 'pure land', sect of Japan have a myth about Jizo-bosatsu as the 'father and mother' of infantile souls trapped on a hellish riverbank through the lamentations of their parents. Instead of offering prayers for the rebirth of these souls the anguished parents are consumed with grief at the decay of their tiny bodies. The stranded infants are thought to spend their days using stones from the riverbank to build for their families little shrines, which nightly demons with iron rods come to demolish.

Kadaklan

The 'greatest' deity of the Tinguian, a people living in the mountainous interior of Luzon, the northernmost island of the Philippines. A thunder god, Kadaklan lives in the sky with his faithful dog Kimat, the lightning, who will bite a house, a tree, or a field whenever the divine master desires that a special ceremony be performed. The origin of Kadaklan is obscure—one suggestion would pinpoint the Spaniards—and he is held in less regard than the tribal ancestors. Funerals are the major events in Tinguian ritual, the prime concern being the safe arrival of the deceased in *maglawa*, the underworld.

Kishimo-jin

The protectress of children. She is the Japanese equivalent of Hariti, 'the snatcher', whom the Buddha dissuaded from stealing and eating children. Moved by the doctrine of compassion, that profound Indian sense of ahimsa, 'no injury to any living being', the demon goddess forswore destruction and became a tutelary deity of children, a universal mother, surrounded by babies, whom she fosters and keeps safe.

The converted ogress was popular in Buddhist India and China, where she was worshipped as the giver of children. Hariti combined the three archetypal activities of the mother goddess: she bestowed life, she fostered life, and she destroyed it. The balance of the divine triad of creation, preservation, and destruction is nevertheless altered by this Buddhist myth. In the depiction of Hariti as a Madonna-like being there is a distinct shift towards benevolence—the idyll of family life.

The cult of Kishimo-jin became popular in Japan towards the end of the thirteenth century. According to legend, she was even seen on one occasion. In shrines from that date onwards her image appears as a mother suckling an infant, while her symbol is the pomegranate, which stands for fertility.

Kuan Ti

The god of war in Confucian tradition. A popular figure in Chinese folklore, Kuan Ti was a leading general during the period of disunity known as San Kuo, the Three Kingdoms (221–65). He is not, however, a Mars figure, warlike and implacable, but rather the god who prevents war. As Kuan Yu, a massive man, nine feet in height, with a beard two feet long, a ruddy complexion, and eyebrows like sleeping silkworms shading his phoenix eyes, which were a scarlet-red, he took up arms in the complicated civil war because he wished 'to pay the state his debt of loyalty and give peace to his black-haired com-patriots'. Ts'ao Ts'ao, the deposer of the last Han Emperor and the architect of discord, had once said: 'I would rather betray the whole world than let the world betray me.'

Kuan Yu was killed by the Sun, a powerful clan established at Ch'eng-tu. Yet his valour and courtesy were a standing rebuke to his contemporaries, then engaged in treachery and violence. The apotheosis of his cult occurred in 1594 when the throne conferred on him the title of *Ti*, great supporter of heaven and protector of the empire. Kuan Ti had become the divine champion, always ready to intervene against all those who disturb the peace—rebels, sorcerers, demons, and foreigners.

Kumang

The mother goddess of the Ibans, the Sea Dayaks of Borneo. Kumang, 'whose back was white', scorched by the setting sun, had charge of paradise, which was the home of Bujang, the first Iban. This land was situated near Mecca, whence Bujang's descendants wandered to Sumatra, then to Borneo, often in the company of tribal divinities. Possibly this legendary migration from West Asia is a reference to the arrival of important ideas, perhaps carried by a few leaders, rather than any actual movement of people. A sense of proximity with the spiritual world is an everyday feature of life in Iban longhouses, villages under one roof, and during each *gawai*, or festival, it is customary to invite the attendance of both ancestors and deities. There are also many tales of the appearance of the god in dreams.

On one occasion Kumang appeared to a shy young warrior and informed him that a petrified bamboo shoot he had found was in fact a charm-stone which would make him a great war leader. Head-hunting was until recent times the crowning proof of manhood, not least because the possession of heads bestowed magical power. War leaders have a *tua*, or guardian spirit. If the tua is the python, it signified that he is guided in battle by his ancestors; if it is the cobra, he is guided by Kling, the god of war. Snakes are the most common guardian spirits, but other tua are wild cats and deer. One normally learns of one's tua by means of a dream.

A nineteenth-century screen painting of Kuan Ti, the Chinese god of war

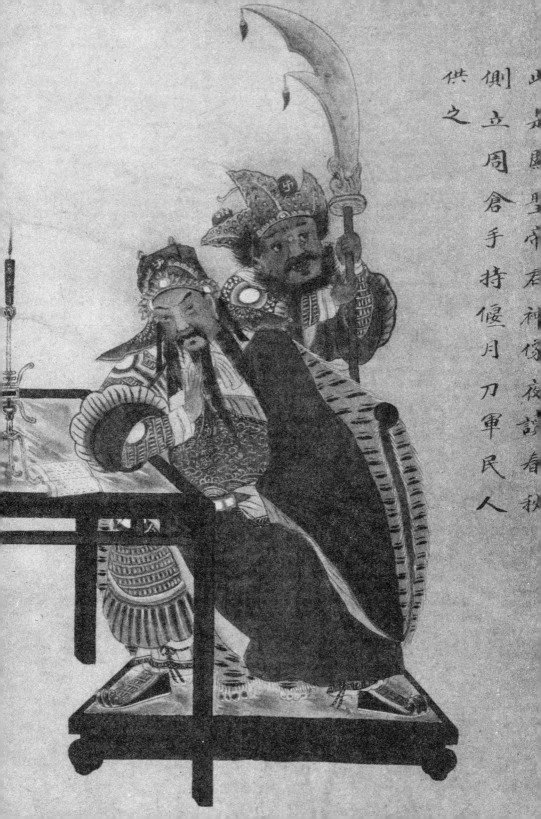

此是關聖帝君神像夜讀春秋
側立周倉手持偃月刀軍民人
供之

A Sung dynasty (AD 960–1269) painted wood statuette of Kwan-yin

Kwan-yin

Kwan-yin of China, Kwannon of Japan—the Madonna of East Asia—is the bestower of children and the all-compassionate mother goddess. The bodhisattva Avalokitesvara, 'the lord who looks down in pity', underwent this metamorphosis in China, possibly through the influence of Tantric Buddhism. As the Goddess of Mercy, she has been second only in popular esteem to A-mi-t'o-fo, Amitabha. A mass of legend concerns her activities as a world-redeeming, world-sustaining divinity, who paused on the threshold of nirvana because of her awareness of the suffering in the world. The androgynous character of this bodhisattva remains a mysterious occurrence: it reaches psychologically into an area where duality has no place.

In Japan the masculine form of Kwannon is predominant. Iconography depicts the bodhisattva in princely form, and even in his own lifetime Prince Shotoku (572–621), the champion of Buddhism, was accepted as an incarnation. Other images possess a thousand eyes and arms, or eleven heads, or a horse's head. This visual complexity is intended to convey an impression of Kwannon's infinite power, compassion, and virtue.

Lao-tzu

The 'madman of Ch'u', the first of the 'irresponsible hermits', according to the Confucians, was Li Er (born 604 BC), but it has become usual in China to refer to the founder of Taoism as Lao-tzu, the Old Philosopher. Though he may have been keeper of the royal archives at Loyang, few details are known of his life. Lao-tzu was 'a hidden wise man', reluctant to found a school and gather a following.

According to legend, Lao-tzu simply decided to leave society. He would have vanished without trace had not the customs official on the border asked him to write a book before he retired from the world. So the sage wrote about 'the proper way to live'. Then he went on. No one knows where he died. Later Taoist mythology was to claim of the final journey into the West that it allowed Lao-tzu to visit India as the Buddha. The reticence of both sages, their profound intimation of the way in which words limit what should really be said, encouraged such an identification, though this myth was put about in the hope of reducing the influence of Buddhist priests among the population. In dealing with competition from Confucianism Chuang-tzu (350–275 BC) had fallen back, too, on an archetypal encounter between Lao-tzu and Confucius. Having washed his hair and left it hanging down his back to dry, Lao-tzu looked like a lifeless body on the arrival of Confucius. When the latter asked how it was that this impression arose, Lao-tzu replied that he 'was wandering in the unborn'. When asked what was to be got by such wandering, he informed Confucius that the result was 'perfect goodness and perfect happiness'. Chuang-tzu asserts that the revelation struck a chord in the visitor's breast, yet it is to be doubted that he would have appreciated the shamanism here, if ever an interview had taken place. The vastness of the universe, and especially the spiritual regions traversed by Lao-tzu, held little attraction for the reforming zeal of Confucius.

Lieh-tzu

A semi-legendary sage, Lieh-tzu provides a perfect example of Taoist obscurity. He 'dwelt on a vegetable plot for forty years, and no man knew him for what he was'. In Chinese tradition the wise man attains to the sublime but performs the common tasks. Like other hsien, immortals, Lieh-tzu rode on the wind, and he delighted in the enigmatic utterances of Taoist philosophy. He told his disciples: 'Saying nothing and knowing nothing, there is in reality nothing that a man does not say, nothing that a man does not know.'

Lung

The dragon of Chinese folklore. Unlike the ferocious and evil creature of West Asian and medieval European mythology, the lung is essentially a benevolent divinity and held in high regard. He is the rainbringer, the lord of the waters—clouds, rivers, marshes, lakes, and seas. In ancient inscriptions the numerous lung were called upon to refresh the earth with rain. These water gods can make themselves as small as a silkworm, or they can become so large that they overshadow the whole world. They can soar through the clouds as well as penetrate to the deepest springs. Their appearance is composite: the horns of a stag, the head of a camel, the eyes of a demon, the neck of a snake, the scales of a fish, the claws of an eagle, the pads of a tiger, the ears of a bull, and the long whiskers of a cat.

The dragon was closely associated with the Chinese emperor, and the five-clawed lung once served as the imperial symbol. Some form of antagonism existed between dragons and the sun, which they often attempted to bite. It was generally believed that 'a pearl of wisdom' reposed in the mouth of each lung. Sages were called 'dragon men', and in his battle with the deluge Yu was given a magic chart by a dragon horse which came out of the Yellow River.

Mi-lo

The future Buddha, at present living as a bodhisattva in Tushita Heaven. In India Maitreya, 'the one who is yet to come', played a minor role, and only after he was introduced into China did he become a major figure. Devotees prayed for rebirth in his paradise, but the Pure Land of A-mi-t'o-fo, Amitabha, eclipsed his refuge during the seventh century. When the cult of Mi-lo was revived 600 years later, the appearance of the bodhisattva had quite changed. He took the form of a fat, jovial man, and he was referred to as the Laughing Buddha. It seems that this alteration was based on legends surrounding the life of a tenth-century Chinese monk with a wrinkled forehead and a mountainous belly. For the inhabitants of K'ai Feng he acted as a barometer for the weather. They could be sure of a fine day whenever he slept on the market bridge, but when he gathered up his loincloth and waddled for cover, they could expect a downpour. Added to Mi-lo's new rotund image was a bevy of children, a feature reflecting the Chinese ideal of a large family.

In Japan Maitreya, as Miroku-bosatsu, is usually portrayed in a thoughful attitude. He sits with his head bent forward on his right hand, while with his other hand he is holding his right ankle raised above the knee of his left leg. Sometimes he carries a minature stupa, a reliquary shrine.

Okuninushi

Literally, 'great land master'. Son-in-law of Susanowo, the storm god of Shinto tradition. He obtained the hand of Susanowo's daughter through stealth, an attribute his father-in-law much admired. At night Okuninushi had tied all the hair of the storm god to the beams of the house and escaped with the daughter. Susanowo appointed Okuninushi as King of Izumo, which the son-in-law ruled with the aid of Sukuna-biko, the dwarf god.

Another king of Izumo, a province facing the Sea of Japan, was Omitsunu, 'beach field master'. This grandson of Susanowo enlarged his realm with pieces of land from Korea and offshore islands; he drew them to the Japanese archipelago with long cord. It should be recalled that the ox-headed storm god had been the first to colonize Korea.

Izumo was under the sway of Amaterasu, the sun goddess, after she sent an expedition against Okuninushi. The descendants of Susanowo were permitted a limited authority, including the 'hidden' world of magic, but all were compelled to acknowledge the ruling family. The contest between the sun goddess and the storm god clearly reflects an early struggle for mastery between leading Japanese clans.

Oni

Japanese demons. In Shinto, the Oni are associated with disease, calamity, and misfortune. These interfering spirits are basically human in appearance, but possess three eyes, a wide mouth, horns, and three sharp talons on both hands and feet. Oni can fly, often swooping down to seize the soul of a wicked man who is about to die. The *Oni-yarahi*, 'demon-expelling' ceremony, takes the form of an annual drama, performed on the last day of the year, in which personified diseases, ill-luck, and disasters are forcibly expelled.

Buddhist monks are thought to be scourges of the Oni, and the Nichiren sect actually holds periodical retreats for driving out evil spirits of all kinds. Nichiren (1222–82) founded his school of Buddhism, according to its own historians, when 'all was dark in Japan . . . Mongol invasions . . . earthquakes, epidemics, famines followed each other, as did our own errors, of we Japanese who had established the

capital at Kamakura, where reigned a military dictatorship embroiled in fratricidal struggles.' He saw the Oni at work everywhere, calling the Zen sect 'an invention of the devil'.

Other demonic spirits are the Tengu, notable for their fury and threatening behaviour. One kind are semi-human with the wings and claws of giant eagles, while a second variety are entirely bird-like. Inspiration for the tengu may have been the Garuda of Hindu legend, though Japanese tradition has explained them as reincarnations of proud and arrogant people, especially priests and soldiers. Tengu-possesion, however, is not accompanied by mischief equal to that of the Oni.

P'an-ku

In Chinese mythology he is the primeval man, born of the cosmic egg. At the outset of the universe, 'the ten thousand things', was an egg. One day the egg split open. The top half became the sky and the bottom half the earth. P'an-ku, who emerged from the broken egg, grew ten feet taller every day, just as the sky became ten feet higher and the earth ten feet thicker. After 18,000 years P'an-ku died. Then, like the cosmic egg, he split into a number of parts. His head formed the sun and moon, his blood the rivers and seas, his hair the forests, his sweat the rain, his breath the wind, his voice thunder and, last of all, his fleas became the ancestors of mankind.

This myth was probably added to Taoist cosmology in the fourth century BC. It is not a creation story so much as an explanation of the Yin-Yang theory. From P'an-ku were derived the Yin and the Yang, the interacting forces within all phenomena. Striking is the lowly position ascribed to man: not the centre of creation, not a colossus in the landscape, but rather a small figure in the great sweep of natural things. The insignificance of men, as formulated in the P'an-ku myth, finds perfect expression in Chinese landscape-painting, where tiny figures are set down amid the magnificence of Nature, mountains and valleys, rivers and lakes, clouds and waterfalls, trees and flowers.

Radin

An eighteenth-century leader of the Ibans, the Sea Dayaks of Borneo. A legend about him concerns a hungry ghost, which visited his people with smallpox. After winning a battle near Betong and taking many heads, Radin

Rati, the demonic Balinese version of the Hindu goddess of maternity and fertility

his place of concealment, singing about the sweetness of human flesh, Radin jumped out and cut down the invisible spirit. He heard something fall, but he could see nothing. Next morning, on going to look at the hornbill carving, he found it had been slashed as if by a powerful knife, and thrown to the ground. Baffled, Radin sought advice from his peers, who told him that the sacred image was too powerful and recommended immediate removal. This he and his people did thereafter using the old longhouse as a burial ground.

Rati
Literally, 'erotic desire'. The Balinese version of the Hindu goddess of maternity and fertility. In her portrayal as a heavily pregnant yet leering woman there is an element of the surreal. The teeming womb and the distended breasts, attributes of the mother goddess, are dramatically juxtaposed with demonic voluptuousness, perhaps a sinister legacy from the island's Polynesian past. Java was always known as 'the island abounding in barley', *yavadvipa*, while Bali seems to have retained its archaic reputation as the island of ghosts, the ancestral spirits dwelling at the sources of the rivers. In Rati the ancient demon-ridden faith of the Balinese finds perfect expression. The goddess taunts those who adhere to the imported ideals of the ascetic.

Shaka-nyorai
In Japan the Buddha known as Sakyamuni, 'the silent sage of the Sakya clan', is the perfect embodiment of virtue. With the exception of the Jodo sect, which concentrates exclusively on the worship of Amida-nyorai, there are shrines dedicated to Shaka-nyorai in every Buddhist monastery, but above all this obmutescent figure is revered by the adherents of Zen.

Although the doctrines of the Ch'an Tsung, or 'inner-light school', were first brought from China in 1191, the real founder of the Zen sect was Dogen (1200–53), who established the great monastery of Eiheiji. Dogen spent four years under the instruction of Chinese masters, and the Japanese today acknowledge that Zen doctrine owes much to Taoism. Like Lao-tzu, the Buddha is supposed to have realized that the experience of Enlightenment was beyond the power of words to convey. Therefore the inexpressible doctrine was born of a smile of Shaka-nyorai before a lotus. The Zen sect is novel, its teaching methods are oral

decided to hold a bird festival, *gawai burong*, and to this feast he invited all the other war leaders and persons of rank. As they were feasting, some of the older guests told him that the image of the rhinoceros hornbill, sacred to the bird god Sengalang Burong, the patron of head-hunters, must be removed from the village three days after the celebration was over, and that the site must be vacated too. Radin adhered to custom in respect of the sacred image, but he did not quit the longhouse, the village under one roof. Some days later his people started to die of smallpox. Then, three nights in succession, as he was lying sleepless, worried by the increasing number of deaths, Radin heard the music of a lovely song, which took apparent pleasure at their plight. On the fourth night Radin took his machete and hid himself inside a roll of matting. When the hungry ghost came near to and intuitive, and it shuns canonical books and texts. Zen masters seek to lead their students to a moment of sudden awareness, *satori*, 'awakening', in which they have an intuitive glance into the very nature of things. It is the non-dual vision. Dogen said: 'If we watch the shore while we are sailing in a boat, we feel the shore is moving. But if we look nearer to the boat itself, we know then that it is the boat which moves. When we regard the universe in confusion of body and mind, we often get the mistaken belief that our mind is constant. But if we actually practise the way of Zen and return to ourselves, we see that this was wrong.'

The great festival of Shaka-nyorai is his birthday, 8 April. Its popular name is Hanamatsuri, 'the festival of flowers'. When deep in contemplation the Buddha sat beneath the Bo Tree, the demon Mara had hurled at him a fiery discus, which turned into a canopy of flowers.

Shoten

The Japanese version of Ganesa, the elephant-headed Hindu god of enterprise, who removes obstacles and vouchsafes wisdom. Incorporated into Buddhist mythology, the cult of this divinity flourished within various esoteric sects, arriving in Japan at the beginning of the ninth century. Shoten was associated with Tantric practices, one of his images being 'double-bodied', the sexual union of male and female. Shoten and Kwannon are thus joined in non-duality: they are the divine couple, the living image of the realization of enlightenment.

Sukuna-biko

The dwarf god of Japan. In Shinto mythology 'the small lord of renown' was the ally of Okuninushi, son-in-law of Susanowo and King of Izumo. Particularly skilful was Sukuna-biko in medicine and agriculture. Though of minute stature and slow gait, the dwarf god knew everything in the world and travelled everywhere. His disappearance remains unexplained—he seems to have been flung from a stalk of millet into space.

Susanowo

Takehaya Susanowo, 'valiant, swift, impetuous deity', is the storm god of Shinto, the native belief of Japan. For his harassment of Amaterasu, the sun goddess, he lost his beard, had his possessions confiscated, and was sentenced to banishment. The world had been divided between three deities, the children of the primeval parents Izanagi and Izanami. The realm of light, including the heavens and the land, was assigned to the sun goddess, the realm of night to Tsuki-yomi, the moon god, while the sea was entrusted to the rule of Susanowo. Unable to contain his violent aspect, the storm god ravaged the land, darkened the sky, and raised against himself the anger of 'the eight million divinities', who restored Amaterasu to her proper place.

Exiled, Susanowo began his wanderings and adventures. At Izumo he gave battle to a serpent with eight monstrous heads. When he cut the carcass to pieces, a sword fell from its tail, and the storm god sent the marvellous weapon to his sister as a token of his submission. The sword, along with a mirror and a jewel, now form the insignia of the ruling family. His other exploits involved the conquest of Korea, the worsting of the plague, and the afforestation of the Pacific coast. He planted the mountains with his own hairs, which became trees. His tomb is thought to exist on the eastern coast of Kii.

T'ai Shan

Literally, 'grand mountain', the most revered of the five sacred mountains of China, honoured alike by Confucians, Buddhists, and Taoists. Annual sacrifices were offered on its summit to Shang Ti by successive emperors each spring, and over the centuries it became the chief centre of pilgrimage. For Taoists, the deity of T'ai Shan is the greatest terrestrial power, and known as Sheng-ti, Holy Emperor. He controls destiny, appoints birth and death, and is lord of the Yellow Springs, the underworld.

Tengri

Literal meaning: 'god' or 'heaven'. The sky god of the Mongols, their original creator deity. Tengri was regarded as the author of all things visible and invisible, the controller of destiny, and the ruler of the world. 'The sky decrees.' This strong belief in fate may have been a Persian inheritance. Like the other northern peoples, however, the Mongols were deeply impressed by natural phenomena. Meteors were considered lucky, for whoever saw such 'a crack in the sky' could at that moment ask of heaven a favour. Hail and thunderstorms were unpropitious. Because of a great hailstorm at Karakorum on 15 August

1246, the enthronement of Guyug as Khan was postponed on the advice of the shamans, the ceremony taking place eventually nine days later on another site. The attributes of Tengri include 'the great', the 'merciful ruler', and 'the rich'. Genghis Khan held himself to be the chieftain most favoured by heaven. His sweeping victories were decreed.

Tripitaka

The historical Hsuan-tsang, the great Chinese pilgrim. In 629 he started overland on the long journey to India, where he underwent instruction in Buddhist metaphysics and made an impression by his own contribution, before returning to Ch'ang-an about 640 loaded down with manuscripts and images. On announcing his desire to return home, his Indian colleagues said in amazement: 'This land is where Buddha was born, and if you visit all the holy places connected with him you have sightseeing enough to keep you busy for the rest of your life. Having got here, surely it is a pity to go away!' Tripitaka had to explain that the message of the Buddha was for all mankind, hence his pilgrimage to India on behalf of Chinese believers who were without full knowledge of doctrine.

The exact date of the coming of Buddhism to China is uncertain. About 65 there was in Shantung a prince who 'recited the subtle words of Lao-tzu, and respectfully performed the gentle sacrifices of the Buddha'. Though in this first reference we find that characteristic mixture of Taoist and Buddhist elements, little is known of early Chinese Buddhism. Eclecticism was the result of circumstances: texts were scarce, and the few available could not be readily translated; ignorance of Indian languages meant that the background to the faith remained obscure; and, not least, the doctrines of the various sects reached the country at different times. To unravel the tangled threads of uncertainty Tripitaka set out for the West, having dreamt that he saw the crystal peak of Sumeru rising from the cosmic ocean. When he tried to cross the mighty waters, a lotus made of rock sprang up under his foot, and safely conducted him like a stepping-stone to the World Mountain. After losing his foothold on the steep sides, Tripitaka found himself borne upwards to the mountaintop by a sudden gust of wind.

Legend has converted the pilgrimage of Tripitaka into the most popular cycle of stories in Chinese folklore. Instead of quietly leaving for India, the pilgrim was supplied with a white horse by the Emperor, and encountered numerous divinities on the adventurous journey. Kwan-yin compelled a dragon to act as Tripitaka's mount after it had emerged from a deep river-bed and devoured the white horse. The Goddess of Mercy also obliged the king of the monkeys to be the guide, adviser, and friend of Tripitaka as a condition of release from punishment earned by celestial misdeeds. The resourceful monkey was none other than Hanuman: he was Sun Hou-tzu, the 'restless, cunning, indestructible one', who lived on jade juice. Born of a stone egg, Sun Hou-tzu could fly, leap 30,000 miles at a time, and handle with amazing dexterity a magic rod. This incredible weapon could accommodate itself to all his wishes; being able to assume cosmic proportions or to reduce itself to the size of the finest needle, so as to fit behind the monkey god's ear. Another helper of Tripitaka was Chu Pa-chieh, a grotesque pig-like divinity, armed with a muck-rake, but almost disarmed by his own coarser passions. Sun Hou-tzu and Chu Pa-chieh got Tripitaka and Sha Ho-shang, 'priest Sha' his mortal companion, into all kinds of scrapes as well as saving them from all kinds of dangers. In *Pilgrimage to the West*, Wu Cheng-en's sixteenth-century novel based on Hsuan-tsang, the knockabout humour reaches extraordinary levels.

Tsao Chun

The Chinese kitchen god, a Taoist deity of remote antiquity. His temple is a small niche close by the cooking stove, long regarded as the most important piece of furniture in the house. Diet is a subject of perennial interest, though one devotee of Tsao Chun attained to longevity by the double gift of not growing old and of being able to live without eating. Tsao Chun is portrayed as a kindly gentleman surrounded by children.

Ukulan-tojon

The water spirit of the Yakuts. In the Lena River valley, as throughout Siberia and Mongolia, it was believed from earliest times that the universe was governed by spirits. Trees, mountains, rivers, lakes, animals: every 'living' thing was animated by an in-dwelling spirit, and decline and death was represented as the spirit's absence. The Altai Tartars use the word *kut* to denote the soul of both human beings and natural objects. Master spirits are those with authority over other spirits, like Ukulan-tojon, lord of all the waters. Others have charge of a particular species or a type of landscape. Always an object of special reverence in North Asia, water was treated with extra respect by the Mongols. Sacrifices were made to effect a safe river crossing, while the unkempt appearance of the invaders of China can be attributed to the taboo on washing themselves or having an article of clothing washed in running water. Moreover, it is the general belief of the northern peoples that certain rivers empty into enormous icy gulfs ruled over by maleficent spirits who devour human souls.

Urashima
The fisher boy of Japanese folklore. He married a sea maiden and lived in a palace beneath the waves. When he was seized by the desire to see his parents again, his wife gave him a casket, which if unopened would ensure his safe return to the deep. Dismayed to learn that centuries had passed since he had left, Urashima opened the lid of the casket. At once a puff of white smoke rose from it and drifted away towards the sea, while he was shaken by a cold wind that turned him into an incredibly ancient man, then a corpse. Today the shrine of Urashima stands on the coast of Tango.

Yakushi-nyorai
Literally, 'the master of remedies', one of the six 'meditation Buddhas'. The Japanese worship this saviour as the one who promised to cure all sickness and to obtain for mankind the remedies it needs.

Yen Wang
Yen Wang of China, Emma-o of Japan—originally Yama, the Hindu god of death—was imported as part of Buddhist mythology. His task was the enforcement of the law of retribution, but the idea that the wheel of rebirth operated automatically outmoded an infernal judgement, leaving 'the king of the devils' as tormentor of the most abominable souls. In China he merged with indigenous traditions about the place of death, the Yellow Springs, *huang ch'uan*. This dreary abode was not unlike our own world, and miners were always worried that they might accidentally break into it. The earliest records of ancestor worship reveal that there was fear of the family spirits; inscriptions are often inquiries as to whether particular illnesses or misfortunes were or were not being caused by dissatisfied ancestors.

In Japan the dark-faced god of death rules over a kingdom thought to be the exact opposite of the Paradise of the Pure Land. The antithesis of Amida-nyorai, Emma-o is the pitiless judge, unswayed by the solicitude of Jizo-bosatsu. Hence the popular proverb: 'Borrow with Jizo's face, but repay with look of Emma.'

Yi
The William Tell of China. In remote times there appeared in the sky no less than ten suns, so that the earth was scorched and oppressed through the excessive heat. A hero, Yi 'the excellent archer', shot down nine of them with a magic bow. The significance of this episode is obscure. Clearly the appearance of several suns was a sign of disorder, just as two suns were visible before the fall of tyrant Chou Hsin, the last Shang monarch, but in Chinese thought arose an early awareness of space.

The Hsuan Yeh, or 'infinite empty space school', argued sometime before 200 that 'the heavens were empty and void of substance. When we look up at it we can see that it is immensely high and far away, having no bounds. . . . The sun, the moon, and the company of stars float in the empty space, moving or standing still. All are condensed vapour.' Because of the fundamental role of Nature in Chinese civilization—that ancient intimacy of man and environment which found expression in the Yin-Yang theory—specialists such as astronomers, astrologers, engineers, and magicians were absorbed into the imperial civil service. Science and sorcery were able to co-exist because of the idea that natural phenomena, like flooding, earthquakes, or eclipses, were connected with supernatural powers. The benevolence of Shang Ti was entreated by the priest king, the Son of Heaven; hence the attention paid to astronomy, whose predictive function in respect of heavenly movements was regarded as a state secret. Observation was a serious business. Systematic records of sun-spots were kept from 28; imperial astronomers must have observed through thin slices of jade or some similar translucent material.

Another legend about Yi concerns the elixir of life. The archer obtained the precious medicine, but his wife stole it, ate it, and flew to the moon. Evidently his bow could not help him in this instance, because 'he was very sad at his irreparable loss'. Thus, Chuang-tzu (350–275 BC) wrote of the Way, the Tao, 'that Yi could never catch a glimpse of it'.

Yin-Yang

The two interacting forces that sustain the Chinese cosmos, 'the ten thousand things'. They are not thought of as being in conflict, but existing together in precarious balance, which if disturbed will bring disasters to mankind. The harmony of the universe depends on this balance—Yin, negative, female, dark, the earth; Yang, positive, male, light, heaven. As the source of weather, Heaven was looked upon by the ancient Chinese as the greater, the realm of Shang Ti, whose benevolence had to be entreated with sacrifices made by the ruler, the Son of Heaven. This perception of the natural forces stemmed from the everyday experience of early agriculturalists in the loess country of the Yellow River valley, where a sudden downpour could alter the landscape dramatically. Nature was a single intricately balanced organism, undergoing continuous alterations, with which man had to learn to respond correctly. It was always a question of attunement to the pre-established harmony of *li*, the universal pattern. So Yu, 'the great engineer', dug the beds of the rivers deeper and kept the dikes low: he sought the natural way, the Tao of water control.

Yryn-ai-tojon

Literal meaning: 'white creator lord'. According to the Yakuts, who dwell along the Lena River in Siberia, Yryn-ai-tojon was the supreme being, whose tethering-post was the pillar of the world, a gigantic tree. From the top of a mighty hill, in the 'navel' of the world, the cosmic tree towered upwards, its branches overreaching the seven floors of heaven, while beneath the earth its roots reached down into the subterranean abysses, where they formed the pillars of the houses of the earth spirits. The bark of the tree never cracked, nor did its luxuriant leaves ever wilt.

At the beginning Yryn-ai-tojon was moving above the primordial ocean when he noticed a bladder floating on the waters. In reply to his inquiry, the bladder announced it was the spirit of evil, the inhabitant of the ground hidden under the water. Then said Yryn-ai-tojon: 'If there really is earth beneath the ocean, hasten and bring me a piece of it'. The evil spirit left the bladder, dived, and returned with a handful of earth, which the white creator lord blessed, placed upon the ocean's surface, and seated himself on it. When the evil one tried to drown Yryn-ai-tojon by stretching out the land, he was amazed to discover that the more he stretched, the stronger it grew, so that at last there existed a whole continent.

The co-operation of good and evil in this myth about the formation of the world is by no means unique in Siberia or Mongolia. It is not, however, a creation myth, since the Yakuts believed 'the universe has always been'. Another version of the story relates that the earth dropped or was let down from heaven. The Kirghis tribes, scattered over a wide area to the west of the Irtish River, held the view that originally there was no water at all. The primeval ox made the lakes and rivers by digging the ground with its horns. The water motif also finds expression in a legend of the Buriats, whose home is the shores of Lake Baikal. Powerful Ulgan, another name for Yryn-ai-tojon, created the land on the water, and placed under the earth disc, in order to support it, three great fishes. Hence, the occurrence of earthquakes was explained as the movement of a fish.

Yu

Semi-legendary Chinese emperor, renowned as an hydraulic engineer. According to the *Shu Ching (Book of History)*, Yu was asked to contain the deluge by Shun, a divine monarch. 'The inundating waters seemed to assail the heavens', Yu said, 'and in their extent embraced the hills and over-topped the great mounds, so that the people were bewildered and overwhelmed. . . . I opened the passages for the streams throughout the nine provinces and conducted them to the seas.' Thirteen years Yu spent 'mastering the waters' without once returning home to see his wife and children. By his skill he brought 'water benefits' to the people—floods ceased and fields were irrigated; to his own family came the privilege of founding the first dynasty, the Hsia. The Yellow River valley permitted irrigation on a small scale and then encouraged not only irrigation but schemes of drainage and flood prevention on an increasingly larger scale. For Confucians, Yu was a paragon of virtue, the ancient standard of public duty: but the Taoists were certain that his organization of labour in hydraulic engineering had represented a divergence from the natural way of doing things. They feared the inhibition of feudal relationships.

EUROPE

Greece Rome The Celtic Lands Northern and Eastern Europe

The outstanding myth-makers in Europe reached the pastures of Thessaly and settled under the shadow of Mount Olympus about 2000 BC. They spoke Greek, an Indo-European language, and brought with them their own gods, whom they installed on the misty Olympian heights under the leadership of Zeus, the sky god. Within a couple of centuries further southward penetration had reached the Peloponnese and there engendered the Mycenaean era, so called because Mycenae was its most brilliant centre. The continental Mycenaean civilization developed alongside the more sophisticated Minoan civilization established on the island of Crete, from which it appears to have acquired the 'Linear B' script, perhaps as a result of occupying Knossos about 1450 BC. The language of the Minoans—termed 'Linear A'—has resisted decipherment, but it is evident from archaeological excavation that the worship given to the mother goddess by this maritime people had an influence on the Mycenaean Greeks. This early phase of Greek religion—an amalgam of Mycenaean and Minoan practices—was brought to an abrupt end by the coming of the Dorians, less civilized Greek migrants from the mountainous lands of the north-west. They overwhelmed the massively fortified cities of the Peloponnese and occupied several islands in the Aegean Sea, including Crete and Rhodes. The consequence of this second migration was the submergence of the Minoan heritage; the Indo-European cult of the sky god was superimposed on an indigenous tradition in which the earth goddess was predominant.

Soon after 700 BC Hesiod tried to unravel the complexity belonging to the Greek myths, a characteristic that can be attributed in part to migration and war. The development of the gods is the subject of his *Theogony*, which seeks universal order through the tracing out of genealogical relationships. The poem relates the progress of Zeus, the events by which this 'cloud-gathering' son of Kronos, the first usurper of the world, achieved his own supremacy. It contains a rich array of gods and heroes dating back to the Mycenaean era, when each important city had a mythical genealogy for its ruling house, and in the exploits of the legendary heroes we encounter a singular feature of Greek mythology. Few traditions possess the equivalent of Jason, Hercules, and Asclepius. In India the theory of the avatar always ensures that the divinity of Rama or Krishna is not forgotten, while in ancient Mesopotamia the travail of Gilgamesh marked him off from other priest kings. In Egypt a very circumscribed mythology stemmed from the unusual domination of the pharaoh and the priesthood: it concentrated on the fate of the soul after death. Among the ancient Greeks we find no such other-worldliness, for the gods were encountered as much in the street as in the temple. The gap between immortals and mortals was never great—both were members of the same community. 'Of one race', wrote Pindar in the fifth century BC, 'are men and gods. Born of one mother we draw our breath, though in strength are gods and men far divided.'

'The Four Horsemen of the Apocalypse' by Albrecht Dürer (1471–1528)

The traveller and historian Herodotus, a contemporary of the poet Pindar, believed that most of the Greek gods were borrowed from Egypt, the obvious antiquity of which deeply impressed him. Although he was wrong to single out this country as the origin of Greek mythology, he did perceive that the Eastern Mediterranean had been a cultural continuum for a very long time. Contacts with Asia Minor must have played a part in the meteoric development of Greek civilization. We are now aware, for instance, that the ecstatic god Dionysus, who came down into Greece through Thrace, derived ultimately from Phrygia or Crete. Only the foolhardy refused his worship, as the Thebans found to their cost. Yet there was already in existence a sceptical attitude towards mythology, an impatience at the scandalous behaviour of the gods. Such a philosophical standpoint did not affect popular Greek religion, though in time it separated *logos*, thought, from *mythos*, myth. Reasoning, first advocated as wisdom by Heraclitus of Ephesus some years earlier, became the instrument for comprehending the intelligible universe. As Heraclitus said: 'This world which is the same for all, no god or man has made; but it is ever, is now, and ever shall be an ever-living fire, with parts of it kindling, and parts going out.' By 316 BC Euhemerus, a Sicilian philosopher resident at the Macedonian court, might argue that all the ancient myths were historical events. His *Sacred History* represented the gods as originally men who had distinguished themselves and who after their death received divine honours from a grateful people.

Conquest of the lands surrounding the Mediterranean Sea, an historical event of the first importance that was almost complete prior to the birth of Christ, made imperial Rome the metropolis of the ancient world as well as the inheritor of its several mythological traditions. While none could resist the tramp of the Roman legions, the conquered peoples discovered to their surprise that the citizens of Rome were quite defenceless against foreign religions. This was particularly true of the relationship between Greece and Rome. The process of assimilation had begun in the second half of the fourth century BC when Rome, as a major Italian power, had come into contact with the city-states of the Greek world. Upstart Rome was needled by its lack of tradition, the absence of a glorious past filled with gods and heroes, and to its historians fell the task of creating a worthy chronology. They obliged. Rome at last found itself in possession of a national tradition dating from the Trojan War all the more complete and harmonious because its historians had taken care to make it so. The embellishment of the legend of Roman origins received state recognition in 239 BC, when the Senate granted its protection to the Acarnanians, harassed by the Aetolians, because they alone of the Greeks had held aloof from hostilities against the Trojans, the ancestors of the Roman people. The classic treatment of this myth occurs in Virgil's *Aeneid*, composed to celebrate the establishment of the Empire by Augustus in 31 BC.

There were other influences on early Romans too. Close at hand were their chief rivals, the Etruscans and the Carthaginians. 'The might of the Etruscans, before the Romans rose to power', wrote the historian Livy, a contemporary of Virgil, 'stretched widely over land and sea . . . from the Alps to the Sicilian Straits.' Rome itself had been ruled by Etruscan kings, and the Romans were aware of the role of Etruria in spreading Greek and West Asian culture among the Italic peoples. Our present ignorance of the Etruscan language precludes judgement: we are uncertain of the original Etruscan

Zeus, king of the gods. A sixth-century BC Greek bronze

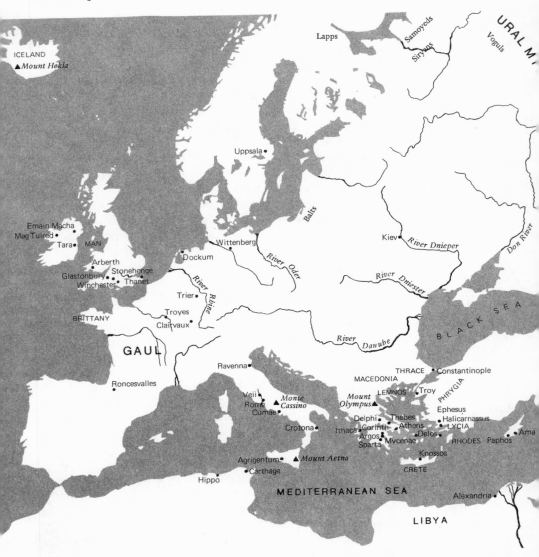

homeland, though Asia Minor seems a likely candidate, and apart from the skill of the
Etruscans in divination, the observation of the entrails of sacrificial beasts, we know
little more than the names of their gods. More details are available on Carthage, the
colony founded in Africa by the Phoenicians in 814 BC, but its impact on Rome was
entirely negative and can be summed up in one word: Hannibal. The ordeal of the
Hannibalic invasion, fifteen years of defeat and devastation (217–203 BC), implanted in
the Romans a phobia of great powers within striking distance of the Italian peninsula.
Rome sought to patrol the Mediterranean lands, striking down any state that showed
any sign of independence, even in 146 BC destroying the reduced cities of Carthage and
Corinth. The consequence of this policy was the collapse of the Roman Republic and
the founding of the Roman Empire.

The architect of Roman dominion was Julius Caesar, who spent the decade before he overthrew the Republic in the conquest and annexation of Gaul, the heartland of the Celtic people. In 55 BC he had reconnoitred the southern coast of Britain, though Roman invasion of the island was begun only a century later. The long campaign in Gaul welded his legions into an invincible army, making him the chief war-lord as well as monarch till he was assassinated in 44 BC. He advanced the Roman frontier to the Rhine, created several large provinces, and, not least, brought the majority of the Celts into direct communication with the ancient world.

The Celts first appear in Germany. From the ninth century BC onwards waves of migrants spread into Gaul, the Iberian peninsula, northern Italy, the Balkans, Asia Minor, and Britain. One wandering band even sacked the city of Rome in 386 BC. The geographical dispersal of the Celtic people explains the lack of unity in their mythology, since each group of migrants encountered different local conditions in settlement. The last migration, for instance, was the invasion of Britain in the first century BC by the Belgians. Although the priests known as Druids have acquired a popular status due to the writings of antiquarians, there is little evidence of their dominant position in Celtic religion. The order may have been restricted to Britain and Gaul. Julius Caesar learned of its teaching that it 'was invented in Britain and taken from there to Gaul, and . . . that diligent students of the discipline mostly travel there to study it.' Moreover, the association of the Druidic grove and Stonehenge has become

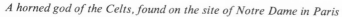

A horned god of the Celts, found on the site of Notre Dame in Paris

so established as a piece of British folklore that we do not often recall that this theory is hardly 300 years old. The function of Stonehenge, a pre-Celtic monument, probably dating from 1500 BC at its final stage of construction, is unknown. Because the Celts chose to rely on oral tradition—Julius Caesar noted that the Druids 'were unwilling, first, that their system of training should be bruited abroad among the common people and second, that the student should rely on the written word and neglect memory'—there are few sources of evidence for their religion, a circumstance ensuring that it will remain forever a mystery. The legendary cycles of medieval Ireland, and the derivative Arthurian tradition in Wales, Brittany, and England, have to represent Celtic mythology.

When in 313 Christianity obtained complete toleration in the Roman Empire, the change of fortune for this West Asian faith had as much effect on the Celts living within the imperial borders as on any of the other peoples. It signalled the general retreat of what Christians termed 'pagan' mythology. In 312 the Emperor Constantine had had a dream, in which Christ appeared to him and told him that if he put a Christian sign on the shields of his soldiers, he would triumph over his rival. Having painted the sign on the shields of at least some of his men, he went on to the Battle of the Milvian Bridge, where his army won a startling victory. Although Constantine delayed baptism until he was on his deathbed twenty-five years later, the edict of 313 set aside discriminatory legislation, and ordered not only freedom of worship but the restoration of all property confiscated from the Church during previous persecution. With the notable exception of Julian, who reigned 360–3, successive emperors issued decrees against non-Christian sacrifices, adoration of images, entry to temples, and magic. Pagan apologists were on the defensive, conceding much of the Church's case. Christian zealots, moreover, seized the opportunity to destroy ancient cult centres, like the Serapeum at Alexandria. In 391 Bishop Theophilus led his militant congregation in an attack on this temple, said to be the largest in the ancient world, and burned it to the ground. Elsewhere temples were either demolished, the stones being used to erect churches, or converted, the clergy purifying them of pagan associations. One of the first to be consecrated at Rome was the round Temple of Faunus, the Roman Pan, which Pope Simplicius (468–83) named St Stephano Rotondo.

A consequence of the policy of adaptation was undoubtedly a lingering paganism. The faithful reported the presence of demons, which the later evolution of the gargoyle may have been intended to frighten away. In 530 on Monte Cassino St Benedict came across a grove sacred to Apollo, where the ancient rites were still observed. When he destroyed the shrine and converted the place to Christian use, Satan appeared to complain, but the Saint kept silence. His companions heard, but could not see, the Devil. In the old western provinces of the Roman Empire the pagan myths openly persisted, especially in the nature cults of the countryside. Christian bishops and saints waged a long struggle against these heretical tendencies, which were partly strengthened by the folklore of the Germanic peoples who poured across the Rhine. Yet medieval Christianity was not without its own legends: among other things the minds of believers were exercised by Antichrist; *dies irae*, the wrath of the last day;

A Celtic god, wearing a ceremonial neck-band and holding a boar

A twelfth-century wall hanging from Hålsingland in Sweden showing Odin (left), Thor, and Frey

relics; the cult of the Virgin; miraculous events, signs, and portents; as well as the omnipresent forces of the evil. The age of belief made its contribution to the store of world mythology.

In the fifth century the Western Roman Empire was overrun by Germanic peoples fleeing westwards from the Huns. Rome itself was looted by the Visigoths in 410 and by the Vandals in 455. Such was the thoroughness of the second sack that these wandering tribesmen have given their name to those who take pleasure in the wilful destruction of beautiful things. The Vandals had crossed from Spain to Africa in 429, only two to three years after crossing the Rhine, and St Augustine lived long enough to witness their seizure of Hippo, the city that was his episcopal see. His famous treatise *De Civitate Dei*, or *City of God*, can be regarded as an attempt to make sense for Christians out of the collapse of Roman authority. Especially galling was the rumour that the fall of Rome was a punishment inflicted by the non-Christian gods for the suppression of their worship in 391–2.

While St Augustine refuted heretical theories of history, the northern invaders completed their conquest of the western provinces. The defeat of the Huns by a combined army of Romans and Visigoths at Troyes in 451 as well as the death of the

Hun war leader Attila two years later were insufficient to save the Western Roman Empire, the victim of internal weakness rather than the strength of Germanic arms. It was unable to withstand the movement of peoples and the hegemony of Western Europe passed into the hands of its traditional enemies. Ever since Julius Caesar had advanced the frontier to the Rhine, the Romans knew that the warlike tribes roaming the forests across that river inhabited another mythological world. Writing in 98, Tacitus mentions the Germanic legend of tribal origin: 'In their ancient ballads, their only form of recorded history, they celebrate Tvisto, a god sprung from the earth, and they assign him a son called Mannus, their progenitor through his three sons.' The Romans were fully aware too that Scandinavia equalled a *vagina nationum*, 'a womb of nations', continually sending forth new waves of migration. What they could not know was that the Germanic settlers of the north belonged to the Indo–European language group from which the Italic tongue had descended. In a similar manner the Angles, Saxons, and Jutes, who had occupied Britain after the withdrawal of the Roman legions in 423, were confronted in the later Viking invasions with an assault by less distant, but more ferocious, cousins.

The original Indo-European speakers dispersed from an unknown homeland about 2500 BC. The branch known to the Romans as the Germani traced their own past back to Scandinavia. Descendants of this stock today include Germans, Dutch, Danes, Swedes, Norwegians, Icelanders, English, and any of their extraction. At the time the Roman Empire fell we have little detailed information on Germanic mythology. Other than brief runic inscriptions, there were no written records till the Christian era, those on Iceland only beginning in the year 1000. It happens that mythological literature was for the most part preserved on this island, which after the 874 migration joined to the Viking world. The greatest contribution to the understanding of Germanic legend was made by the Icelandic scholar and statesman Snorri Sturluson (1179–1241), whose *Prose Edda* comprises a handbook for poets on the world of the ancient gods, providing explanations of metaphors based on the old myths. The Viking Age, 750–1050, saw the development of a vigorous cosmology revolving round the heroic deeds of Odin, Thor, and the brother-sister deities, Frey and Freya, and it is this late tradition that Snorri interprets for us. Elsewhere in Western Europe the Germanic conquerors soon converted to Christianity. The reign of Charlemagne (768–814) represents the triumph of the Christian Church; the Frankish kingdom acted as the champion of the Catholic faith, embattled with heretics and pagans alike. In his campaigns against his Saxon kinsmen Charlemagne was conspicuously intolerant of non-Christian practices. While the inhabitants of Scandinavia remained undisturbed, the activities of missionaries carried the faith beyond the borders of the Franks. In 597 Augustine landed on Thanet with a mission to convert the English.

Russia was only converted to Christianity in 989, when the converts joined the Eastern Orthodox Church, not the Roman Catholic Church. This event opened the way for the eastern tradition of Christendom to expand northwards to the shore of the Arctic Ocean and eastwards to the shore of the Pacific Ocean. Greek missionaries found a primitive mythology among the Slavs, but the old beliefs did not long survive the official abolition of pagan worship for the reason that Christianity exercised a civilizing influence. The Slavs and the Balts, their closest linguistic neighbours, appear to have possessed gods with names strikingly reminiscent of Indo-Iranian and Thraco-Phrygian deities. Indeed, the Slavic *rai*, paradise, has been acknowledged as a direct borrowing from the Iranian *ray*, meaning heavenly radiance, or beauty. The storm god Perunu, the wielder of the thunderbolt, received sumptuous worship at Kiev till the tenth century, and he is one of the few Slavic deities about whom we have details, albeit from the account of the discontinuation of his cult. The rest of the mythology of Eastern Europe remains lost in the mists of the pre-Christian era.

Lastly, in the northernmost parts of Europe there are still to be found the scattered remnants of an ancient people, the Uralians. The Lapps of Finland, the Samoyeds of Russia, along with several smaller groups inhabiting the tundra, preserve in their folklore the traditions of a people that must have begun to scatter about the fourth millennium BC. Their beliefs are similar to those held by the tribesmen of Siberia, a link strongly suggesting an original shamanism. Evidence of the former activities of medicine-men, spirit-possessed priests, is provided in the accounts given by early visitors to the Lapps. An eighteenth-century Danish traveller witnessed the trance into which such a medium fell, after a series of whirling dances. During the time that he was unconscious of the immediate surroundings—his spirit it was said having journeyed to the land of the dead in order to master the spirit afflicting his patient—the medium could handle burning logs and swing an axe against his knees without suffering the least harm. On his return to consciousness, he announced the nature of the malady and the length of time it would take for the sick person to recover. Traces of sorcery are evident, too, in the ancient beliefs of the Finns, Voguls, and Hungarians, all of whom have descended from Uralian stock. The idea that every living thing was animated by a spirit appears to have been extended by the Hungarians to every limb and organ. Each had its separate soul; a chronicle of 899 records that for magical reasons the Hungarians ate the hearts of captives.

Achilles

The hero of Homer's *Iliad*, the ninth-century BC epic account of the siege of Troy, which probably took place four centuries earlier. Son of the Thessalian King Peleus and the nymph Thetis, Achilles was an invincible warrior but given to inexplicable fits of anger. He quarrelled with the other Greek chieftains, sulked in his tent, and across the battlefield he dragged the body of the Trojan champion Hector, whom he had slain in single combat. According to legend, Thetis sought to make Achilles immortal, by dipping him in the subterranean River Styx, and succeeded with the exception of the heel by which she held him. This one vulnerable spot a poisoned arrow from the bow of Paris found out, and Achilles died prior to the fall of Troy.

Aeneas

The famous Trojan-Roman hero; the son of Anchises and the goddess Venus-Aphrodite.

The Romans believed that an important element among them came from Asia Minor—Trojans who escaped the sack of Troy by the Greeks and followed Aeneas. This myth received classic statement in Virgil's *Aeneid*, an account of the wanderings of fugitive Aeneas till his settlement in Italy. Imperial interest in the epic poem was pronounced. From Spain in 26 BC Augustus, the first Roman Emperor, wrote to Virgil expressing a wish to have a draft or portions of the *Aeneid* which had been begun about that time. Virgil celebrated the destiny of the Romans as the divinely inspired rulers of the ancient world: it was a sentiment close to the heart of the victor of Actium.

After sailing to Crete, where he learned in a dream that Dardanus, ancestor of the Trojan royal family, hailed originally from Italy, Aeneas continued to Epirus upon the eastern Adriatic coast, and then on to Sicily and Carthage before making landfall near the rock-hewn sanctuary of the Cumaean Sibyl. The diversion to North Africa occurred because of a sudden storm sent by the goddess Juno, who had constantly pursued him with her hatred during the voyage. This animosity appears to owe something to the fierce antagonism of Hera for Hercules, the Greek hero. At Carthage, Venus ensured that Aeneas and Dido, its Queen, fell deeply in love. When, in obedience to the command of Jupiter, he left her, she burned herself to death on a funeral pyre.

Of interest is Aeneas' visit to the underworld. The Sibyl bade him arm himself with the golden bough, and together they descended to 'the land of shades'. When Aeneas encountered Dido there and tried to speak to her, she turned away in silence. But then he came upon his father Anchises, who disclosed to him the future glories of Rome, reaching their climax with the reign of Augustus. The remainder of the *Aeneid* relates the unification of the Trojans and the Latins into a single nation, which was the great mythical achievement of 'pious' Aeneas.

Aesir

In Germanic mythology, the two races of the gods were the *aesir* and *vanir*. Snorri Sturluson (1179–1241) thought that aesir derived from the word Asia, making Thor a grandson of Priam of Troy and Odin his descendant in the twentieth generation. The vanir were originally inhabitants of the land on the Don River, 'formerly called Vanaquisl'. Although this interpretation of Scandinavian tradition receives no support today, it is not unlikely that the vanir were late arrivals from Asia Minor and that their initial rivalry with the aesir represents an accommodation within the earlier mythology. Odin was chief of the aesir, while the goddess Freya took a leading role among the vanir, not least at the time these two races were syncretized.

Pitted against the gods was a race of frost giants, the descendants of Bergelmir, survivor of the bloody deluge caused by the slaying of Ymir. It is evident that the gods were in the hands of fate and inexorably moving towards their doom, the *ragnarok*. On this day, the forces of evil would overcome the gods and their allies, the *einherjar*, the slain champions beloved of Odin. Two human beings, Lif and Lifthrasir, should survive the cataclysm: they will re-people the new earth and worship Balder, son of Odin, in the new heaven.

Antichrist

In medieval Christian mythology, the prodigious tyrant of the last days, the arch-enemy of Christ. It was a notion that combined Persian dualism with Judeo-Christian apocalypse. Antichrist first appeared in *Revelation* as the pseudo-messiah 'who opposeth and exalteth himself above all that is called God, or that is worshipped. . . . And it was given unto him to make war with the saints, and to overcome them: and power was given to him over all kindreds, and tongues, and nations.' In the Middle Ages, however, he was portrayed not only as a world tyrant but also as an airborne beast with a huge head, flaming eyes, ass's ears, and iron teeth.

The coming of Antichrist was tensely awaited. In 1096 Pope Urban said that, since the tyrant's arrival was imminent and the Holy Land would be the centre of his power, it was crucial that Christians expel the Moslems from Jerusalem. Thus he launched the First Crusade. When the threat of invasion by Saracens, Tartars, or Turks did not fuel the myth, Europe tended to find his supporters within itself. Satan became 'the father of the Jews', and bloody persecution ensued. But if most people believed that Antichrist was to be a Jew, there were many who believed that he would be the son of a bishop or a nun. Anticlericalism and Antichrist became strangely entwined. As Pope Boniface VIII wrote in 1296: 'Antiquity relates that laymen show a spirit of hostility towards the clergy, and it is clearly proved by the experience of the present time.' During the Reformation it comes as no surprise to discover that Protestants regarded the Pope as Antichrist while Catholics returned the compliment with regard to Luther.

Aphrodite

The Greek goddess of love. Unlike her Roman counterpart Venus, with whom she was identified, Aphrodite was not only a deity of sexual love but also of affection and all the impulses that underpin social life. Her amorousness may be partly explained by one of the legends concerning her birth. When Kronos cut off Ouranos' phallus with a sharp sickle, he flung the immortal member into the sea, where it floated amid white foam. Inside the divine flesh a goddess was nurtured, whom the Greeks called Aphrodite, 'she who came from the foam'. In this way she reached 'sea-girt Cyprus', where two important shrines

A Greek terracotta figure of Aphrodite, goddess of love, rising from a shell

were built for her worship at Paphos and Amathos, the latter being dedicated to a bearded form reminiscent of the Assyrian Ishtar. In fact Aphrodite travelled the opposite way: she came from Cyprus, an island under West Asia influence since earliest times. It was competition with Hera, the indigenous earth mother and wife of Zeus, that caused her to specialize as a love goddess, becoming in time the mother of Eros, a deity with whom, originally, she had nothing whatever to do. Older aspects of her cult—a Greek metamorphosis of the Sumerian Inanna—survive in her names. Aphrodite was Apostrophia, 'she who turns herself away'; Androphonos, 'man killer'; Tymborychos, 'gravedigger'; Anosia, 'the unholy'; Epitymbidia, 'she upon the tombs'; and, above all, Pasiphaessa, 'the far shining' queen of the underworld. The Athenians regarded her as 'the oldest Moirai'—the senior of the Fates. As a goddess of love, Aphrodite collected special epithets too, like Kallipygos, 'she of the beautiful buttocks'; Morpho, 'the shapely';

and Ambologera, 'she who postpones old age'. At Corinth there were even temple prostitutes.

According to legend, the Horai received Aphrodite on Cyprus, whereupon they covered her nakedness with proper attire. These divinities were the daughters of Themis, the goddess responsible for order, justice, and the seasons. The first statue of the naked goddess was made by the sculptor Praxiteles and erected at Cnidus on the south-west coast of Asia Minor in the fourth century BC. The Cnidians revered the cockle, because it was believed that the love goddess had grown inside a cockle-shell.

The unfaithful wife of Hephaistos, the crippled smith god, Aphrodite had several children by the war god Ares. When the outraged husband devised a trap of subtle chains and caught the lovers together in bed, he called the Olympian gods to witness his shame. But they all laughed, except Poseidon, who promised a fitting atonement on behalf of the gods. Only then did Hephaistos consent to unchain Aphrodite and Ares.

Most beloved by Aphrodite was Adonis, the Syrian god killed by a wild boar. Born of an incestuous relationship between a king and

Apollo in his chariot from a Greek wine cup

his twelve-year-old daughter—possibly the King of Lebanon who was deceived by Princess Myrrha—Adonis was so handsome that Aphrodite and Persephone, the queen of the dead, quarrelled over his possession. Their violent dispute was brought before Zeus, who ruled that for a third part of the year Adonis was to dwell by himself; for a third part with Persephone; and for a third part with Aphrodite. Thus the Syrian god died and revived annually, while his guilty mother was turned into a tree that wept a spicy gum: myrrh.

Of historical interest are the two stories that connect Aphrodite with Troy. So potent was the love goddess that she even compelled Zeus to fall in love with mortal women and to

neglect her rival Hera, daughter of Kronos and Rhea. In return Zeus compelled her to be enamoured of the Trojan herdsman Anchises. Disguised as a Phrygian princess, she visited the cattle-pens, dazzling the poor man with her beauty. Although the terror of Anchises after their night of love was justified, he had the compensation of knowing that their son Aeneas would be the founder of the Latin nation in Italy. For having slept with the goddess—a costly privilege for any mortal—Anchises was either lamed by lightning or blinded by bees. While Aphrodite was instrumental in saving a remnant of the Trojans through providing them with the leadership of Aeneas after the fall of the city to the Greeks, she contributed to the fatal conflict herself. In order to be judged the most beautiful of the goddesses by Paris, the son of Priam and Hecuba, when he was serving as a shepherd,

Aphrodite promised him the hand of Helen, already the wife of the Spartan King Menelaus. The abduction of Helen by Paris brought about the Trojan War.

Apollo
Twin brother of Artemis, the virgin huntress, and son of Zeus and Leto, a Titaness. Called by the Greeks Phoebus 'shining'. Cultic associations with Asia Minor predate those of Greece: Leto was said to have given birth to Apollo and Artemis in Lycia, though the place most closely associated with Apollo's birth was the sacred island of Delos. At birth he said: 'Dear to me shall be the lyre and bow, and in oracles I shall reveal to men the inexorable will of Zeus.'

According to one legend, the young Apollo went to Delphi at the age of four days in order to slay there the earth serpent which had tried to molest his mother during pregnancy. This python, a son of Gaia, sent up revelations through a fissure in the rock; a priestess, the Pythia, inhaling the potent fumes, was thus inspired to give voice to cryptic utterances—the prophecies of the Delphic Oracle. Apollo killed the great snake and took its place. Another legend makes the dispossessed creature a she dragon named Delphyne, 'the womb-like': hence Delphi.

Of his amorous adventures, noteworthy were the affairs with Koronis, the mother of the medicine god Asclepius; with Daphne, a wild virgin from Thessaly, who became a laurel to avoid ravishment; with the nymph Dryope, whom he approached in the guise of a tortoise; with the boy Kyparissos, 'cypress', a kind of double of Apollo himself. Daphne and Kyparissos must derive from the god's older habitat, the wild regions of the north. Apollo was originally the patron of shepherds: after his installation at Delphi he acquired power over archery, music, and medicine. The Romans built their first temple to Apollo in 432 BC. They may have adopted him from Greek settlers or from the Etruscans, whose divinity Veiovis was identified with Apollo.

Artemis
When the moon shone, Artemis was present, and beasts and plants would dance. In honour of the goddess male and female dancers performed, and the villagers of Arcadia, in the Peloponnese, attired their girls with phalluses. The Athenians sensed the pre-Greek origins of the virgin huntress Artemis, the goddess of

wild places and wild things, and her cult was restricted to the surrounding countryside where *arktoi*, 'bear virgins', attended her. The vestiges of human sacrifice could be found in her worship: blood was drawn from a slight cut on the throat of a male victim by the female devotees of the sometime bear goddess.

Greek legend tells how Actaeon had the misfortune to come, while hunting, upon Artemis as she was bathing. She changed him into a stag and he was pursued and torn to pieces by his own dogs. In an older version the naked goddess was approached by the hunter covered with a stag's pelt. Like Athena, Artemis sometimes wore the frightful mask of the Gorgon on her neck, for with Athena and Hestia, the mild guardian of the home, she was one of the goddesses over whom Aphrodite had no power. In Asia Minor, however, Aphrodite was often identified with Artemis in the aspect of a virgin huntress.

Korythalia, 'laurel maiden', Artemis was the daughter of Zeus and Leto, a Titaness, and the twin sister of Apollo. When the giant Tityos attacked Leto on her way to Delphi, he was slain by one of Artemis' shafts or by a blow from Apollo. Odysseus saw the offender in Hades: the giant was chained and two vultures tore ceaselessly at his liver.

Arthur
Hic jacet Arthurus, rex quondam, rexque futurus. 'Here lies Arthur, king that was, king that shall be.' This inscription on his tomb at Glastonbury catches the flavour of his legendary life and un-death. In Wales, Cornwall, and Brittany, during the medieval period, there was a firm popular belief that Arthur was not dead but would return to deliver his people from their enemies. He was the focus and inspiration of late Celtic mythology.

In one of the earliest references to Arthur, namely the *Historia Brittonum* of Nennius, a ninth-century Welsh monk, he was described as *dux bellorum*, 'leader of troops'. Like the Irishman Finn MacCool, he was a warrior who defended his country against foreign invaders. But his legendary character by far outshone whatever historical fame he may have had. In romance, King Arthur and the Knights of the Round Table were the paragons of chivalry.

Athena in a belligerent mood. A Greek bronze of about 450 BC

Son of Uther Pendragon, King of Britain, and Igraine; wife of Duke Gorlois of Cornwall, Arthur was conceived out of wedlock and brought up by the wizard Merlin. By pulling the magic sword Excalibur from a stone from which no one else could extract it, he revealed himself, though then a child, as the predestined king. Crowned at the age of fifteen, in Wales, he soon showed his skill as a military commander, even reaching the city of Rome in one campaign. Against Merlin's advice Arthur married Guinevere, who loved Sir Lancelot and was unfaithful to the king. Disaster struck his kingdom in the shape of a rebellion raised by Mordred, his nephew. A great battle was fought, nearly all of the Knights of the Round Table slain, and Arthur himself sorely wounded. Excalibur was thrown into a lake, and in a boat three fairies took Arthur away to Avalon, or Avallach which has been identified with Glastonbury.

Asclepius
In Greek mythology, the patron of medicine and son of Apollo. He not only cured the sick, but recalled the dead to life. This rare authority over Hades may have derived from the circumstances of his own birth. Koronis, a lake nymph, was impregnated by Apollo, yet dared to take in secret a human being as a second lover. So furious was the god on discovering the infidelity that he sent his sister Artemis to slay Koronis. This she did with a pestilence. When the fire was already blazing round the lake nymph on the funeral pyre, Apollo felt compassion for his unborn son, and removed him from the corpse. In this manner Asclepius came into the world and was taught the art of healing by Chiron, the wisest of the Centaurs. The success of this instruction was so great that Zeus, fearing lest men might contrive to escape death altogether, killed Asclepius with lightning; but at Apollo's request he placed the medicine god among the stars. His chief temple was at Epidaurus, near Argos, and sacred to him there were serpents—the only species with the power to slough its skin. At Rome the worship of Asclepius was introduced from Greece in 293 BC, for the purpose of averting a plague.

Athena
Or Athene. The daughter of Zeus and Metis, 'counsel', Athena sprang into being fully formed and fully armed from the head of her father, after Zeus had swallowed the pregnant Metis. The smith god Hephaistos may have assisted with his axe at this birth. A warlike virgin, Pallas Athene eschewed senseless violence, unlike the war god Ares, and relied on the boldness of wisdom. She successfully disputed with the sea god Poseidon who should rule Athens: Zeus judged her the winner because she had planted the olive tree. There existed, however, a dark side to her character, since she was Glaukopis, 'owl-eyed', and Gorgopis, 'Gorgon-faced'.

Athena was patroness of craftsmen, especially smiths, weavers, and spinners. This explains her title of Hephaistia, the associate of the smith god. But not all was well between god and goddess, as the myth of Erichthonius makes clear. To avoid losing her virginity to Hephaistos, she thrust him from her, or miraculously vanished from the bridal bed. The spilled semen of the smith god fell to the ground, where it grew into the serpent Erichthonius. The three daughters of Cecrops, the first King of Athens and a half serpent man, were given a box by the goddess and told not to look inside it. Curiosity overcame two of them, and the sight of the divine child snake drove them mad. Athena, however, did not withdraw her protection from the city, indeed she always remained the energetic goddess of action. It was an active support that aided Odysseus on his epic voyage home from the Trojan War.

Balder
'The bleeding god' of Germanic mythology. Renowned for his good looks and his wisdom, Odin's second son was a northern derivative of Adonis, Attis, Tummuz, and Osiris. The return of the dying Balder would occur in the new world, the green land risen from the sea, after ragnarok, the destruction of the gods.

Balder was killed by a shaft of mistletoe, since time immemorial in Europe a mysterious and sacred plant. Hodr was the blind god who, used as a catspaw by Loki, flung the deadly shaft. When Balder fell, the gods were thrown into confusion and uncertainty, till Frigg suggested that someone ride to *hel*, the place of death, in order to find out the ransom desired. This dark abode was really a prison, filled with the souls who would fight against the gods at ragnarok. Its queen Hel possessed a palace called Sleetcold, and she tyrannized those who were sent to her, having died of disease, old age, or accident, instead of meeting a glorious end in battle. Balder was known as the 'god of tears' because his brother Hermodr, rode back on Sleipnir, the eight-legged stallion of Odin, with news that the condition of release from hel was that all created things should weep for him—as they did, all except Loki, whom the gods bound for this impudence. But the German peoples always believed one day, after the cosmic catalysm, the un-dead Balder would return to a rejuvenated world. In the event the dying-and-rising son of the Christian deity took over his place in the hearts of northern men.

Bestiaries

Collections of material on animals, usually legendary; a vogue in the Middle Ages. Most famous of the fabulous beasts was the Unicorn, a creature with a single horn and an admiration of virgins. Most deadly was the Cockatrice, also known as the Basilisk, a small serpent, scarcely six inches long. So venomous was its breath that the wretched creature dwelt in a self-created desert. Most amazing was the Asian Bonnacon, a beast with bull's head and a horse's body. So curved were its immense horns that it could not use them for defence. However, it was not devoid of protection, since when it ran away it discharged excreta on its pursuers. Over three acres could it cover with this fiery substance, dangerous to plants, animals, and men.

Bor

Literally, 'born'. According to Germanic legend, the primeval cow Audumla, 'the Nourisher', licked the icy rocks which were salty to her taste. By the evening of the first day there appeared from the ice, at the spot where she was licking, the hair of a man; on the second day, a man's head; on the third day, an entire man. This was Buri, 'the born one', handsome, tall, and strong. He begat a son called Bor who took to wife Bestla, the daughter of a frost giant: they had three famous sons—Odin, Vili, and Ve. These deities killed the old giant Ymir, who had been sustained by the milk of Audumla. From Ymir's corpse they created the world, his gushing blood having drowned nearly all the other frost giants.

Bran

Son of Febal. He is the royal hero of the eighth-century Irish epic *The Voyage of Bran and His Adventures*. Sea voyages fascinated Irish story-tellers, who distinguished between *echtrai*, 'adventures', and *immrama*, 'voyages', the latter involving visits to otherworld isles. The tale of Bran combines both, and begins with a silver branch covered in white blossom, a woman in a strange raiment, and her song of the wonders to be found in the world beyond the sea, with its many islands, each of them larger than Ireland, its beautiful women and sweet music, a world where treachery, sorrow, sickness, and death were not known. Thither sailed Bran and his men. Among the places he visited were the Island of Joy, where heedless all gape and laugh, and the Island of Women, from which Bran only agreed to depart after much persuasion by a homesick comrade. Arriving in Ireland, he discovered that he was unknown, except as a legendary voyager to the otherworld, and so he set sail again. The homesick member of his crew, however, jumped ashore and became a heap of ashes.

Bres

Legendary Irish king. Son of Elatha, a prince of Fomoire, a race with single arms and legs, and Eriu, a woman of Tuatha De Danann, 'the peoples of the goddess Danann'. Their son was called Eochaid, 'the beautiful', and he grew twice as rapidly as other boys. Bres had another name, Gormac, 'dutiful son', but he did not live up to it. The Tuatha gave him the kingship of Ireland in the hope that his reign would ensure peace and good will between themselves and the Fomoire. But Bres proved unworthy; he humiliated the warriors with menial tasks and oppressed the common people. Deposed, he fled and raised a formidable army from the Fomoire. At the Second Battle of Mag Tuired, a scene of fearful slaughter, the Tuatha won the day. The war between these mythical peoples is most likely an echo of early struggles for ascendancy between migrant tribes. When the Tuatha first landed, they resolutely burned their boats 'in order that they themselves should not have to flee therein from Ireland'.

Cormac mac Airt

The Irish Solomon. His famous reign could have been 226–66, when Tara enjoyed a period of unprecedented prosperity. A contemporary was Fin MacCool, who led his band of warriors in great deeds. The wisdom of Cormac derived from a wonderful golden cup. If three lies were spoken over it, into three pieces it would break; whereas three truths told made it whole again. The King also possessed a musical branch, made of silver with three golden apples on it. When Cormac shook the branch, the sick, the wounded, and women in childbed would fall asleep until the next day. Both the magic cup and branch were gifts from Manannan mac Lir, 'a renowned trader who dwelt in the Isle of Man'. At Cormac's death, they vanished.

Coronation
The ancient West Asian idea of the divinely appointed monarch took root in Europe at Charlemagne's coronation by the Pope on 25 December 800. The inability of the Eastern Romans to relieve Lombard pressure on Rome in 753 had caused Pope Stephen II to cross the Alps in order to ask for Frankish military intervention in Italy. The Franks defeated the Lombards and gave to the Papacy the territory at Ravenna formerly in the hands of Constantinople. Despite strong opposition from the Eastern Romans, who insisted on the principle of one empire, Constantinople was forced to concede to Charlemagne the title of Basileus, 'King'.

The Christian rites for the coronation of kings always made it very clear that the temporal monarch was in some sense being ordained, for he was sacramentally anointed and had the hands of the bishop laid upon him in the same manner as at the ordination of a priest. The Church justified the Crown, just as the old Hebrew kings had held office as Yahweh's anointed. 'Ruling by Divine Right under God' was a myth predestined to entangle politics with religion, as happened during the seventeenth century in England.

Cuchulainn
Semi-legendary Irish hero, said to have lived in the first century. His father was Lug, a Tuatha chieftain. Cuchulainn was a youth of extraordinary beauty, stature, and gaiety, the favourite of ladies and poets, yet he changed into an appalling spectacle 'when the battle-frenzy was upon him'. His body trembled violently; his heels and calves appeared in front; one eye receded into his head, the other stood out huge and red on his cheek; a man's head could go into his mouth; his hair bristled like hawthorn, with a drop of blood on each single hair; and from the ridge of his crown there arose a thick column of dark blood like the mast of a great ship. The archetypal warrior, seized by such a paroxysm, was terrible to behold. On one

occasion, when his chariot was 'graced with the bleeding heads of his enemies', he charged round the fortress of Emain Macha screaming for a fight. Very quickly, a way had to be found to abate his immense fury. And one was found. Out of Emain Macha came 150 women, naked, with vats of cold water, to calm the warrior. Cuchulainn, embarrassed or perhaps amazed at such a display of womanhood, looked away, at which they thrust him in the first vat of cold water. It burst asunder. A second vat boiled. The third became only very hot. Thus was the hero subdued, and the fortress saved.

The ancient heroes of Ireland were fierce head-hunters, daring cattle-rustlers, and mighty eaters. Their feasts as well as their fights were conducted on a superhuman level. Often a challenge or a boast in the hall led to a contest, so as to determine which warrior should carve the champion's portion, the first slice of the roast pig. Cuchulainn, however, was without equal: sets of weapons he shattered with his strength; chariots he reduced to fragments; whole armies he faced single-handed; monsters fled his deadly blows; few dared to challenge him; while he was the admiration of women. The cycle of tales about Cuchulainn greatly influenced the development of Arthurian tradition, in Wales, Brittany, and England.

Cupid
The Italian Cupid or Amor, the Greek Eros—god of love, son of Aphrodite, by either Zeus, Ares, or Hermes. Cupid was thought of as a beautiful but wanton boy, armed with a golden quiver full of 'arrowed desires'. According to a late legend, Venus became jealous of beautiful Psyche, 'the soul', and ordered her son to inspire her with a love for the ugliest of all men. It happened that Cupid himself fell in love with Psyche and, invisible, visited her every night. He ordered her not to attempt to see him and when, overcome by curiosity, she violated his command, he deserted her. Psyche wandered about the world seeking him, overcoming many obstacles placed in her way to Venus, until at last Jupiter granted her immortality and the lovers were reunited. The Greco-Roman conception of the love god, however, lacks the brilliance and subtlety of his Hindu counterpart, Kama.

Cyclopes
Literally, 'circle-eyed'. The one-eyed giants of

Greek mythology. Hesiod in his *Theogony*, composed soon after 700 BC, claimed that they gave to Zeus his special weapons, thunder and lightning. In the *Odyssey*, at least 150 years earlier, Homer had described the Cyclopes as 'overbearing and lawless'; they were ferocious pastoralists, given to cannibalism. Odysseus came up against their brutish leader Polyphemus, the son of Poseidon, in his cave near Mount Aetna in Sicily. By blinding the one-eyed giant in his drunken sleep with a brand, Odysseus and his surviving men were able to escape, though they earned the undying hatred of the sea god. The two legends jar and the Cyclopes, those strange giants with the single eye set in their foreheads, remain forever mysterious.

Daedalus
Legendary Greek craftsman. At the command of Minos, King of Crete, he designed and built the Labyrinth, in which was hidden the

Odysseus blinding the cyclops Polyphemus

Minotaur, a monstrous creature born of the strange love of Pasiphae, the Cretan queen, for a sea-born bull. Minos had asked Poseidon for a sign when he was contending with his brothers for the throne, and it happened that the splendid bull that god sent from the waves inspired in Pasiphae an ungovernable passion, which was gratified by means of a bronze cow into which she slipped so as to deceive the beast. Again this was the handiwork of 'cunning' Daedalus.

According to legend, Daedalus was imprisoned by Minos for revealing the secret of the Labyrinth, but escaped by constructing wings for himself and his son Icarus. Despite his father's warning the boy flew too close to the sun, the wax holding together his wings melted, and he fell into the sea and was drowned. Daedalus himself managed to touch down safely on Sicily.

Dagda
Literal meaning: 'the good god'. The ancient Irish deity of life and death; with one end of his staff he could kill nine men, but with the other

end he restored them to life. Dagda was chief of the Tuatha De Denann, and a mighty aid to these mythical peoples at the Second Battle of Mag Tuired. He was Aed, 'fire'; Ollathair, 'all-father'; Ruad Rofessa, 'lord of great know-ledge'; and the god of druidism or magic, *draidecht*. Among his sacred possessions were an inexhaustible cauldron, two marvellous swine—one always roasting, the other always growing—and ever-laden fruit trees.

His daughter was Brigit, goddess of fire, fertility, cattle, and poetry. She appears in Gallic and British inscriptions as Brigindo and Briganta; aspects of her personality passed to St Brigit (453–523), especially generosity. The Christian saint drove her father to despair, so freely did she hand out family property to the poor. Her good wishes were legendary: 'a great lake of ale of the King of Kings'; 'the family of heaven drinking it through all time'; 'Jesus to be among these cheerful folk'; and 'vessels full of arms to be given away'. St Brigit's Day is in fact the old festival of spring.

Danann

The mother of the ancient gods of Ireland and patroness of the Tuatha, the wizards. She may have had connections with rivers: her Hindu equivalent would be Danu, 'the waters of heaven', an early goddess. The same root is evident in European rivers: Don, Dnieper, Dniester, Donwy. The Tuatha De Danann, 'the peoples of goddess Danann', dominated Ireland before the coming of the Sons of Mil, the ancestors of the present inhabitants. After their defeat by the Sons of Mil, they were awarded the underground—'the hills and fairy regions, so that fairies under ground were subject to them'. The 'little people' of the popular fairy lore of Christian Ireland are therefore reductions of earlier pagan divinities.

Demeter

Demeter of Greece, Ceres of Italy—the goddess of vegetation and fruitfulness, especially corn—had several consorts, including Zeus and Poseidon. When the amorous sea god began to pursue Demeter, she was already engaged in seeking her abducted daughter Persephone. Demeter turned herself into a mare and mingled with grazing horses. Poseidon perceived the trick, and coupled with her in the shape of a stallion. Their offspring were a mysterious daughter and a black stallion. By Zeus the corn goddess bore

Persephone, the dying and reviving daughter. According to Orphic tradition—one of the Greek 'mystery' cults—Rhea as Demeter had forbidden Zeus to marry. At this the sky god sought to rape his mother. When Rhea turned herself into a serpent, Zeus did likewise, and as serpents they coupled together. When in turn Zeus enjoyed their daughter Persephone, he also assumed a serpent-like form and begot Dionysus.

The Athenians were ardent worshippers of Demeter. They claimed that Triptolemos, a legendary ancestor, had invented the plough and agriculture, and therefore civilization. It was he who started the rites at Eleusis, where artists showed him as a youth riding in a chariot and holding a sceptre and corn ears. Triptolemos, 'threefold warrior', may have been originally a war god, a slayer of people. The chthonic aspect of the Eleusinian mysteries was pronounced: 'Demeter's people' meant to the Athenians the dead.

Dies Irae

Literally, 'day of wrath'. The preoccupation of medieval Christians was the end of the world; they anticipated the Last Judgement, followed by the Millennium. After the fall of the Roman Empire in the West there was a revival of the belief in the end of time. The year 1000 likewise excited mythological speculation, as did famines, plagues, and earthquakes. Most influential were the views of the visionary Joachim of Fiore (1145–1202). He divided history into several ages and said that in 1260 would be the fulfilment of the Age of the Spirit, which had begun with St Benedict (480–550). At that time mankind could expect a new revelation, the coming of Antichrist, and the last days of wrath. This myth, written down at the behest of the Papacy, exerted a potent influence on medieval thought, and in its vision of a future world where the Holy Roman Empire and the Church of Rome would give place to a free community of perfected beings who have no need of clergy or sacraments or scripture, it anticipated modern millennial theories.

Dionysus

In Greek mythology, the youthful deity of vegetation, wine, and ecstasy. The son of Zeus by Semele, a Theban princess, Dionysus was 'the roaring one', a 'bull-horned god', because he often manifested himself as a bull, rampant with fertility and power. Dionysus' mother,

Dionysus and maenads; from a fifth-century BC amphora painted by Kleophrades

tricked by jealous Hera, demanded that her divine lover come to her in his true form and, since Zeus was the god of lightning, she was consumed to ashes. From her charred remains, however, Zeus took the unborn child and sewed it up in his thigh until it reached maturity. Thrace and Phrygia vied for the honour of Dionysus' birthplace, though he may have come from the island of Crete: to the Greeks, he was a foreign deity of incredible power—the Thebans refused his worship and were driven to legendary madness and murder. Dionysus was Dimetor, 'twice mothered'; Enorches, 'the betesticled'; Arsenothelys, 'the man-womanly'; Endendros, 'he in the tree'; Omadios, 'eater of raw flesh'; Mystes, 'the initiated'; while as Bromios and other titles he presided over the drunken frenzy of his devotees.

The chthonic aspect of Dionysus is evident in an alternative tale of his birth: serpentine Zeus coiling with Rhea, who had transformed herself into a snake to avoid her son's advances, begot Persephone, the wife of the underworld god Hades. Then again the writhing sky god mated, but with his daughter Persephone, who bore Dionysus. The snake is an arcane symbol of earth and water: like a river winding its way, the serpent creeps silently along the ground; it dwells in the earth and issues forth like a spring or a new shoot from its hole. Above all the serpent can

penetrate the tomb, and in sloughing its own skin represent the resurrection of the dead.

Dionysus was a popular deity, most of his followers being women—the maenads. They engaged in riotous, ecstatic dancing on mountains, and performed ceremonies which involved the rending of flesh—even human flesh. Worship of the great remover of inhibition was gradually tamed in the development of seasonable processions and sacred drama. Nevertheless, the wildness of Dionysus, his far-reaching influence over human emotions, remains imprinted on several legends. Most famous was the tragedy of Pentheus, King of Thebes. He attempted to stop the worship of the god but was torn to pieces by the maenads in their orgiastic fury—these wild devotees were actually led by his own mother.

Dionysus was always associated with the vine, but he was not, like his Roman counterpart Bacchus, solely a god of wine. In 186 BC the Roman Senate passed severe laws against the orgiastic rites of the imported 'mystery' cult. It is likely that several thousand people were executed before the official cult of the wine god Bacchus took root in Italy.

Dives

The medieval Christian personification of the rich man. Dives was doomed to hell fire, while his exact opposite the beggar Lazarus reposed in the bosom of Abraham. In iconography Dives appeared as the epitome of meanness, weighed down with his money-bag and tormented by devils.

Druids

An ancient Celtic order of priests, teachers, diviners, and magicians. The name itself is thought to relate to an oak tree or *drus*. Julius Caesar reports that the Druids met annually at a site believed to be the centre of Gaul; he also mentions a Chief Druid. The only detailed account of a Druidic ceremony we have was recorded by another Roman writer. It occurred at the time determined by the growth of mistletoe on an oak. A druid in a white robe climbed the tree and cut with 'a golden sickle' the branch of mistletoe, which was caught as it fell on a white cloak. Two white bulls were then sacrificed, and a feast took place. The meaning of this rite, like much else connected with this priesthood, remains obscure.

Empedocles

A native of Agrigentum in Sicily, this Greek philosopher flourished during the fifth century BC. Apart from writings and lectures, Empedocles was renowned for his success in curing diseases as well as his active support of democratic principles. Legend says that he disappeared in the flames of Mount Aetna, his intention being to confirm the report that he had become a god. This motive was imputed to him when the volcano threw up one of his bronze slippers. Fire may have been the cause of his teacher's death, too: the citizens of Crotona in Italy had set alight the school of Pythagoras some years before. Clearly a fraternity of philosophers had to run a city-state if it was not to be victimized like the Pythagoreans. The archetypal incendiary was, of course, Herostratus, who in 356 BC burned down the great temple of Artemis at Ephesus so as to immortalize himself.

Erinyes

Literal meaning: 'the angry ones'. They were the avenging deities of Greek mythology, the Furies who pursued the outragers of custom. These three chthonic goddesses, born of the blood of mutilated Ouranos in Gaia's womb, were imagined as ugly women, with serpents entwined in their hair, carrying torches and whips. They were pitiless, both in life and death; but, unlike Satan or other West Asian spirits of evil, the Erinyes were never wantonly malignant. Their names were Alecto, 'the never ending'; Tisiphone, 'voice of revenge'; and Megaira, 'envious anger'.

The Erinyes tracked down those who wrongly shed blood, and especially the blood of the mother. Thus they pursued Orestes because, despite the fact that he had acted in compliance with the direct command of Apollo, he had committed matricide. Sent abroad by his mother Clytemnestra while his father Agamemnon was away at the siege of Troy, so that she might enjoy her illicit affair with Aegisthus, Orestes came back to the city of Argos after Clytemnestra and Aegisthus had murdered Agamemnon on his return from the war. In revenge the son slew his mother and her lover. According to the dramatist Aeschylus (525–456 BC), the Erinyes were only persuaded to abandon their persecution after the acquittal of Orestes by the Areopagus, an ancient council over which Athena presided. The verdict of the trial calmed the anger of the Furies, and they were henceforth known as the Eumenides, 'the soothed goddesses'. It is likely, however, that the Greeks referred to them by this euphemism because they were frightened to use their real name.

Finn MacCool

Or Finn mac Cumaill; Fionn MacCumal. The *Fianna*, the old cycle of epic tales concerning Finn and his son Oisin, celebrate the splendours of the Irish kings in the third century. One of them, 'The Pursuit of Diarmaid and Grianni', is the prototype for the story of Tristan and Iseult.

A band of tried warriors, the Fenians, 'Finn's people', only admitted to their ranks the brave, the learned, and the able. One test would have disqualified most candidates: 'No man was taken till in the ground a hole had been made, such as would reach to the waist, and he put into it with his shield and a fore-arm's length of a hazel stick. Then must nine warriors, having nine spears, with a ten furrows' width between them and him, assail him and at the same time let fly at him. If he sustained injury, he was not received into the fellowship.'

Frey

Most famous of the vanir were the twin deities,

Frey and Freya, the son and daughter of Njord, the handsome sea god. In Germanic mythology the brother-sister gods were instrumental in bringing together the two divine races, the aesir and the vanir, so that Frey became assimilated with Frigg, the wife of Odin.

Frey means 'lord' and Freya 'lady', a circumstance suggesting connections with the cult of the sacred marriage in ancient West Asia. In the Uppsala temple, according to Adam of Bremen, there was about 1200 an image of Frey with a pronounced phallus; the priests actually called him Fricco, 'the lover', and his Roman counterpart was Priapus, the son of Dionysus, and Aphrodite. Just as Frey was the most handsome of the gods, having authority over rain, sunshine, and natural fruitfulness, so Freya was the most beautiful of the goddesses, sharing with Odin one half of the slain. On her journeys she used a trap driven by a pair of cats.

Frigg

In Germanic mythology, the wife of Odin, and the mother of the gods. A fertility goddess, who 'will tell no fortunes, yet well she knows the fates', Frigg must have come north before the vanir and in this movement lost the active aspects of her divinity. When Balder dreamed of impending harm, Frigg extracted a promise from all created things except the mistletoe that no harm should befall her son. Otherwise Frigg tended to be a rather passive deity: she knew the future but had no power to affect it.

Gawain

In Malory's *Morte d'Arthur*, published by Caxton in 1485, Sir Gawain is the perfect knight, the strict upholder of chivalry and the enemy of Sir Lancelot. In *Sir Gawain and the Green Knight*, an earlier alliterative poem, we find this reputation tested, and found wanting, in his strange encounter with Bercilak de Hautdesert, the Green Knight. This adventure began in King Arthur's hall on New Year's Eve, when a green giant challenged the knights to a beheading contest. Sir Gawain accepted and severed the stranger's head in a single blow. To the amazement of the company, the giant behaved as though nothing had happened. Calmly stooping, he picked up the head, and mounted his green charger. Then did the grisly lips move on the bloody head and bid Sir Gawain to meet him at a lonely chapel a year from that day—to receive his

share of the axe's keen edge. After many incidents, and temptations not entirely resisted, Sir Gawain kept the appointment, but flinched when the green giant swung his weapon. Although he returned to Camelot, Arthur's residence, with only a slight flesh wound, Sir Gawain was made to realize the inner wounds of his own imperfection.

Originally Gawain must have had solar connections: his strength waxed to noon and waned thereafter. He also owes something to Cuchulainn, the archetypal warrior of the Irish epics. They both wore a magic belt that rendered them invulnerable. The female enchantress whom Sir Gawain met on his quest was Morgan le Fay, the half-sister of King Arthur. She is also identified with Nineve, the mistress of Merlin.

Gogmagog

Or Gourmaillon, the giant figure cut into the chalk hills near Cambridge. Although the age and identity of this pre-Celtic figure remains a mystery, as do the other chalk-cut figures to be found in southern England, there can be little doubt that it was connected with the fertility rites of prehistoric religion. An Elizabethan edict actually forbade Cambridge undergraduates from attending festivities then held near Gogmagog; they were too lewd.

The legend of giants in Britain is old. In his *Historia Regum*, written in the twelfth century, Geoffrey of Monmouth states that the island was once peopled by a race of giants. They died out, and Trojan settlers led by Brut captured the last two. The name of Britain came from Brut the giant-killer.

Gorgons

In Greek mythology, three frightful sisters named Stheno, Euryale, and Medusa. They had snakes for hair and to look on them turned people to stone. Medusa, who alone of the trio was mortal, had at first a beautiful form, but she was changed by Athena into a winged monster because she slept with Poseidon, the sea god. The hero Perseus slew Medusa by never looking directly at her, but only at her reflection in his shield. Later traditions placed the Gorgons in Libya.

Other winged creatures were the Harpies, usually represented as women with bird's wings, sometimes as birds with women's heads. They lived in horrible places and had an insatiable hunger, which gave their faces a pallid, pinched appearance.

Grail

Sangreal, the Holy Grail. One of the most widespread legends of the Middle Ages. The Grail was said to be the vessel of the Last Supper and, at the Crucifixion, the one that received the blood which flowed from the spear thrust in Christ's side. Brought to Britain by Joseph of Arimathea, the rich man who buried Christ and founded the Christian settlement at Glastonbury, the Grail was later lost and its quest preoccupied King Arthur's knights. It was still in Britain, poets were quite sure, but in a mysterious castle surrounded by desolate lands and stretches of water. The custodian of the Grail was the Fisher King, who lay wounded and immobile, neither living nor dead. The recovery of the Fisher King, and the renewal of his blighted domain, was thought to depend on the successful completion of the quest. Only Sir Galahad, however, had a vision of the whole Grail.

The Church was always uneasy about the legend. It so patently retained links with the

Hades holding court in the underworld. A Greek vase-painting

insignia and utensils of pre-Christian rites. In the background stood the Celtic cauldron, whether the one used by the hag Ceridwen to prepare the three drops of inspiration, or the one capable of restoring the dead to life, the cauldron of rebirth discovered at the bottom of an Irish lake.

Grendel

The monster of the seventh-century Anglo-Saxon epic poem *Beowulf*. 'Grim and greedy, brutally cruel' was Grendel, the 'gruesome prowler of the border land, ranger of the moors, the fens, and the fastness'. To rid the Danish King Hrothgar of this terror, the young warrior prince Beowulf set a trap and in the fierce struggle tore off Grendel's arm. Later, Beowulf slew the monster's enraged mother and, finding Grendel on his deathbed, cut off his head. Four men were needed to lug the trophy back.

Hades

In Greek mythology, one of the world-ruling sons of Kronos; the brother of Zeus; and the husband of Persephone. At the division of the universe after the overthrow of Kronos, Zeus took the sky, Poseidon the sea, and Hades the underworld; the earth was to be shared between them. 'The house of Hades' was the habitation of the shades, the dead. Its ruler had the name Polydegmon, 'receiver of many guests', on account of the multitudes who streamed through its portals. Hades was a subterranean Zeus—*chthonios*, of the dark realm, as opposed to the cult of the sky god, *hypsistos*. So fierce and inexorable was the god of death that his worshippers used to avert their eyes when making a sacrifice. They called him Pluto, 'the giver of wealth', because no one wished to pronounce the dreaded name of Hades. This title refers of course to the blessings of the earth: crops, minerals, and clear water from springs. Hades as a place for the dead was a late development, but even then this dim realm bore no resemblance to the Christian hell. It was never a place of punishment.

Hecate

Literally, 'the distant one'. Associated by the Greeks with the moon, Hecate had a beneficent influence over such activities as farming, but she was also a goddess of the dark hours—ghosts and witchcraft fascinated the distant one who dwelt 'on tombs', at places 'where two roads crossed', or 'near the blood of murdered persons'. The Athenians propitiated her zealously, placing offerings of food at cross-roads each month. Hecate was the cousin of Artemis, the divine huntress.

Hephaistos

The Greek smith god. He was lame as a result of having interfered in a quarrel between his parents, Zeus and Hera. So angry did Zeus become that he flung his son out of Olympus and let him fall heavily on the island of Lemnos. A late variant of the legend states that Hephaistos was born a dwarfish figure, with a limp, and that in disgust Hera threw him into the deep, where he would have drowned had not sea nymphs rescued him.

Hephaistos appears to have been imported from Asia Minor. He was associated with subterranean fires; the Greeks thought Lemnos showed signs of volcanic activity. In Athens, along with other centres of industry, the fire god was transformed into the deity of craftsmen who used fire for their trades. His own workshop was located within Mount Aetna in Sicily, an idea the Romans adopted for their analogue Vulcan.

Hera

Literally, 'lady'. The earth goddess of Argos, a pre-Greek deity, assimilated as the daughter of Kronos and Rhea, and the sister-wife of Zeus. She was the protectress of marriage, childbirth, and the home. Often her jealousy and quarrelsomeness led to disaster for gods, heroes, and men, when she harried Zeus' mistresses and persecuted their children. Against the baby Hercules, whom Zeus begot on Alcmene, she sent two serpents, but the infant hero strangled them in his cradle. This ancient superman, however, was eventually the victim of Hera's 'harsh anger'. When Zeus bore Athena without her assistance, Hera gave birth to Typhaon without him. This terrible creature resembled neither gods nor men, and is reminiscent of the monster Typhon, which challenged Zeus on behalf of the original earth goddess Gaia.

Hercules

Or Heracles. The greatest of the heroes in Greek mythology. Son of the Theban Alcmene and Zeus. Hercules' life was shaped by the animosity of Hera, who pursued him with relentless hostility. She drove him mad so that he killed his own family. To expiate this dreadful crime he undertook the famous twelve labours. They were: the killing of the Nemean lion, a feat he achieved with his bare hands; the killing of the Hydra, a nine-headed dragon sacred to Hera; the capture of the Arcadian stag; the killing of the Erymanthian boar; the cleansing of the Augean stables, which contained 3,000 oxen; the killing of the Stymphalian birds, vicious creations of the war god Ares; the capture of the bull which Poseidon had sent to King Minos of Crete; the capture of the flesh-eating horses of Thrace; the seizure of the girdle of the Queen of the Amazons, the nation of female warriors; the capture of the oxen of Geryon, a Spanish king with three heads, six hands, and three bodies joined together at the waist; fetching the golden apples of the Hesperides, female guardians of the fruit that Gaia gave to Hera

*Hercules killing the Stymphalian birds; from a
sixth-century BC Attic vase*

at her marriage with Zeus; and, finally, bringing the three-headed dog Cerberus from the
underworld.

Hercules was a popular figure with the
ancient Greeks, who had a conspicuous
predilection for semi-divine heroes. Of his
mythical contemporaries—Perseus, Theseus,
Jason, or Asclepius—he came the closest to
full divine honours. In the fifth century BC
Pindar called him *heros theos*, 'hero god'.
Another unusual thing about this superman
was that he had no grave. His remains did not
belong to any city or state; from the funeral
pyre he was translated directly to Mount
Olympus. Without hesitation the Romans
later adopted Hercules as the god of physical
strength.

Hermaphroditos

Son of Hermes, the divine messenger, and
Aphrodite, the goddess of love. According to a
Greek legend, this lovely boy of fifteen visited
Asia Minor, and excited the passion of
Salmakis, the nymph of a fountain near
Halicarnassus. When Hermaphroditos spurn-
ed all her advances, Salmakis prayed to the
gods that she might be united with him for
ever. The wish was granted and her opportunity came as he bathed in the enchanted
waters of the fountain. Salmakis boldly
embraced Hermaphroditos: the nymph and
the wonderful boy merged physically, and
since then hermaphrodite has meant female
boy—yet not like Phrygian Attis, who cut
away his manhood.

Hermes

In Greek mythology, the son of Zeus and the nymph Maia. A popular deity, Hermes was the messenger of the gods who often led men astray. As a *psychopompos*, 'leader of souls', he escorted the dead to the underworld, the realm of Hades. This function explains the later identification of the Germanic god Odin with Mercury, the Roman version of Hermes: Odin was father of the slain.

Hermes was looked upon as the patron of good luck and fortune, the patron of merchants and thieves. Winged sandals helped him steal the cows belonging to his half-brother Apollo, while winged thoughts saved him from Apollo's rage, for he gave as a trespass-offering his invention, the lyre. He was also the god of roads and a god of fertility, aspects that were included in the *hermeia*, quadrangular pillars with a bust of the god set on top and a phallus carved below. In their earliest form these wayside shrines of his were just heaps of stones, and travellers, seeking his protection, would add one to the heap. As time went on, the customary gesture became the pouring of a libation of oil. In the third century BC Theophrastus, making fun of superstition, wrote that a certain man 'when he goes by the carved shafts at cross-roads, pours oil on them from his flask, falls on his knees, makes an obeisance, and only then moves on'. Today the mountainous roads of Greece are provided with small Christian pillar shrines, the saintly descendants of the hermeia.

Janus

An old Italian deity, represented with two faces, looking different ways. His double-gated temple on the Forum in Rome had a symbolic significance: it was open in time of war and closed in time of peace. Janus may have been connected with the fortunes of war because any army had to pass through a gateway in order to start a campaign. An *ianua*, 'entrance gate', has two sides and presumably represents the two possible outcomes of any future event—success or failure.

From this military association Janus developed into a god of all 'beginnings'. The month of January was sacred to him—today Europeans continue to look forwards and backwards at this time—while as Janus Quadrifrons, 'four heads', he presided over the four seasons. The Romans named Janus first in any list of gods invoked in prayer.

Jason

Legendary Greek hero and leader of the Argonauts, the stalwarts who sailed to Colchis in the ship *Argo* to seize the Golden Fleece. Jason crossed a sea of marvels, accomplished difficult tasks, circumvented the guardian dragon, and returned with the fleece and the power to topple a usurper. Part of this success was due to the magic of a Colchian princess, Medea, whom Jason made his wife, with assistance from the goddess Athena. Medea seems to have been associated with dismemberment. When the *Argo* hastened away with its prize, she suggested that they cut up her brother Apsyrtus and throw the bits overboard in order to slow down the swift pursuit of their father, King Aietes. This the Argonauts did, forcing the Colchians to gather up the remains for a decent burial. When the heroes returned to Greece, Medea persuaded the daughters of King Pelias of Iolcus to cut their father to pieces and boil him, so as to restore him to youth. This they did, with the expected consequence, and thereby avenged the death of Jason's own father.

After a few years Jason deserted Medea for Glauce, but the former wife was revenged by killing Glauce and their children. The hero himself died when a piece of the rotting *Argo* fell on his head. The myths collected around Jason are an amalgam of diverse elements: the hero's name, for instance, means 'healer' and suggests that he began as a rather different figure.

Juno

In Roman mythology, the queen of heaven and wife of Jupiter. Her origin is obscure, but she seems to have been an Italian mother goddess. At Rome she was worshipped along with Jupiter and Minerva. As the genius of womanhood, she ensured fecundity, childbirth, and marriage. The month of June, once called Junonius, was considered to be the most favourable month for weddings. At Veii, an Etruscan city, Juno had the second name Regina, 'queen'. Later she was identified with the Greek goddess Hera.

Jupiter

Or Jove. The Latin version of the Indo-European sky god. Together with Juno and Minerva, he formed the trinity of gods worshipped in the temple situated on the Capitoline Hill of Rome. The cult of Jupiter Optimus Maximus, 'best and greatest', was instituted under the Etruscan kings, their own highest god being called Tinia.

Originally a sky god connected with the elements and the agricultural cycle, Jupiter developed into a special protector of the Roman people. Added to Tonans, 'thunderer', and Fulgur, 'wielder of lightning', were such titles as Imperator, 'supreme commander', Invictus, 'invincible', Triumphator, 'triumphant', and Praedator, 'booty snatcher'. With the development of urbanization and the increasing importance of the city, it was only natural that the tutelary deity, like Marduk in Babylon, should have risen to greater preeminence, while his associate Mars shed agricultural associations for a more bellicose disposition. Under the name of Jupiter Capitolinus, he presided over the Roman games, always an important feature of ancient city life. The introduction of emperor worship, a means of testing the loyalty of a subject as much as an official religion, did reduce Jupiter's political function somewhat, though traitors were still thrown down from the Tarpeian rock on Capitoline Hill. He was no longer the sole embodiment of the greatness and prosperity of the Roman Empire. Instead, he became the divine guide of the world, directing the destinies of mankind from afar. Cicero, who in 43 BC had his head and hands cut off for advocating a return to republican principles, equated Jove with *numen praestantissimae mentis*, 'the awful presence of a supreme mind'. It was a conception not unlike the monotheism of Christianity, to which the conversion of Emperor Constantine in 312 meant the beginning of the end of the pagan era in Europe.

Kronos

Or Cronos. In Greek mythology, Kronos was the Titan son of Gaia, earth, and Ouranos, sky. He emasculated his sky father and seized control of the world. Marrying his sister Rhea he followed the example of Ouranos in disposing of his sons, because of the warning given by an oracle that he would be displaced by one of them. Kronos swallowed the children as soon as they were born, but on Gaia's advice his wife gave him a stone wrapped in swaddling clothes instead of the infant Zeus, who was taken secretly to Crete in order to grow up in safety there. When Zeus had attained full stature, he obliged Kronos to vomit up his brothers and sisters—Poseidon, Hades, Hera, Hestia, and Demeter—as well as

release his uncles and aunts whom Kronos had chosen not to unfetter on the deposition of Ouranos. The most important of these were the Cyclopes, single-eyed giants, who in gratitude gave Zeus thunder and lightning, thereafter his emblems and instruments of power. In the ensuing struggle Kronos and the Titans lost: the former was exiled along with a portion of the Golden Age to the Isles of the Blest, at the outermost edge of the earth, while the Titans were thrown into Tartarus, a land situated beneath Hades. The inhabitants of Tartarus—in time others joined the enchained Titans there—were not so much great offenders as offenders of the great.

Rhea, the wife and sister of Kronos, was identified with Cybele, the mother goddess of Phrygia. The ecstatic dances of her devotees, noted for the loud clashing noise involved, were said to have drowned the cries of the Zeus child hidden in the Cretan cave from Kronos. Clearly this is a mythical explanation of the ritual connected with the orgiastic worship of a West Asian earth goddess.

Kul

The Siryan water spirit, an evil being living in deep waters. It had a human shape. Among neighbouring peoples, however, Kul-jungk or 'fish spirit' did not have a malevolent character, but was regarded as the genius of fishes. Immemorial custom decreed that on the breaking up of the ice on rivers, in late spring, a fish-like image made of wood or birch bark be taken along to the fishing place. Thus a portion of the first catch was dedicated to the fish god, who like the bear god Leib-olmai assisted northern men in their hard struggle for survival.

Lancelot

Lancelot du Lac, Launcelot of the Lake; the most attractive and splendid of King Arthur's knights, even though he betrays his allegiance to his lord, disgraces the ideal of stainless chivalry, and renders himself, through his adulterous love for Queen Guinevere, incapable of the quest of the Holy Grail. He was stolen when one year old and reared by the Lady of the Lake, Nimue, who also bestowed on Arthur the unfailing sword, Excalibur. Sir Lancelot was the ideal knight, from the female standpoint, for his love of Guinevere shaped his entire destiny. After the un-death of Arthur, Lancelot became a priest and tended the King's grave.

Leib-olmai

Literal meaning: 'alder man'. The bear man, or bear god, honoured by the Lapps: he it was who gave luck to the hunter, preventing injury in the skirmish with the bear. At bear feasts the hunters' faces were sprinkled with extract of alder bark, a ritual in honour of Leib-olmai.

An unfriendly forest spirit, quite the opposite of the bear god, was Ovda, the assailant of Finnish woodsmen. Ovda wandered in the forest as a naked human being, but its feet were turned backwards. Sometimes it appeared as a man, sometimes as a woman. The method of destruction used by Ovda was ingenious: it enticed people to dance or wrestle, and then tickled or danced them to death.

Limbo

The realm of the virtuous pagan dead. Christianity dealt with the problem of those who lived virtuously before the coming of Christ and unbaptized infants by placing these souls in a special part of Hell, called Limbo. Here they suffered no pain, but were excluded from heavenly bliss. In the *Divina Commedia* the poet Dante (1265–1321) is guided through this place by Virgil, a resident himself.

Loki

The 'mischief maker' of the Germanic gods. Fickle and false, clever and cunning, the trickster god Loki was 'the father of lies'. Probably a personification of the forest fire, one of the most destructive agencies known to ancient peoples, 'the sly god' ultimately would hasten ragnarok, the twilight of the gods. Through his enmity Balder descended to hel, the prison of death, and the forces of evil mustered on the Vigrid plain for the final battle.

Of an ogress Loki begot three dreadful offspring: the wolf Fenrir, the sea serpent Jormungandr, and Hel, queen of hel. These evil creatures, along with the subjects of Hel, formed the army against whom the gods under Odin and Thor fought vainly in the ragnarok. Then Loki, as the fire giant Sutr, reduced everything to ashes.

Lucretia

The rape of Lucretia was the crime that toppled the semi-legendary Etruscan kings of Rome. In 510 BC Sextus Tarquinius, the son of King Tarquinius Superbus, violated this Roman matron, who stabbed herself and died.

Lucretia's funeral roused the people and their anger was turned by the eloquence of Lucius Junius Brutus into a desire for the abolition of the monarchy. Thus later Roman historians construed the mythical foundation of the Republic.

Manannan mac Lir

The eponymous hero of the Manxmen. He was their first king and a great magician or medicine-man. *Inis Manann*, the Isle of Man, may have been an early centre for trade: Manannan was 'son of the Sea', *mac Lir*, the most renowned pilot in the west of Europe, and the trader who gave to King Cormac of Ireland the magic cup and branch. A sea god, Manannan appears in Irish and Welsh stories along with other wizards or magician kings.

Mars

Next to Jupiter, Mars enjoyed the highest honours at Rome. Exalting military power and glory, the Romans raised this war god far above the status of his Greek counterpart Ares. The Greeks had conceived Ares as an unpopular deity—bloodthirsty, brutal, he was a braggart, even a coward. Mars, on the contrary, was considered the father of Romulus, who built the walls of Rome. The war god also protected farmers and herdsmen.

Merlin

The archetypal wizard of Arthurian legend. He brought together the royal couple who were to become Arthur's parents, King Uther Pendragon and Igraine, who at the time was the wife of the Duke of Cornwall. He accomplished the seduction by magic arts, and then he himself watched over Arthur's youth, preparing him in secret for the hour of his destiny. According to one tradition, he also used his magic to build Stonehenge. The stones came from Ireland and they were erected as a monument to British nobles killed by the Saxons. Another work to his credit was the Round Table, a copy of which may still exist at Winchester.

Merlin himself had been begotten upon a king's daughter by a mysterious youth who came at night to her nun's cell. In his *Historia Regum*, written in the twelfth century, Geoffrey of Monmouth reckoned that Merlin's father was a demon. So potent an influence did his prophecies have on medieval Europe that they were included in the *Index* by the Council of Trent. Merlin's end was

The Winchester round table, said to have been the work of Merlin

testimony of the overwhelming power of the fairy world, a recurrent notion in Celtic mythology. Because of his love for Nineve, possibly the daughter of a Sicilian siren, he taught her enough magic lore to be placed under one of her spells. Thus he was trapped forever in an enchanted wood. As he told Sir Gawain, who once passed him: 'I am also the greatest fool. I love another more than I love myself, and I taught my beloved how to bind me to herself, and now no one can set me free.'

Minerva

The Roman goddess of wisdom and the arts, identified with the Greek Athena. Her name may contain the same root as *mens*, meaning thought. Her cult was widespread in Italy, though only at Rome did she take on an extremely warlike character. There Minerva was represented with a helmet, shield, and a coat of mail; and the spoils of war were dedicated to her.

Moirai

The Greek goddesses of Fate. Their genealogy is confused and reflects their change from chthonic deities associated with death to the controllers of human destiny, those who decide what must befall the individual. There were usually three Moirai: Klotho, 'the spinner'; Lachesis, 'the apportioner'; and Alropos 'the inevitable'. A late idea was that the Fates span a length of yarn which represented the alloted span for a mortal.

Naglfar

A ghastly ship made from the nail parings of the dead. Hence the obligation among Germanic peoples to ensure that none went to the grave with nails unshorn. At ragnarok, the destruction of the gods, the *Naglfar* would slip its moorings in the violent seas whipped up by the enraged sea monster Jormungandr.

Num

The sky god of the Samoyeds. The heavens were supreme in Uralian cosmology, the Voguls even believed that their sky god Numi-torem sent down animals to the forests and fishes to the rivers. No representation of Num was fashioned by the Samoyeds, but a myth tells how he sent birds to explore the watery chaos at the beginning of the world, and made land from the mud that one of them brought back in its beak. In Finnish traditions an eagle flew over the limitless waters, searching for a dry spot to lay its eggs. Suddenly it caught sight of the knee of the sorcerer Vainamoinen protruding above the surface of the water. There the eagle made a nest and laid its egg. When the slumbering sorcerer felt some discomfort in his knee, he stirred, changed the

position of his limbs, and inadvertently caused the egg to fall into the water. It broke at once: the yolk became the sun and moon, while the pieces of shell formed the earth and the stars.

Vainamoinen, the archetypal magician of the far North, was the son of Ilmatar, the air goddess. A cultural founder hero, he invented the zither and his playing of this ancient instrument filled the forests with delight. Wild animals grew tame and the turmoil of the elements ceased. Vainamoinen also led an expedition to find the arcane *sampo*, which seems to have 'ground out' prosperity.

Odysseus

Or Ulysses to the Romans. This Greek hero was King of Ithaca, a small island in the Ionian Sea. He took part in the Trojan War and earned the title Sisyphides for his devious schemes, the most successful of which was undoubtedly the wooden horse. Deceived by various ruses, the Trojans dragged this wheeled contraption into their impregnable city, and with it the Greeks hidden in its hollow belly. Odysseus was among these soldiers, who emerged at night and opened the gates to their waiting comrades.

After the sack of Troy, Odysseus began his homeward journey to Ithaca and this, the subject of Homer's *Odyssey*, composed in the ninth century BC, took ten years, even though the goddess Athena gave Odysseus her special protection. His adventures were many: in Sicily he acquired the undying enmity of Poseidon by blinding the sea god's son, the Cyclops Polyphemus; he encountered the Laestrygones, a cannibal race; on Circe's island he resisted spells, with the aid of Hermes, and compelled the enchantress to restore to human shape his men who had been turned into swine; his crew narrowly avoided shipwreck by the alluring Sirens, the bird women of storms, and by monstrous Scylla, a six-headed inhabitant of a cave in the straits between Italy and Sicily; he visited the Lotophagi, 'lotus-eaters', descended to the underworld, and spent years on the island of the nymph Calypso; before, the lone survivor, he returned in disguise to Ithaca and found his palace occupied by fifty suitors. He persuaded his wife Penelope to promise her hand to the suitor capable of bending a mighty bow. Only Odysseus could string it, and with its deadly shafts he slew the suitors to a man. In the fight his only allies were two faithful servants and his young son Telemachus.

Odin

In Germanic mythology, the one-eyed deity of battle, magic, inspiration, and the dead. The elder son of Bor by the giantess Bestla, Odin was 'supreme as well as being the oldest of the gods'. Writing in the thirteenth century, Snorri Sturluson, the outstanding Icelandic scholar and statesman, thus endeavoured to account for the rise of Odin during the Viking period (750–1050), when the war god took over many of the functions of the sky god. 'He had his way in all things. Mighty as the other gods may be, yet they all serve him as children do their father.' Odin was Alfodr, 'father of the gods'; Valfodr, 'father of the slain'; Veratyr, 'lord of men'; Bileygr and Baleygr, 'shifty-eyed' and 'flaming-eyed'; Glapsvidir, 'swift in deceit'; Fjolsvidr, 'wide in wisdom'; Farmatyr, 'god of cargoes'; Oski, 'wish giver'; Sidfodr, 'father of victories'; and many more *ekenames*, nicknames, given to Odin 'for something he did'.

Odin—sometimes Voden, Woden, Wotan, Wuotan—probably meant wild or furious. He inspired the frightful *berserkers*, maddened warriors who rushed naked into the midst of the fray. As Valfodr, he adopted as his sons all the casualties of battle: Valhalla, the hall of the slain, was filled with *einherjar*, the souls of champions gathered there by the Valkyries. At an early stage Odin must have displaced Tyr, the Germanic derivative of the original Indo-European sky god, for the one-handed Tyr was called 'son of Odin'. Tyr was an old synonym for 'god', and the chief myth by which the deposed Alfodr was remembered shows him as the guardian of the sky. When he stopped the wolf Fenrir from devouring 'the light' of heaven, namely the sun and moon, his hand was bitten off in the wolf's jaws. While Tyr—the Tvisto noted by Tacitus in 98—adjusted to a lesser role as a war god in late Germanic mythology, Odin and his two brothers, Vili and Ve, were elevated into the rank of creator deities. Odin, the Alfodr, existed 'from the beginning of time'; he 'created heaven and earth and sky and all within them'; and he ruled 'with absolute power'.

Odin, Vili, and Ve—the sons of Bor—fought Ymir, the senior frost giant. They slew the mighty giant, and so much blood poured from his wounds that all the frost giants got drowned except Bergelmir and his wife. The sons of Bor then took Ymir's carcass to *ginnungagap*, the primordial abyss, and made the soil from his flesh, the mountain crags from his bones, and boulders from his toes. Out of the excess of blood they formed the lakes and seas. Maggot-like within the carcass of Ymir, innumerable dwarfs grew up, and at the word of the gods they acquired human intelligence and shape. Their dwelling-place was inside the earth and the rocks. Ymir's skull was made into heaven, the means of suspension being four dwarfs, and the giant's brains, flung into the wind, became the clouds.

This creation-and-flood myth was given a biblical overtone in the sixteenth century, when Bergelmir was not saved by 'climbing up on to his mill', but by 'going up in his boat'. The other great myth of Bor's sons concerns the creation of men. One day they discovered on the sea-shore two logs of driftwood, which they picked up and whittled into mankind. Odin gave 'the precious soul', Vili the understanding as well as the emotions, and Vi the faculties and form. It is a story that chimes with the original duty of Odin as a wind god, a leader of souls rushing through the air. An entry of 1127 in the *Old English Chronicle* relates how one night many people observed huntsmen in the sky. The 'were black, huge, and hideous, and rode on black horses and on black he-goats, and their hounds were jet black, with eyes like saucers, and horrible. This was seen in the very deer park of the town of Peterborough, and in all the woods that stretch from that town to Stamford, and all through the night the monks heard them sounding and winding their horns.' Even after conversion to Christianity, it seems that the furious host of Odin Atridr, 'the rider', continued to haunt the Germanic skies.

A factor in the ultimate decline of Odin worship and the rise of Christianity in northern Europe was undoubtedly the increased emphasis on violence, which roughly coincided with the era of Viking expansionism. The fatalistic warriors of the longboats were fascinated by the concept of ragnarok, the destruction of the gods. Just as the cycle of Germanic mythology started at a world awash with Ymir's blood, so the final scene was a battlefield on the immense plain of Vigrid, where the gods were predetermined to gush out their own blood. Ragnarok, the twilight of the gods, commenced with the death of Balder, Odin's second son, and the realization by the gods that, in Loki, the forest fire and the murderer, they had tolerated the growth of evil. Although they secured Loki with chains, they knew that it was too late. The end was at hand: 'a wind age, a wolf age'. The wolf Fenrir managed to swallow the sun and bite the moon, while Jormungandr the sea serpent boiled up the deep, blowing clouds of poison all over the earth and sky. On the Vigrid plain the forces of evil were mustered—Fenrir and Jormungadr along with Loki and Hrymr who led the frost giants—and against them marched the gods and the einherjar, in full knowledge of their impending defeat. Then Yggdrasil, the cosmic ash, trembled as terror seized the world. In the mêlée fell Odin, Thor, Tyr, the wolf Fenrir, and the sea serpent as well as myriad combatants, till at last Surtr, the 'black' fire giant form of Loki, pitched flames over the earth and turned heaven to cinders. The description of this catastrophe bears a striking resemblance to what happened in the volcanic eruptions on Iceland, like that of Mount Hekla in the eighteenth century. After the ragnarok, possibly a purely Scandinavian idea, 'the earth shall rise up green and fair out of the sea, and plants shall grow where none shall be sown. An idyllic age will ensue, Snorri wrote, and all 'shall live in love'.

Other myths about Odin tell of his feats in the various worlds. *Svipall*, 'changing', he wandered in disguise, most often as an old man with a staff—one-eyed, grey-bearded and wearing a floppy brimmed hat. To obtain the gift of wisdom Odin had thrown one of his eyes into the well of Mimir, a renowned sage. Connected with the underworld, this mysterious well was located under one of the roots of Yggdrasil. Another version is that Odin received Mimir's severed head, which he preserved with herbs and magic spells. A Celtic parallel is the speaking head of Bran. Quite different is the wisdom-winning myth in which Odin hung himself upon the cosmic ash in order to learn the secret runes. A 2,000-year-old naked man found preserved in Tollund bog, Jutland, in 1950, may have been hanged on a sacrificial gallows in remembrance of Odin. Lastly, the inspiration of poetry, a wonderful mead created by dwarfs from honey mixed with the blood of Kvasir, a supremely wise man, Odin obtained through stealth.

Oedipus

Literal meaning: 'swollen-foot'. Son of Laius, King of Thebes, and Queen Jocasta. His father, having learnt from an oracle that he

was doomed to perish by the hands of his own son, exposed Oedipus on a mountainside, immediately after his birth, with his feet pierced and tied together. The child was found by a shepherd, who took him to the childless King and Queen of Corinth; they brought Oedipus up as their own son.

In his youth Oedipus was told by the Oracle at Delphi that he would kill his father and marry his mother and, horrified, he resolved never to return to Corinth. Ignorant of his true ancestry, he set out for Thebes and on the road encountered King Laius, whom he slew in a quarrel over the right-of-way. Near the city he answered the riddle of the Sphinx, then a plague to all travellers, and for defeating this monstrous female winged-lion, the Thebans made him their king. He married the widowed Jocasta and so, unwittingly, fulfilled the prophecy. In time he became aware of the patricide and incest: this self-discovery caused him to blind himself before going into exile, where in the grove of Colonus near Athens the Eumenides finally released Oedipus from an earthly existence. Jocasta hanged herself shortly afterwards.

Oisin

Or Ossian. 'Little deer', the Irish hero who spent 300 years as King of *tir na n-Og*, 'the land of youth'. In a wood he encountered a mysterious being with the beautiful body of a woman, but the head of a pig. She declared that the head was due to a Druidic spell, promising that it would vanish the very minute he would marry her. This happened, and they lived happily in 'the land of youth' for many years. When Oisin wished to visit Ireland again, his wife told him centuries had passed, but if he must go, then he was to ride on a white steed and let not his own foot touch the ground. Unfortunately, he slipped, and in an instant the marvellous steed was dead and Oisin lay on the ground a blind old man.

Orpheus

Legendary Greek poet and hero. The son of Apollo and the muse Calliope, Orpheus was a great musician, his playing moved not only animals and plants but even rocks and the elements. When his wife Eurydice died of a snake bite, Orpheus descended to the underworld, where his lyre 'drew iron tears' from Hades, god of death. His wife was delivered up to him, but according to one legend he lost her again. His grief for Eurydice led him to despise other women, who in revenge tore him to pieces under the excitement of their Dionysiac orgies. The doctrines of Orphism, a Greek 'mystery' cult, were derived from poems attributed to Orpheus.

Ouranos
Hesiod in the seventh century BC traced the genealogy of the Greek gods back to the divine pair Ouranos and Gaia, sky and earth. Passionate was their relationship, since Ouranos 'drawing near and spreading out in all directions, eager from love, enveloped the earth in all directions'. But it was also destructive: Ouranos permanently coupling with Gaia meant that the sky could hold back their children in the earth's womb. One of these buried offspring, Kronos, the youngest son, determined to overthrow the sky father of hated name. Gaia having conceived a mighty sickle with sharp teeth, Kronos swung this weapon so well that he cut off Ouranos' phallus within the earth's body. Emasculated sky was thus separated from earth—pushed asunder as in West Asian myth by the first of the gods—and from his blood Gaia conceived the 'strong ones', the Erinyes, the Titans, and other creatures, while the fallen phallus engendered in the sea Aphrodite. Ouranos then passed into oblivion and Kronos ruled the universe, taking to wife his sister Rhea. This period was the Golden Age, when the Titans lived. But Kronos, too, disposed of his sons, being warned by an oracle that he would be displaced by one of them, till Zeus was born and rescued from this fate by his mother. After a long struggle his children, led by Zeus, defeated Kronos and the Titans, whom they dispatched to Tartarus deep beneath the surface of the earth.

The deposition of Ouranos recalls the narrative in the *Song of Ullikumi*, an Hurrian myth of the second millennium BC. Kumarbi dealt with his tyrannical father in a more drastic way. He swallowed the divine member, becoming pregnant with several 'terrible gods', including the storm god Teshub, who was destined to cause his own overthrow. In Hesiod the theogonic succession is Ouranos, Kronos, Zeus. Two centuries earlier Homer still knew of the primeval waters; 'Okeanos from whom the gods are sprung'; but for Hesiod the original chaos of the murky deep is allegorized as the child of Ouranos and Gaia. Okeanos becomes the surrounding waters where earth meets sky.

Pan
The Greek worshippers of this goat-horned, goat-legged god were none too certain whether he was a single deity or a group of deities. Legend makes Pan the son of Hermes, and the favourite of Dionysus, the fertility god. His birthplace was Arcadia, the pastoral state in the centre of the Peloponnese. Pan played on the syrinx and haunted caves and lonely rural places. He was playful and energetic, but irritable, especially if disturbed during his siesta. He could inspire fear, a sudden groundless fright, in both men and animals. By blowing on a conch shell he created panic when Zeus led the gods against Kronos and the Titans. Like other Olympians, he enjoyed chasing nymphs, and especially Echo.

The death of Pan was reported during the reign of the Roman Emperor Tiberius (AD 14–37). A ship sailing from Greece to Italy was becalmed off the island of Paxos. Suddenly a voice from the shore three times cried, 'Tammuz!' The pilot, whose name was Tammuz, answered, and the voice said, 'Tell them that great Pan is dead.' When the vessel drifted shoreward elsewhere, the pilot shouted that the god was dead, whereupon arose the sound of great weeping. On arriving in Italy the pilot was summoned by the Emperor, and scholars called in to interpret the event decided that the Pan in question was not the god but a demon of the same name. In all probability the mariners were privy to a ceremonial lament for Adonis, or even the Babylonian Tammuz. Early Christians took comfort from the story, believing that it marked the beginning of the end of the pagan era.

Persephone
Persephone of Greece, Proserpina of Italy— the queen of the underworld—was abducted by Hades, son of Kronos and Rhea. She was playing with the daughters of Okeanos, the circular ocean, picking flowers on a lush meadow, when she beheld the hundred-blossomed narcissus planted by the earth mother Gaia to please the god of death, Hades. As Persephone bent to pluck it with both hands, a chasm appeared in the ground, and from it rose Hades, who seized her and carried her down to his realm. Immediately the springs of fertility ran dry: vegetation languished, animals ceased to multiply, and the hand of death touched mankind. The mother of Persephone—Demeter to the Greeks, Ceres to the Romans—wandered upon the earth,

with two burning torches in her hands. She would neither eat nor wash. Zeus finally intervened and ruled that his subterranean brother must give up the captured bride unless she had, by some word or deed, consented to her abduction. It happened that she had eaten a pomegranate seed at Hades' behest, which was adequate to ensure that henceforth she divided her time equally between her husband and her mother.

Persephone could have been a pre-Greek goddess of the underworld. As Kore, 'the maiden', she was the power of growth within the corn itself, an extension of the corn goddess Demeter, her mother. Her annual disappearance and the distress it caused was only matched by the joy of the gods on her return to Mount Olympus. The myth was in fact an account of the sacred drama performed

Pan playing knuckle bones with Aphrodite; from the back of a fourth-century BC Greek mirror

at Eleusis, near Athens. During the summer heat, after the harvest was gathered in, the corn goddess vanished beneath the parched earth, like the corn stored in underground silos. The Eleusisian mysteries included a sacred marriage as well as other initiation rites common to the fertility cults of West Asia. In Athens 'Demeter's people' was a euphemism for the dead.

Perseus

Legendary Greek hero. The son of the Argive princess Danaë and Zeus, who came to her in the form of a golden shower. Perseus killed the Gorgon Medusa and presented her head to the goddess Athena, who had given him a mirror shield.

Perunu

The ancient Slavic thunder-god. He was the pre-eminent deity, even a creator god, and at Kiev he had an important cult centre till the tenth century. Though there are obvious parallels with the Germanic Thor, an overlap suggesting influence, it is likely that Perunu derived from an autochthonous cult of the thunderbolt in Russia. His name is connected with the oak, the oak forest, or the oak-wooded hill. Details of a ritual for rain-making survive: a chaste girl, naked and draped with flowers, whirled ecstatically in the middle of a ring, invoking the fructifying moisture of Perunu. Whirling and drinking seem to have played a not inconsiderable part in his worship. Perunu was portrayed as a man, usually 'carved out of wood with a silver head and a gold moustache'.

Poseidon

A leading member of the Greek pantheon. The son of Kronos and Rhea, and the brother of Zeus and Hades, Poseidon was the ruler of the waves, a sea god liable to attacks of tempestuous rage. He rode the deep in a chariot pulled by splendid golden sea-horses. In his hands was a mighty trident, a weapon capable of stirring the waters to fury, like the sudden Aegean storm. Poseidon was a turbulent, independent deity, midway in function between the docile partner of the earth mother and the dominant sky father type. He sired numerous sea creatures of an equine nature, his wife being the sea goddess Amphitrite. Together with Apollo, he is said to have built the walls of Troy. In the *Odyssey*, composed by Homer about 850 BC, he is represented as the implacable foe of Odysseus, who had blinded his one-eyed son Polyphemus.

Priam

The aged King of Troy at the time of its siege and destruction by the Greeks. The war seems to have taken place in the later part of the thirteenth century BC. According to legend, hostilities broke out as a result of the flight of Helen to Troy. The daughter of Zeus and Nemesis, the personification of retribution, Helen was the wife of Menelaus, King of Sparta, but she eloped with Paris, one of Priam's sons.

In the earlier part of his reign Priam

supported the Phrygians in their struggle against the Amazons, the nation of female warriors dwelling near the borders of the world. When the Greeks landed on the Trojan coast, Priam was too old to take an active part in the war. His sons led the Trojans, and especially Hector, who in single combat fell to Achilles. At the sack of the city Priam was killed by Pyrrhus, Achilles' son. Helen herself returned to Sparta with Menelaus and lived quietly there until her death. In the underworld, however, she was said to have deserted her husband for Achilles.

Prometheus

Literal meaning: 'forethought'. The Greek fire god and friend of mankind; the son of the Titan Iapetus and Clymene, a nymph, and brother of Atlas, Menoetius, and Epimetheus. Hostile to Zeus, the sons of Iapetus found their match in the wide-seeing sky god, though Prometheus himself gained a Pyrrhic victory by enduring torture and not revealing his secret knowledge of future events. He was aware that if Zeus had a child by the sea goddess Thetis, their son would displace Zeus as chief of the gods. Zeus struck down 'overweening' Menoetius with lightning, obliged 'stubborn' Atlas to prop up the sky, gave disastrous Pandora to 'foolish' Epimetheus, and chained 'subtle-counselled' Prometheus on a rock, sending in the daytime an eagle to consume his immortal liver, which was restored each succeeding night. The hero Hercules may have released the suffering fire god, without the consent of the Olympian gods.

According to Hesiod, writing in the seventh century BC, there were five races, corresponding to the five ages of the world: these were the Golden, the contented subjects of Kronos; the short-lived Silver, who were made impious by Prometheus; the ferocious Bronze, unnamed devotees of Ares, warriors predestined for the underworld; the Heroic, their more honourable successors; and, finally, the Iron, whose members include Hesiod and ourselves. The iron race will not cease from grief and destruction till Zeus sweeps it away, like its four predecessors. The original abundance of the earth—from which mankind sprang—was withdrawn by Zeus after Prometheus had taught men to cheat the former of his due share of sacrifices. Also taken back was fire, an element indispensable for civilization. Prometheus dared to steal a flame, either from the workshop of Hephaistos or from the hearth of the gods on Mount Olympus, and Zeus retaliated by promising the creation of evil. This was Pandora, 'all-gifted', whom Hephaistos constructed at Zeus' request. Despite the warning of Prometheus about not accepting gifts, Epimetheus welcomed Pandora and her jug, from which issued 'all the baneful cares of mankind'. Thereafter the division between mortals and immortals was clearly apparent.

Prometheus is an ambivalent figure. He contains two conflicting aspects of the divine helper: fire was his gift to mankind, in some tales even life itself; but the price of technological advance was the grief and destruction typical of the Iron Age. Two steps forward and one step back: compared with the Golden Age, perhaps three steps backwards. Yet Prometheus remains an appealing symbol, the personification of the unconquerable will opposing greater power, forever chained and suffering but confident of the ultimate triumph of his cause.

Pwyll

Welsh nobleman and hero of one of the parts of the *Mabinogion*, the medieval cycle of legends. Pwyll encountered grey-clad Arawn, the magician—king of the underworld, *annwfn*, and they agreed to exhange forms and responsibilities for a year. Later he married Rhiannon, but lost her temporarily to the deceitful Gwawl, the disappointed suitor who had the support of her family. By ingenuity he recovered her, but his own people were annoyed by their childlessness and Rhiannon suffered a miserable fate. Though a son was eventually born, the family continued to be dogged by ill luck, even after the death of Pwyll. Years of desolation passed before the spell put on them by Gwawl's kin was lifted.

Pwyll was called chief of Dyfed, his lands in south-west Wales, and chief of the underworld, annwfn. The latter title he appears to have gained through submission and patience, yet the former he nearly lost because of his marriage to Rhiannon. She was clearly associated with horses—at her first appearance she rode 'the swiftest steed'—and may have been the 'great queen' Epona, the Celtic goddess known from Roman inscriptions. Epona was portrayed astride a mare, and her authority extended to the journey of the soul after death. Gwawl meant 'light', so that behind the conflict arising at the wedding feast was probably the ancient ritual of seasonal combat.

Quirinus

In Roman mythology, a war god associated with Jupiter and Mars. Quirinus was originally worshipped by the Sabines, who occupied the highest part of the Central Apennines. A colony of these people dwelt on the Quirinal Hill, and several great families at Rome were proud to recall their Sabine lineage. According to the historian Livy, writing in the first century BC, the successor of Romulus, the founder hero, was the Sabine Numa Pompilius, whom the Romans invited to become king owing to the fame of his piety. Though Numa was alloted, in retrospect, a house on the Quirinal Hill, an attraction for tourists still in Livy's time, it is unlikely that any of the historical kings of early Rome were other than Etruscans, then the dominant people in Italy.

Relics

The preservation of objects, believed to contain virtue because of former associations, is very ancient. The Christian cult of relics also started early in connection with the remains of martyrs. After St Ignatius was devoured by lions in 107, only the larger bones remaining, these were carried to his native city of Antioch and kept 'as an inestimable treasure left to the Church by the grace which was in the martyr'. Belief in the efficacy of such relics led to the division of remains among many churches and believers. Soon theft, trade, and deception were added to the cult. St Augustine (354–430) complained how persons, disguised as monks, wandered about selling relics of the martyrs and other fake amulets. Where genuine relics were known to exist, Christians confidently expected miracles to take place. In 415 the disinterred body of St Stephen wrought miraculous cures and pilgrims flocked to his shrine in Jerusalem.

It became the custom to carry relics as a means of protection from evil influences. In 1066 William the Conqueror went into action at Hastings wearing round his neck a string of relics given to him by the Pope. Voices were raised against the cult—Alcuin (735–804), the ecclesiastical adviser of Charlemagne, said that it was better to copy the example of the saints than to treasure their bones—but it continued with unabated vigour throughout the Middle Ages.

Roland

At Roncesvalles in 778 the Basques annihilated the rearguard of Charlemagne's army, which was withdrawing from a campaign in Spain to deal with a rising among the recently conquered Saxons of Germany. The Frankish commander, Roland, died in the action. Legend embroidered the defeat, and in the eleventh-century *Chanson de Roland* the fallen warrior emerged as a Christian hero overwhelmed by the forces of Islam. The poem represents the feudal system in epic action and reveals the surprising depth of Christian hatred for the followers of Mohammed. Proud, brave, and ruthless, Roland refused to sound his horn for reinforcements until it was too late. Then the effort caused 'blood to flow from his mouth and burst from his forehead'.

Romulus

Legendary founder and first King of Rome. Romulus and Remus were sons of Mars and a Vestal Virgin, Rhea Silvia. The war god having forced Rhea Silvia, the infants were set adrift in a small boat on the flooded Tiber, but it was washed ashore and they were rescued and suckled by a she wolf. Faustulus, the royal herdsman, discovered and adopted them. Grown to man's estate, they founded Rome, but strife arose between the brothers, in which Remus was slain. The city, a haven for runaway slaves and homicides, suffered from a shortage of women, which Romulus overcame by arranging for the capture of Sabine maidens at a festival. After ruling for forty years Romulus vanished and became the god Quirinus.

During the late fourth century BC the Romulus myth first rivalled that of Aenaas as the supposed city founder. The she wolf had been the symbol of nationality since the establishment of the Republic in 510 BC. Although imperial patronage gave to Aeneas the official glory (on the nine hundredth anniversary of the traditional foundation of Rome in 148, coins were issued which gave pride of place to the city's Trojan origins) interest in Romulus and Remus never diminished.

Saturn

An ancient Italian corn god, identified by the Romans with the Greek Kronos, but having more in common with Demeter, the goddess of vegetation. Saturn was said to have derived his name from sowing; *satus* meant sown. His festival, the Saturnalia, took place in December and lasted seven days: our Christmas revels are its dim survival. The planet Saturn is named after him, as also is Saturday.

Seide

The sacred stone of the Lapps. They were natural stones, unfashioned by human hands, but usually water-moulded rocks of curious shape, even resembling human beings or animals. Such gnarled, convoluted, weather-worn stones were often placed together in a sacred place and were then believed to represent a family. Boons and predictions of future events could be obtained from these stone gods.

Besides the seides of stone, the Lapps had also wooden ones. They were either tree stumps embedded in the soil, or posts driven firmly into it. The Samoyeds of Russia are known to have traditions concerning upright stones, which on certain mountain peaks in the Urals were thought of as 'bearers' of the universe. They had a practical as well as a symbolic function: they actually supported the sky. The idea of a sky pillar occurs in the mythology of various northern peoples. Examples were the 'evergreen' tree by the temple at Uppsala and the Irminsul column destroyed by Charlemagne during his wars against the Saxons at Eresburg in 772.

Sermenys

The long funeral feasts of the Balts. When the Teutonic Order carried the Christian religion to Prussia and Lithuania with fire and sword, in the thirteenth century, they were amazed at the elaborate attention paid by their Indo-European cousins living there to the burial of the dead. It was the custom when a person died for relatives and friends to feast for a month or more. Certain tribes knew how to freeze the corpse so that an even longer period could elapse before cremation. Such mortuary practices date back to remote times, as the signs of fly larvae having fed on Bronze Age skeletons in Central Europe indicate, but we know that the Balts were concerned to ensure a proper departure for the land 'beyond the hill . . . where the sun is'. The souls of the deceased, however, were also thought to transmigrate into trees, flowers, animals, and birds. Hence the prohibition which is still sometimes found on pruning trees and mowing the grass in old cemeteries.

Sibyl

A prophetess. In Roman mythology the best known was the Cumaean Sibyl, who assisted Aeneas in his descent to the underworld. In the *Aeneid*, written at the close of the first century BC, Virgil treats Cumae as a place where Daedalus, flying from Crete, built a temple to Apollo, and dedicated his wings in it. He also describes as a labyrinthine network of caves the prophetess' sanctuary. 'Cleft out is the flank of Cumae's rock into a cavern terrific. To it a hundred broad accesses lead, a hundred their mouthways. From it a hundred come the streams of sound, the Sibyl's answerings.'

The *Sibylline Books*, a collection of oracular sayings which were believed to foretell the future, came to Rome during the reign of Tarquinius Priscus, a legendary Etruscan king. 'A foreign woman' offered to sell this ruler nine volumes. When her offer was declined, she burned three of them and offered the remaining six at the original price. When that was declined, she burned three more and offered the last three at the price first asked for the nine. This Tarquinius Priscus had to accept. The books were kept in the Capitol by a college of priests, and might only be consulted by order of the Senate. They finally disappeared when the Vandals sacked Rome in 410.

Sisyphus

'The craftiest of men', according to the ancient Greeks, and punished for his trickery by endless labour in the underworld. Throughout eternity he was required to roll a marble block to the top of a hill only to have it plunge back down just as it reached the crest. The symbol of futility, Sisyphus had been an avaricious King of Corinth.

A second victim of frustration was Tantalus, whom Zeus begot upon a nymph. His misbehaviour on Mount Olympus—either he divulged to mortals the table talk of the gods or passed to them the food of the gods, nectar and ambrosia—forced Zeus to banish him to Tartarus, the prison beneath the underworld. There Tantalus stood in water up to his chin, but was unable to quench a raging thirst, since the water always responded to the movement of his head. Likewise a bunch of luscious grapes remained just beyond his reach.

Svantevit

In Slavic mythology, a four-headed war god.

His attributes were a sword, a bridle, a saddle, and a white horse. Svantevit possessed several major temples, each with a guard of more than a hundred men.

Svarozic

The ancient Slavic fire god, especially the fire used to dry grain. His father was Svarog, who was identified with Hephaistos, the Greek smith god. Svarozic's name survives today in the Rumanian *sfarog*, meaning torrid.

Taliesin

The Welsh wizard bard. He may have lived in the sixth century, the age of the chieftain who became the 'King Arthur' of later romance. Taliesin's legend and poems survive in the *Mabinogion*. The witch Caridwen once prepared in her cauldron a magic brew which, after a year's boiling, was to yield three blessed drops. Whoever swallowed these drops would know all the secrets of the past, the present, and the future. By accident this happened to be Gwion Bach, the boy who helped to tend the fire beneath the cauldron. When boiling drops fell on his finger, he put it in his mouth, and then, realizing his danger, fled. Caridwen pursued him relentlessly. After numerous transformations, the ravenous witch as a hen ate the fugitive boy disguised as a grain of wheat.

Thrown into the sea at last, he was caught in a fish-trap, and called Taliesin by those who saw him, because of his radiant brow. His knowledge dumbfounded king's bards and amazed the common people. 'I am old, I am new,' he said. 'I have been dead, I have been alive. . . . I am Taliesin.'

Teutates

A Celtic war god worshipped with human sacrifices in Gaul. His name may derive from the word 'tribe' or 'people': Gallic, *touta*; Irish, *tuath*. On one hand it is suggested that Teutates, as Julius Caesar called him, was the chief of the Gallic pantheon; on the other, that this is not the name of an individual deity but of a general attribute that could be applied to different deities. If a war god, Teutates would have been identified with Mars.

Theseus

Legendary Greek hero. The Athenians ascribed to this prince numerous exploits that were the beginning of democracy. He deposed tyrants, freed his fellow citizens from terror, and ended onerous tribute to foreign powers. Most famous was the slaying of the Minotaur, a bull-headed man fed by the Cretans on seven maidens and seven youths exacted annually from Athens. In this adventure he was assisted by Ariadne, a Cretan princess, who supplied him with the skein of thread that permitted him to escape from Daedalus' labyrinth after he had killed the Minotaur. In this myth perhaps we have a garbled version of far older tales of the sacred bullfight dating from the pre-Greek era of Cretan history.

Other feats of Theseus were the defeat of the Amazons and the capture of their queen, Antiope; his successful alliance with King Pirithous of Thessaly against the Centaurs, aggressive horse-men; and his daring descent to the underworld with Pirithous so as to abduct Persephone, queen of the dead. In this raid they met strong opposition, Theseus only getting away through intervention of Hercules. At the Battle of Marathon in 490 BC the departed hero was believed to have helped the Athenians repulse the Persian invaders.

Thor

When the Anglo-Saxons accepted the Roman calendar about 300 they named the fifth day *Thunres-daeg*, Thursday, after the Latin *Jovis dies*, Jupiter's day. For hot-tempered, red-headed Thor was the Germanic version of the Indo-European thunder god: his peers were Jupiter, Zeus, Indra, and the Hittite weather god. Though acknowledged as the arch-enemy of the frost giants, Thor was in many aspects— his strength, his size, his energy, his huge appetite—more like one of the giants than one of the gods.

Two goats drew his chariot across the sky; their names were Toothgrinder and Toothgnasher. His three magic weapons were the hammer, really a thunderbolt; iron gauntlets with which he handled the hammer-shaft; and a strength-increasing belt, capable of increasing his size by a half. Writing just before 1200, Adam of Bremen described the three gods worshipped in the great temple at Uppsala thus: 'Thor, the mightiest of the three, stands in the centre of the building, with Wodan and Fricco on his right and left. Thor, they say, holds the dominion of the air. He rules over thunder and lightning, winds and rain, clear weather and fertility. . . . When plague or famine threatens, sacrifice is offered to Thor.'

The most famous journey to Giantland was the occasion that Loki accompanied Thor, and they encountered Skrymir, 'Vasty', a frost giant so immense that the gods inadvertently slept in the thumb of his empty glove, thinking it was a room. When Thor attempted to hammer in the skull of the sleeping giant, Vasty awoke in the belief that either a leaf or a twig had brushed his brow. Afterwards they came upon the city of Outgard, the summit of whose battlements they could not see even though they pressed back the crowns of their heads on the napes of their necks. Inside the great city Thor and his companions failed in a number of contests, the thunder god himself being wrestled down on one knee by 'an old, old woman'. Only on the journey home did the gods appreciate that Skrymir and Outgard were illusions, stupendous creations sent out by the timorous frost giants to baffle mighty Thor.

Once Thor and the giant Hymir went fishing together for the sea serpent Jormungandr. A colossal hook baited with a giant ox caught in the monster's throat, and Thor would have landed the prize had not the sight of Jormungandr rising from the depths of sea terrified Hymir. In panic the giant cut the line and then dived overboard—to escape the wrath of the frustrated fisherman. Another giant who annoyed Thor was Hrungnir. The thunder god was recalled from his pastime of hunting *trolls*—those shadowy ex-giants of Scandinavia, somehow reduced in stature and potency to become confused with elves and dwarfs—and asked by the gods to be their champion against the stone giant Hrungnir, the pursuer of Odin. In single combat Thor felled Hrungnir with his hammer, but sustained injury himself, a piece of whetstone having got stuck in his head.

The hammer, the sole protection of the gods against the giants, figures in one of the oldest poems in the *Eddas*, the collection of Icelandic epics. Dating from about 900, the 'Thrymskvida' relates how the hammer was stolen by the giants and hidden in the bowels of the earth. This intelligence Loki brought from Thrymr, the frost giant king, as well as the terms by which it could be redeemed: namely, that Freya marry Thrymr. The goddess refused point blank, and so it was decided by the gods that Thor should go instead. Overcoming his extreme reluctance to don a dress, Thor set out disguised as Freya, with Loki pretending to be a maidservant. At

the nuptial feast Thrymr was astonished when the 'bride' ate a whole ox, eight salmon, all the dainties intended for the ladies and washed the lot down with three barrels of wine. Cunning Loki explained away the singular appetite: the 'bride' had been too excited to eat or drink for a week before the marriage. Then Thrymr took out the hammer, which Thor grasped and with it laid low all the giants in attendance.

The thunderbolt of 'the Thunderer' was saved. The gods had gained a temporary respite in their long struggle with the giants. But after a time they would be overwhelmed at ragnarok, the destruction of the gods, Thor slaying Jormungandr but meeting his own death too in that titanic struggle.

Tinia

The Etruscan storm god: the equivalent of Roman Jupiter or Greek Zeus. Tinia-Jupiter was in fact introduced to the city of Rome during the period of the Etruscan monarchy (c 650–510 BC). Tinia held boundaries sacred, watched over them, and ensured their inviolability.

Tristan

For the *trouvères*, the troubadours of medieval France, Tristan was the ideal lover. They acquired the legend of Tristan and Iseult from Brittany, but its ancestry reaches back through Cornwall, Wales, Ireland, and Scotland to an unknown era. Elopements and wooings were a favourite theme of Celtic mythology.

Urdr

The Golden Age in Germanic mythology ended when 'the three giant maids came from Giantland', because they brought with them Time. Their names were Urdr, 'past', Verdandi, 'present', and Skuld, 'future': collectively these three sisters were known as the Nornir and dwelt round the well of Urdr, situated beneath the third root of the cosmic ash Yggdrasil. They were the Fates, to whom Odin and the gods owed obedience. The Anglo-Saxons called Urdr by the name of Wyrd, which meant fate or destiny, and they maintained their belief in the tremendous power of the three sisters long after the arrival of Christianity. The Weird Sisters in

A stone pillar in Uppsala showing Thor in his boat fishing for the sea serpent Jormungandr

Shakespeare's *Macbeth* clearly owed something to the Nornir.

Valkyries

In Germanic mythology, the personal attendants of Odin, father of the slain. They rode over the battlefields of the world to choose those who must die. One of the soldiers in the army of Harald Hardradi, King of Norway, dreamed of a Valkyrie shortly before his side were defeated by King Harold at Stamford Bridge in September 1066. He thought he was on the King's ship, and saw a great witch wife standing on the island, with a fork in one hand to rake up the dead and a trough in the other to catch the blood. In the *Eddas*, Icelandic epics of the ancient gods, the Valkyries became woman warriors who were equally at home serving drink in the hall or riding out armed for battle. Their main task was bringing back to Valhalla, the hall of the slain, the souls of fallen champions, *einherjar*, the adopted sons of Odin Valfodr.

Vesta

The Roman hearth goddess. She was the same as the Greek Hestia, daughter of Kronos and Rhea, and associated with the fire burning on the hearth. Vesta received worship in every house, while at Rome, as the national protectress, she resided in an eternal flame, housed inside a circular temple on the Forum and attended by six Vestal Virgins. Any violation of their vow of chastity was cruelly punished: guilty priestesses were buried alive.

Virgin Mary

In the person of the Virgin Mary the earth goddess—the 'great mother' of ancient religions—succeeded in re-establishing something of her former position. At first the Virgin was not honoured above other saints, but from the fourth century onwards there was a marked growth in the devotion accorded by Christians to Mary. In 431 the Council of Ephesus, which met in a church supposed to contain her mortal remains, confirmed the title of Theotokos, 'God-bearer', which was translated into Latin as *Mater Dei*, mother of God. It subsumed the vision of St John of Patmos as described in *Revelation*. 'And there appeared a

'The journey to the other world' of Germanic mythology, carved on a stone slab. The tall figure between the warriors in the centre is thought to be a Valkyrie

great wonder in heaven: a Woman clothed with the sun, and the moon under her feet, and upon her head a crown of twelve stars.'

She was *Mater Virgo*, virgin mother, the primal material prior to its division into the multiplicity of created things; *Stella Maris*, star of the sea, the immaculate womb of the divine font as well as the primeval waters over which the Spirit moved; and the Tree of Jesse, the world-axle, and the branch upon which 'the spirit of the Lord shall rest'. Inherited attributes though these were, clearly an accretion of folk tradition, the Church had to come to terms with the cult and legends of the Virgin. Popular pressure outweighed theological nicety. In vain St Bernard (1090–1153), the champion of Catholic orthodoxy, tried to stem the tide. A monk of Clairvaux, his old abbey, saw in a vision the dead saint with a dark spot on his breast, caused by his refusal to accept the Immaculate Conception. Adjustment even continues today: in 1950 Pope Pius XII proclaimed by the Bull *Munificentissimus Dei* the dogma of the bodily ascent into heaven of the Virgin Mary. Likewise in the Eastern Church the popularity of her cult is evident in the plethora of icons, sacred images.

The Virgin always comforted those who fell into deep despair. According to one medieval legend, a poor knight sold his wife to Satan for great riches. When the unfortunate woman was taken to meet the Devil by her husband, in order to complete the bargain, she sought refuge in a church and commended herself to the Virgin. Unknown to the knight, the Virgin took the place of his wife, and went to the mouth of Hell. There she forbad Satan to have power over those who called on her, and then dismissed him. She asked the knight to give away his wealth, which he did, thereafter gaining more riches from her.

There were real grounds for infernal frustration. The Virgin eased the pain of 'poor souls' in Purgatory, the dwelling-place of those guilty of venial sins, and she even saved from Hell those who had died in mortal sin. 'I complain daily to God of these injustices', a medieval chronicler has the Devil remark. 'But He is deaf where His Mother is concerned and leaves her lady and mistress of Paradise.' On an earthly level the Virgin succoured the needy and cured the sick. Modern centres of the cult in western Europe were established at Lourdes in 1858 and Fatima, Portugal, in 1917, after reports of her manifestation at these places.

Wayland
The smith god of the Anglo-Saxons. The Icelandic *Eddas* tell of the encounter of Volundr, or Wayland, and his two brothers with three swan maidens by the shore of a lake. For seven years they lived in love together, then one day the princesses flew away. Distraught, the brothers sought their lost loves, each taking a different path, but Wayland was seized by Nidud, a rival king, who claimed the smith had stolen his gold. As a punishment he cut Wayland's leg sinews and removed his forge to a remote island. The unsteady smith god, however, got his revenge by killing Nidud's two sons, who came secretly to see his treasures, and by sending their severed heads studded with precious jewels and mounted on silver, to King Nidud.

Witches
The scapegoats of late medieval Europe. A witch was commonly, though not always, believed to be a female who practised *maleficium*, the art of doing harm by occult means. In league with the Devil and associated with wild and desolate places, she was thought to turn into a vampire or bird, or possess the power of flight, so as to attend a coven of her fellows, where they fed on the human flesh provided by one of their number. A delicacy was newly born babies.

Witches were not always hunted as heretics. Charlemagne had passed laws against witch hunts on the ground that belief in the existence of witches represented pagan superstition. The position changed in the thirteenth century when the Inquisition was established to search out and extirpate heresy. In 1252 Pope Innocent IV allowed the use of torture in trials, an instrument the inquisitors used to verify the existence of witchcraft. In 1484 Pope Innocent VIII issued the Bull *Summis desiderantes affectibus* which made witchcraft a heresy and gave the Inquisition enlarged powers. The creaking structure of medieval society, badly damaged by the Black Death, was ready for its most infamous holocaust. The numbers burned at the stake are unknown: the craze started in the fifteenth century and reached its height only in the late sixteenth century. A glimpse of this mythical terror can be obtained from surviving details. Around Trier, in the years 1587–93, 368 witches were burned, leaving two villages with only one female inhabitant each. Moreover, both Catholics and Protestants hunted witches, as they tracked down Anabaptists, to demonstrate their doctrinal rectitude and zeal. Martin Luther had four witches burned at Wittenberg.

Yambe-akka
Literally, 'old woman of the dead'. In Lapp mythology she had charge of the underworld, which appears to have been imagined as a similar place to the world, except that the departed spirits walked on air. Prior to the advent of Christianity, death does not seem to have severed the bond of union between spirit and body, and Siryan tradition relates how, while a person slept, the spirit could emerge in the form of a mouse. So the souls of the departed sometimes assumed other animals, birds, or insects. A frequent choice was the butterfly, flitting through the sunlit clearings of the northern forests during the short months of summer.

Lapps buried their dead attired for a long journey. Birch-bark shoes were the traditional footwear, and in the grave of an old man they would put a staff for him to lean on. Clothes and ornaments were always heaped on the coffin of a maiden in the belief that men who had died unmarried were likely to propose to girls with a dowry. Until the grave fell in, indicating complete physical decay of the body, it was the custom for relatives to cook food in the cemetery. If the dead were not given their rights, they might become resentful and, coming back from the underworld, disturb the peace of their survivors. Missionaries have noted too a burial custom akin to the Irish wake: 'funeral beer' was consumed in vast quantities, once the mourners had dipped their fingers into it and wetted their faces.

The entrance to the underworld was thought of as the mouth of a river that gave into the ocean of ice. Yambe-akka ruled this gloomy realm, though some legends have an old man rather than an old woman as the 'bearer' of the earth, since hell supported the land of the living and earth tremors occurred whenever their old hands trembled.

Yggdrasil
The cosmic ash of Germanic mythology. Its branches overhung all the worlds and struck out above the heavens. It had three mighty roots: one reached down to Giantland, where stood the wisdom well of Mimir; the second ended in foggy Niflheim, close by the well

of Hvergelmir, 'the roaring cauldron', and dragon Nidhoggr, 'dread biter', which gnawed the root from below; the last was embedded in heaven and beneath it was the sacred well of Urdr, where the gods had their judgement seat.

Yggdrasil means 'the horse of the terrible one', Odin. Since this god discovered the secret of runic wisdom by hanging himself on the cosmic ash—that is, sacrificing himself to himself—Yggdrasil must have been regarded as a tree of knowledge. Parallel with the Cross, the death of Odin has a separate ancestry, sacrificial trees having existed in northern Europe from earliest times. Christian missionaries like St Boniface (c 674–754) cut them down, to the terror and rage of the people: till he was himself cut down at Dockum near the Frisian coast.

Zaltys

The Indo-European Balts—Lithuanians, Prussians, and Letts—revered a harmless green snake, the Lithuanian zaltys. A symbol of fertility, the gentle serpent had a place in every house: under the bed, in a corner, even at table. Zaltys was loved by Saule, the sun goddess, and to kill it was sacrilege. This deity seems to have been a weeper. The sight of a dead zaltys brought tears to her eyes; the red berries on the hill were her tears. The Balts regarded the sun as jug or ladle, her light a golden liquid. Another mysterious, wealth-bringing animal was the Aitvaras, a flying zaltys which emitted light. After the formal conversion of Lithuania to Christianity in 1387 the peasant belief in the green serpent continued unabated, so that in folklore encountering a snake meant either marriage or birth. This notion represents a survival of the general prehistoric worship of snakes.

Zeus

The supreme deity in Greek mythology—the usurping son of the Titans Kronos and Rhea. In the *Theogony*, written soon after 700 BC, Hesiod states that Zeus was 'wise in counsel, father of gods and men, under whose thunder the broad earth quivers'. He defeated his father Kronos, and forced him to yield up not only his swallowed children, such as Poseidon and Hades, but also the imprisoned offspring of Ouranos, his grandfather. In gratitude the primeval Cyclopes presented Zeus with his powerful arms: thunder and lightning. The defeated Titans—the descendants of Ouranos

and Gaia—Zeus confined in Tartarus, the realm beneath the underworld.

A composite figure, the sky god of the Greeks was active in the daily affairs of the world, but he was never looked upon as a creator deity. The origins of the world were far distant: they were entangled, Hesiod notes, in the myths concerning Ouranos, sky, and Gaia, earth. The Dorian invasion of Greece about 1200 BC resulted in the superimposition of the Indo-European sky father cult on an indigenous Minoan-Mycenaean tradition in which the earth goddess was predominant, just as in India the Aryans submerged the Indus valley culture. Although the pre-Greek Hera survived as the wife of Zeus, it was he as Nephelegeretes, 'the cloud gatherer', who ruled over all things. His other names were Ombrios, 'rain god'; Kataibates, 'the descender'; Keraunos, 'lightning'; Gamelios, 'god of marriage'; Teleios, 'giver of completeness'; Pater, 'father'; and Soter, 'saviour'; while Hades, the god of the dead, and Poseidon, the sea god, could be seen as extensions of Zeus' power in their special realms. They were given separate mythical forms, yet the writ of Olympian Zeus, 'the wolfish', Lykaios, ran everywhere, and he alone judged winners and losers. He also consorted with a string of goddesses, nymphs, and women, either to produce further offspring, like Apollo and Artemis, or to absorb the females' special powers. Despite Hera's jealousy and wrath, Zeus' illicit children remained the chief actors on the cosmic stage. Hercules was easily the most conspicuous single figure in Greek mythology.

Zeus even managed to subsume Cretan traditions in his personal myths. It was to this island that he was spirited away when Rhea gave Kronos a stone wrapped in swaddling clothes instead of the infant Zeus. Thither too he brought the Phoenician princess Europa when that maiden foolishly dared to mount him as a tame sea bull. In Crete she became, by Zeus, mother of Minos and other worthies. Another tradition in which Zeus played a crucial role was Orphism, a mystery religion of considerable popularity under the Romans. Here he was 'the foundation of the earth and of the starry sky . . . male and immortal woman . . . the beginner of all things, the god with the dazzling light. For he has hidden all things within himself, and brought them forth again, into the joyful light, from his sacred heart, working marvels.'

AMERICA

North America Central America South America

Men entered the American continents from Siberia over a temporary land link during the final stages of glaciation. If it is accepted that East Africa was the place where our ancestors first became differentiated from their cousins the great apes, and this view of the family tree of man appears to be the correct one, then it makes the trek on foot from there to Tierra del Fuego a journey of epic proportions. The Indian tribes living on the bleak and rocky tip of South America are among the most primitive people on the planet. They survive and in their folklore survive traces of the mythology that the first settlers brought into this part of the world so many millennia ago. The Yahgan and Ona tribesmen of Tierra del Fuego, fishermen and hunters respectively, have maintained an initiation ceremony remarkable for its anti-feminine character. Although there is disagreement about the origin of this curious attitude, a primitive parallel of the Fall, the ascendancy of the male is unquestioned and reflected in the sex of the creator deity. Their text might well be the words of Yahweh to Eve: 'I will greatly multiply thy sorrow and thy conception; in sorrow thou shalt bring forth children; and thy desire shall be to thy husband, and he shall rule over thee.'

The warrior was the central figure in the majority of pre-Columbian societies. The Aztecs, the dominant people of Central America on the arrival of Hernando Cortés and his Spanish soldiers in 1519, were excessively puritanical. It was evil for a warrior to exhibit any interest in women, since a diversion of attention from the practice of arms might have weakened the Aztec supremacy. Adultery was a shameful crime punishable by death: yet to die in battle was the supreme purification. While other tribes did not share the rigour of the Aztecs, the importance of the brave cannot be gainsaid. The Plains Indians of North America, for example, insisted upon both fasting and sexual continence before a band of warriors set out for either hunting or war.

In the seventeenth century, when the systematic settlement of North America from Europe was beginning, there existed more than 2,000 independent Indian tribes. Many of these peoples were sworn enemies, a state of affairs the European immigrants turned to their own advantage, so that no effective resistance could be organized. The Plains Indians took readily to horses and guns, but the diversity of the Indian peoples themselves precluded a grand alliance. The scattered tribes had reached stages of civilization ranging from simple hunters and fishermen to advanced town-dwellers with elaborate social divisions. The humble Menomini on the shores of the Great Lakes, a tribe which subsisted by gathering wild rice, had little in common with their maize-growing Iroquois neighbours: yet both these peoples appear nomadic in comparison with the Pueblo in Colorado, where the cultivation of maize sustained large hilltop settlements and perhaps the most developed mythology in North America. Today the 300 surviving Indian tribes live on reserves. The process of concentration and betrayal started in earnest during the nineteenth century, when

A medicine woman from a North-Western American tribe

The middle palace at Palenque, the great Maya city on the edge of the Yucatan plain

railways linked the coast of the Atlantic Ocean with that of the Pacific and farmers destroyed the natural flora and fauna of the Great Plains. The tribes which were not farmers have seen the greatest changes in their way of life: just as the buffalo no longer roams beyond the pen of the zoological gardens, so the Indian hunting party now tracks little more than the route to the reservation supermarket.

Before the Indian tribes of North America became the object of tourist curiosity that they are today, they possessed a remarkable variety of mythologies. Most fascinating are the beliefs of the peoples living along the northern coast of the Pacific Ocean.

Renowned for their predilection towards tribal rivalry, whether it took the form of kidnapping raids or ceremonial display, the Haida, Snohomish, or Quinault tribes also surprised the first Europeans with the range of their cosmological ideas. The mysterious Coyote falls into perspective when it is remembered that these people believed that animals were the original inhabitants of the land, and that they were exactly like men except in two instances. They were much bigger and they could put on and take off their fur like clothes. When human beings were created by the changer god Kwatee, he turned these colossal animal people into the ancestors of present-day animals, birds, and fish. The Quinaults say that he changed things in order to prepare the world for the men he was to make from his own sweat and from dogs. Although potent deities such as Kwatee approach the status of a supreme being, there is no tendency towards monotheism outside the traditions of the Maidu in California, the Algonquins of the Middle West, and the Selish in Canada. These tribes, however, would seem to be of great antiquity.

Even older civilizations existed in Central and South America. When for some unknown reason the aggressive Olmecs abandoned their settlements on the Gulf of Mexico about 400 BC, this represented the end of an occupation lasting nearly 1,000 years. Meanwhile the Mayas of the great peninsula, the Yucatan, had started to build with stone, under the influence of the Olmecs, and soon to arise were their extensive ceremonial centres: the complexes of courtyards, pyramids, and temples, all richly decorated. Somewhat remote from the centre of cultural development, which was situated on the high Mexican plateau, the Mayas evolved a distinct civilization of their own, though in the tenth century either refugees or adventurers from the Toltec city of Tollan appear to have founded a new state in north-west Yucatan. The fall of the Toltecs about 980 was due to a dynastic dispute and the insurrection of subject tribes. The Toltec nobles seem to have retreated from Tollan with their last ruler, Quetzalcoatl, and taken ship to Mayan territory, where they built the city of Chichen Itza. After its overthrow in the thirteenth century, and a period of complicated political strife, the Toltec and Maya nobility combined to set up another capital at Mayapan, the first walled city in that area. In terms of religion, the coming of the Toltecs meant the introduction of new deities, beliefs, and ceremonies, especially the large-scale practice of human sacrifice. Antonio de Herrera, the official historian of the Indies for the King of Spain, wrote in 1598 that 'the number of people sacrificed was great. And this custom was brought into Yucatan by the Mexicans.'

Of the Olmec religion we know very little. There is no firm evidence to suggest that human sacrifices were made to the earth goddess, even in her terrifying alligator form, nor are the jaguar masks of her consort proof of ritual killing. Sacrifices may have taken place in this ancient, and almost lost, civilization but, on surviving data, the first people to institutionalize the practice were the Toltecs, who dominated the high plateau from about 750 till 980. Yet the Toltecs seem lukewarm in comparison with the fierce Aztecs, when the annals tell us proudly of the tens of thousands of victims whose hearts were torn out on solemn occasions. In Tenochtitlan, the amazing island-city the Aztecs created on floating rafts in Lake Texococo, human sacrifice formed an integral part of daily life. The origin of the builders of Tenochtitlan, 'cactus rock', which had a million inhabitants, remains obscure, but their impact upon Central America in the century of their ascendancy was profound. Wars against rival cities had the objective of providing captives for sacrifice: they were known as 'flower wars'. The 'blossoming

heart' and blood of the victim had to be offered to the gods, in particular the sun god Tonatiuh, who needed all the strength that men could give him. According to the Aztecs, man was responsible for the maintenance of the cosmos—by feeding the gods with blood and by observing a strictness bordering on madness in social behaviour. A primitive people when they arrived on the Mexican plateau, the Aztecs exaggerated the brutality in the indigenous religion they inherited and submerged the spiritual striving that so patently disdained the flesh. Nevertheless, a deep sense of unfitness pervaded Tenochtitlan, whose inhabitants inflicted upon themselves severe punishments: bodies were lacerated with cactus thorns, ears and tongues pierced with osiers, and hearts cut out of not unwilling victims. Compulsion and fear sustained the despotic Montezuma, the Aztec Emperor, on the landing of Hernando Cortés, but so did the fanatical belief of his own people. The swift collapse of the empire, and the virtual annihilation of the Aztecs, were connected as much with fatalism as fire-arms. Cortés was divine Quetzalcoatl returned to claim his own.

At the same time as the Aztecs commenced the series of campaigns that laid the foundation of their power, high in the Andes the Incas were putting together a state which in area was comparable with the Roman Empire. About 1438 the city of Cuzco was nearly sacked by a rival people: desperate street fighting ensued, and the man of the hour, Pachacuti, a young prince, assumed the Inca crown. He set out to conquer and annex not only the territory of the defeated attackers, but the whole of the rest of the Pacific coast. Under his vigorous direction, and that of his son Topa Inca Yupanqui, who ruled from 1471 to 1493, Cuzco was transformed into the capital city of a far-flung empire. In spite of their ignorance of the wheel and an elementary script the Incas succeeded in the administration of numerous provinces and peoples. The nobility was expanded by the incorporation of noble families belonging to conquered tribes so as to provide additional officials and military officers, while the Inca army received into its ranks defeated warriors and fresh recruits. A policy of population removal did much to diminish old antagonisms and foster new loyalties.

The origin of the Inca dynasty is wreathed uncertainly in the mists of legend. At the end of the eleventh century it is said that three men and a woman came into the mountains, climbing up the steep slope from the jungles of the Amazon. Arriving in the hills above Cuzco, this small group camped and placed on the ground a wedge of gold, which they claimed had been entrusted to them by their father, the sun. They had been told that where the wedge sank into the ground was the place for them to live. This happened in Cuzco itself. Two of the brothers then transformed themselves into sacred rocks and for several generations of brother-sister marriage, the Inca family ruled as a petty dynasty. The assault on the city occurred when the other tribes living in the vicinity appreciated the growing pretensions of the Incas. The consequence of the struggle was establishment of Inca authority throughout the Andes mountains.

Archaeology has made it apparent that the Incas were latecomers in the history of pre-Columbian Peru. For two millennia before their seizure of Cuzco, Indian peoples had been farming, weaving cloth, worshipping in impressive temples, making elaborate pottery, and working metal. The Mochica culture, whose main sites are situated near the Ecuadorian border, flourished between 100 BC and AD 800. It has

Quetzalcoatl, deity and cultural founder-hero of Central America

bequeathed a startling array of artefacts to museums, but the absence of a native record of historical events leaves the mythologer with scant information concerning beliefs. For this reason the pre-Columbian civilizations of South America are inevitably represented by Inca religion.

Our knowledge of the Incas derives from Spanish observers of Francisco Pizarro's conquest, which was complete in 1525. Only remnants of the Inca army held out for another fifty years on the Atlantic slope of the Andes, where the tropical forest aided guerrilla warfare. Their last refuge, the abandoned city of Machu Picchu, was not discovered till 1911. What stands out in the account of Inca religion is the divine mission of the ruler. Both his person and his authority were manifestations of the beneficent sun god Inti. From pity of men's poverty and backwardness Inti had sent down to earth his children, the Incas.

Just as the dense forest of the Amazon basin provided natural cover for the Inca refugees in the sixteenth century, so it has offered protection to the indigenous Indian tribes till the last few decades of our time. The movement into the interior of Brazil is a recent event. Little was known about the Amazonian peoples before the 1940s, and these tribesmen knew even less about modern civilization. The arrival of prospectors, settlers, and anthropologists has changed much, but even today there remain bands that have only the slightest contact with outsiders. Brazil's drive westwards encountered a strange and significant set-back in the conversion of the Villas Boas brothers to the Indian way of life. These three adventurers were overwhelmed by the beauty and cultural richness of the tribes of the Xingu River. They stayed in the jungle, lived with the Indians, and did their utmost to protect them from speculators, politicians, missionaries, and disease. They argued that until 'civilized' people created conditions among themselves for the integration of the Indians, any attempt to integrate them would be the same as introducing a plan for their destruction. Whether or not the work of the Villas Boas brothers will appear to future generations as a useless gesture remains to be seen, but from the point of view of the mythologer it is exemplary. Their respect for the values and ideas of the Indian has stimulated at least the collection of folklore and myth.

In 1540 the voyage of Francisco Orellana up the 'river of the Amazons' had confirmed earlier rumours of an island inhabited by rich and warlike women, who permitted occasional visits from men, but endured no permanent residence of males among them. The Spaniards found themselves under attack from groups in which woman acted as leaders and took the foremost place in the fight. These Amazons were 'very tall, robust, fair, with long hair twisted over their heads, skins round their loins, and bows and arrows in their hands'. Although the skirmish was enough to give the longest river in the world its name, there can be little doubt that the myth had no firmer basis than the practice of certain tribes whose women bore arms. Even in the Caribbean Sea the landing parties from the ships of Christopher Columbus had met female islanders who fought bravely alongside their husbands and brothers.

Today the islands of the Caribbean are populated by peoples of European and African descent. The massive transportation of black slaves to the New World in order to work on plantations and the reckless use of the native Indians by the *conquistadores* in their pursuit of riches has brought about this great change. The original Caribs appear to have possessed traditions like those of the Arawak tribes of South America—their supreme being was a remote sky god who 'lived in the sun'—but for the

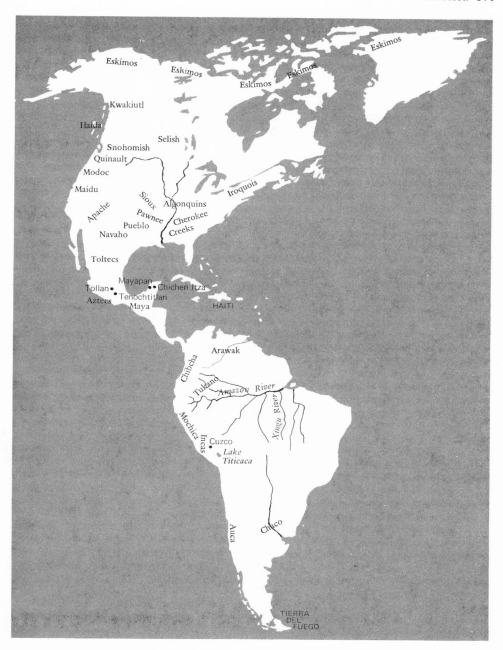

mythologer these poorly recorded legends of the past are less significant than the living cults of the ex-slaves, the best known of which is the Voodoo of Haiti. *Zombi*, a soulless body, has passed into the English language, yet till the last few decades it was the custom to dismiss Haitian beliefs as a species of degenerate magic, especially as its deities appear in living form by taking possession of devotees. Thanks to the labours of one or two scholars we can now appreciate that Voodoo, primarily an African faith in origin, has absorbed diverse elements without loss of its own inner consistency. Saints and symbols have been fused with Voodoo mythology to such an extent that Christian missionaries are helpless. This remarkable occurrence may have been due to the capture and transportation of *hougans*, 'spirit masters', the priests and adepts of West African religion. They would have provided the continuity of doctrine that otherwise a mixture of displaced persons, thrown into a new environment, must have forfeited.

Agwé

The Haitian sea god. Elaborate ceremonies take place to feed this proud deity, the Voodoo worshippers sending down to his magnificent submarine palace ships loaded with gifts.

Ah Puch

The Maya god of death. He was portrayed as a skeleton or a bloated corpse, adorned with bells. As Hunhau the chief of demons, he presided over the ninth and lowest of the underworlds, the horrible *mitnal*. In modern folklore he survives as Yum Cimil, 'lord of death', prowling the houses of the sick in his endless search for prey. The Maya have always had a great fear of death, unlike their more warlike neighbours, and the Spanish conquerors were amazed at the overwhelming grief and sorrow expressed by the bereaved. It was the custom during the day for them to weep in silence; and at night, when the earth duplicated the darkness of Hunhau's realm, they raised loud and awful cries, unbearable alike for passers-by or those living near.

The bodies of the humble were buried under the floors of their houses or behind them: their mouths were invariably filled with ground maize, and jade beads placed in their hands as money. The bodies of the socially esteemed were burned, their ashes being placed in great urns, and shrines built over them. In northern Yucatan ashes were even put in hollow statues made of pottery or of wood.

Ai Apaec

A late name for an active god of the Mochica. From archaeological evidence it seems that this pre-Inca civilization possessed a remote, almost indifferent, supreme being and creator deity, who was a sky god; beneath his throne, usually placed on a high mountain, ranged the mobile Ai Apaec. This god shared the feline mouth of the nameless creator deity; also he wore snake-head ear-rings and a jaguar head-dress. Possibly Ai Apaec was the son of the mountain god.

Amotken

The creator deity of the Selish, one of the oldest of the North American Indian peoples. According to their cosmology, the universe comprises an underworld, earth, and heaven, all of which levels of habitation are supported by a gigantic pillar or post. Amotken dwells in heaven, solitary and alone: he is an old man, wise and kind, never-changing in concern for his creation. Coyote acts as his messenger but exhibits none of the trickery associated with him among Californian tribes. One creation myth relates that Amotken made five young women out of five hairs taken from his head. When he asked them what they wanted to be, he received five different replies. The first wanted to become the mother of wickedness; the second the mother of goodness; the third mother earth; the fourth the mother of fire; and the fifth the mother of water. Amotken fulfilled their wishes and said that at first wicked men shall be in the majority, but later on the good will rule over the world.

Angakoq

One of the names of the Eskimo shaman, or medicine-man. Since the religious ideas of the inhabitants of the Arctic lands were never formalized, the *angakoq* is the repository of lore, the judge in matters of tradition, and the means of communication with the spirit world. Both men and women can become angakoq, magicians, but it is said that women lack the courage to do evil. An angakoq who can call down misfortune on his fellows is known as an *ilisitsoq*: his victim would be attacked by one of his magic animals, a *tupilak*, usually in the form of a seal.

A person becomes an angakoq by acquiring the protection of a *tornaq*, 'guardian spirit'. There are three specific kinds: those in the shape of human beings, those in the shape of stones, and those who inhabit bears. The last are believed to be the most powerful of all. Through the agency of the tornaq, a medicine-man cures the sick, controls the weather,

Pueblo Hopi deities of lightning (left) and corn (right)

secures good hunting, and propitiates the hungry sea goddess Sedna.

Asgaya Gigagei
Literally, 'red man'. The thunder god of the Cherokees, a tribe long under the domination of the Iroquois. They also have lesser gods known as 'thunder boys'.

Ataensic
According to the Iroquois, Ataensic was both the sky woman and the earth goddess. She is said to have died giving birth to the twins Hahgwehdiyu and Hahgwehdaetgah. After her death Hahgwehdiyu created the world from her corpse.

Atius Tirawa
The creator deity of the Pawnees. He is said to have ordered the courses of the sun, moon, and stars. The Pawnee tribes were so named because the warriors dressed their hair like 'a horn'. The conception of Atius Tirawa may owe something to European settlers, whom the Pawnees encountered on the Great Plains, but astral worship was always a feature of their belief.

Awonawilona

Literally, 'all-container'. The dual creator deity of the Pueblo Zuni. Awonawilona existed before all else: by his-her volition did he-she create life. 'The mists of increasing and the streams of growing' flowed from his-her being, when it assumed the shape of the sun and fecundated the primeval sea. Green scum formed over the endless waters and became firm, then divided into Awitelin Tsta, earth mother, and Apoyan Tachi, sky father. From this divine pair sprang all living things.

In four wombs stirred the seeds of life. Inside each womb teemed unfinished creatures, crawling over one another in the darkness, writhing like reptiles as they tried to gain the warmth of the sun's rays. Among them was Poshaiyangkyo, the foremost and wisest of men. He contrived to escape. He found a passage and followed it upwards and outwards, till he came to the light. There in the shallows of the world ocean, standing silently in the lapping waters, Poshaiyangkyo besought the sun to release the creatures still imprisoned in the fourfold womb of Awitelin Tsta. So it was that Awonawilona sent the divine twins to the place of generation. They cleft the earth with thunderbolts and, being light, they descended on threads of spiderweb. In the wombs they instructed the living things how to make themselves ready for birth. Most of those for whom Poshaiyangkyo had prayed were thus led upwards by the divine twins, but there were numerous casualties since some fell back and only escaped later as monsters, cripples, and idiots.

The first men, however, were strange when they reached the light. They had adapted to the womb world and possessed scales, short tails, owl's eyes, huge ears, and webbed feet. The first sunrise they greeted in howling terror. Their adjustment to life on the surface of the earth was gradual, though the medicine-man Yanaulaha contributed greatly to this difficult process.

Bochica

The cultural founder hero of the Chibcha Indians, whose early civilization in Colombia was probably the most advanced after that of the Incas. Bochica arrived from the east and wandered the land as a bearded man. He instructed the Chibcha ancestors in moral laws and taught them how to make things. At last he disappeared in the west leaving his footprints on certain rocks. Yet his severe moral teachings were opposed by a woman named Chie, who urged men to rejoice and make merry. Although Bochica turned Chie into an owl, she still helped the work god Chibchacum to flood the country of the Chibcha, who in distress appealed for aid to their founder hero. Bochica appeared in a rainbow, sent the rays of the sun to dry up the waters, and caused an outlet to carry away the flood of the sea. Since that time Chibchacum has lived underground and supported the world on his shoulders.

Chac

The Maya rain god, counterpart of the Aztec Tlaloc. Though portrayed with two curling fangs and tears streaming from his eyes, Chac was a friend of man, the lord of wind, thunder, lightning, rain, and fertility. Sometimes he was worshipped not as a single god but as four gods, one for each of the cardinal points.

Chalchihuitlicue

Literal meaning: 'lady precious green'. The Aztec water goddess, a personification of youthful beauty and ardour, Chalchihuitlicue was portrayed as a river from which grew a prickly pear tree laden with fruit which symbolized the human heart.

Chiminigagua

The creator deity of the Chibcha culture in Colombia. Having made large black birds, which carried light over the mountain peaks, Chiminigagua left the rest of creation to others. The goddess Bachue, 'large-breasted', was the mother of mankind, the father being her son. Their cosmic task fulfilled, they returned to the sacred lakes as serpents.

Cinteotl

The Aztec maize divinity. In April people offered to him their blood, dropped upon reeds which they displayed at the doors of their houses. Closely associated with Xochipilli, the flayed god of flowers and lord of souls, Cinteotl was a god whose penitence ensured for mankind a regular supply of food. He was under the protection of the water god Tlaloc, and he had various feminine forms.

Coatlicue

Literal meaning: 'the serpent lady'. She was the Aztec earth goddess, and the mother of Huitzilopochtli, the tribal god of the Aztecs.

Although one of the wives of the cloud serpent Mixcoatl, who was also the god of hunting, Coatlicue was magically impregnated with Huitzilopochtli. One day while she was sweeping a feathery ball descended to her like a lump of thread, and she took it and put it in her bosom. After the housework was done, she looked without success for the ball, from which legend says she became pregnant without sin. This miraculous conception awakened the fury of her existing offspring, 400 sons and daughters aggrieved by the apparent slight on the family honour. They would have killed their earth serpent mother had not Huitzilopochtli emerged fully armed from her womb and set about his brothers and sisters, many of whom he slew.

Coatlicue was the earth serpent goddess. She was of especially horrible aspect: her skirt was of writhing snakes, her necklace of human hearts and hands supported a skull pendant; her hands and feet were clawed; her breasts were flabby; and her diet was the corpses of human beings. Coatlicue represented the devouring mother who was at once the womb and the grave. Under the Aztecs land was not owned by anybody. The earth was Coatlicue: she freely gave to men her fruits but no person could expect to cultivate a specific portion of the goddess in perpetuity. Officials would rightly declare after two or three years that the goodness of a plot was exhausted and the time had come for it to be left fallow.

Coyolxauhqui
Literally, 'golden bells'. According to the Aztecs, when earth serpent goddess Coatlicue was pregnant for the last time, her innumerable offspring were horrified. They were so convinced that their mother had committed some dreadful crime that they plotted to kill her before she could give birth. Coyolxauhqui disapproved and rushed ahead of her brothers and sisters to give warning. But from the great cave where Coatlicue dwelt the newly born Huitzilopochtli stormed, fierce and fully armed. He slew Coyolxauhqui and savaged the star children hard on her heels. After the fight, he returned to his mother who told him about his sister's goodness. So he cut off the head of Coyolxauhqui and threw it up into the heavens to become the moon, where the golden bells of her cheeks could still glitter.

Coyote
The trickster deity of south-western North American myth—a distant cousin of Reynard the Fox. Among the Maidu Indians, an ancient Californian people, the creator deity Wonomi yielded place to Coyote his adversary; but it was not because the adversary was stronger, but because, as Wonomi admitted sadly, men had followed him and not their creator.

After the creation of the world, Coyote and his dog Rattlesnake came up out of the ground. Coyote watched Wonomi create Kuksu, the first man, and Laidamlulum-kule, or Morning Star Woman, his spouse. But when the trickster tried to create people too, he laughed and they were made glass-eyed. Coyote watched the easy way of life that Wonomi had given to the ancestors of mankind, and he decided that it would be more interesting to add sickness, sorrow, and death. Coyote was even pleased when the first person to die was his own son, from a bite given by Rattlesnake. Perhaps the trickster expected that the secret of rejuvenation imparted to Kuksu might save the boy. In the event the corpse's submersion in a lake, which Wonomi had taught the first man to use as a method of shedding years, failed to restore Coyote's son. So Kuksu buried the body, saying: 'This is what you must do till the world is changed.' Later it is said that Coyote killed himself and roamed the world as a spirit.

Coyote is a mischievous, cunning, and destructive force at work within creation. Mysterious and monstrous are his antics, just as the obvious pleasure he obtains from causing troubles and upsets is a chilling aspect of daily experience. The Maidu, and other south-western tribes, know that they can expect to suffer from his endless trickery.

Damballah
Damballah Wedo is the powerful serpent god of Voodoo mythology. In the sky above the island of Haiti he manifests himself in the company of his wife, Ayida, as a rainbow. They encompass the world, an entwined pair of serpents representing sexual unity.

On earth the river snake Simbi acts as a lesser Damballah: he is the patron of springs and rains. Dan Petro, however, is the stern 'snake up the tree', a legacy of the revolt of slaves against the Napoleonic forces that, by 1804, had made Haiti the second free colony in the New World, following the United States of America. Yet the three cosmic serpents, Damballah, Simbi, and Petro, are rather aspects of the life-force than opposed deities. In iconography Damballah Wedo is identified with St Patrick, the sender of the serpents of Ireland into the sea.

Dohkwibuhch

In Snohomish mythology, the dilatory creator-changer deity. Mankind, this north-western Indian tribe believes, was dissatisfied with the way Dohkwibuhch had made the world. Though the first men could not talk together because of the different languages given to them by Dohkwibuhch, they soon discovered that everyone bumped their heads against the sky, which for an unknown reason was very low. It happened also that people climbed up high in the trees and went into the 'sky world'.

A wise man devised a plan. He said that if all the people and all the animals and all the birds pushed at the same time, the sky could be lifted away from the earth. In order to co-ordinate this incredible sky pushing it was agreed that the cry 'Ya-hoh' would be the signal to raise the long poles prepared for the task. So the moment came; the cry was heard and the sky pushed until it reached the place where it is now. But a few people did not know about the sky pushing. They were hunting elk and, just as the people and the animals and the birds pushed the sky upwards, they followed the game into the sky world. Stranded there, the elk and the hunters became the stars of the Big Dipper.

Dzelarhons

The Frog Princess of Haida mythology. The Haida, an important Indian tribe of fishermen living on the Pacific islands of Canada, refer to Dzelarhons as the Volcano Woman too. She arrived from the sea with six canoe-loads of people, which means an entire tribe in an area where dug-out canoes reach 40 or 50 feet in length. Her husband was Kaiti, the bear god.

Dzoavits

A huge ogre. According to the Shoshoneans, a relatively primitive people of Nevada and Utah, Dzoavits stole the Dove's two children. Although Eagle and Crane assisted Dove in their recovery, the monster pursued them so closely that they had to hide in one of Weasel's holes. Even then Dzoavits would have found the fugitives had not Badger intervened. When the huge ogre asked Badger where Dove and her children were concealed, he directed him into a specially prepared hole, threw hot rocks in on him, and plugged the hole with a stone.

Ek Chuah

Literally, 'black war leader'. This Maya deity, represented with a black-rimmed eye, was fierce and violent. He also concerned himself with those who had died in battle. A friendly aspect, however, was his patronage of mer-chants, since he sometimes appeared carrying a bundle of merchandise on his back like an itinerant salesman.

El Dorado

The gilded king. The Spaniards reaching America in the sixteenth century heard rumours of a mysterious people whose cities were paved and plated with solid gold and of a kingdom ruled over by a priest king, called El Dorado, because his body was covered in powdered gold. This garbled account of the Incas encouraged the conquistadors in their pursuit of wealth. Two overriding motives drove these men: acquisitiveness and religious zeal. Above all they sought an adequate financial return for the enduring dangers of battle and voyage. Many of the casualties suffered by the army of Hernando Cortés resulted from soldiers loaded down with booty attempting to cross the swamps surrounding Tenochtitlan.

El-lal

A legendary hero of the Indian tribes of Patagonia. His father, Nosjthej, wishing to eat him, had snatched him from his mother's womb. El-lal owed his rescue to the in-tervention of Rat, who carried him to the safety of his hole. Having learned from this substitute father the sacred lore, El-lal emerged into the world, making himself its lord by means of his invention—the bow and arrow. He had further battles with fierce Nosjthej as well as indigenous giants, all of whom he overcame, but at last he decided to quit the earth. Thereafter, he said, men would have to look after themselves.

Enumclaw

Literally, 'thunder'. Once two brothers, Enumclaw and Kapoonis, were hunting for guardian spirits that would make them great medicine-men. It happened, according to Indian tradition in Washington, that Kapoonis found a fire spirit, and with it he could make lightning. Meanwhile Enumclaw became expert in throwing rocks. So worried was the sky father by this acquisition of power that he translated Enumclaw as the thunder spirit and Kapoonis as the lightning spirit.

Erzulie

The goddess of love in the Voodoo pantheon. Erzulie is not the earth mother, nor the mother of men, but rather she is the *loa*, or goddess, of elemental forces—the ideal, but tragic, mistress. She lives in fabulous luxury and appears powdered and perfumed. She is lavish with her love as with her gifts. On the fingers she wears three wedding rings, since her husbands are the serpent god Damballah, the sea god Agwé and the warrior hero Ogoun.

As Erzulie Ge-Rouge, she huddles together her knees drawn up and her fists clenched, while tears stream from her eyes. She weeps over the shortness of life and the limitation of love.

Estsanatlehi

Literal meaning: 'the woman who changes'. The most respected deity of the Navaho Indians—hunters living in the semi-arid area of Arizona. It is said that Estsanatlehi never remains in one condition, but that she grows to be an old woman, and in the course of time becomes a young woman again. She passes thus through an endless course of lives, always changing but never dying. The apotheosis of the seasons, Estsanatlehi dwells in a floating house on 'the great water in the west . . . and here the Sun visits her, when his journey is done, every day that he crosses the sky'.

According to legend, primeval man and woman once observed a black cloud descend on to a mountain. 'Surely something has taken place', said the first man. 'Let us go and see.' So the primeval couple trudged to the summit of the mountain and were surprised to find a baby girl there. This happened to be Estsanatlehi, who was the daughter of Naestan, 'the woman horizontal', and Yadilyil, 'the upper darkness'. The first woman picked up the baby and carried it home. Fed on pollen brought by the sun god Tsohanoai, Estsanatlehi grew into a woman within eighteen days.

On another occasion the changeling goddess felt lonely in her marine home. She had no companions there. She thought she might make people to keep her company, so one day, she used small pieces of her own skin to create men and women.

Ga-gaah

The wise crow. When this divine bird flew from the kingdom of the sun, the Iroquois say, he carried in his ear a grain of corn which Hahgwehdiyu, the good creator deity, planted in the body of the earth goddess. This maize—the staple of the Iroquois Indians—was the great gift to mankind.

Ghede

In the Voodoo mythology of Haiti, the hungry figure in black top hat, long black tail coat, and dark glasses posted at the eternal crossroads, where pass the souls of the dead on their way to *guinee*, the legendary place of origin and the abode of the gods. Ghede is wise beyond all others, since as god of death he holds the knowledge of all those who have lived. He is also 'the lord of life', a phallic deity: he sustains the living, increases their number, and resurrects the dead. In the chamber dedicated to his worship a sculptured phallus lies side by side with the grave-digger's tools.

As the guardian of the dead, the cross of Baron Samedi, as Ghede is sometimes called, is in every cemetery, while the graves that are under the protection of his female counterpart, Maman Brigitte, are marked by a pile of stones. As the lord of love, Ghede is noted for his unpredictable obscenity and his inordinate desire for strong rum. He is liable to arrive at a ceremony for another loa and outrageously disrupt the proceedings. His possession of devotees cannot be controlled by the hougans, 'spirit masters'. Several years ago a group of Ghedes—all of them hougans possessed by the god and wearing his black attire—forced their way into the presidential palace, where they demanded money. These swashbucklers were satisfied, and eventually left: how could the President refuse the comic symbol of dynamic life and inevitable death?

Gluskap

According to the Abnaki Indians, a tribe of Algonquin stock, Gluskap is a cultural founder hero who retired from the world after performing amazing feats on behalf of gods and men. Once he even rode on a whale. Like King Arthur of Celtic tradition, Gluskap is expected to return one day and save his people.

Guinechen

Literally, 'master of men'. The supreme being

of the Auca tribes of Chile, the staunchest opponents of Inca, and later Spanish, rule. He was also called Guinemapun, 'master of the land'. His authority extended over natural phenomena and the fertility of men, animals, and plants. A parallel deity was Pillan, to whom were attributed such events as sudden storms, floods, and volcanic eruptions. But the ultimate source of ill was Guecufu, the malevolent spirit that sent the deluge.

Hahgwehdiyu
In Iroquois mythology, the good creator deity; son of the sky goddess Ataensic, and twin brother of Hahgwehdaetgah, the evil spirit. Hahgwehdiyu shaped the sky with the palm of his hand, placed his dead mother's face in the sky as the sun, while from her breasts he made the moon and stars. To the earth he gave her body as the source of fertility, thereby making Ataensic into the earth goddess. It was Hagwehdaetgah who placed darkness in the west, invented earthquakes and hurricanes, and challenged the goodness of his brother's handiwork. At last the twins fought a duel with the huge thorns of the giant crab-apple tree, sharp as arrows. Fortunately for mankind, the long struggle ended in the defeat of Hahgwehdaetgah and his exile to a subterranean realm.

Hiawatha
Iroquois tradition makes Hiawatha a sixteenth-century sage. He was instrumental in bringing about the confederation of the five Iroquois tribes known as 'the five nations'. The hero of Longfellow's poem was an Algonquin chief.

Hisakitaimisi
Or Hisagitaimisi. 'The master of breath', the supreme deity of the Creek Indians, the mound builders of the south eastern United States. Closely related to the sun, Hisakitaimisi is also known as Ibofanga, 'he who sits above'.

Huacas
Sacred things. Beneath the remote creator deity Virococha, and the more active sun god Inti, the Incas worshipped innumerable nature gods, believed to be manifest in *huacas* such as rocks, oracles, or idols.

Huitaca
In Chibcha mythology, the goddess of in-dulgence, drunkenness, and licence. As Chie, she opposed the severe moral code of Bochica, the Colombian hero, and for her impudence she was turned into an owl.

Huitzilopochtli
The only deity of purely Aztec origin, Huitzilopochtli, 'blue hummingbird on the left', was a god of war. At the outset of their conquest of the Mexican plateau, Huitzilopochtli addressed his fellow Aztec chiefs thus: 'My mission and my task is war.... I have to watch and join issue with all manner of nations, and that without mercy.' After the foundation of Tenochtitlan in 1325, the greatest temple of this island city was dedicated to this wilful war god.

Huitzilopochtli was believed to be the sun, the young warrior who was born each day, who defeated the stars of the night, and who was aided in his western death and resurrection by the souls of warriors. Moreover, his symbols of authority—the humming bird and fire—correspond with the attributes of Xochipilli, the lord of flowers and the guardian of souls. Both deities are intimately linked with notions of rebirth. In the sixteenth century, too, the Franciscan historian Bernardino de Sahagun noted that on the feast of Huitzilopochtli 'the priests offered to the idol flowers, incense, and food, and adorned it with wreaths and garlands of flowers'. But on other occasions the war god received offerings of a more bloody nature. Along with the flayed god Xipetotec, continues Sahagun, he was given sacrifices of all prisoners—'men, women, and children. The owners of prisoners handed them over to the priests at the foot of the temple, and they dragged them by the hair, each one his own, up the steps'. Having killed them, extracted their hearts, flayed the corpses, and dismembered their limbs, the priests sent portions of the flesh to the ruler and the nobility to eat. The native historian Ixtililxochitl explains the continuous military activities of the Aztecs as a method of obtaining prisoners for sacrifice to their voracious gods. These ritual killings, of course, fermented the political antagonism that they were intended to prevent.

The Aztec god Xipetotec, who gave food to mankind by having himself flayed alive

Hunab

Or Hunab Ku, 'the single god'. The remote creator deity in Maya belief. He renewed the world after the three deluges, which poured from the mouth of the sky serpent. The first world was inhabited by dwarfs, the builders of the great ruined cities; in the second lived the *dzolob*, or 'offenders', an obscure race; the third world saw the Maya themselves; the present one peopled by a mixture of tribes will also end with a flood. This alternation of destruction and renewal is a reflection of the duality in Maya religion. Chac, the rain god, tended the new shoots of the tree, while the god of death, Ah Puch, sought to nip off the seed leaves.

Ictinike

The deceitful son of the sun god in the mythology of the Iowa, a principal Sioux tribe. From Ictinike many of the Indian peoples learned their war customs, and for this reason he is sometimes looked upon as a war god. In the tales of his adventures the dominant themes are treachery and deceit.

Igaluk

One of the names of the Eskimo moon god. In Alaska Igaluk is the supreme deity: he directs natural phenomena. Under his authority are all the creatures that elsewhere belong to the sea goddess Sedna.

The Eskimo people of Greenland say that the sun and moon are brother and sister. Once in the winter, long ago, during the Arctic night, people began to sport in the igloos, with the lamps out. Then one by one the man took outside the women they had been with, and lighted torches to see who they were. Thus it was that the moon man discovered his playmate had been the sun woman, his own sister. In horror the sun tore off her breasts and threw them down in front of the moon. Then with a flaming torch in her hand, she rose into the sky. Her brother chased after her, but the torch he carried went out, so that it only glowed. Now they have a house in heaven, divided into two rooms; and the moon has not the brilliance of the sun.

Inti

The Inca sun god. He was looked upon as the ancestor of the Incas, whom he had sent down to earth in order to assist the development of civilization. The identification of Inti with the Inca crown led to the merging of their worship. After the death of Pachacuti Yupanqui Inca, the founder of the empire, his dried body and that of his consort were the centre of an impressive annual rite. Their bodies were removed from a palace tomb, seated on gold-covered biers, and taken to sit in the great temple dedicated to the sun god.

At Machu Picchu still stands the 'hitching post of the sun', *intihuatana*, a ceremonial shadow clock which was used in the observance of Inti's course. Around these large stone pillars would gather priests, wise men, and astrologers so as to ascertain the pattern of cosmic events. But Inti was always regarded as a kind and generous deity, like his wife the moon goddess.

Itzamna

In the Maya pantheon, the most active and important deity. Son of the creator god Hunab, Itzamna was the lord of the heavens, and also lord of the day and night. He was represented as a kindly old man with toothless jaws, sunken cheeks, and a pronounced nose. A cultural hero, too, he invented writing and books, established religious ceremonies, and 'divided the land'. Itzamna, often identified with the sun, was entirely benevolent, never being held responsible for any destruction or disaster.

Ixchel

In Maya mythology, the angry old woman who emptied the vials of her wrath upon the earth and assisted the sky serpent in creating the deluge. Ixchel was the goddess of floods and cloudbursts, a malevolent deity likely to cause sudden destruction in a tropical storm. The consort of Itzamna, 'lord of the heavens', she was zealously appeased and propitiated by sacrifices. In her oldest form Ixchel appears as a clawed water goddess, surrounded by the symbols of death and destruction, a writhing serpent on her head, and crossbones embroidered on her skirt.

Ixtab

The Maya goddess of suicide. Ixtab was portrayed as dangling from the sky with a rope round her neck; her eyes were closed in death and her cheeks already showed the first signs of decomposition. It was believed that suicides by hanging, warriors killed in battle, sacrificial victims, women who died in childbirth, and members of the priesthood went directly to paradise. Ixtab came to fetch these lucky souls. In the delectable shade of the cosmic tree, *yaxche*, the inhabitants of paradise could rest from labour, and escape from all suffering and want.

Iyatiku
The corn goddess of the Keresan Puebloes. From *shipap*, her underground realm, mankind first emerged, from there infants today are born, and thither go the dead. The Cochiti Puebloes regard Mesewi as the hero who led the ancestors of the tribe out of shipap.

Jaguar
The fanged god of pre-Columbian religion in South America. Statues of deities with staring eyes and double fangs exist dating from very early periods. In Mochica culture the remote creator deity of the mountain had a feline appearance. Among the tribes of Bolivia, where the jaguar is indigenous, men still go out to kill the animal single-handed and armed only with a wooden spear in order to win the status of warriors. Yet it would seem that the close association between medicine-men and jaguar spirits elsewhere represents a survival of an ancient taboo placed on the jaguar and puma. The jaguar is the power, the ambivalent force, which the adept has to master. It is also the personification of fertility in the widest sense, witness the statues of jaguars coupling with women.

Kanassa
In Kuikuru mythology, the creator deity and the bringer of fire. At the beginning, relate the Kuikuru Indians of the Xingu River in Brazil, Kanassa could not see what he was doing. He drew a ray in the mud at the water's edge, but as it was dark, he could not see and stepped on his own drawing and was stung by it. As soon as the ray had hurt him, it plunged into the water. In anger Kanassa said: 'I just made her, and already she has wounded me. It's all the firefly's fault, because he doesn't give any light.' Then he remembered the king vulture, *ugwvu-cuengo*, was the master of fire. So he devised a plan—and like the sun god Kuat in Kamaivran tradition—Kanassa seized one of the bird's legs and obliged it to bring down an ember from the sky. Although the frogs tried to squirt water over the flames of the fire that Kanassa made, the sacred light was not lost and a serpent helped the god to carry it safely away from the lagoon.

Kasogonaga
According to the Chaco tribes, the original inhabitants of the Pampas, rain was produced by a female spirit hanging in the sky. This was Kasogonaga. A variant myth cites a red ant-eater, while the creation of the world was achieved by a gigantic beetle, which also created the spirits and the first man and women. The latter were stuck together until he parted them.

The hunters of the Pampas seem to have had no supreme being. There were benevolent spirits, even deities addressed as grandfather or mother, but the various tribes lacked a consistent cosmology. Rival brothers explained duality in one tribe, another thought that the rainbow killed by its tongue, and a third blamed the stars. Even the legendary hero Carancho, sometimes identified with the hawk, found himself bedevilled by a fox.

Kici Manitu
Literal meaning: 'great spirit'. The supreme deity of the Algonquins, the most widely diffused of Indian peoples. Kici Manitu created heaven, earth, men, animals, and plants. Mankind he made from earth and a spirit he breathed into the body, but the rest of creation proceeded through intermediaries.

According to the Arapahoes, a western Algonquin tribe, 'the ancestor with the sacred pipe' wandered over the huge watery waste at the beginning of the world. This was Kici Manitu, 'weeping and fasting', as he searched for the place where earth would arise. With a loud voice he called together all water birds and reptiles, the creatures that already existed, and asked for assistance. So it was that the turtle knew where earth could be found, and the water fowl were able to bring back portions in their bills. Kici Manitu dried the clay upon his pipe, made the world, and took delight in its beauty. Even the arrival of Bitter Man, the personification of disease, old age, and death, could not mar that moment.

On the other hand, the Delaware tribe visualizes the universe as 'the true Big-House', the centre post of which is the staff of Kici Manitu, 'the father'.

Kononatoo
Literally, 'our maker'. The Warau Indians of Guiana believe that Kononatoo wished them to live in heaven. They descended to earth when a young hunter discovered a hole in the sky, but have been unable to return there

because a fat woman got stuck in it. Moreover, the disobedience of the Warau on earth saddened the creator deity and deterred him from making another entrance to heaven. It appears that two girls swam in a forbidden lake and the offspring of one of them, begotten by a water god, started the species of serpents. The extreme reluctance of the Warau to bathe must relate to this myth.

Koshare
According to the Pueblo Indians, the Koshare were the first men. A certain goddess wanted to amuse her companions and so she rubbed a ball of skin off herself in order to make the Koshare. In Navaho legend the goddess Estsanatlehi used the same method of creation. Today the Koshare are the clowns who enliven the Pueblo dance with their absurd antics. They perform a critical function, since their satirical comments and posturings on the times are beyond censorship.

Kuat
The sun god in Kamaiuran mythology. In the beginning, according to this Amazon tribe of the Xingu River, all was dark. It was always night. People dwelt around the termite hills. In the confusion life was squalid. The brothers Kuat and Iae, the sun and the moon, did not know what to do. They could not make light. Since the birds already possessed day in their village, the sun decided to steal it from Urubutsin, 'vulture king'. He sent the flies with an effigy, full of maggots, but Urubutsin could not make any sense out of the hum of flies. When one of his subjects eventually interpreted the message, the chief bird realized that the delicious maggots were a gift and that the flies bore an invitation to the birds to visit the sun and eat many more.

So it was that the birds shaved themselves bald and started out. Meanwhile Kuat and Iae had hidden themselves in another effigy. As soon as Urubutsin landed on it in order to eat, the sun grabbed one of his feet and held it fast. Deserted by the other birds, Urubutsin agreed to let the sun and moon have day, which was brought as a ransom. He also explained the alternation of day and night, ending with assurance that day 'will always come back'.

Kukulcan
Possibly the Maya wind god, counterpart of the Aztec plumed serpent Quetzalcoatl.

According to Maya records, a conqueror named Kukulcan arrived in Yucatan by sea from the west in or shortly after 987. Kukulcan, 'feathered serpent', clearly recalls Quetzalcoatl, the name or title of the Toltec leader who quit the great city of Tollan in the face of an insurrection of subject peoples. Kukulcan, therefore, seems to be a cultural founder hero as much as a god of wind.

Kumush
According to the Modoc Indians of northern California, Kumush was 'the old man of the ancients'. Once he went down with his daughter to the underground world of the spirits. In this beautiful realm it was the custom for the spirits to sing and dance at night, but when daylight came, they returned to their resting places and became dry bones. After six days and six nights in the land of the spirits, Kumush decided to return to the upper world and take some of the spirits with him. So he collected in a big basket lots of bones. Three times he attempted to climb the long and steep road out of the underground realm; twice he stumbled, and the spirits, shouting and singing, leapt from the basket and returned to their places; but on the third attempt he spoke to them angrily, telling how marvellous was the world above. Stepping into the blaze of the sun's rays outside the entrance to the underground road, Kumush threw down the basket and called out: 'Indian bones!'

Then he opened the basket and selected the bones of the different tribes. His final choice was the Modoc Indians, his brave and chosen people. 'Though you will be a small tribe and though your enemies are many,' said Kumush, 'you will defeat all who come against you.' Then he finished his arrangement of the world, travelled along the sun's road, and built for himself and his daughter a house in the middle of the sky. There they live today.

Kururumany
According to the Arawak Indians, who live in the Orinoco basin of South America, Kururumany was the creator of men, while Kulimina formed women. The creator deity introduced death into the world as soon as he learned of the corruption of mankind. He also added such things as serpents, lizards, and

A medicine man, the North American Shaman, of the Blackfoot Indians

fleas. Beyond Kururumany, however, there appears to a remote and indifferent first cause, Aluberi. It may be that Kururumany was originally looked upon as a world-building ant god, the agent of an otiose supreme being.

Kwatee

Or Kivati. The changer or trickster god of the Indian tribes resident in the Puget Sound region of Washington. It was Kwatee, 'the-man-who-changed-things', and his mythical assistants who transformed the ancient world into the world which we know today. Originally the colossal animal people, like Spider, Ant, Beaver, Fox, and Coyote, owned the land and there were no human beings. But Kwatee, the Quinault Indians say, 'went up and down the country changing things . . . as he was getting the world ready for the new people who were to come'.

When the giant animal people tried to stop his activities, Kwatee made ordinary animals out of them. One would-be assassin became the deer, another the beaver. Then Kwatee rubbed his hands over his own body until he made little balls of dirt and sweat. These he changed into people, the first Indians. On his wanderings he created other people from dogs and showed them how to use stones as mallets and cutting tools. More heroic was the killing of the monster living in Lake Quinault. When the cavernous throat of this beast opened to swallow Kwatee's brother and his canoe, the changer god tossed hot rocks into the lake. The water boiled and the monster rose to the surface, dead. Slitting the monster's stomach he released his brother, who had changed into the father of hermit crabs.

Old and tired at last, Kwatee reviewed his work of transformation and perceived that he had made all the changes he could make to help mankind. He sat on a rock, watching the sun disappear over the western rim of the ocean, and after the sunset he pulled a blanket over his face, thereby turning himself into stone.

Legba

Derived from the West African ancestor god Lebe, 'the old man at the gate' in the Voodoo cult of Haiti is Legba, a god or loa identified with the sun. 'Open the road for me,' pray his devotees, 'do not let any evil spirits bar my path.' Whereas Legba commands the divinities of the day, Carrefour has dominion over the spirits of the night. The latter is conceived

of as an energetic moon man, capable of good and evil actions.

Manco Capac

Or Ayar Manco. The semi-legendary founder of the Inca dynasty. There are three versions of the myth. In the first, four brothers and four sisters proceeded in the general direction of Cuzco, looking for somewhere to settle. During the journey Ayar Cachi, who possessed magical strength, was walled into a cave by his brothers who feared his destructive tendencies. Then Ayar Oco turned himself into a sacred stone and Ayar Ayca became the protector of the fields, leaving the last brother, Ayar Manco, to seize Cuzco with his sisters, one of whom he married. She was Mama Ocllo.

In a second version the sun god Inti, seeing how wretched men were, felt pity for them and sent to earth on an island in Lake Titicaca his two children Manco Capac and Mama Ocllo, brother and sister, to establish civilization. They travelled northwards carrying with them a wedge of gold. Wherever this sank into the ground, they were instructed to settle. In the soil of the plain on which Cuzco stands this occurred. From this city, the dynasty they founded conquered all the Andean peoples. A variant has three brothers and a sister.

According to the third version, eagerly recorded by Spanish historians, the Inca crown acquired divine status because of Manco Capac, an astute ruler with a love of display. His splendid clothes and the elaborate customs of his court impressed a gullible people. Manco Capac, however, was supposed to be the first Inca emperor.

Masewi

The twin brothers of Pueblo mythology are Masewi and Oyoyewa, whom the universal mother sent into the world to place the sun correctly in the sky and assign people to their clans.

Mavutsinim

The Kamaiura Indians, inhabitants of the Xingu River in Brazil, say that in the beginning there was only Mavutsinim, the creator. He turned a shell into a woman and begot a son, the first man. Then Mavutsinim took away the child and the tearful mother went to a lagoon, turning into a shell again. 'We are the grandchildren of Mavutsinim's son,' declare the Kamaiura.

Mictlantecuhtli

The Aztec god of death, who ruled in the restful and silent kingdom of the dead, *mictlan*. When the Emperor Montezuma Xocoyotzin received intelligence of impending disaster, the sorcerers' view of inextinguishable fires, comets, and strange birds, he sent emissaries to Mictlantecuhtli laden with sumptuous gifts—the skins of flayed men. He yearned for the peace of mictlan, since he was gripped by uncertainty and apprehensive over the rumours of Quetzalcoatl's return.

Napi

Literal meaning: 'old man'. The creator deity of the Blackfoot Indians, a tribe of Algonquin stock. It is suggested that Napi is a god of light rather than a solar deity. This would make his name 'dawn-light-colour-man'.

In character the Old Man is a curious mixture of opposite attributes. At the creation of the world he is spoken of as the thoughtful and wise sky father; but, in other dealings with mankind, he displays an impishness, even a spite worthy of the trickster god Coyote. The Blackfeet, however, are sure about his immortality. They say that he has simply withdrawn into the mountains and has promised to return one day. Natos, 'the sun', appears to have taken the place of Napi as their supreme deity: his wife is Kokomikeis, 'the moon'. According to legend, all the children of Natos and Kokomikeis were eaten by pelicans, except Apisuahts, 'the morning star'.

Having created the world and set it in order,

A Navajo sand picture of a holy man (centre) guarded on the right by Nayenezgani

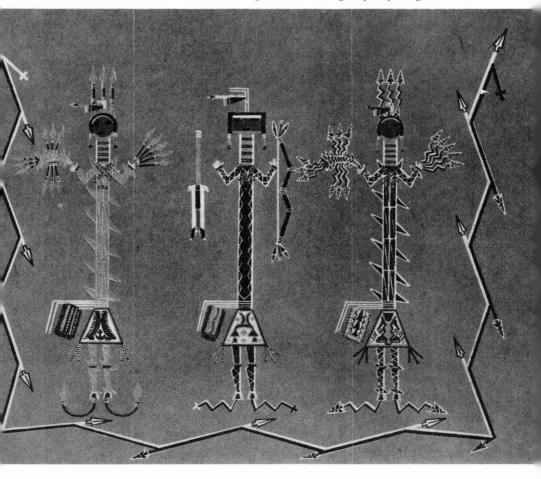

Napi made the first people out of clay. By a river he introduced himself to them, and was surprised at a question from the first women. She asked: 'How is it? Will we always live, will there be no end to it?' He replied: 'I have never thought of that. We must decide. I will toss this chip of wood into the river. If it floats, when people die, in four days they will breathe again; death will last four days. But if it sinks, there will be no end to death.' Napi threw the chip in the river and it floated. The first women picked up a stone and said: 'If it floats we will always live, but if it sinks people must die.' The stone immediately sank and Napi said: 'You have chosen.' Later the woman's baby died so that she realized what she had done.

Nayenezgani

Literally, 'slayer of alien gods'. Along with Tobadzistsini, 'child of the water', the Navajo Indians say that Nayenezgani dealt fearful blows to the spirits of evil threatening the world. The two brothers, Nayenezgani and Tobadzistsini, may be seen as war gods, but they are more like cultural heroes. As the offspring of Estsanatlehi, 'the woman who changes', and Tsohanoai, the sun god, Nayenezgani appears to be a lord of light, while Tobadzistsini, moist and dark, is his opposite, a lord of darkness.

Once the two brothers encountered Nastse Estsan, the benign Spider Woman. They were on their way to the house of the sun god when they noticed smoke rising from the ground. Looking closely they found it came from the smoke hole of a subterranean chamber, into which led a ladder. Having climbed down the rungs of this smoke-blackened ladder, the two brothers were greeted by Naste Estsan, who told them that their journey to the Tsohanoai's abode would lead them past four places of danger. They were the rocks which crush the traveller; the reeds which cut him to pieces; the cacti which tear him to pieces; and the boiling sands that overwhelm him. To aid them in their quest Naste Estan presented two charms: a feather to subdue enemies and a feather to preserve lives.

After many adventures, thanks to the magical feathers, Nayenezgani and Tobadzistsini reached the square house of the sun god and beheld its handsome occupants. Two young women there stood up without a word, wrapped the two brothers in a bundle, and placed them on a shelf. On his return Tsohanoai demanded to know who it was that had dared to call in his absence. His wife cautioned him, but the enraged sun god pulled the visitors from the bundle and proceeded to test their strength. First, he threw them on to sharp spikes, but the two brothers tightly clutched Naste Estan's feathers. Secondly, the sun god tried to steam them without avail. As a final assay he forced them to taste a smoking-pipe filled with poison. A caterpillar warned of the danger and gave them something to put into their mouths. Thus was Tsohanoai satisfied with the two brothers and he acknowledged them as his own sons. When he asked about the purpose of their visit, they told him of the *anaye*, 'monsters or evil gods', who devour men, and requested that he furnish them with divine weapons. Though he informed the two brothers that the chief anaye, the giant Yeitso, was also his son, Tsohanoai let them have powerful arms, including a chain-lightning arrow, a sheet-lightning arrow, a sunbeam arrow, and a rainbow arrow.

Nayenezgani and Tobadzistsini then left through the sky hole, *yagahoka*, and descended to earth via steep, shining cliffs in order to do battle. They encountered scaly Yeitso by a lake and slew and scalped the monster with a little help from Tsohanoai. Next Nayenezgani alone killed dreadful Teelget, a great four-footed beast with the horns of deer. Using a tunnel burrowed into the monster's hide by a gopher, he succeeded in reaching Teelget's enormous heart, which he pierced with an arrow of chain-lightning. The enraged anaye virtually ripped itself to shreds with its horns to get at Nayenezgani, before slumping dead to the earth.

The third kind of anaye to meet their doom were the Tsenahale, huge eagle-like beasts that almost crushed Nayenezgani in their talons. Again the lightning arrow found the mark and the hero was able to dispose of this terror: the parents were destroyed, their plucked feathers changing into smaller birds like wrens and warblers, while the young Tsenahale became the eagles from which later men obtained plumes for head-dresses. Nayenezgani's other exploits were ridding the world of the Binaye Ahani, 'the people who slay with their eyes'; the defeat of Tsenagahi, 'the travelling stone', a mischievous rock spirit; and the beheading of a ferocious bear.

Ogoun

The Voodoo warrior hero of Haiti, a divinity

related to the Nigerian iron god Ogun. There are many Ogouns: the fighter; the politician; the victim, head drooping and arms outstretched like the crucified Christ; the magician; the impairer, *ferei*; the gate keeper, known as Ogoun Panama, 'the straw hat'; and the guardian of fire.

Ogoun never receives libations of water. Instead, rum is poured on the ground, and a match is set to it, so as to produce his sacred colour, red. When in possession of a devotee the fierce god wants a strong drink, he will shout: 'My testicles are cold!'

Oi

According to the tribes living along the Xingu River in Brazil, the remote past belonged to such legendary nations as the Oi, who were very tall and had a curious habit of singing in chorus as they walked. Since the Oi have disappeared only in recent times, the Indian peoples have remembered their chant and can still intone it today. Another mythical nation was the Minata-Karaia, whose men had a hole in the top of their heads that produced a high, loud whistle. They also had bunches of coconuts growing from under their armpits; these fruits they snatched, broke against their heads, and ate.

Ometecuhtli

Literally, 'the dual lord'. Above the other gods in the Aztec pantheon, far above the events of the world, stood Ometecuhtli, the androgynous master of duality and the source of all existence. Outside space and time, 'beyond the stars', this supreme being was the unity of contraries—male and female, light and dark, movement and stillness, order and chaos. Below Ometecuhtli was the great spirit of the world, Tezcatlipoca, and his rival Quetzalcoatl, whom the Aztecs regarded as in temporary exile. At last the plumed-serpent lord would return to inaugurate a new religion.

Pachacamac

Literally, 'earth-maker'. An ancient creator deity of Peru. He may have originated among the coastal peoples as a fish god. The Incas adopted his cult and his name appears in the title of several rulers. According to a creation myth, Pachacamac forgot to provide the first man and woman with food. When the man died of starvation, the woman accused the sun of neglect, whereupon this god made her fertile. Pachacamac killed the son that she bore and cut the corpse into pieces, from which grew vegetables and fruits. A second son, named Wichama, he was unable to catch, but he slew the first woman. In revenge for his mother's death, Wichama pursued Pachacamac, driving him into the sea.

Pachamama

The earth goddess of the Incas. She received sacrifices of llamas and other animals. Before the first Incas entered Cuzco, their capital, they killed a llama. One of the four sisters in the party caught the animal, removed the lungs, and inflated them with wind. Carrying this bloody standard of Pachamama and the golden wedge of the sun god Inti, they entered the city. Worship of the earth goddess survives today, and she has also been identified with the Virgin Mary.

Page Abe

Literally, 'father sun'. Creator deity of the Tukano Indians, who live in the upper reaches of the Amazon, along the Colombian-Brazilian border.

In the beginning, say the Tukano, there were the sun, Page Abe, and the moon, called Nyami Abe or 'nocturnal sun'. Since Nyami Abe had no wife, he was lonely and tried to force the sun's wife: hearing of it, Page Abe deprived the moon of his feather head-dress and ordered him to keep away from the family. Never again did the sun and the moon share the same quarter of the sky. After this dispute, Page Abe created the earth and placed on it animals, plants, and men. In this work he was aided by a semi-divine being called Pamuri-mahse, but it was the sun's own daughter, Abe Mango, who descended to earth in order to teach the Tukano people how to live well. Her gifts were fire, buildings, pottery, weaving, and cookery.

Pamuri-mahse

In Tukano mythology, a semi-divine assistant of the sun god and creator deity Page Abe. The Amazonian Indians say that Pamuri-mahse brought down to earth many dangerous beasts, including the large snakes of the river. One large snake with seven heads fell in love with a young girl and it would have carried her off had not a medicine-man and a dog intervened. After a fierce struggle, they succeeded in killing all seven heads. Then the medicine-man brought firewood and burned the snake's carcass, but the black smoke that arose from the large bonfire was carried by the wind to the sea, where it fell as rain on the waves and the snake was reborn.

Pinga

In certain Eskimo myths the moon god Igaluk is subordinate to the mysterious Pinga, 'the one on high'. This goddess acts as the guardian of game, the controller of the hunt, the protectress of the living, and the helper of the *angakut*, 'medicine-men'. Another helper of the shamans is Asiaq, the goddess of weather.

Potlatch

Literally, 'giving'. An extravagant festival held by the Indian tribes of the northern Pacific coast, especially the Haida, the Nootka, and the Kwakiutl. The ceremonial destruction or giving away of possessions by chiefs and leading warriors establishes superiority in social or political status, or permits the assumption of inherited rights. One chief might 'shame' another by destroying valuable pots, killing slaves, and burning down houses. If the other chief failed either to give away or to destroy more things, then he would lose public esteem. According to legend, the first *potlatch* was concerned with the exchange of feathers, long regarded as sacred objects by the North American Indians.

Punotsihyo

According to the Blackfeet of Montana, the earth belongs to Punotsihyo, 'the ground man'. He is highly respected and receives many sacrifices. Aisoyimstan, 'cold maker', freezes the earth or blankets it with snow. He is portrayed as a man, white in colour, with white hair, and dressed in white clothes, who rides a white horse.

Quetzalcoatl

The plumed serpent god of Central America. He was the giver of breath and the god of winds. At the same time he was a creator deity, identified with the sun, and the god who descended into the land of the dead, mictlan, where 'he fell like one dead'. On his recovery, perhaps aided by his double, he gathered up the precious bones there, returned to the earth and, sprinkling them with his own blood, he turned them into human beings.

The mystery surrounding the figure of Quetzalcoatl derives from his dual character. On one hand he is patently a deity at the centre of an amazing myth: as a man, on the other hand, he has acquired the legendary status of a cultural founder hero. In his *History of Things of New Spain*, written in the sixteenth century, Bernardino de Sahagun wrote: 'In the city of Tollan reigned many years a king called Quetzalcoatl. . . . He was exceptional in moral virtues . . . the place of this king among these natives is like King Arthur among the English.' The temple pyramid dedicated to Quetzalcoatl in this advanced city had been built by the Toltecs, whose ninth emperor priest he was. Three centuries after the collapse of Toltec power the rulers of Aztecs were pleased to call themselves 'successors of Quetzalcoatl'. He was regarded as the greatest historical king: he started the cultivation of maize; he introduced weaving, the polishing of stone, and the making of feather mantles; he taught men how to measure time and study the movements of the stars; he invented the calendar along with its fixed ceremonies and days of prayer; he expounded religious doctrines. The brutal Aztecs, who exaggerated the Toltec obsession with human sacrifice, used the Quetzalcoatl myth to prop up their military state. However, they also inherited the prophecy that, one day, this king would return from the sea and reclaim his throne. It was a fatalism that Hernando Cortés exploited in 1519-21 when he posed as the undead Quetzalcoatl.

Myth recounts the fall and exile of Quetzalcoatl. His enemy was Tezcatlipoca, a chief warrior, who weakened the king by 'giving him his body'. That is to say, Quetzalcoatl was tempted into drunkenness and sensuality. Anguish then consumed his heart and, after a mock death in a stone box, he ordered the abandonment of the city of Tollan. He burned his palace, buried his treasures, and, putting on his insignia of feathers as well as his green mask, he departed in great sorrow. Reaching the sea-shore, Quetzalcoatl may have immolated himself on a funeral pyre and rare birds have arisen from his ashes. Or, as was generally believed, he sailed eastwards on a raft of serpents after saying he would return. Historically, the deposed ruler could have arrived in Yucatan, since shortly before 987 Mayan records note the coming of Kukulkan, 'the feather serpent', and the foundation of a new state there.

Sedna

The sinister sea goddess of Eskimo myth-

An Aztec turquoise mask thought to represent either Quetzalcoatl or Tonatiuh

ology. Only an angakoq, 'medicine-man', can withstand the sight of her hideous one-eyed form.

Various legends account for her wild temper and her dominion over *adlivun*, 'those beneath us', the unholy dead. Daughter of giant parents, Sedna was an unmanageable child, who would seize on flesh and eat it whenever the opportunity arose. One night she started to eat the limbs of her mother and father as they slept. They awoke in horror, grasped the voracious daughter, and took her in a boat far out to sea. Cast overboard, Sedna clung on to the side of the boat, and her father had to cut off her fingers one by one to make her let go. As the severed fingers touched the waves they turned into whales, seals, and shoals of fish. Then fingerless Sedna sank to the bottom of the sea where she now dwells and keeps strict guard over all who live there.

Another version represents Sedna as 'she who did not wish to marry'. She refused suitors and only favoured a bird or a dog. The enraged parents dumped her fingerless in the sea. Her one-eyed father, however, had one hand, the three fingers of which he used to seize the dying. The family deformity and its connection with the dead, therefore, suggests that Sedna's descent to the bottom of the sea was nothing more than a myth to explain her enthronement as mistress of the underworld.

Adlivun, her dreadful domain, housed the spirits of those who disobeyed her during life. In some places the Eskimo people believe that these unfortunate souls return to their villages in flapping clothes, as malevolent spirits. The antithesis of Sedna's realm is *qudlivun*, the solace of those who had a mean life, or those who were generous to others.

Si

The Mochica moon god. The fanged Ai Apaec gave place to another deity, a radiant and armoured war god, who was the prototype of the later moon god. The great Si assumed the hegemony of the gods because of his control of the elements, storms, and the calendar.

Sinaa

The feline ancestor of the Juruna, an Indian tribe living along the Xingu River in Brazil. Sinaa's father was an enormous jaguar, his mother a woman. For an unknown reason both father and son had eyes set in the back of their heads. Sinaa was very old, 'but he became young again each time he took a bath, pulling his skin off over his head like a sack'. The end of the world will come, according to the Juruna, when Sinaa finally decides to pull down the enormous forked stick that supports the sky.

Sta-au

The ghosts of wicked people. According to the Blackfoot Indians, the shadow of a person is his soul. Usually the deceased inhabit a certain range of hills, but in the case of malignant spirits they loiter near encampments and cause harm to the living, especially after sunset.

Tawiscara

The Huron spirit of evil. The twin grandsons of the moon, Tawiscara and Ioskeha, represent the antithetical forces in Nature. In their bloody fight for supremacy Ioskeha armed himself with the horns of a stag, while Tawiscara could only seize a wild rose. For this reason the evil one was driven off, bleeding 'flint stones', and Ioskeha became the guardian deity of the Hurons, Mohawks, and Tuscaroras.

Tecciztecatl

In Aztec mythology, he was the old man who carried a large white seashell on his back. Tecciztecatl, 'old moon god', represented the male form of the planet, even its rising from the ocean.

Tezcatlipoca

Literally, 'smoking mirror'. His name refers to the black obsidian mirror when used by Aztec magicians to descry the future. Tezcatlipoca had several aspects: he was the patron of warriors and identified with Huitzilopochtli; he was the original sun knocked out of the sky and turned into a tiger by Quetzalcoatl; he was a trickster god associated with witches, thieves, and evildoers in general; and, not least, he was an all-powerful deity who could take or give life. Details survive of a custom whereby a youth impersonated Tezcatlipoca for a year and then was ritually killed in the spring, his heart being offered to the sun.

Tieholtsodi

In Navaho mythology, the water monster. Tieholtsodi was formerly an enemy of mankind, but now has become less antagonistic, though he is still believed to be responsible for cases of drowning. As king of the ocean, he was unable to resist the demands of Tonenili, the rain god, and Hastsezini, the fire god, when they rescued the first Navaho from the deep.

Tlaloc

The rain god of ancient Mexico, worshipped

by the Toltecs and their successors, the Aztecs. He was the controller of clouds, rain, lightning, and mountain springs. His kingdom received the spirits of those killed by thunderbolts, water, leprosy, and contagious diseases: it was named the earthly paradise, *tlalocan*.

Tlauixcalpantecuhtli
In Tollan a destructive deity identified with the planet Venus. In Tenochtitlan the Aztecs retained this Toltec apprehension and thought that in his different phases Tlauixcalpantecuhtli, 'lord of the house of dawn', threatened ill to the various social classes.

Tlazolteotl
In Aztec mythology, the goddess of filth. She was associated with witchcraft and the purification of sin, acting as a go-between for the penitent in respect of the god Tezcatlipoca, 'the mirror that smokes'. The Aztecs saw Tlazolteotl essentially as the power behind all forms of unclean behaviour: her special terror was sex. In order to preserve the fanaticism of warriors at Tenochtitlan a corps of prostitutes was maintained, recruited from ordinary families in the city. The young girls, devotees of the goddess, were trained and periodically turned loose on the military barracks. After such festivals these black-mouthed instruments of Tlazolteotl were seized upon and ceremonially killed.

Tonapa
Or Conapa, 'heat-bearing'. One of the divine assistants of Viracocha, the creator deity of ancient Peru. He may have been bound and set adrift upon Lake Titicaca as a punishment for rebellion against Viracocha. Tonapa's symbol, a cross, and his iconoclasm led early missionaries to associate him with Christianity.

Tonatiuh
The Aztec sun god. The fourth in a series of suns, Tonatiuh gave power to warriors and because of his heat and thirst, he received the hearts and blood offered in the daily sacrifices. The Aztecs conceived of this god as a power being constantly burnt up, threatened by the colossal task of its daytime birth and journey as well as its struggle and death at night. Only through continuous sacrifice and moral virtue would the sun be sustained. The ancient Mexican insight into life, the notion that happiness comes from toil and suffering, was

Tlaloc, Aztec god of clouds and rain, holding bowl containing rain

undoubtedly debased in the Aztec use of mass slaughter of ritual victims, but not for one moment can it be suggested that these militaristic tribesmen deviated from their profound beliefs. The coming of Christianity to Mexico had been foretold; this new dispensation was brought by Quetzalcoatl incarnated as Hernardo Cortés.

Tonenili
Literally, 'water sprinkler'. The rain god of the Navaho Indians of Arizona. A deity given to having fun and playing tricks, Tonenili carries a water pot. In the tribal dances he is represented by a masked man who enacts the part of a clown. In the myths, too, he is the fool who dances about in order to show that he is pleased with what is happening.

Tsohanoai
The Navaho sun god. He is conceived of as a man who carries the sun on his back. At night Tsohanoai, 'sun bearer', is said to hang the sun on a peg on the west wall of his house.

Tulungusaq
In Alaska the Eskimo people believe that the crow father Tulungusaq was aided by a swallow in giving form to the world. This

4

192 America

legend appears to owe something to North American Indian traditions, for there is no distinct creation myth in Eskimo religion. The groups living in Greenland simply hold that the earth 'dropped from above' and that people 'came up out of the earth'. Overpopulation was prevented by the sea goddess Sedna, who took pleasure in drowning many men.

Eskimo art reflects the absence of the notion of creation. There is no real equivalent of our words 'create' or 'make'. The closest term means 'to work on'; it is a restrained kind of activity, like the aim of the Eskimo carver of ivory to release the characteristic form of the piece in hand.

Tzi-daltai

The fetishes worn by Apache Indians in New Mexico. They are usually carved from lightning river wood, generally pine or cedar, or fir from the mountains. Miniature statues in form, tzi-daltai are 'medicine' and offer protection to the wearer, like the sacred feathers given to the Navaho heroes Nayenezgani and Tobadzistsini.

Uaica

The Asclepius of the Juruna, an Indian tribe living along the Xingu River in Brazil. One day Uaica, out hunting in the forest, noticed a lot of dead animals under a large tree. When he approached the heap of beasts, he felt dizzy, fell down, and went to sleep. In his deep dream he saw Sinaa, the jaguar ancestor of the Juruna, who talked to him. This happened on several occasions till the deity told him to keep away.

Uaica obeyed. He also made a drink from the bark of the tree: from this potent brew he acquired many powers. Uaica became a great medicine-man who could take away disease with the touch of his hand. Sinaa would come into his dreams again, and through their conversation all the needs of the people were supplied. Pressed by the Juruna, Uaica consented to marry, but his wife was unfaithful to him. Through this shortcoming and the attempt of her lover on Uaica's life the Juruna lost the medicine-man. It happened that Uaica, who had eyes in the back of his head, saw the swinging club, and instantly he disappeared into the hole it made on striking the ground. Uaica said: 'I shall not return. Arrows and clubs will be your lot. I tried to teach what Sinaa wished, but now I go.' Later the medicine-man is said to have beckoned the Juruna to follow him underground, but they were too baffled and frightened to do so.

Ueuecoyotl

Literally, 'old old coyote'. The trickster god of ancient Mexico: his spontaneity was greatly feared by the puritanical Aztecs, especially when his irresponsible gaiety involved sex.

Uixtocihuatl

In June the Aztec women celebrated the festival of Uixtocihuatl, 'the salt goddess'. Old women and young girls danced together wearing flowers on their heads, the climax of the ceremony being a human sacrifice at the pyramid of Tlaloc, the rain god.

Vai-mahse

Literal meaning: 'master of animals'. The Tukano Indians of the upper reaches of the Amazon look upon Vai-mahse as the most important spirit of the forest. A dwarf with a body painted red, Vai-mahse controls the game of the hunter, the fishes in the rivers, and the herbs beneath the trees. Certain hillocks are sacred to him and care is taken not to earn his displeasure. Vai-mahse's deadly weapon is a short wand, highly polished and red in colour. His overriding interest in fecundity explains his unkindness to pregnant women and young mothers, to whom he sends sickness—because he was not the cause of their pregnancy.

Other forest spirits are the Boraro, 'white ones'. They are tall, with hairy chests and huge phalluses; their ears stick forwards and their feet backwards; while the lack of a knee joint causes them difficulty in rising from the ground after a fall. Should a Boraro be seen carrying a stone hoe, it is certain that he is on the lookout for someone to devour.

Viracocha

The supreme being of the Incas: a storm god and a sun god. Of great importance in Peru even before the rise of the Inca Empire, Viracocha was represented with the sun for a crown, thunderbolts in his hands, and tears descending from his eyes as rain. He was Illa, 'light'; Tici, 'the beginning of things'; while Viracocha itself may have meant 'the lake of creation'. Lake Titicaca, according to one tradition, was the site of the creation of the sun, moon, and stars. Yet in his legendary wanderings on earth, he assumed the form of a beggar. The ragged and reviled mendicant was probably connected with the unique feature of Viracocha, his cosmic tears. The living waters were the tears of the creator deity, who knew the sufferings of his creatures and still felt obliged to sustain their lives.

Viracocha made the earth, the stars, the sky, and mankind. But this first creation did not please him, so he swept the world in a deluge, killing the first men, who were probably giants. Then he made new and better men, among whom he wandered as a beggar teaching the rudiments of civilization as well as working numerous miracles. A late cosmology, however, describes five ages. The first was the age of Viracocha, when the gods ruled and death was unknown; the second was an age of giants, the worshippers of Viracocha; third came the age of the first men, who existed on a very primitive level; fourth, that of the *auca runa*, 'warriors', the authors of early civilizations such as the Mochica; and fifth that of the Inca rule, ended by the coming of the Spaniards in 1531. Viracocha himself disappeared across the Pacific Ocean, 'travelling over the water as if it were land, without sinking'. The Incas did not forget this god in spite of their elevation of Inti, the sun god.

A Pacific Indian dance apron with a beaver motif, possibly a stylised version of Wishpoosh

Wakonda

'The power above', the great mystery of the Sioux, the supreme hunters and warriors of the Great Plains of North America. Related to the Iroquois word *orenda*, 'magic power', and the Algonquin *manitu*, 'spirit', Wakonda is the source of all wisdom and power, the everlasting fount that sustains the world and enlightens the medicine-man. The Dakota Indians also worship Wakonda, but as the mighty thunder bird and antagonist of the trickster god Unktomi.

Watauineiwa

Literal meaning: 'most ancient one'. Although Charles Darwin considered that the Indians of Tierra del Fuego lacked any idea of religion, later investigation has revealed this not to be the case. The Yahgan tribe prayed to Watauineiwa, a benevolent sky god who made and sustained the world. Among the Ona, their neighbours, the supreme being was Temaukel. He was said to be without body, wife, and children. Souls, *kaspi*, travelled to the place of Temaukel after death. Initiation rites practised by the Yahgan and the Ona, like those of the Australian Aborigines, were the

preserve of the men: indeed, their central myth was a celebration of the superiority of the male, following an initial period when the female was dominant. Today the inhabitants of Tierra del Fuego are a vanishing people.

Wishpoosh

According to the Nez Percé Indians of Washington, the beaver monster Wishpoosh refused to allow anyone to fish. Whenever a person came to the lake where he dwelt, he seized the fisherman with his giant claws and dragged him to the bottom. So it was that the Nez Percés asked the trickster god Coyote for help. Coyote fashioned a huge spear with a long, strong handle, and fastened it to his wrist with a flaxen cord. Then he went to the lake to catch some fish.

Wishpoosh seized the trickster god but received a lunge from the long spear. At the bottom of the lake Wishpoosh and Coyote fought so fiercely that the surrounding mountains drew themselves back. When the beaver monster strove to escape downstream Coyote speared him firmly enough to be borne along with him. Their titanic struggle widened rivers, tore through hillsides, and created immense gorges. Having gained the Pacific shore, Wishpoosh plunged into the waves, seizing whales and eating them to renew his strength, while Coyote paused for a rest. Cunning and change assisted the tired champion. He turned himself into a branch of fir and floated out to Wishpoosh, who inadvertently swallowed him. Inside the beaver monster's stomach, Coyote changed himself back into his animal shape and assaulted the heart with a sharp knife. He hacked and hacked till Wishpoosh was dead.

Out of the enormous corpse Coyote created a new race of people. They were the Indians of the north-western coast and forest: the Chinook, the Klickitat, the Yakima, and the Nez Percé. What Coyote forgot to do in this flurry of creation was to give these tribes eyes and mouths. Later he realized his error and put it right, but his knife had become so dull that he made some of the mouths crooked and some too large. This accounts, say the Nez Percé Indians, for their ugly mouths.

Wiyot
In the mythologies of certain Indian tribes of California, Wiyot fathered a race of beings which preceded mankind. As these people multiplied, the land grew southward and groups of people migrated in that direction. Wiyot seems to have died from poison: Coyote, the trickster god, may have had a hand in the demise of his chief, since he leaped upon the pyre, tore off a piece of flesh from the body, and swallowed it.

Wonomi
Literally, 'no death'. The sky father and supreme being of the Maidu Indians of California. He is also known as Kodo-yapeu, 'world creator'; Kodo-yanpe, 'world namer'; and Kodo-yeponi, 'world chief'. Having made human beings and set the natural processes in motion, Wonomi ruled supreme until his adversary Coyote appeared. This trickster god, however, was able to displace the sky father because of one reason: men followed Coyote and not Wonomi. The souls of the dead can still attain to the sky father's 'flowerland' above the clouds, as his continued solicitude indicates, but beneath the floor of the sky it is the trickster god who holds sway.

Xaman Ek
The snub-nosed god of the North Star. He was 'the guide of the merchants', and the Maya compared his benevolence with that of the rain god Chac. Merchants used to offer incense to Xaman Ek at altars along roadsides.

Xipetotec
Literally, 'the flayed lord'. An enigmatic Aztec deity. Xipetotec possessed two aspects: he was the newly planted seed, a god of agriculture and vegetation, the one who gave food to mankind by having himself skinned alive just as the maize seed loses its skin when the young shoot begins to burst forth; he was also the lord of penitential torture, the symbol of sacrifice, the way of spiritual liberation. The latter aspect was made explicit in the illnesses Xipetotec sent to mankind: smallpox, plague, scabs, blindness. Like Quetzalcoatl, the flayed lord had a profound interest in mictlan, the underworld.

Xiuhtecuhtli
In Aztec cosmology the fire god Xiuhtecuhtli was the great pillar. Running through the whole universe, extending from the fireplace in mictlan, 'the land of the dead'; through the fire in the homes of the earth, the domain of the serpent goddess Coatlicue and her usual consort Tlatecuhtli, a fantastic frog armed with enormous teeth, who is often portrayed as the devouring grave; straight through to the heavens, was the mysterious spindle of the fire god. As a *psychopompos*, 'leader of souls', Xiuhtecuhtli assisted the spirits of the deceased in their absorption into the earth.

Xochipilli
The Aztec god of flowers and lord of souls. Four years after their deaths, according to the Aztecs of ancient Mexico, the souls of warriors became richly plumed birds. As the god of flowers, red-faced Xochipilli was the personification of the spirit, the flayed flesh of his portraits representing his indifference to material forms.

Xochiquetzal
Literal meaning: 'most precious flower'. The Aztec goddess of the flowering and fruitful surface of the earth. Her association with the underworld was celebrated at festivals for the dead when she was offered marigolds. According to legend, Xochiquetzal graced the world with flowers and beauty during the reign of Quetzalcoatl, but after his departure from Tollan and the collapse of historic Toltec power she was less active and bounteous. The Aztecs looked upon her as giver of children.

of penitence, while his death by cooking in a kettle may have represented some form of spiritual detachment. Self-torture and ritual killing were the two sides of the Aztec religion of suffering.

Yanauluha
The great medicine-man of Zuni mythology. After the first men had emerged from the wombs of the earth mother, they realized how unusual their own appearance was. Having adapted to life underground, they were strange creatures, black and scaly, with short tails, owl's eyes, huge ears, and webbed feet. In the uncertainty of that day they turned to the wisdom of Yanauluha, who had brought a vessel of water from the primeval ocean, seeds of plants, and a staff which had power to give life. He taught the Pueblo Zuni the arts of civilization: agriculture, husbandry, and the regulation of social life. His potent medicine staff, painted in bright colours and decorated with feathers, shells, and stones, represents the foundation of Zuni religion; it is the emblem of the first chief priest.

Yolkai Estsan
According to the Navahoes, Yolkai Estsan, 'white shell woman', was created at the same time as her sister Estsanatlehi, 'the woman who changes'. Estsanatlehi appears to be an earth goddess, related to the seasons and the land, whereas Yolkai Estsan is connected with the sea.

Yum Kaax
Literal meaning 'lord of the forests'. The Maya agricultural deity. He seems to have absorbed a handsome young corn god in later time. Though impressive statues exist of this youthful god with a retreating forehead, we do not know his name. Like Yum Kaax, he was under the protection of the rain god Chac, who may have assumed the general role of a fertility god.

Zombi
A soulless body. In the Voodoo cult of Haiti, a zombi is the slave of a magician. The soul may have been removed by magic from a living person, or the body of someone recently deceased may have been brought up out of the grave after the soul had been separated from it by regular rites of death. As the lord of the dead, Ghede has the power to animate corpses as zombis.

Xochipilli, the Aztec lord of souls and god of flowers, wearing a warrior's helmet

Xolotl
The dog or animal. An Aztec deity with a deformed shape, often shown with backward turned feet, he was regarded as the dispenser of misfortune. As lord of the evening star, Xolotl pushed the sun down into the darkness of night, though he was also looked upon as Quetzalcoatl's double. His burst eye was a sign

A wayside shrine carved out of a clay bank in Ibo territory, Nigeria

AFRICA

Sahara The West Coast East and South Africa Madagascar

Mythologies abound in Africa. Tribes possess their own traditions, and even where they share a language with their neighbours, like the Bantu-speakers of East and South Africa, it is the diversity of local belief that surprises rather than the evidence of a common heritage. Factors making for this mythological variety are several. First, there is the size of the continent itself, along with the accompanying range of climate. Some tribes wander the open plains, herding cattle and hunting game; others raise crops on fertile riverside clearings amid dense equatorial jungle: these peoples would find the habitat of the Bushmen unendurable. Once the sole inhabitants of the area south of the Zambezi River, the Bushmen were decimated by incoming Bantu tribesmen and by later white settlers, until today surviving tribes eke out a living on the fringes of the Kalahari Desert. A second factor, therefore, is the migration of peoples, an historical process about which we are only dimly aware. Recorded history starts late in Africa so that inferences have to be drawn from oral tradition, supplemented where possible by information collected in the journals of travellers and explorers. The last factor to be taken into account is the presence of separate ethnic groups. North of the immense Sahara Desert this situation is transparent in the relation of the indigenous Berbers and their Arab conquerors. Only in the mountainous interior of Algeria and Morocco are vestiges of the old Berber culture preserved. Nevertheless, West Africa is the part of the continent with the greatest concentration of different peoples, since between the Senegal River and the headwaters of the Congo River there are 2,000 known languages and dialects.

Almost all African peoples believe in a supreme god who is omniscient and omnipresent. The Akan of Ghana refer to this deity as Brekyirihunuade, 'he who knows and sees all', while the Zulu of South Africa simply call him 'the wise one', uKqili. God's 'great eye', according to the Ganda people of Uganda, keeps perpetual watch everywhere and at all times: it never blinks. Nothing can be hidden, assert the Yoruba of Nigeria, because his vision includes 'both the inside and outside of man'. A sky god, the deity is thought of as father, mother, grandfather, elder, supreme ancestor, friend, and companion. The Koma of Ethiopia, a tribe which sacrifices dogs—their king eating the tail at an annual reinvestiture—call the sky 'god's belly'. When lightning strikes cattle, the Zulu say that uKqili 'has slaughtered for himself among his own food . . . he is hungry; he kills for himself.' Thunder, on the other hand, is represented sometimes as the god at play. Though looked upon generally as benevolent, the ways of the sky god are inscrutable, and he also sends men their ills. The Akamba of Kenya suppose Asa, 'the father', to have said, 'It is I who made the people; whom I love, he will thrive; and whom I refuse, he will die.' Yet the Herero of South-West Africa simply explain death as god calling away old people.

A myth current in Liberia offers a quite different explanation for the origin of mortality. Once Sno-Nysoa, the creator god, sent his four sons into the world. He wished them to return, but they wanted to stay, and Earth, too, tried to keep them. Then Sno-Nysoa used his power and took his sons back to heaven. When they could

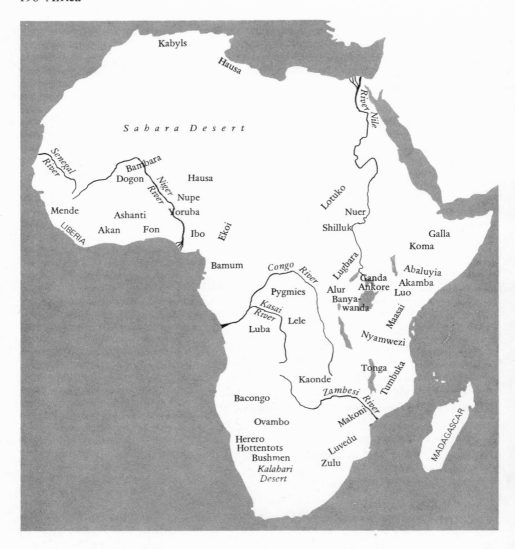

not wake up in the morning, he said to Earth: 'I have called them home. I leave their bodies with you.' Since that time Sno-Nysoa has used his power to take men away from the world, and the way to the deceased is blocked, on account of the Earth's attempt to keep the divine children. Before Sno-Nysoa and the Earth quarrelled, however, sickness, suffering, and death were unknown. Mankind considered what should be done. The result was that a cat was sent to the medicine-man, to fetch a remedy which should cure the sick and awake the dead. On the way back, the cat, putting the medicine on the stump of a tree, took a bath in a river. Then she forgot about her errand. So they sent the cat to look for the medicine, but she did not find it, and went back to the medicine-man again. He was angered at the cat's carelessness, and cursed it roundly. Moreover, he said that 'thereafter, though a tree be cut, if the stump remain, the tree will grow again; but when men die, it will be the end.'

The wrath of the medicine-man is crucial. He is the intermediary between god and man. Africans, like most other peoples, feel that they cannot or should not approach divinity alone or directly, and must do so through the mediation of special persons. Among the Maasai of East Africa, for instance, the medicine-men, or *iloibonok*, come from one clan and trace their hereditary powers back for ten generations to the first who fell, full-grown, from the sky. While all Maasai can address En-kai, 'sky', in prayer, the iloibonok are in daily communication with him through dreams, trances, and signs. His sanction, through them, must be obtained for any important action. Under the protecting eye of these experienced initiates in the sacred ways unfolds the pattern of tribal life: birth, marriage, coming-of-age, and death. Ancestors hardly impinge on the consciousness of the Maasai, since they have no distinct notion of personal survival after death. The corpse is normally left in the bush to be eaten by hyenas: at most the relatives of an elder would pile heavy stones on top. The souls of old men, they believe in particular, may return in the form of snakes.

Deities of the Yoruba pantheon, Nigeria

With the exception of the nomadic Maasai, ancestor cults feature prominently in the mythologies of East and South Africa, whereas in West Africa an extended pantheon offers more scope for worship and speculation. There is room for divinities other than the creator god as well as the accidents of fate and fortune so necessary for mythological development. A folklore personage like Anansi, or Mr Spider, appears to be almost a national hero in Sierra Leone. This trickster is shrewd, designing, and selfish; from the safety of a tree Mr Spider enjoys the sport he has helped to create by his subtle wit and takes advantage of the victims to supply himself with food. Neither the elephant nor the hippopotamus can cope with him, and they are tricked into a contest that brings both of them to death. 'You might be stronger,' he reflects, 'but you are also more stupid.'

In Dahomey there still exist innumerable shrines to local gods, their worship little affected by Islam or Christianity. Beneath Mawu, the moon, and her twin brother Lisa, the sun, often conceived as the androgynous creator deity Mawu-Lisa, preside their offspring, the gods associated with the weather, the earth, the forest, and metal; the latter, the Fon people consider, was formed from divine excrement. Many priests are dedicated to the service of the Fon gods, *vodu*. According to tradition, Mawu-Lisa set the universe in order before she-he made vegetation, animals, and men. They celebrate this in a four-day week, the first day of which is believed to be when Mawu-Lisa established the universal order and when she-he created man from water and clay. On the second day the earth was made habitable for men. On the third day man received sight, the gift of speech, and understanding of the world about him. On the fourth, and last, day of creation Mawu-Lisa presented man with technology.

The Fon, a warlike tribe, must have appropriated the gods of their vanquished foes, since they possess a syncretic pantheon. But conflict that occurs within a homogeneous group has to be fitted into the divine scheme, too. A Yoruba myth pins the blame firmly on the trickster god Edshu. Once this mischievous deity came walking along a path between two fields. He noticed in either field a farmer at work and decided to play a trick on both of them. He donned a hat that was on one side red but on the other white, green in front and black behind. Later that day the two farmers walked back to the village and talked of the stranger they had seen but, whereas one of them said that he had worn a red hat, the other insisted with equal conviction that the hat had been white. The conversation soon turned into an argument, each farmer accusing his fellow of blindness or intoxication, till at last they came to blows. When they drew their knives, they were brought by neighbours before the headman for judgement. Edshu was among the crowd at the trial, and when the headman admitted his own bewilderment, the trickster god revealed himself, made known his joke, and displayed the hat. 'The two farmers could not help but quarrel', he said. 'I wanted it that way. Spreading strife is my greatest joy.' The personification of the four directions of the world, as represented in the colours red, white, green, and black, Edshu reveals how restricted is the viewpoint of mankind. As William Blake remarked: 'The roaring of lions, the howling of wolves, the raging of the stormy sea, and the destructive sword, are portions of eternity too great for the eye of man.'

Divine favour is, of course, sought by sacrifice. Propitiation offerings are made

A Dahomey hougan (spirit-master) consulting Fa—the messenger of Mawu—about the future

during drought, famine, or serious illness; otherwise they may be intended to ward off attack, evil, or misfortune. The usual sacrificial objects are animals like cattle, sheep, goats, dogs, and fowl, but evidence exists to show that human beings were formerly used. The Makoni of Rhodesia have a legend of strangulation at a rain sacrifice. Long ago a drought lasted for a whole year. When the *wanganga*, the medicine-men, ordered the sacrifice of a noble virgin, it happened that a girl of marriageable age innocent of a man could not be found. Therefore the wanganga advised that a young girl, who had not yet reached puberty, be imprisoned until she was ready for marriage. Though this took two years, in the course of which no rain fell and all the cattle died, the plan was strictly kept. At last the moment of sacrifice came, the maiden was strangled by the wanganga, and her body buried in an antheap beneath the roots of a great tree. For three days the Makoni people danced round this tree, which grew till it reached the sky. Then the morning star appeared, the crown of the tree spread across the sky, blocking out the moon and stars, and a tempest arose. The leaves of the great tree were torn off the branches and tossed into the sky as clouds, storm clouds that for thirty days without cease poured the waters of heaven over the parched earth. Such, say the Makoni, was the origin of the rain sacrifice.

In modern times changes have taken place in Africa. The long isolation of the continent has come to an end through slavery, imperialism, urbanization, money, communications, missionaries, and, most recently, independence. The old religions are in retreat, while the African idea of a supreme deity has been incorporated in Islam and Christianity. Many temples have disappeared, but the ancestor cults continue with some vigour. Yet there remain numerous living mythologies, not all of which have been properly recorded, as a testimony of the rich past of what was after all the cradle of mankind.

Abassi

The zealous god of the Efik. Although on the advice of his wife Atai, the sky god Abassi let a human couple settle upon the earth, he greatly feared that they might not only become his equals, but excel him in wisdom. Atai promised to see that such a thing did not come about. Therefore, the man and wife were forbidden either to procreate or to work, and even their meals were to be taken in heaven 'when Abassi rang his dinner bell'. In the course of time the couple began to disregard these rules: they tilled the soil, cooked for themselves, and produced children. They had forgotten Abassi, who pointed out this deplorable state of affairs to his wife. Once again Atai promised to take a hand in the matter. She sent death to the husband and wife, and caused discord between the children. The price of apparent independence for mankind, this Efik myth suggests, was the advent of death and evil.

Adroa

God of the Lugbara, whose tribal territories stretch across the border of Zaire and Uganda. He is conceived of in two aspects: as transcendent Adroa, 'god in the sky', remote from mankind and *onyiru*, 'good'; as immanent Adro, 'god on earth', close to mankind and *onzi*, 'bad'. The fountainhead of all power and authority, this ambivalent creator deity established the social order through the tribal ancestors, whose 'words' represent customary law. The relationship between Adroa and the ancestors is obscure, though the Lugbara say: 'We forget them and send a ram to the mountains.'

Propitiation of the immanent Adro was formerly achieved through child sacrifice, but since the 1930s rams have been substituted as victims. Adro dwells on earth, especially in rivers. Though invisible to ordinary people, he may become visible to a person who is about to die. Adro is tall and white; he has half a body—one eye, one ear, one arm, and one leg, on which he jumps about. His children, *adroanzi*, frequent streams, large trees, and rocks. Providing one does not look back at adroanzi, who like to follow human beings at night, there is no danger. Otherwise these guardian spirits of the dead will kill. *Adro onzi*, 'bad God', is clearly associated with death.

Aigamuxa

In Hottentot mythology, strange man-eating monsters who are occasionally encountered among the dunes. Aigamuxa have their eyes set on their instep, so that to discover what is going on they have to get down on hands and knees, and hold up one foot.

Ajok

Or Adyok, Naijok. The Lotuko, a Sudanese people, believe that whereas by nature Ajok is benevolent, he must be kept so through constant sacrifice and prayers. Man rather than the deity is seen as the cause of discord. A family quarrel, for example, was the cue for death's entry into the world.

Once a child died and the distraught mother implored Ajok to restore it to life. The supreme deity did so, but the father of the child was displeased: he scolded his wife and killed the child. Then Ajok said: 'You cried and asked to have the child restored to life, but never will I do so again. Hereafter, death is permanent for a Lotuko.'

Anansi

Mr Spider: the great trickster of West African legend. Originally credited with the creation of the world, Anansi has been transformed into a cultural founder hero. His exploits form cycles of popular stories and they are even relished as far away as the West Indies. Only in his encounter with the Wax Girl is Mr Spider beaten. When she 'no duh talk', he struck her with his legs and stuck fast. Angered, 'he conk um, he chest fas'n'. Finding himself trapped, Mr Spider 'begin fo' talk soffle, he beg, he beg ... do' go clean.' But there was no reply and no escape, according to the tale in Sierra Leone, for 'he fash'n so 'pon dah wax we'en den people all duh beat um, dat make he flat till today.'

Andriambahomanana

In Madagascan mythology, the first man. When god saw that Andriambahomanana and his wife, Andriamahilala, had many children,

and even grandchildren, he asked them what kind of death they wanted. The first man chose to die like a banana plant, which soon puts forth shoots anew, while the first woman was sent to the moon, where she dies every month, to be born again the following month.

Asa

Literally, 'father'. God of the Akamba people of Kenya. Asa is 'the strong lord', above the spirits, but also a merciful deity. He is Mwatuangi, 'distributor'; Mulungu, 'creator'; and Mumbi, 'fashioner'. A god of consolation and sustenance, Asa intervenes when human help is slow or ineffective.

Azra'il

According to the Hausa-speaking people in Tunisia, it was the angel of death, Azra'il, who brought early mortality into the world. The first people lived for centuries. One virgin had lived for 500 years before she died. When Moses found her anklets, he prayed to Allah that he might be allowed to see the owner. Allah brought the woman from the grave, but she complained to Moses about this resurrection, since world weariness plagued her spirit. Moses then asked that Allah might let people die earlier, and so Azra'il was instructed to make sure that all should pass away after sixty or seventy years.

Chiuta

Literal meaning: 'great bow in the heavens'. The supreme deity of the Tumbuka in Malawi; sometimes he is referred to as Mulengi, 'creator'. Chiuta is a powerful god, self-created, and omniscient. Moreover, he is Mwenco, 'owner of all things', and Wamtata-kuya, 'eternal'. Above all else Chiuta is a rain god, the succour of a people often afflicted by drought.

Chuku

Literally, 'great spirit'. The supreme deity of the Ibo of Eastern Nigeria. Chuku is 'the first great cause'; also he is Chineke, 'creator'. The Ibo hold that he is essentially good and only good comes from him. The origin of death is explained by a messenger myth. Once Chuku sent a dog to men with the message that if anyone died, the body should lie upon the earth and be strewn with ashes, after which the dead person would come back to life. The dog was delayed by hunger and tiredness, so Chuku sent a sheep with the same message.

The sheep, too, stopped on the way in order to eat, and on arrival it had forgotten the wording of the message, and said to men that a corpse was to be buried in the earth. When, now, the dog arrived with the correct message, it was not believed. 'We have been told to bury the dead,' the Ibo said, 'and this is what we have already done.' So death was established on the earth.

Certain trees are sacred to Chuku. Offerings and sacrifices take place in groves and beneath trees in home compounds. Assistance is also sought from Ale, the earth goddess and daughter of Chuku. And, like their West African neighbours, the Ibo seek to propitiate their ancestors and other spirits.

En-kai

Literally, 'sky'. The rain god of the Maasai in East Africa. En-kai, a remote deity, is Parsai, 'the one who is worshipped', and Emayian, 'the one who blesses'. In their rituals the nomadic Maasai use grass.

Gu

In Fon mythology, the heavenly blacksmith. On the second day of creation Mawu-Lisa, the creator god, sent Gu to make the earth habitable for mankind, and 'this work he has never relinquished'. Alternatively, Gu is conceived of as a magical weapon given by Mawu to Lisa, when she told him to go to the earth and clear the forests, and show human beings the use of metal so that they might fashion tools.

Hai-uri

A monster greatly feared by the Hottentots. One-legged, one-armed, one-sided, and semi-invisible, the surprisingly agile Hai-uri can leap over clumps of scrub in its pursuit of human prey. Tikdoshe, the malevolent dwarf of Zulu tradition, has a similar anatomy, and takes delight in fighting men. Defeat means death, but victory can mean the acquisition of magic, since Tikdoshe will offer to show the victor 'lots of medicines'.

Heitsi-eibib

Legendary hero of the Hottentots. Son of a cow and some miraculous grass, eaten by the cow, Heitsi-eibib is a great magician, a patron of hunters, and a superb fighter. Only he could

A carved figure of Chuku, the 'great spirit' of the Ibo of Nigeria

rid the Hottentots of the monstrous Ga-gorib, 'thrower down'. This creature was in the habit of sitting on the edge of a great pit and daring passers-by to throw stones at him. The stone always rebounded and killed the thrower, who then fell into the pit. When Heitsi-eibib approached Ga-gorib, he declined to aim a stone, until he had diverted the monster's gaze. Then he struck Ga-gorib under the ear and tumbled him into his own trap. Another version of the contest relates the near defeat of Heitsi-eibib, who was chased round the pit before he slipped and fell into it. Though he managed to escape, the hero was hard pressed and only succeeded in pushing Ga-gorib into the pit after a prolonged wrestle. According to legend, Heitsi-eibib was killed on numerous occasions, after which he resurrected himself: his cairns are dotted over the Hottentot lands.

Holawaka

The mythical bird sent by god to tell the Galla of Ethiopia that they would not die. Holawaka was to say that when men found themselves growing old and weak, they were to slip off their skins and become young again. On the way the bird met a snake which was eating a dead animal. It promised to let the snake hear the message in return for sharing the carcass. So Holawaka altered the meaning and said: 'Man will die when he is old, but the snake will change its skin and grow young again.' Afterwards this was the case.

Imana

Literally, 'almighty'. God of the Banyarwanda people of Ruanda, an area unvisited by Europeans before 1894. This densely populated kingdom retained intact till very recent times its ancient mythology. For the Banyarwanda 'the invisible world is a fearful reality'. One part is called *ijuru* and exists beyond the rock which is the sky we see. Beneath the soil is the other part, known as *ikuzimu*. The three-storeyed universe of the Banyarwanda appears to be slowly degenerating, getting old, and wearing out: it would entirely collapse without the support of Imana, the author and sustainer of the universal order.

Imana 'alone knows all things'. He is Hategekimana, 'the only ruler'; Hashakimana, 'the one who plans'; Habyarimana, 'the sole giver of children'; Ndagijimana, 'the protector of possessions'; and Bigirimana, 'owner of all things'. Conceived as a powerful person,

Imana 'has very long arms' and is even found in 'fearful places', but his influence is thought always to be beneficial for human beings. He is remote, the distant source of all gifts. A legend, however, suggests a more active aspect of the god. Once a man borrowed beans from different people. When repayment of loans was demanded, he always managed to wriggle out of the debt. But Death, one of his creditors, insisted on repayment, and would have seized the man had not Imana intervened to save him. It would seem that the god did not so much condone the man's behaviour as respond to the invocation of his own sacred name.

Imana coexists with Death. At the beginning he hunted Death, a kind of wild animal. He ordered men to remain indoors so that his quarry should not find a hiding place. When an old woman went out to her banana grove, Death asked her protection, and was allowed to hide under her skirt. Imana, in order to punish her, decided then that Death should stay with men. A second myth of the loss of immortality blames woman too. There was a family consisting of husband, wife, and mother-in-law. The wife had a great dislike of the mother-in-law and felt it as a relief when the latter died and was buried. Three days after the funeral she visited the grave and found that it was full of cracks, as if the dead woman was about to emerge. Returning with a heavy pestle, she pounded down the earth and shouted, 'Stay dead!' On the two following days the same incident was repeated, but thereafter the wife discovered no cracks. The strength of the deceased was exhausted. Although this delighted the wife, her action ensured that for mankind the possibility of resuscitation was lost forever.

The Banyarwanda consider that the spirits of the dead, *bazimu*, are gloomy and unpleasant. While bazimu sometimes come back to this world, returning to the places they used to live, the majority stay in ikuzimu. The diviners, *bapfumu*, offer a certain defence against the dead; they interpret the will of Imana, thereby indicating the wisest course of action. On the other hand the sorcerers, *barozi*, are secretly in league with the bazimu. If found they are usually killed. The inhabitants of *ijuru*, the concealed land in the sky, are less frightening, and seem to be minor divinities.

Itherther

The primeval buffalo of Kabyl mythology.

The Kabyls of Algeria preserve in their legends something of the ancient notions of the Berber peoples, who flourished in northern Africa before the Arab Conquest (643–700).

In the beginning there were on earth a buffalo, Itherther, and a female calf, Thamuatz. Both emerged from a dark place under the earth called Tlam, to which they did not wish to return. Achimi, their bull offspring, ran off and came to a village built by the first men. When the villagers tried to capture him, he hastened back to his parents. Meanwhile a wise ant explained to men about the young bull and also told Achimi about other animals. Although the ant suggested that it was better for an animal to serve man, who could drive off predators and offer plenty of food, the young bull did not choose to take this advice. Instead Achimi returned home, coupled with his mother and newly born sister, and exiled his father.

So it was that Itherther found himself wandering the mountains. He could not forget the cow Thamuatz. Every time he remembered her did his semen run into a natural bowl of rock. From this semen the sun engendered the game animals—the first were gazelles—and Itherther was a mother to them. All the wild animals of the world originated from the bowl, except the lion. The first lion, the Kabyls say, was a cannibalistic man.

Jok

Literal meaning: 'creator'. God of the Alur tribesmen of Uganda and Zaire. He is also known as Jok Odudu, 'god of birth'. The Alur believe that the world is full of spirits, *djok*, and consider that their ancestors manifest themselves in snake forms or in large rocks. Black goats are sacrificed to Jok, especially when the Alur need rain.

Juok

God of the Shilluk, tribesmen living on the upper reaches of the River Nile. Shilluk cosmology represents the universe as the two divine loaves, *opunne*, the heaven and the earth, divided by the great river, the Nile. Juok, a deity of many facets, is omnipresent; he gave the Shilluks cattle, millet, and fish for their sustenance, and is still the giver and sustainer of life through his breath. He also 'liftest up' the sick.

Nyikang, a semi-legendary king, is usually invoked as an intermediary when Juok is addressed in prayer. Possibly Nyikang acts as a manifestation of the supreme deity on the earthly loaf. Society appears to have been established by this ancestor, who is never spoken of as having died. Nyikang either 'went up', or 'became the wind'. His successors, later occupants of the 'divine throne', are said to have continued his mission, the upholding of human society. The Shilluk call their king 'child of god', 'last-born of god', and 'reflection of the ancestors'.

Kaang

Or Kang, Cagn, Kho, Thora. In Bushman mythology, the creator deity, a remote sky god. It is said that Kaang made all things, but met with such opposition in the world that he went away. In the arid fringes of the Kalahari Desert, the harsh habitat of the wandering bands of Bushmen, rain falls only rarely and then as a sudden heavy storm accompanied by a strong wind. When this happens, the Bushmen say Kaang is 'god of rain, wind, and breath'. Otherwise he is regarded as the invisible spirit within natural phenomena, but especially manifest in the *kaggen*, mantis, or the *ngo*, caterpillar. The relationship between Kaang and I Kaggen, the praying mantis spirit, is hard to clarify, but it would appear that the former is rather the 'great magician', whose strength lies in one particular tooth.

Kaang was provoked by the disobedience of the first men that he made. So he sent to the earth both destruction and death, removing his own abode into the top of the sky. Mankind were ungrateful in spite of the presence of his own sons, Cogaz and Gcwi. These divinities had descended to become chiefs; they made digging sticks with sharp stone points and showed men how to dig with them for roots. Kaang's daughter married a snake, and henceforth the snakes were called 'Kaang's people'.

The adventures and exploits of Kaang form the basic cycle of Bushman mythology. Once he was eaten by an ogre, who then vomited him up. On another occasion he was killed by thorns; the ants picked his bones clean, but this dying and rising god reassembled the skeleton and resurrected himself. The moon, say the Bushmen, Kaang created from an old shoe.

The principal enemy of the creator deity is Gauna, or Gawa, or Gawama, the leader of the spirits of the dead. Though weaker than his rival, Gauna seeks to disrupt his creation and harass the lives of men and animals. The origin of this antagonistic deity may well have been the pantheon of an enemy people. But the Bushmen dead themselves also play a conspicuously evil part in the affairs of the world. Ghosts dwell in a dim nether world from which they wish to escape. Graves are considered to be places of danger, for the departed have an unhappy desire to drag the living with them into the nether world. The breaking of taboos seems to be the way of releasing these malicious ancestors. By proper conduct alone are the Bushmen able to avoid the wrath of Kaang and the dead. However, there are communal rites, including a dance of exorcism, that can be used as a defence against Gauna.

Kazikamuntu

Literal meaning: 'root of man'. The first human being of Banyarwandan mythology. Created by Imana, the supreme deity, he had many children, but strife arose between his sons. Their original disagreement, the Banyarwanda say, accounts for the dispersal of men into different tribes.

Kalumba

According to the Luba in Zaire, the creator deity Kalumba knew that Life and Death would soon approach mankind. He, therefore, commanded a goat and a dog to keep watch on the roadside and to allow Life to pass, but not Death. These animals quarrelled, and the goat left the dog on duty. Death—'wrapped up in grass-cloth, tied to a pole, as for burial'— safely passed the sleeping dog. But the next day, when the goat was left on duty, Life came along and was mistakenly captured.

Katonda

Literally, 'creator'. The Ganda, an East African tribe with a strong monarchical tradition, conceive of their supreme deity's authority in ancestral terms. He is the father of the gods living in heaven, just as the first king is the father of the men living on earth. The Ganda believe in the profound influence of the dead on the living. Great care is taken to ensure that the ghosts of sorcerers, suicides, and abnormal births cannot return to cause trouble. Ghosts of past rulers and outstanding men, sometimes considered to be incarnate in certain animals, are looked upon as guardian spirits. Elaborate rituals surround the cult of dead kings, while ordinary ancestors are offered beer and warmth.

Katonda is Lissoddene, 'the big eye' in the sky. He is Kagingo, 'master of life'; Ssewannaku, 'the eternal'; Lugaba, 'giver'; Ssebintu, 'master of all things'; Nnyiniggulu, 'lord of heaven'; Namuginga, 'he who shapes'; Ssewaunaku, 'the compassionate'; Gguluddene, 'the gigantic one'; and Namugereka, 'he who apportions'.

The Ganda say that Katonda 'saves the afflicted according to his will'. He is the final judge, though he may express his will through the actions of gods and men. So Katonda exercises his control over the natural world by means of nature spirits, *balubaale*. There are over fifty balubaale, some of whom are deified heroes, others simply personifications of natural phenomena and human activities. Walumbe is death and Kibuka, war. At death each ghost visits the underworld of Walumbe, and then returns to the tribal burial ground, where the corpse is interred. Until recent times the Ganda had a highly developed priesthood for their gods, and at many temples they maintained oracles. If a woman medium were employed as the mouthpiece of the divinity, she was regarded as a holy bride and remained chaste all her life.

Khonvum

The supreme spirit of Pygmy belief. 'In the beginning was god; today is god; tomorrow will be god.' Formless and eternal, Khonvum makes contact with men by the intermediary of an animal, usually a chameleon. After the creation of the world, he lowered from the sky to the earth the first men—the Pygmies. He also provided for these primitive hunters and fruit-gatherers the plentiful fauna and flora of the equatorial forest. The nightly chore of Khonvum is the renewal of the sun; he collects broken pieces of stars in his sack and tosses armfuls of them at the sun, so it can rise again next morning in its original splendour.

Khuzwane

The Luvedu, a southern Bantu tribe living in the northeastern Transvaal, are singularly uninterested in cosmological speculation. Although they name their god Khuzwane, 'the creator', and say that when he created man he left his footprints on rocks which were still soft, the apparent remoteness of the rest of creation from their daily lives discourages the growth of legend. The preoccupation of the Luvedu is the present order of Nature, over which they believe their own 'divine' queen has control. A complex ritual surrounds her person—to shield her from evil influences and to preserve the strength of her magic. Signs of her vitality are said to be the immunity of the queen from disease and the effectiveness of royal rain charms. People still recall with terror the years following the death of Queen Majuji II in 1894. The tribal lands were ravaged by drought, locusts, famine, and disease. Perhaps a third of the population followed all the cattle into death. The death of a queen, the Luvedu explain, is a matter of her personal volition.

Kintu

Semi-legendary King of Uganda. An immortal, Kintu was in the habit of visiting Katonda, the supreme deity, in order to submit reports of his work on earth. These meetings took place on a hill. One day Katonda told the King not to visit him again; he also entrusted Kintu with a sack, from which the latter was not to part, and which no one else was to be allowed to touch. Under the influence of strong drink, Kintu forgot his instructions, went to the hill and left his sack there. Wrathful Katonda deprived Kintu of his immortality, and sent to Uganda sickness and death.

Kwoth

The great spirit of the Nuer tribesmen living in the southern Sudan. Kwoth, their god, has neither form nor fixed abode, but manifests himself in natural phenomena. The Nuer believe that he is compassionate and spares the poor and the miserable. The universe came into existence as an expression of his will, and is sustained by his activity. A just and righteous deity, Kwoth is said to punish the wicked—'sooner or later'.

Lebe

According to Dogon tradition, Lebe was the first ancestor to die. They have, in fact, two categories of ancestors: those who lived before death had made its entry into the world of men, and who, therefore, were and are immortal, and those who lived after the entrance of death, and were, therefore, mortal. Lebe was a very, very old man, who called upon Amma, the supreme deity, for release from his worn-out body. He died but his relatives, thinking he was sleeping, tried to wake him up. When the body began to decompose, they placed it in a hole they had dug in the ground. Years later the Dogon resolved to move to another land and it was

decided to take Lebe's bones with them. When they opened the grave, they found a serpent instead of his remains. Since the serpent followed them on their journey, they were sure that it was Lebe, the first of the living dead.

Le-eyo

The great ancestor of the Maasai. One day Le-eyo learned that if a child should die, he was to say, when he discarded the body: 'Man, die, and come back again; moon, die, and remain away.' Now a child did die, and when he threw away the corpse he said instead: 'Man, die, and remain away; moon, die, and return.' The next time a child died, his own in this case, he tried to use the correct charm, but found he had forfeited the chance of restoring the child to life by his action on the previous occasion. The moon, not man, has retained the power to come back again.

Leza

According to the Kaonde in southern Africa, the supreme deity Leza summoned to his presence the honey bird and gave it three calabashes, all of them closed at both ends. The honey bird was to take these to the first human beings, and tell them that they might open two of the calabashes, which contained seed. The third, on the other hand, was not to be opened until Leza himself had come to earth and given instructions concerning its contents. On the way, however, the honey bird could not contain its curiosity, and opened the calabashes. While two did contain the promised seed, the third calabash held death, sickness, all kinds of beasts of prey and dangerous reptiles. Neither the honey bird nor Leza could recapture these unpleasant things, and so it was that men had to build huts and shelters for their protection.

Mawu-Lisa

God of the Fon, a warlike people of Dahomey. The turbulent history of the Fon kingdom, its defeats and its victories, is reflected in the composite character of the Fon pantheon. Gods were imported from conquered tribes, in order to secure their benevolence, and on occasions the usurpation of a foreign dynasty also led to important changes in worship. The dual deity Mawu-Lisa, for example, came from Aja, to the west of Dahomey.

Although Mawu-Lisa is thought of as a

A pot in the shape of Mawu-Lisa, creator-deity of the Fon of Dahomey

creator deity, the Fon sometimes say that there existed a god prior to Mawu-Lisa. This was Nana Buluku, an androgynous deity, and the progenitor of the dual creator. At the beginning of the present world, however, the Fon recognize only the existence of Mawu-Lisa and their offspring, vodu, sky gods and earth gods. It appears that Mawu-Lisa 'created', 'shaped', and 'ordered' the universe out of a pre-existing material.

In the dual Mawu-Lisa, Mawu is female and Lisa male. They are *xoxo*, 'twins', and their union is regarded as the basis of the universal order. It is a concept that has parallels elsewhere. In Chinese mythology the primordial woman, T'ai Yuan, sometimes combined in her person the masculine Yang and the feminine Yin—the two interacting forces that sustain the cosmos. Likewise among the Zuni Indians of North America, Awonawilana, the creator and sustainer of the world, is he-she. The Fon identify Mawu with the moon, night, fertility, motherhood, gentleness, forgiveness, rest, and joy; and they associate Lisa with the sun, day, heat, work, power, war, strength, and toughness.

Fon cosmology envisages the earth as floating on water, the source of rain and the springs beneath the surface of the ground. Above the earth circle the heavenly bodies on the inner surface of a gourd. Serpentine power, personified as Da, son of the divine pair, assists in the ordering of this cosmos. A serpent, he has a dual nature rather than a female-male identity. When he appears in the rainbow 'the male is the red portion, the female the blue'. Above the earth Da has 3,500 coils, xasa-xasa, and the same number below: together they support Mawu-Lisa's creation. A way of describing this cosmic inter-relationship would be to say that Mawu-Lisa is thought and Da is action. Other vodu of course are assigned parts in the government of the world: the sky is under the charge of androgynous Heyvoso, 'thunder'; the earth owes allegiance to the dual deity Sakpata, whose dreadful weapon is smallpox; the sea and the waters are the domain of Agbe-Naete, twins of the opposite sex; and to Age is given the barren wastes.

Echoes of Da Aido Hwedo, the cosmic serpent, can be found in Haiti and Surinam. In the former great care is taken never to arouse the anger or jealousy of this deity. On bethrothal young couples offer gifts to the ever-watchful great snake.

Mokele-Mbembe

A fabulous beast reported by early European visitors to West Africa. The size of an elephant, the Mokele-Mbembe had a long neck, a single horn or tooth, and a strong serpentine tail. Although it attacked small boats and inhabited marine caves, its diet was said to be vegetarian.

Mukuru

The remote sky god of the Herero people of South-West Africa. Mukuru 'is all alone', without parents or companions. He is a benevolent deity, showing his kindness through life-giving rain, healing the sick, and upholding the very old. Even death is taken as a benign act—the calling home of god's creatures. Since Mukuru 'does only good', the Herero say, 'we do not make offerings to him'. The implication is that they are unnecessary, the trappings of a priestly cult.

Mulungu

God of the Nyamwezi people of Tanzania. It is said that Mulungu cannot be reached by worship. Through intermediaries—a hierarchy of spirits—communication takes place, leaving mankind very much at the bottom of a long ladder. The loneliness of the first men could well account for their rejection of a medicine of immortality: the first woman advised that death would return them to the spirit world. This idea occurs elsewhere in southern Africa, where far-sighted persons are supposed to have become uneasy at the prospect of overpopulation and welcomed the intervention of death, so that 'the sons of men might qualify for admission to heaven by means of physical decay'.

The Nyamwezi believe in a monster spirit of evil, armed with boxes of diseases and misfortune, and it is this being who wields the scythe of death. Mulungu is not seen as indifferent; he is Kube, 'the one who embraces all'; rather is he remote, at a distance, Limi, 'the sun'. Another of his titles is Likubala, 'he who counts every step'.

Mwambu

According to the Abaluyia tribesmen of Kenya, the first human couple, Mwambu and Sela, lived in a house on stilts. They were always careful to pull up their ladder because there were amanani, 'monsters', prowling about on the earth. The house, a miniature version of the heavenly abode that the creator god Wele had made for himself, remained the home of Mwambu and Sela, but their children descended to the ground and began the colonization of the earth.

Mwuetsi

In the mythology of the Makoni tribe of Rhodesia, the primeval man and the moon, Mwuetsi. The sky god Maori created Mwuetsi, gave him a horn filled with ngona oil, and put him to live at the bottom of a lake, but Mwuetsi insisted that he moved to the earth. When he discovered that the earth was desolate, without grasses, bushes, trees, and animals, Mwuetsi wept bitterly. 'I tried to warn you', said Maori. 'You have started on a path at the end of which you shall die. I will, however, give you one of your kind for two years.' Thus was created Massassi, a maiden and the morning star; he also let her have a fire-maker. With the aid of Mwuetsi's horn of ngona oil Massassi bore grasses, bushes, and towering trees. They lived in plenty till the time came for Massassi's departure. The distress of Mwuetsi was so great that Maori decided to give him another woman; she was called Morongo, the evening star. From their union came chickens, sheep, goats, cattle, and children. Although told of his impending death and warned not to produce further offspring, Mwuetsi still slept with Morongo. As a result she gave birth to lions, leopards, snakes, and scorpions. Afterwards Morongo preferred the snake and Mwuetsi turned to his daughters, but one day he forced Morongo and the snake bit him. Then Mwuetsi sickened; rain did not fall; plants withered; streams ran dry; animals and people died. From the *hakata*, 'sacred dice', Mwuetsi's children learned their sick father should return to the primeval lake. They strangled Mwuetsi, buried him, and chose a new king. Later Morongo was buried near his grave.

This is a myth of the development of the world. Ngona oil is potent stuff, connected with lightning, the quickening spark of life. Another Makoni legend tells how a king once broke the horns from the moon. New horns appeared immediately, but mankind was left in possession of two mysterious ngona horns. Mwuetsi continued on his way to death, like the temporarily injured moon, leaving in his children's hands the custody of the world.

Ngewo

God of the Mende tribesmen in Sierra Leone.

He is also known by what appears to be a much older name—Leve, 'the high-up one'. The Menda say of traditional usage 'this is what Leve brought down to us long ago'. As Ngewo, the sky god is remote from the affairs of men, though they believe that it is the deity's power which manifests itself indirectly in natural phenomena. Thus he sends rain to fall on his 'wife', the earth. Between Ngewo and mankind are the spirits—ancestral spirits and genii, *dyinyinga*. The latter are associated with rivers, forests, and rocks; the former have cults designed to facilitate communication between men and the sky god.

After the rites of *tindyamei*, 'crossing the water', the departed soul reaches the land of the dead. On his journey the deceased is assisted by the objects deposited in the grave, which is called 'a house', because 'on the other side' the spirits expect to receive presents from the newcomer. To deny a person the burial rites is tantamount to condemning his spirit to remain on earth and, in consequence, to be haunted by it. The land of the dead, according to the Mende, is rather like the world of the living. Ancestors are not feared, and often appear in dreams as messengers, bringing words of warning or advice. Illness in a family, for instance, may be discovered to have resulted from a failure 'to feed' a certain ancestor. Offerings include rice, chicken, and tobacco. At important points in the calendar, such as sowing, the Mende sacrifice to the ancestral spirits, whose aid is necessary to ensure a good crop.

The propitiation of dyinyinga follows a settled pattern, too. An example would be the sacrifice made to the 'angered' spirit of a river which regularly overflows its banks during the autumn rains. Genii take various physical forms: *tingoi* appear as beautiful women with soft white skins, and they are usually benign; *ndogbojusui*, white men with long white beards, are bent on mischief, but a subtle man can outwit them and obtain substantial gifts. The Mende believe that boldness is required when handling dyinyinga. Either one takes control of the genii, or the genii takes control of oneself.

Mende magic, *hale*, invokes the aid of dyinyinga as well as Nwego. But there is an interesting myth to explain the remoteness of the sky god. In the beginning Nwego told men to go to him for everything they needed. They went, however, so frequently that he said to himself, 'If I stay near these people, they will wear me out with their requests.' So he made for himself another place far away, and while they slept, he went off there. Since that time Nwego has not deserted his creatures, but has forced mankind to be less dependent on him.

Njambi

The creator deity of the Lele people. His greatest gift, after life itself, is the tropical forest—'a mighty house'. It is the source of all good things and the antitheses of the dry grassland.

Njambi 'owns men', protects, orders them, and avenges injustice. Animals in the forest are also under god's control, though they have been given to the Lele for their food. The spirits, *mingehe*, look to Njambi too. They inhabit the deep forest, and influence both the fertility of women and the hunting of men. Sorcerers are used to deal with the capricious mingehe.

Nommo

The model of creation in Dogon cosmology. Amma, the supreme deity, appears to have created a cosmic egg, which was divided into two twin placenta, each with a pair of twin *nommo*, emanations of the godhead. These sons of god, after the twenty years of creative gestation had passed, became involved in worldly affairs, such as agriculture and war. The development of each person follows the underlying nommo principle. Hence the newborn baby is the head of nommo; as a herd-boy he is its chest; at betrothal he is the feet; at marriage he manifests the arms; while on initiation into adulthood he becomes 'the complete nommo'. For some unknown reason the Dogon say that the starting of creation was 'the star which revolves round Sirius', citing as proof its heaviness, the weight of 'the germ of all things'. The Fon, another West African people, have a similar creation myth in that Mawu, their supreme deity, is helped in ordering the world by an assistant named Da, 'the first created being'. Da set up the four pillars that support the sky, formed the waterways, and from his own excreta made the mountains and the metals of the earth.

Ntoro

Literal meaning: 'spirit'. The Ashanti believe that every person receives a sunsum, 'ego', and a kra, 'life-force'. They also say that a man transmits his ntoro to his child. In this sense sunsum and ntoro are synonymous. The kra might be thought of as a tiny portion of the creator deity that lives in every human being. In earlier times there existed twelve distinct ntoro groups and members of each group were thought to manifest the same characteristics. Membership involved the observance of certain taboos and the use of set greetings. Today, the Ashanti are the less strict about ntoro divisions and the notion of the inherited 'spirit' is more individualistic.

The twelve traditional ntoro were thus described: the tough, the human, the distinguished, the audacious, the eccentric, the fanatic, the chaste, the truculent, the virtuoso, the fastidious, the liberal, and the chivalrous. A myth explains how the bosommuru ntoro, 'distinguished spirit', first arose. Long ago a man and a woman came down from the sky, as did a python, which made its abode in the Bosommuru River. Since they lacked desire and a knowledge of reproduction, the couple had no children. One day the python asked if they had offspring, and on being told they had not, it said it would cause the women to conceive. The python sprayed their bellies with water, and uttered certain words, after which it told them to return home and lie together. In due course the first children were born and they took Bosommuru as their ntoro, each male passing on this ntoro to his children. This is the reason why those belonging to this group will bury a dead python should they chance to encounter one.

Nyame

Literal meaning: 'shining one'. In Akan mythology he is the supreme deity. Nyame is called Nana Nyankopon, 'grandfather Nyame who alone is the great one'; Amowia, 'giver of light'; Amosu, 'giver of rain'; Amaomee, 'giver of sufficiency'; Brekyirihunuade, 'he who knows or sees all'; Abommubuwafre, 'consoler'; Nyaamanekose, 'comforter'; Nana, 'great ancestor'; and Borebore, 'creator-architect'.

Eternal and unequalled, Nyame is a god to whom people may confidently turn in times of distress or hardship. The Akan stress the faithfulness of their god. They also credit him with making life a joy for creatures. He 'opens up for man an appetite for life, makes life worth living for him'.

The twin nommo of the Dogon of Mali

Nzambi

God of the Bacongo people of Angola. Identified with the sun, Nzambi is self-existent, almighty, and 'knows all'. The Bacongo say: 'He is made by no other, no one beyond him is.' Nzambi, 'the marvel of marvels', is kind, a deity who 'looks after the case of the poor man'. Indeed, the sky god appears to show kindness even to the most destitute members of society. Incapable of evil or wrongdoing, he 'is just and merciful', the ruler and sustainer of the universe, a fount of goodness.

Individual differences, however, the Bacongo attribute to Nzambi. Not only does he create individuals, but he also gives them different tastes and soul qualities. They say: 'What comes from heaven cannot be resisted.' A special relationship is said to exist between the creator deity and man, sometimes expressed as 'man is god's man'.

Ogun

The Yoruban iron god and war god. According to legend, he was originally a hunter who descended by a spider's thread upon the marshy waste that existed prior to the formation of the earth. By nature Ogun is hard, fierce, and terrible, but he is not an evil deity. Rather does he demand rectitude and adequate respect for his gift of mental implements—the source of wealth and victory. In the past he was given human sacrifices. Blacksmiths sacrifice dogs every fortnight and at his annual festival the people dance and eat dogs, for three days.

Olorun

Literal meaning: 'owner'. The head of the Yoruban pantheon, which contains 1,700 divinities. He is Olofin-Orun, 'lord of heaven'; also he is Olodumare, 'almighty' and 'supreme'. To the Yoruba of Nigeria, this sky god is the discerner of hearts—'he who sees the inside and the outside of man'. Active in celestial and terrestrial affairs, Olorun is able to do all things; he is the enabler of all who achieve any ends. No one has ever seen this 'king who cannot be found by searching', yet as Olodumare he is omnipresent: a mighty, eternal rock, forever constant and reliable.

Olorun created the universe, appointed night and day, arranged the seasons, and fixed the destiny of men. Whenever a misfortune befalls a bad person, the Yoruba say 'he is under the lashes of god'. Death was his creation too. At first men did not die. They grew to an immense size, after which they shrank into feeble old people. Because there were so many of them creeping around, men prayed to Olorun, begging him to free them from long life, and in this way the old ones died.

Like the other gods in the Yoruban pantheon, Olorun is served by priests. They enjoy an important social status, virtually nothing being done without their ministration. The training period for priests can last as long as three years.

Onyankopon

Literal meaning: 'the great one'. According to the Ashanti, the universe is 'full of spirits', but as Bore-Bore, 'the creator of all things', Onyankopon was the god who made them all. Below the pantheon of gods, *abosom*, and minor deities, *asuman*, are the lesser spirits which animate trees, animals or charms; and then there are the ever-present *nsamanfo*, the spirits of the ancestors. Onyankopon is Otumfoo, 'the powerful one'; Otomankoma, 'the eternal one'; Ananse Kokroko, 'the great wise spider'; and Onyankopon Kwame, 'the great one who appeared on Saturday.'

At first the sky god Onyankopon lived very near to men. He was obliged to remove his abode to the top of the sky because a certain old women used to knock her long pestle against him when she pounded yams. As soon as the crone realized what had happened, she instructed her many children to collect all the mortars they could find, and pile them one on top of the other. They did so, till they required but one mortar to reach Onyankopon. She told them to take one from the bottom of the pile and put it on the top. They did so, the pile wobbled and fell, and the tumbling mortars killed many people. After this incident 'the great one' remained at a distance from men, but he is never considered to be inaccessible to the individual; unlike abosom he does not have special priests.

The abosom derive their power from Onyankopon. They are said to 'come from him', to be 'parts of him', and to act as intermediaries and messengers between him and other creatures. For 'the great one' sent the rivers and the sea, who were his children, 'to receive honour from men, and in turn to confer benefits on mankind.'

A nail fetish figure of the Bacongo of Angola

Osawa

The sky god Osawa, according to the Ekoi, sent a frog to men with the message that death would be the end of all things. At the same moment he sent a duck with the message that they should arise from the dead. Unfortunately, the frog alone accomplished Osawa's errand, since the duck was beguiled by palm oil, and men did not hear its message of hope.

Pamba

The Ovambo god. Pamba, 'chief', is the creator and sustainer of life. The matrilineal Ovambo declare, 'the mother of pots is a hole in the ground; the mother of people is god'.

Pemba

According to the Bambara peoples of the Niger River, the creation of the world is a continuous process. Pemba and Faro, they say, descended from the sky, but at first it was Pemba who sought to govern the world. He was a wood spirit, the maker of the first woman, and the king of trees. Musso-koroni, the first woman, planted Pemba in the soil and her human and animal offspring shed blood in sacrifice to his divinity. But she did not like Pemba's thorns, ceased to be his consort and instead, Musso-koroni wandered the world causing disorder and sadness. The water spirit Faro too disliked the growing power of Pemba and so he uprooted him. Thereafter, the Bambara assert, the harmony of daily life has depended on the creativity of Faro, and his spirits.

Rugaba

Literally, 'giver'. The Ankore, a Ugandan people, look upon their god as a potent creator deity. He is Ruhanga, 'creator'; Kazooba, 'sun'; and Mukameiguru, 'he who reigns in the sky'. Rugaba is the great one 'who sets things in order, creates everything, and gives new life'. The Ankore also say 'god's smile brings life', whereas his displeasure means sickness and death. The other observers of human behaviour are two kinds of spirits: emandwa, guardian spirits of the tribe, benevolent and helpful; emizimu, family spirits, are more aggressive and punish bad actions.

Ruhanga

God of the Ugandan Banyoro tribes. Ruhanga's providence is personified in a spirit of plenty and fertility, supplying the Banyoro with children, animals, and harvest. Though his concern for the happiness of men is evident in another spirit, the guardian of health, Ruhanga is also the author of disease, sickness, and death. Formerly the dead came back to life, except for the animals. All that was required to accomplish this resurrection was the expression of joy among the living. However, one woman refused to dress up in her best clothes and meet the newly risen, because her pet dog had died. 'Why should I go', she asked, 'when my dog is gone?' Ruhanga heard this and said: 'So people don't care what becomes of the dead. They shall no longer rise again, for death will terminate their lives.

Sasabonsam

According to the Ashanti, the hairy Sasabonsam has large blood-shot eyes, long legs, and feet pointing both ways. Its favourite trick is to sit on the high branches of a tree and dangle its legs so as to entangle the unwary hunter. Belief in this forest monster is on the wane, but its curious mythical relation might have been the Sciapod of medieval Europe. A Sciapod was a man with one foot so large that he could lie on his back and use it as a sunshade.

Soko

The Nupe, a semi-nomadic people living in northern Nigeria, revere Soko. At the beginning this creator god told men how to take the advantage of certain cosmic forces by means of ritual, kuti. But he also put the power of witchcraft into the world. The dead, according to the Nupe, are intimately linked with Soko and act as intermediaries for the living. However, the latter have to be on guard against deception as the following folk-tale indicates.

Once a hunter went into the bush and found an old human skull. When the hunter asked aloud what had brought it to this pass, the skull answered: 'Talking brought me here.' Excited, the hunter ran off and informed the king about the talking skull. Baffled, the king decided to send guards out with the hunter into the bush to find out if he had spoken the truth. The king ordered the guards to kill the hunter if he had lied. When the guards and the hunter reached the skull, the latter was dismayed to find that all his entreaties were ignored. In the evening of that day the guards told the hunter to make the skull speak, and when he could not they slew him, and departed. The skull then asked: 'What brought you here?' And the dead hunter's head replied: 'Talking brought me here!'

Sopona
The Yoruban god of smallpox. He prowls about 'when the sun is hot, robed in scarlet'. Though zealously propitiated, he lacks the authority of Esu, whose task is checking upon the correctness of worship and sacrifices, and reporting to Olorun on the deeds of men and divinities, *orisa*. Sopona is an erratic manifestation of disease, a sudden calamity, while Esu represents the watchfulness of heaven, judging the blameworthy and the blessed.

Tchue
A Bushman cultural founder hero. His deeds and transformations were 'many, many and not one'. He was a genius of fruit; also was he at different times a fly, a lizard, an elephant, a bird, and a water hole. From Tchue too came the gift of fire.

Tilo
God of the Tonga tribes of Zambia and Malawi. Although Tilo is associated with lightning, the word can also mean 'the blue sky'. An active deity, this sky god 'kills and makes alive': he protects the individual, while his absence brings disaster and despair. When a person is overwhelmed by difficulties, he exclaims, 'Tilo has forsaken me!' He is Mlengi, 'creator'; Nyangoi, 'everlasting'; Wanthazizose, 'almighty'; Mkana Nyifwa, 'he who cannot die'; Kajati, 'self-creator' Mtaski, 'saviour'; Msungi, 'sustainer'; Mlezi, 'food giver'; and Mlengavuwa, 'rain maker'.

In the figure of Tilo the Tonga succeed in combining two fundamental notions—divine limitlessness, an overarching potency, and divine intervention, a personal regard. As Lesa, he is the 'great father', who nurses and cherishes the family of man. As Lesa too, he is the awful presence within natural convolutions. 'Heaven never dies,' they say, 'only men do.'

Tohwiyo
Literally, 'founders'. The divine founding ancestors of Fon clans. When the earth was still sparsely populated the sons of Fa, 'the word of Mawu-Lisa', came from the sky to preach 'the doctrine of destiny, and to foretell that supernatural beings would appear and found family lines'. These tohwiyo started the

clans, instituted their laws, and organized their cults. The comparative lateness of this event in Fon mythology is a reflection of the hard struggle this people had to liberate themselves from the Yoruba.

Tsoede
The Nupe cultural founder hero. Having seized the throne by killing his uncle, Prince Tsoede extended the frontiers of the Nupe kingdom and introduced his subjects to the rudiments of technology. He showed them how to work metals and how to build canoes. Other legendary innovations included the institution of marriage and the arrangement of sacrifices.

Unkulunkulu
Literally, 'chief'. The Zulu, once the most warlike nation in southern Africa, conceive of their sky god's omnipotence in political terms. He is uGuqabadele, 'the irresistible'; uGobungqongqo, 'he who bends down even majesties'; and uMabonga-kutuk-izizwe-zonke, 'he who roars so that all nations are struck with terror'. Like their armies of old, the sky god tolerates no physical opposition.

Unkulunkulu—sometimes called uKqili, 'the wise one'—is a self-originating deity. The Zulu describe him as uZivelele, 'he who is of himself'. Having 'come into being, he gave being to man', whom he raised 'out of beds of grass'. Unkulunkulu is a creator god whose ways are incomprehensible and mysterious. Man knows 'nothing of his mode of life, nor of the principles of his government. His smiting is the only thing we know.' For Unkulunkulu controls lightning as uDumakade, 'he who thunders from far-off times'. The maker of all things, he was also indirectly responsible for the coming of death to the earth. Once he sent a chameleon with the message of eternal life, and a lizard with the announcement of death. The chameleon was slow and stopped at a bush in order to eat, so that the lizard arrived first. When the chameleon got to mankind, it was dismayed to find that the message of the lizard was accepted as the correct one. The message myth is widespread in Africa, though a sheep or a dog may act as the messenger. In Rhodesia the Bemba proverb, *Ulufyeny-embe ali-fwa nakali* (The chameleon is dead long ago), sums up precisely the attitude to this creature, so worthy of death because it failed to deliver the message of life.

An interesting contrast is found in the story

of man's desire for death told by the Bamum of Cameroon. Njinyi, 'he who is everywhere', had created men healthy and strong. He was, therefore, unable to understand that many of them suddenly became cold and stiff, and asked Death if it was he who caused this. Death replied that men themselves desired to die, and declared that he could demonstrate this truth. While Njinyi concealed himself behind a banana hedge, Death sat down by the wayside. The first person to come along was an old slave, who bewailed his lot and said: 'Oh, the dead are lucky! If only I had never been born!' Suddenly he fell down dead. The next to come that way was an old woman. As soon as she complained about the troubles of life she sank down lifeless to the ground. Death then said to Njinyi: 'Do you see how they call me?' Njinyi went away grieved, since his creatures did call upon Death.

Unkulunkulu's answer to the loss of immortality was the institution of marriage, so 'that children may be born and men increase on earth'. He also provided men with 'doctors' for the treatment of diseases, and fire for the preparation of food. Health, fertility, and increase are clearly the sky god's concerns—'the source of being is above which gives life to men'—but his dislike of human misbehaviour is manifest in thunder and hail. Zulu reaction to these natural phenomena is 'Put things in order!' They, however, consider that cattle belong to Unkulunkulu, they are his gifts to mankind, and when lightning strikes them, they simply say that 'he has slaughtered for himself among his own food'.

The departed are not altogether forsaken by Unkulunkulu, though the Zulus believe that unremembered ghosts become impotent and irrelevant. The dwelling-place of the dead is situated in the sky; it is said that the stars are the eyes of the dead looking at the human world. The Bushmen, too, hold that the stars were formerly animals or people.

Utixo

God of the Hottentots: a benevolent deity who inhabits the sky, sends rain for the crops, and speaks with the voice of thunder. The first men, according to Hottentot mythology, were endowed with the gift of rising again after dying, like the legendary hero Heitsi-eibib. Mortality is explained, as in most other African traditions, by a messenger myth. The moon is said to have sent the hare with the message that men would not die forever.

When the hare got confused and informed men that they would not rise again, the moon was so annoyed that it split the hare's lip with a powerful blow.

Wele

Literally, 'high one'. the supreme deity of the Abaluyia of Kenya, a group of northern Bantu peoples. He is Khakaba, 'the distributor', and Isaywa, 'the one to whom sacred rites are paid'.

Wele created heaven and 'supported it all round by pillars just as the roof of a round hut is propped up by pillars'. Then he created two assistants, and together they placed the moon and the sun in the sky. But these luminaries fought each other: first the moon knocked the sun out of heaven; then the sun hurled down its eldest brother, 'throwing him into the mud. Afterwards he splashed the moon all over with mud to stop him from being resplendent.' Wele had to separate the rival brothers and decree that the sun would shine in the day, while the night would belong to the pale moon.

The next creations were clouds, the cock of lightning, stars, rain, rainbows 'by which god stops rain', air, and 'the cold air' which causes hailstones. This was the work of two days. The creation of the earth followed, along with the first man, named Mwambu, and the first woman, Sela. Then Wele stocked the earth with animals and completed the making of the universe 'in six days'.

A myth concerns the marriage of the sun to an Abaluyian maiden. A beautiful girl, who had refused all the young men of her village, was carried to the sun by a rope. There she was received by the mother of the sun, who told her that her son wished to marry her. When the sun, conceived of as a wealthy chief, returned from his garden, he courted the maiden and won her with the present of his rays, which she placed in a covered pot.

After several years of marriage and the birth of three sons, she asked her husband for permission to visit her parents. Together with her children she descended to earth by the rope, and found a joyous welcome in her village. Her father, as custom decreed, killed cows because of her long absence from home. When she and her sons returned to the sun's dwelling, she opened the pot containing the rays so that they could shine upon the earth. As a result many cows fell into her father's homestead and the whole earth was warmed by the sun's rays. Thereafter the land was fruitful and people lived in plenty.

While the stars assist the sun and moon, the Abaluyia dread the appearance of a comet, since it is the sign of impending and ill-fated war. In the past all kinds of ceremonies were performed to avert such disasters. Yet Wele himself allows unpleasant events as a punishment for misconduct. Death, for instance, was only introduced into the world through man's meanness. Because a farmer once refused to share his food with a hungry chameleon, he was cursed. The chameleon said: 'I am leaving now, but you all may die.' On the other hand the generosity of a snake secured the chameleon's blessing and immortality.

Were

Literal meaning: 'father of grace'. The Luo of Kenya have numerous names of their supreme deity. He is Wuonwa, 'our father'; Wuon Kwere, 'father of the ancestors'; Wuon ji, 'father of all'; Ja Mrima; 'the one with a temper'; Jan' gwono, 'the kind one'; Jahera, 'the merciful'; Nyakalaga, 'the ancient one'; Janen, 'seer'; Wuon Ogendi, 'father of all peoples'; Wuon lowo, 'lord of the earth'; Hono, 'worker of miracles'; Ratego, 'almighty'; Jalweny, 'great warrior'; Polo, 'god of heaven'; Piny k'nyal, 'unconquerable'; Wuon oru, 'lord of the future'; Ruodh Ruodhi, 'king of kings'; and Wang Chieng, 'eye of the sun'.

A potent and active diety is Were, whom the Luo believe causes both the births and deaths of individuals. Nature is securely under his control, and he uses the thunderbolt to strike down wrongdoers. Offerings and sacrifices are made to Were under large trees, in which his presence is often discerned. The closeness of the divinity is a feature of Luo life: prayers, invocations, and signs are commonplace. Every social event is reported to Were and the elders call down his wrath on the disobedient members of the tribe. The usual time for worship is in the morning, though young people ask the moon, 'his other sun', for marriage partners and children.

Zanahary

The supreme deity of the Madagascan pantheon. A multiple deity with female and male aspects as well as celestial and terrestrial manifestations. According to one creation myth, Zanahary made the earth, but left it desolate. Thereupon Ratovoantany, 'self-created one', shot up like a plant from the ground. When surprised and curious Zanahary descended from heaven to visit Ratovoantany, this new divinity was drying clay images of human beings and animals that he had made in the sun. He was unable, however, to give these figures life. Zanahary offered to vitalize them, but insisted that he take them up to heaven. Ratovoantany refused. As a compromise, they agreed that Zanahary was to give life, but also to take it back when these creatures died. Their bodies were to remain always with Ratovoantany. Hence the Madagascan custom of placing corpses on the ground.

A variant is the quarrel between the heaven-Zanahary and the earth-Zanahary. Once the latter formed different creatures out of clay, including men and women. Anxious to get hold of the women, the god of heaven offered to let the sun shine on the earth, but was reluctant to endow all the figures with life. At last he was compelled to oblige, but the earth-Zanahary refused to give up the now living human beings until they had had offspring. A bitter argument arose, and since then the heaven-Zanahary has done everything in his power to take back the life from all the creatures of the god of earth.

The wife of Zanahary is Andriamanitra, queen of heaven. A legend recounts that her contribution to the creation of mankind was the flesh and the form; other deities provided the bones, the blood, and the breath of life, or spirit.

OCEANIA

Polynesia Melanesia Micronesia Australia

Oceania has exerted a singular fascination over the European mind. Travellers, painters, anthropologists, and psychologists have been drawn to the Pacific Ocean by an expectation that there they might find primitive cultures which illustrate how the early ancestors of all mankind lived and thought. Although this assumption has been attacked by modern scholars, it remains true that in the Australian Aborigines today we have men who are not far short of being 'living fossils'. The age-old isolation of Australia, clearly evident in its archaic animals, such as flightless birds, egg-laying mammals, and marsupials, does find a parallel in the unique physical type of the aboriginal inhabitants. Of the Stone Age tribesmen of the central mountains of Papua, the world's second largest island, little is known at present, but it would appear that they may have maintained, too, a very primitive way of life through lack of contact with more advanced societies. The Pacific islanders, on the other hand, possess legends of migration and in their myths freely transfer divinities from island to island. A striking characteristic of Oceanic mythology in general is its closeness to what Carl Jung calls the archetypes, which are said to bring into our everyday consciousness an unknown psychic life belonging to a remote past; but, with the exception of central Papua and Australia, the area has not been sealed off from outside influences and a view of its preservation of the earliest intellectual and spiritual ideas cannot be sustained.

Oceania, in fact, contains four major traditions: Polynesia, Melanesia, Micronesia, and Australia. Polynesia, the easternmost cultural area, extends in a great triangle from New Zealand to Hawaii and Easter Island, and contains in its centre the island clusters of Tonga, Samoa, Tahiti, and Tuamotu. In this huge area there have been several migrations, but it is thought that the chief one was the arrival of the first Polynesians from South-east Asia by way of Micronesia. These settlers came about 2,000 years ago and carried with them an established pattern of culture, which has given a remarkable homogeneity to the mythology of the scattered archipelagos they colonized. The immense distances between islands—Hawaii is more than 4,000 miles from the northern island of New Zealand—have brought about local variations, a different emphasis in a legend here and a new concept of divinity there, but they are better described as modulations of a common theme. The Polynesian favourite, Maui, belongs to no particular island, and his trickery enlivens the legends of different gods and goddesses.

The Maori people of New Zealand, the supreme cosmologists and mythologers, explain the breaking of the one into the many as a conflict between the sky god Rangi and his children, imprisoned in the earth womb of Papa by their father's endless love-making. Like the Greek Ouranos, Rangi had to be separated from his docile spouse and forced upwards as the sky, but he was not emasculated in the conflict with his sons.

A Raratongan ironwood carving of the sky god Rangi with his sons

After this cosmic adjustment, and a struggle for supremacy between Rangi's children, the numerous beings hidden in the earth womb found themselves free to increase and multiply. The ultimate victor of the divine battle was the warlike Tu-mataugena, god of fierce human beings. His long struggle with the storm god Tawhiri-ma-tea, the Maoris say, caused the great inundation that formed the Pacific Ocean. The Hawaiians, on the other hand, make their remote god of generation, Kane, the creator deity. His withdrawal was ascribed to the ingratitude and misbehaviour of the first men. Kane, Ku, and Lono, moulded Kumuhonua, the first man, out of wet soil, gave him for wife Lalo-honua, and made him a chief to rule over the whole world. The first human couple lived happily until Lalo-honua met Aaia-nui-nukea-a-ku-lawaia, 'the great seabird with the white beak that stands fishing', and was seduced to eat the sacred apples of Kane. She went mad and became a seabird, while her husband was condemned to die.

The composite divinity of Kane, Ku, and Lono instituted death as a punishment for Lalo-honua's transgression. Lono-nui-noho-i-ka-wai, 'great Lono dwelling in the waters', was a messenger god; Ku-ka-o-o, 'Ku of the digging stick', joined together the notions of good harvests, catches of fish, successful outcomes, and human continuity; and Kane, the chief deity, was a sky god, namely Kane-i-ka-pahu-wai, 'Kane with a calabash of water', and Kanehekili, 'Kane the thunderer'. He was, however, sometimes associated with the sorcery god Kahoali, possibly because that god ruled the underworld. In Polynesia the souls of the departed were believed to travel to one of two lands: the souls of chiefs and outstanding men went to the paradise of the gods, an airborne island; the souls of ordinary people made their way to a shadowy place situated either beneath the ocean or the ground. The Hawaiians thought of the underworld as *lua-a-milu*, 'the pit of Milu', after the truculent chief Kane thrust down 'to the nethermost depths of the night'. It was entered through clefts in the earth, called 'casting-off places', and these were found in every inhabited district.

The journeys of Polynesian heroes to the sun, to the underworld for fire, or to the heavens, are reminiscent of the sorcerer's quest after the spirits which determine sickness and health, life and death. In the Maori legend of Hakawau and the supernatural head, the hero and the sorcerer are actually combined in the same person. It is a feature of mythology that is less pronounced in the other Oceanic traditions. Yet common to all of them are man-eating legends. At the time of the discovery of the Pacific islands by European voyagers, cannibalism was practised extensively and shipwrecked sailors had to be as cautious as did visitors from other archipelagos. Though the inhabitants of the Hawaiian Islands seem to have preferred 'manslaying' rather than 'man-eating' customs, they have preserved details of the gruesome practice of cannibalism. Famous was Ka-lo-aikanaka, 'Lo the man-eater', a fierce chief of enormous strength and appetite. This warrior, tattooed with figures of birds, sharks, and other fishes, was driven from his ancestral home because of his relish of baked human beings. A related myth is the oven of food obtained from the body of a god, who once came as a stranger to an island and took a wife. When there was a famine, he built and heated an oven, then got into it and was covered with earth. After the time had elapsed for the body to be cooked properly, the people opened the oven and discovered all sorts of cooked food, while the man himself, perfectly untouched, was seen approaching again from the sea. A stream of fresh water was also found welling up at the sea where he had emerged after digging his way half a mile from the oven.

Melanesia, the central cultural area, is made up of the large island of Papua, a ring of volcanic archipelagos, including the Admiralty Islands, Solomon Islands, Banks Islands, New Britain, New Hebrides, and New Caledonia, and, somewhat separate from the rest, the Fiji Islands. In striking contrast to the mythology of Polynesia, what stands out here is an amazing heterogeneity, which may have been encouraged by the apparent absence of the idea of a supreme deity.

In his formative study *The Melanesians*, which was published in 1891, R. H. Codrington noted that no supernatural being occupied a very elevated place in their world. On the contrary, 'the Melanesian mind', he wrote 'is entirely possessed by the belief in a supernatural power or influence, called almost universally mana. This is what works to effect everything which is beyond the ordinary power of men, outside the common processes of nature; it is present in the atmosphere of life, attaches itself to persons and to things, and is manifested by results which can only be ascribed to its operation. When one has got it he can use it and direct it, but its force may break forth at some new point. . . .' Although modern scholars have questioned the supposed impersonality of mana, and suggested that it is a supernatural quality rather than an impersonal force, the description of Melanesian religion as a mixture of spirit and ancestor worship in Codrington's pioneer work has not been displaced. Because the Melanesians have, or had until very recent times, cosmogonic myths that assume the pre-existence of the world and its chief characteristics, and merely describe subsequent alterations in shape and form, there is little scope for the activities of potent deities. A creator figure like Qat was a *vui* 'spirit', not a god; he lived and thought like men, his superior knowledge and powers derived from a sure hold on mana.

Good and evil are explained by the New Britain islanders in the opposition of two brothers, To-Kabinana and To-Karvuvu. Unfortunate and unforeseen were the consequences of the half-witted brother's actions, his inept imitation of To-Kabinana's magic. For To-Karvuvu created the first shark, the symbol of terror in the Pacific Ocean. The perpetual rivalry between these twins is a reflection of the unending fluctuation of human destiny, and contains in it the subtle notion that mishaps arise as much from foolishness and misplaced endeavour than the conscious hostility of the environment. Man, the inhabitants of New Britain assert, must seek for equilibrium within society and within the natural surroundings. Other culture myths take up this theme, though in Papua the emphasis is on fertility and reproduction.

The northernmost cultural area is Micronesia, a constellation of scattered islands. There are four main archipelagos—the Gilbert, Marshall, Mariana, and Caroline groups of islands. Remote from world trade routes, Micronesia was until the end of the Second World War neglected by scholars, and even today we have no comprehensive study of its mythological traditions, which appear to combine elements from both Melanesia and Polynesia. Moreover, it is possible to discern themes that originated in Europe and became mixed with the indigenous materials sometime after Magellan reached Guam in 1521. This is certainly true of folklore collected in the Gilbert Islands by Sir Arthur Grimble. To the activities of Christian missionaries are due the notion that death came to the world as a consequence of the first people damaging a sacred tree.

The old religion of the Micronesians placed great emphasis on ancestor worship. The *ani*, 'deified ancestors', were carefully propitiated by the Caroline islanders, who coupled their totemic cult with that of local deities. Ani were honoured in the shape of a special bird, animal, fish, or tree in which they were supposed to reside, and with which

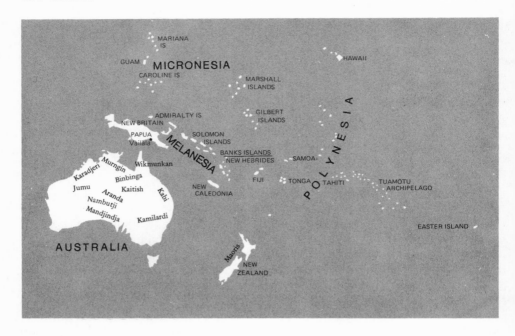

they were identified. The dead, however, travelled to one of two final resting places: they went either to a submarine paradise, *pachet*, or to a gloomy underworld, *pueliko*, whose portals were guarded by two malevolent hags. As in other parts of Micronesia, the cause of misfortune and wickedness was blamed on a trickster brother, Olofat. This god of fire bore responsibility for such diverse things as the teeth of the shark and the prevalence of adultery. By assuming innumerable transformations, Olofat succeeded in upsetting the world and escaping the consequences of his action. Less disruptive were cultural founder heroes such as Lugeilan, the inventor of tattooing and hairdressing as well as a teacher of agricultural skills.

When in 1788 Britain annexed the last cultural area, Australia, there were some 300,000 Aborigines divided into more than 400 tribes. These people had no knowledge of agriculture, metallurgy, pottery, or writing, and lacked domesticated animals, except for the dingo: they had adjusted to the inhospitable environment by a nomadic way of life, hunting and gathering wild fruits. No date can be placed on the arrival of the Aborigines in Australia, but it would seem that at some unrecorded time bands of food-gatherers moved southwards from the Indonesian archipelago, and spread over the continent, giving rise to the development of distinct languages and dialects. In spite of their low level of material culture these tribes have evolved a complex social order and religion. Allowing for local variations, the main features of the latter are belief in a detached sky god, and in lesser but more active deities, often cultural founder heroes; the close association of myth and ritual, where legendary events are even relived by those taking part in certain ceremonies; secret initiation rites for men; and totemism, the linking of individuals and groups with natural phenomena.

Among the Aranda in central Australia there is an awareness of a primordial celestial being, *erina itja arbamanakala*, 'him none made', who was alive before *alchera*, 'dream time'. During the 'dream time' the spirits sleeping beneath the ground arose and wandered the earth, shaping the landscape, making man and teaching the arts of survival. Their work done, these totemic ancestors subsided once more into sleep. While the Aranda have largely forgotten the primordial sky father, as have other groups with similar myths, they look back with intense nostalgia to the time when the chthonic deities walked the tribal lands. In initiation rites, a preserve of the men, the communication of the sacred traditions of the tribe about alchera is of central importance. These symbolical ceremonies represent a survival into modern times of an incredibly ancient system of spiritual instruction, and they involve a ritual eating of the primal father, since initiates drink the fresh-drawn blood of the older men. In former times this blood was obtained from a man who was killed for the purpose, just as portions of his body were eaten. On one recorded occasion, at the end of the nineteenth century, the blood-letting and cannibalism was practised on the initiates when two boys looked up and observed what they were forbidden to see. Although it is said that the first initiation rites were carried out in such a way that all the young men were killed, such a dramatic reversal of roles was unusual, not least because the consumption of blood coupled with the circumcision of the initiate is always intended to separate the boy from his mother and join him to the body of the warrior descendants of the totemic ancestors. About twelve months after the ordeal of circumcision, the initiate to manhood undergoes a second ritual operation: subincision. The opening of this phallic womb is intended to make him more than a man. Not surprising, therefore, was the interest shown by the Australian Aborigines in the Christian communion rite when they learned about it from the first missionaries.

Ahoeitu

A legendary Tui Tonga, king of Tonga. 'There first appeared on the earth the human offspring of a worm or grub, and the head of the worm became Tui Tonga. His name was Kohai. . . . The descendants of the worm, his subjects, became very numerous.'

One day, long ago, the god Eitumatupua climbed down from the sky on a great tree, and he took as his wife Ilaheva, a worm descendant. The god then returned to the sky, while the woman and their child, Ahoeitu, remained on earth. As soon as Ahoeitu grew up he determined to visit his father above; Ilaheva told him that he would find Eitumatupua catching pigeons. So Ahoeitu climbed the tree, met his father, and in joy they pressed noses. Yet the happiness of Eitumatupua over the arrival of the earthly son angered his celestial brothers, the children he had begotten in the sky. They, therefore, ambushed Ahoeitu and tore him to pieces, then cooked and ate him. Eitumatupua suspected the crime and ordered Ahoeitu's brothers to 'come and vomit'. Having recovered all the pieces of the earthly son, the

sky father remade him with the aid of magic herbs. Then he said: 'You have killed Ahoeitu. He shall descend as the ruler of Tonga, while you, his brothers, remain here. But they pleaded for forgiveness and in time Ahoeitu's brothers were allowed to climb down the great tree. The descendants of Ahoeitu, which means 'day has dawned', became successively Tui Tonga.

Alchera

Literally, 'dream time'. The remote period of time in which the ancestral spirits of aboriginal tribes in Australia walked the earth. The chthonic ancestors are believed to have returned to their abode underground.

Altjira

The otiose sky father of the Aranda tribes in central Australia. He is conceived of as a man in the sky with feet like an emu; his wives and daughters have feet like dogs. Strange or malformed feet are a common feature of spirits or ancestors in aboriginal belief. Witness such epithets as 'foot dog', 'foot body', 'toes-feet-rough', and 'bone foot'.

Altjira is *erina itja arbamanakala*, 'him none made'. His name is also connected with the verb to dream; he is, therefore, looked upon as the remote deity of the 'dream time', when the subterranean ancestral spirits left their slumber to roam the earth. Altjira gave the world its present form and then removed himself to the top of the sky, while the other 'eternal ones of the dream' sank back into their earthly abode. The Aranda say that today Altjira is indifferent to mankind.

Atea

In Tuamotuan mythology, the original moving sky space, a shapeless being. Atea was made into the sky god and Fa'ahotu became his wife. According to one legend, the firstborn of Fa'ahotu was the magician Tahu, but he died of starvation when nursed on her flat bosom. As other children followed this short path to the grave, Atea and Fa'ahotu exchanged sexes and the sky was the father-mother who suckled the young.

One of the great conflict myths in Polynesia was the struggle between Atea and Tane-mahuta, which the Maoris conceived of as the separation of the sky father from the earth mother, Rangi and Papa respectively. The Tuamotu islanders believed that Atea tried to capture the young god Tane, and sent a host of lesser deities after him. After Tane escaped from his pursuers on earth and wandered the clouds, he became so hungry that he killed and ate one of this ancestors, which was the beginning of cannibalism. On reaching manhood, Tane declared war on the sky god and, using the thunderbolts of his ancestor Fatutiri, 'thunder', he slew Atea. One of the dynasties of the Tuamotu archipelago claimed descent from the overthrown ruler of the sky.

Auwa

The sacred places of origin of the *pulwaiya*, 'ancestors'. Among the Wikmunkan tribesmen of northern Australia, the auwa, or totem centres, are the nests and breeding places of birds and animals. Each auwa has its own peculiar characteristics, though there is always water near by in the shape of a stream, lagoon, or water hole. The totemic ancestors are thought to reside and to play about the vicinity of the auwa. Near these subterranean spirits the great tribal ceremonies take place, and in some areas it is possible to find old rock paintings which relate to these rituals.

Bagadjimbiri

The Karadjeri in north-western Australia attribute everything to the two ancestral brothers called Bagadjimbiri. Prior to their rising from the ground as two dingos, the earth was featureless. There were no trees, no people, no animals—nothing lived. The Bagadjimbiri made water holes; from a toadstool and a fungus they shaped genital organs for the first sexless people; they also instituted the rite of circumcision.

After the two brothers had become gigantic men reaching up to the sky, and travelled throughout the land, they got into a dispute with a cat man called Ngariman, whom they had annoyed with their laughter. Ngariman and his relatives killed the Bagadjimbiri with spears. So enraged was Dilga, their earth goddess mother, that milk came out of her breasts and flowed underground to the place of the murder. There it emerged in a torrent, drowning the culprits and reviving the victims. After a time the reborn Bagadjimbiri decided to pass away; their corpses turned into water snakes and their spirits rose into the sky as great clouds.

Baiame

The totemic ancestor of the Kamilaroi tribe of New South Wales. An ancient sky god and 'father of all things', Baiame was master of life and death—the archetypal medicine-man. He invented the stone fish trap and he answers invocations for rain, while his favourite wife, Birrahgnooloo, sends floods on request.

Bamapana

The trickster hero of the Murngin in northern Australia, 'a crazy man'. To the open horror and hidden delight of these aboriginal tribesmen Bamapana was obscene and broke clan incest taboos. The quarrels and misunderstandings he caused were innumerable.

Banoi

One of the names used in the New Hebrides for the land of the dead. In this part of Melanesia it is believed that the spirit of the deceased lingers for several days before leaving the world of the living. Possibly an underwater realm, banoi has all the amenities found above except for gardens, because there is no work. Tradition holds that the ghostly inhabitants segregate themselves according to the mode of death: thus, those who have died of cough keep together.

Banks islanders say that the nether world, which they call *panoi*, is as near to the earth as death is near to life. Their subterranean land of the dead seems even a beautiful place, where festivals and social activities offer solace to those who 'have come to stay'. Fainting, or a temporary black-out, was always thought of as a brief visit to panoi. Yet a ghost, *tamate*, does not appear to have knowledge of distant things like a vui, a spirit or demigod: he is essentially a man who has died.

In the Solomon Islands the ghost, *tindalo*, of a chief or great man is revered as a link with the unseen world, a powerful ally in moments of crisis. Unpropitiated, however, the ghost can prove a dangerous enemy. Ghosts that haunt the sea are believed to be very terrible in appearance and behaviour: composed of fishes, they attack lonely canoes or swimmers.

Bobbi-bobbi

One of the ancestral snakes of the Binbinga, an aboriginal people living in northern Australia. Once the snake Bobbi-bobbi sent a number of flying foxes for men to eat, but these large bats managed to escape from the oven. Therefore, the snake, who was underground watching them, took out one of his ribs and threw it up. Using the bone as a boomerang the men killed the flying foxes for cooking. They later made a hole in the sky with it, and this angered Bobbi-bobbi, who seized hold of his rib when it fell back to earth. Since two of the young men tried to save the sacred boomerang, they were pulled down into the snake's mouth.

Another snake spirit was Ulanji. For some unknown reason this ancestor climbed rocks in order to bite off the heads of flying foxes. He also took out two ribs and his heart. Binbinga initiates are told that the snake father requires their foreskins.

Bue

In Gilbertese mythology, son of a woman magically impregnated by the sun. Bue travelled to the east by canoe, seeking his father and his inheritance of cleverness, *te rabakau*, and knowledge, *te ataibai*. Like the Polynesian hero Maui, the determined Bue assaulted the sun god and obtained his desire. Although the father tried to hamper the later exploits of the son, Bue was the cultural founder hero. He taught men how to build canoes and houses, how to raise winds by magic, how to ensure health and prosperity, and how to compose dance chants.

Dhakhan

The Kabi tribe on the Queensland coast of Australia worship Dhakhan, the rainbow, an ancestral spirit part fish and part snake that resides in deep water holes. He appears in the sky as a rainbow when he is passing from one water hole to the other.

Djanggawuls

The divine trio of north Australian mythology. Two sisters and a brother who came to the earth via *beralku*, the island of spirits or the dead, and gave the landscape its shape and vegetation. This they accomplished with the aid of sacred sticks, called *rangga*, some of which were left behind at certain places as sacred objects. From the red-plumed solar deities, the Djanggawul sisters, came the first men and women, also called rangga. The rites of these ancestral sisters and brother, which are mainly concerned with fertility, are now carried out by men, though originally they were the possession of women. Such a change may have been brought about by rape, as was the case in another tradition.

Dudugera

In Papuan mythology, the leg child who became the sun. One day a woman who was in a garden near the ocean, seeing a great fish sporting in the surf, walked out into the water and played with it. Some time later the woman's leg, against which the fish had rubbed, began to swell and become painful until at last she got her father to make a cut in the swelling, when out popped a baby.

Dudugera, as his mother called the child, grew up in the village but his aggressiveness made him unpopular with the other boys. Fearing lest he might come to harm, Dudugera's mother determined to send him to his father. They went down to the beach, whereupon the great fish came, seized him in his mouth, and carried him far away to the east. Before this happened, Dudugera warned his mother and her relatives to take refuge under a great rock, for he was about to become the sun, the terrible affliction of the world. So they did as Dudugera suggested, and from the shade of their sanctuary, they watched the heat of the sun wither people, plants, and animals. To prevent the total annihilation of life his mother tossed lime into the face of the sun as it rose one morning, which placed clouds between the earth and the merciless sun rays.

The Papuans account for the comparative dullness of the moon by a myth of premature birth. Once a man digging a well found deep in the earth a small bright disc. This was the moon which, escaping from his hands, rose into the sky. Had it remained in the ground until the period of gestation was over, the moon would have acquired greater light. A variant has the moon escape from a water jar.

Goga

The Massim people of Papua believe that the origin of fire was an old woman named Goga. The first men stole it from her. A rain goddess and a fire goddess, Goga tried to quench the stolen firebrand by a downpour but, fortunately for mankind, a snake preserved the flame on its tail.

Another fire myth relates how the first men noticed smoke rising from the sea. They sent various animals after a flame, and it happened that the dog managed to steal a blazing brand from the island of the fire goddess.

Gora-daileng

In the Caroline Islands, the god who punished the wicked after death. Gora-daileng lived by a subterranean river of unknown length. Having tortured wicked souls by fire, he was in the habit of pushing them into this river so that the strong current would bear them away to oblivion.

Hakawau

The pre-eminent Maori sorcerer. He attained to fame by his overthrow of the magical wooden head belonging to the sorcerers Puarata and Tautohito. This potent head bewitched all persons who dared to approach the stronghold in which it was kept, and the fame of its power spread throughout New Zealand. The death of so many people was the general topic of conversation in the islands, and, at last, Hakawau decided he would test its strength by a personal visit. With a single human companion, the old sorcerer set out, unceasingly working at his enchantments, and repeating incantations, which might ward off evil genii. They passed the rotting corpses of their predecessors, to the dismay of his companion, but Hakawau had already learned from his own familiars that the malignant spirits of Puarata and Tautohito were not as powerful as at first appeared. Moreover, his army of good spirits was able to take the fortress and, when in desperation Puarata

appealed to the magic head, it could no longer bellow aloud as in former times, but uttered only low moans and wails. Climbing over the palisades of the gateway, Hakawau publicly demonstrated his own superiority as a sorcerer, and after a brief inspection of the sacred places of the stronghold, he and his companion departed, unharmed and satisfied. His final action was to clap his hands, at which every person inside the palisades died. Thus were Puarata and Tautohito overthrown.

Haumea

The mysterious fertility goddess of Hawaiian mythology. Haumea was sometimes identified with the earth goddess Papa: she was 'the prolific one', and 'the woman from a distant land', who gave birth to 'strange noisy creatures'. By rebirths it was said Haumea changed herself from age to youth and returned to marry her children and grandchildren. Although the goddess attended at childbirth, taking delight in the natural increase of people, she would also destroy. Most celebrated of all was her connection with magic fruit trees and a stick 'that attracted the fish'. One could order these sacred trees to produce food, though an accident to the 'fish tree' scattered fish through the waters all about Hawaii.

Hiyoyoa

Among the Wagawaga tribes of Papua, the underworld. At death the soul, *arugo*, is said to leave the body and journey to *hiyoyoa*, a realm beneath the sea. The white-skinned and smooth-haired lord of the dead is Tumudurere. In his gardens the arugo work, as visitors from the world of the living testify. Indeed, it is claimed that certain plants were brought back from there.

Icho-Kalakal

A semi-legendary chief. According to the Caroline islanders, Icho-Kalakal was the leader of a great invasion from the south, presumably Melanesia. Whether or not he was daunted by the massive stone fortifications on some of the islands we do not know. These gigantic enclosures were the handiwork of the divine twins Olo-sipa and Olo-sopa.

A Hawaiian carving of a woman, possibly a deity

Iki-haveve

Literally, 'belly don't know'. The Papuan description of the ecstatic cult that arose in Vailala about 1919. People were seen 'taking a few quick steps in front of them and would then stand, jabber and gesticulate, at the same time swaying the head from side to side; also bending the body from side to side from the hips, the legs appearing to be held firm'. Such ecstatic possession, an indirect consequence of colonial penetration, found its cult leader in an old man named Evara. He prophesied the coming of a steamer, carrying the spirits of the ancestors on board, who would bring with them the 'cargo'. Anti-European sentiments were evident in his revelations, since the expected gifts included rifles. However, the idea of a return of the dead was somewhat complicated by the belief that ancestors were white. Later Evara prophesied that an aeroplane would bring the sacred cargo of plenty.

The paraphernalia of modern technology everywhere appeared: an instance was imitation radios for making contact with the ancestors. Tribal customs and beliefs were abandoned as the ecstatic Papuans anticipated the millennium. The deep interest in European material goods, the root of the 'cargo cults', was reflected in the mythical attire of their new god Ihova: he wore a coat, shirt, trousers, hat and shoes. Though the Vailala outbreak was almost over in 1923, its legacy was the modern 'cargo cult', stimulated by the Second World War. Aeroplanes, ships, vehicles, supply bases bewildered and intrigued peoples emerging from Stone Age levels of culture. They were also interested after the end of hostilities when the United States Army began to exhume the bodies of its dead. The forlorn watchers of intercontinental flights remain today as witnesses to the mythical possibilities of cultural change.

Kahausibware

A serpentine female spirit revered in the Solomon Islands. Long ago, when the fruits of the earth grew without labour, Kahausibware made men, pigs, other animals, and trees. But she also introduced death into the world. When the first woman left the first baby with the snake spirit, and went off to work in her garden, the infant screamed ceaselessly. Unable to tolerate the din, a weakness incidentally shared by the ancient Mesopotamian gods, Kahausibware coiled herself round the baby and strangled it. The mother returned while the snake's body was still partly wound round her child, and seizing an axe she started to hack the snake to pieces. Though Kahausibware had the power to rejoin the severed parts, she disliked this treatment and made off to a distant island. As she swam away, she flung out this taunt: 'Who will help you now?' Since that day things were never the same.

A culture myth of the Admiralty Islands also revolves round a snake spirit. Once a woman entered the forest and met a serpent. After some initial reluctance the woman agreed to marry the serpent, and she bore a boy and a girl. Then the serpent sent her away so that he alone could nurture the children. When they were quite big, he told them to catch and cook some fish. But they warmed the fish with the sun's rays, and ate the food, still raw and bloody. At this the serpent said: 'Spirits you are, eaters of raw meat. Perhaps you will eat me.' And he commanded the boy to crawl into his belly, but the child was afraid and asked the reason for this order. 'Bring out the fire', replied the serpent, 'and give it out to your sister! Then gather coconuts, yams and bananas.' The boy did as he was bid, and with the flame they cooked the vegetables. When the children had eaten, the serpent asked, 'Is my kind of food or yours better?' They answered, 'Yours! Our kind is bad.' In this manner, say the Admiralty islanders, were the rudiments of society first introduced.

Kai-n-tiku-aba

Literal meaning: 'tree of many branches'. The sacred tree of Samoa. According to the Gilbert islanders, who migrated northwards from Samoa about 1400, Kai-n-tiku-aba sprang from the spine of Na Atibu, the father of the gods, who died that the world could be made ready for mankind. People actually grew as fruit on the branches of Kai-n-tiku-aba. One man, however, broke the tree: he was Koura-abi. What roused him to this sacrilege was the excrement dropped by the branches on his head. Because of Koura-abi's violence the people of the tree were scattered and sorrow entered the world of men.

Kamapua'a

Literally, 'hog-child'. A popular figure in

Ku, Hawaiian god of war and helper of Kane. Image of feathers on basketry frame

Hawaiian mythology. With his enormous snout he dug the earth and 'raised a great mound, a hill for the gods, a hill with a precipice in front'. Possibly this legend refers to a stronghold belonging to a powerful family of the pig god's descendants.

Despite numerous attempts on the life of infant Kamapua'a, he grew up into an energetic and powerful deity. He would uproot with his snout the crops of his enemies, defeat them in battle, savagely wielding a club in his human hands, and carry off as booty all their valuables. A welcome ally in the interminable wars of Hawaii, Kamapua'a married the two daughters of a leading chief and rendered him loyal service on the battlefield, capturing the 'feather capes and helmets' of many rival chiefs.

Once, as a handsome man, Kamapua'a attempted to woo the fire goddess Pele. She refused him with insults, calling him 'pig and the son of a pig'. Soon they were hurling abuse at each other, and as their divine supporters arrived the quarrel changed into a fight. Pele's relations poured flames on the pig god, while his friends threatened to extinguish the volcanic fires with fog and rain. 'Hogs ran all over the place. The pit filled with water. . . . And Pele yielded, and Kamapua'a had his way with her.'

The amorous and warlike aspects of the pig god alternate in his cycle of legends. Occasionally they can be seen to explain natural phenomena. At a certain place he once saw two pretty women and pursued them. They were goddesses and disappeared into the earth. When the enormous snout dug for them, two springs of water burst forth, thereafter known as 'the springs of Kamapua'a'.

Kane

In late Hawaiian mythology, the chief god of generation: he had a 'dazzling' phallus like the Polynesian trickster hero Maui. He was 'the ancestor of chiefs and commoners' as well as the maker of the three worlds—the upper heaven, the lower heaven, and the earth.

At the beginning Kane dwelt in darkness. Then light was created, and Ku, an ancestral deity, along with Lono, god of the heavens, helped Kane to fashion the earth and the things on the earth. Later they created man and woman, but the misbehaviour of this pair forced Kane to leave the earth and retire to heaven, after he had made mankind subject to death. That his original intention was to live among people can be seen from the title given to the world: Ka-honua-nui-a-Kane, 'the great earth of Kane'.

Human sacrifice was never paid to Kane, because 'life is sacred to him'. His images were rare, a tall conical stone often sufficed for altars. His powers, however, were clearly perceived: he was Kane-hekili, 'thunderer'; Kane-wawahi-lani, 'breaking through heaven'; and Ka-uila-nui-maka-keha'i-i-ka-lani, 'lightning flashing in the heavens'. The bloodlessness of Kane worship contrasts with that of many other Hawaiian gods. The sorcerer god Kahoalii, for instance, used to receive the eyeball of a fish and that of a human victim. The drinking of a victim's eye with kava as an offering to a deity was common in Polynesia, though the Tahitians reserved the eye for their king.

Kane was often associated with the squid god Kanaloa, the Hawaiian Tangaroa. Kanaloa was 'evil-smelling', vindictive, and the opponent of Kane's creatures. He has been identified with the Christian devil and the land of the dead. Like Kane, Kanaloa was thought of as a deity living in a human body on a paradisal island, floating in the clouds near the Hawaiian Islands. The magical island was called Kane-huna-moku, 'hidden land of Kane'.

Kava

Literally, 'bitter'. An intoxicating drink brewed from the root or leaves of a plant of the pepper family. It is important in Polynesian ceremonies, though the drink is sometimes used to quiet hunger. In a Tongan myth, a king went to visit a place troubled by famine. Since there was no food to offer him, a noblewoman had her baby dressed and cooked like a baked pig. When he discovered the deception, he said, 'I am not a man-eater. Take it away and give it a chief's burial.' This they did. And the next morning the people noticed that a plant had come up out of the child's grave. The king told them to tend this plant, the kava, which would be their curse or blessing, according to the way they used it.

Kumu-honua

Literal meaning: 'earth beginning'. The first man of Hawaiian mythology. His wife was called Lalo-honua, 'earth below'. The original garden made for mankind by the god Kane contained fruits and animals, all of which were available to Kumu-honua and his wife, except for a sacred tree. The apples and the bark of this tree were forbidden, but like the biblical pair they broke the law and were expelled. A great white albatross drove them out. In one version of the myth it is a 'great seabird with a white beak' that persuaded Lalo-honua to eat the sacred apples of Kane.

Kunapipi

The mother goddess of the aboriginal tribes of northern Australia. Now a vague, otiose, spiritual being, 'the old woman' once travelled across the land with a band of heroes and heroines, and during the ancestral period she gave birth to men and women as well as creating the natural species. A 'rainbow serpent' went before in order to prepare her way.

Laufakanaa

The wind god of Ata, a low Tongan island. According to legend, the sky god Tamapoulialamafoa sent Laufakanaa down to the earth as the ruler of Ata and the controller of winds. 'If there is a vessel that has bad winds', said Tamapoulialamafoa, 'and men come to you, Laufakanaa, and ask for your aid, then you must give fair winds to that vessel.' When the Tongans, therefore, had need of perfect sailing conditions, it was customary for sailors to visit Ata and present to Laufakanaa bread cooked with the oil of grated coconut.

Though this offering apparently pleased the wind god, he was never identified with the coconut tree. Instead, the Tongans say, Laufakanaa brought down from heaven and planted on Ata the banana and several edible roots. He is also credited with the invention of the fishing net. His name means 'speak' *lau*, 'to silence', *fakanaa*, and it is interesting in this occupation myth that the Tongans assume the pre-existence of sky and sea. Maui, the trickster hero of Polynesia, fished up numerous islands with a strong fish hook, but others like Ata were thrown down from heaven. The latter were called *makafonua*, 'land stones'. A variant, however, does include Ata in the land-fishing of Maui, who hauled it from the sea, jumped ashore, and stamped heavily on the highest mountain. 'As he stamped, the earth shook, and the mountain crumbled away beneath his feet, and rolled down into the valleys below, till they were filled up to the level on which he stood. This he

did to four of the seven hills, leaving the other three untrodden, for he was weary of the work.'

Lioumere

A ghastly spirit of the Caroline Islands. When this female demon with long iron teeth used to visit an island, the people were usually cautious in their behaviour. But there was one man who coveted her iron fangs so much that he made a plan. Getting Lioumere to grin at the antics of a very ugly clown, he rushed forward and dashed them out with a stone. At once there was a scramble for the iron fangs because of their magical power.

Loa

In the Marshall Islands, the supreme being and creator deity, a parallel of the Tahitian Ta'aroa. At the beginning Loa, or Lowa, dwelt alone in the primeval sea. Loneliness and boredom made him raise up reefs and sandbanks, create plants and birds, and station a god at each of the cardinal points. From Loa's leg emerged Wulleb and Limdunanij, the first man and the first woman. When their offspring conspired to kill Wulleb, he fled and fell to earth, where from his leg came two more sons. Edao, the younger one, became a great magician and had many adventures, not unlike those of Olofat.

A variant myth relates that Wulleb and Lejman, male and female worms living in a shell, were the first human beings, a notion echoed in the Tongan Islands. The worms raised the upper part of the shell to become the sky, leaving the lower as the earth. Loa here remains in the background as the first cause.

Lugeilan

According to the Caroline islanders, Lugeilan came down from the sky to teach men for the first time. His specific contributions were tattooing, hairdressing, and agriculture. Lugeilan was always connected with the coconut palm.

The Micronesian hero Olofat was his son. This trickster often visited heaven and on one of his visits he brought the secret of fire down from the sky. The cunning and deceit of Olofat probably led to the identification of Lugeilan with the bird god Luk, the god of death and disease.

Mangar-kunjer-kunja

Literal meaning: 'fly-catcher'. The Aranda of central Australia say that the world was originally covered by the ocean with only a few hills protruding from the salt water. On the slopes of these primeval hills lived the *rella manerinja*, 'two grown together'. These undeveloped beings had their eyes and ears closed; instead of a mouth they had a small hole; their fists were closed; and their arms and legs were both attached to the trunk. For a long time they lived in this symbiotic state. Then the level of the waters fell and Mangar-kunjer-kunja, a lizard ancestor, came and separated them with a stone knife. Afterwards he cut all the openings, giving them eyes, ears, nostrils, and so on. His next gifts, after performing the rites of circumcision and subincision, were the stone knife, fire, the spear, the shield, the boomerang, and the *tjurunga*, a sacred object linking man with his ancestor and affording protection from harm. Finally Mangar-kunjer-kunja regulated their marriage system.

A variant has two beings called *numbak-ulla*, 'self-existing ones', descend from the sky. They found a creature with the appearance of human beings all doubled up into a ball. After a time it began to take shape as two persons and the numbakulla assisted in this evolution, before transforming themselves into fly-catching lizards.

The lizard is taboo for Aranda initiates, the penalty for its killing being an abnormal craving for sex. Other aboriginal tribes possess myths of incomplete men, but the celestial assistants are often birds or bird-men. According to Kaitish tradition, in 'dream time' two hawk-men, *ullakupera*, flew down and transformed numbers of unfinished, or potential, creatures into men and women; they circumcised and subincised the men and cut the vulva of the women. Another tribe, on the other hand, considers that the first man originated as a lizard.

Marawa
The Melanesian spider spirit. According to the Banks islanders, Marawa was both the friend and foe of Qat, the other potent vui, 'spirit'. Not only was Marawa responsible for making man a mortal being, but even more he directly opposed Qat's conquest of the sea. Nightly he replaced the chips which Qat had cut from the tree trunk he was making into a canoe. When Qat surprised him one night, Marawa agreed to help Qat and together they out-manœuvred the latter's brothers, who were jealous and vindictive. Once they trapped Qat

in the hole of a land crab and toppled a stone on the top of him. To their bewilderment, the brothers returned home and found the intended victim sitting by the side of his wife, the beautiful Ro Lei. Marawa had assisted Qat in his miraculous escape.

Matagaigai
A Papuan tree spirit. The male is described as an ordinary man, but the female has one large and one small breast. Matagaigai only appear to people when they are ill: should their fingers sink into the patient's flesh, then death is certain. Malevolent are the swamp spirits, or *matabiri*, ugly creatures with huge bellies and swollen cheeks. They like to put 'medicine' on people.

Maui
The diminutive Polynesian culture hero and trickster. He appears in myths from New Zealand to Hawaii and enjoys a reputation as a kind of Hercules. Usually a youngest son, sometimes an abandoned child, either abortive or premature, Maui was thrown into the sea by his mother, Taranga, who first wrapped him in a tuft of her hair. Saved by his great ancestor, Tama-nui-ki-te-Rangi, he eventually returned to earth and rejoined his family. Then it was that his mother called him Maui-tiki-tiki-a-Taranga, 'Maui formed in the top knot of Taranga'.

The best known of Maui's legendary exploits were fishing up islands from the bottom of the sea, snaring the sun to slow it down in its passage, lifting the sky to give men more room on earth, and getting fire. In Maori myth, Maui used the jaw bone of his ancestress, Muri-ranga-whenua, as his enchanted weapon. With its keen point he drew land from the sea, but his brothers, ignoring his warning, sliced it all up, thus causing the island-studded triangle of Polynesia and the mountains of New Zealand. With the mighty jaw bone and a flaxen rope Maui also assaulted the sun. The hero undertook the task 'when he began to think that it was too soon after the rising of the sun that it became night again'. He caught the sun in a noose and dealt him many fierce blows, till weak from its wounds the sun could only creep along its course.

A Maori carving of Maui from the inside of a tribal meeting house

The Tongans say that the sky is sometimes dark because of the poker which Maui used to force it upwards. It happened that he was preparing an earth oven when his poker got jammed in the sky, then much lower than today. Infuriated, Maui reversed it and pushed up the sky upwards. An Hawaiian legend, however, recounts that he performed the sky-lifting feat to gain the favour of a certain woman.

The source of fire is variously interpreted. Some traditions explain that Maui stole the secret of fire from 'the mud hens' while they were roasting bananas. Each time he approached these celestial chickens they scratched out the flames. When he finally managed to seize the smallest hen, she told him that fire was in the tree called *wai-mea*, 'sacred water', and showed him how to obtain it. According to the Maori version, it was the ancient fire goddess, his relation, who pulled out her nail to give Maui a flame. But his trickery almost got the better of his judgement in this adventure because he asked for more flaming nails than he could handle safely.

Other tales surrounding Maui concern his birth, marriage, and death. Of interest is the story of Hina and Maui recorded in the Tuamotu Archipelago, which is east of Tahiti. The wayward Hina deserted her husband the monster eel Te Tuna, and searched the world for a new lover. She cried aloud: 'I am a woman to be possessed by an eel-shaped lover; a woman come all the way hither to unite in the struggle of passion upon the shore . . . the first woman thus to come utterly without shame seeking the eel-shaped rod of love.' Nobody dared to satisfy Hina's desire, for fear of the wrath of the monster eel, till Maui was directed to her by his own mother. At first Te Tuna took no notice of their liaison, but the taunts of neighbours eventually roused him to anger. Amid darkened skies, thunder rolls and lightning flashes, and an empty sea, littered with stranded monsters, the rivals Te Tuna and Maui compared their manhood. With his gigantic phallus in hand the trickster hero struck down three of the eel monster's frightful companions, overawed his rival, and claimed the day. Thus did Hina, the archetype of the faithless wife, confidently change husbands. Later Te Tuna made another attempt on Maui but he was 'rent apart', a victim of the trickster's superior magic. From the buried head of Te Tuna grew the first coconut tree.

The Maoris regard Hina as Hine-nui-te-po, the goddess of death. They believe that Maui found her fast asleep. He tried to pass through her body but the twittering of birds woke her up, and she squeezed him to death. If Maui had passed safely through Hine-nui-te-po, then no more human beings would have died, since death itself would have been destroyed. But on Hawaii the irrepressible trickster was supposedly killed by the inhabitants, who found his activities irksome. It is said that his blood made shrimps red and gave the colours to the rainbow.

Menehune
A mythical race of pygmies. The Hawaiians believed that they were 'about two feet in height'. Their 'bow-legged' forms were encountered in the forests, where travellers needed to be on guard. They shot tiny arrows at the careless or the inquisitive, but left alone they lived happily in caves.

The Menehune later migrated to New Zealand and became mixed up in the minds of the Hawaiians with the Maoris. Traditions of little men are found throughout the Pacific Ocean. While in distant Java they were credited with the construction of temples, in Tonga they acted as foresters, planting whole islands 'in a single night', and in Fiji invisible dwarfs with 'fuzzy mops of hair' taught the people how to sing and dance.

Minawara
Minawara and Multultu—the two ancestral heroes of the Nambutji tribe in central Australia—are kangaroo men. They emerged from a heap of debris carried by 'the flood', and travelled southwards, walking on all fours. When they camped they made a little hole and slept there, covering themselves with rubbish. A rat man saw this, and reprimanded them severely. 'Don't do what I do,' he said. 'You two sit in the shade beside the tree.' Since then, *alchera*, the 'dream time' of the ancestors, the kangaroo, has rested in the shade. Having got a tail from under the rubbish, Minawara and Multultu continued their journey into the desert, where they donned feathers. Their mucus and lungs were tossed away as stones: likewise a rib became a standing stone, which the Nambutji still grease with red ochre. The kangaroo men put on a spear-thrower their testicles, then took them back again, and so they went off holding each other by these parts. This archaic myth, a

secret of the men in the tribe, forms the centre piece of Nambutji initiation rites.

Mokoi

Literal meaning: 'evil ghost'. The Murngin in northern Australia believe that death is rarely caused by old age: instead they ascribe a fatal disease or accident to a mokoi, or to ritual uncleanliness. Thus Yunlungur, the ancestral snake spirit, devoured two women and their offspring because they had broken an incest taboo. An evil ghost, however, is said to strike down a victim because of the black magic of a sorcerer. The Murngin have great fear of these men, and in time of need turn to good magicians for aid. The latter are distinguished by the small bag that hangs down from a head band. In a contest with a mokoi the magician would invoke his own familiars.

Naniumlap

In the Caroline Islands, the god of fertility and festivity. Naniumlap ensured that plants grew, animals fattened, and women bore children. Sacred to him were the turtle and certain other creatures, which only chiefs might eat.

Nareau

Literal meaning: 'spider lord'. The creator deity of Gilbertese traditions. At the beginning Nareau walked alone on Te Bo ma Te Maki, 'the darkness and the cleaving together'. He was Nareau te Moa-ni-bai, 'spider lord the first of things'. Then entering the primordial substance, he created out of sand and water two beings, Na Atibu and Nei Teukez. From their union sprang the gods; Te Ikawai, 'the eldest, Nei Marena, 'the woman between', Te Nao, 'the wave', Na Kika, 'octopus lord', Rüki, 'the eel', and a multitude of others. The last was Nareau the younger, also known as Te Kikinto, 'mischief maker'.

Nareau te Moa-ni-bai considered that his work was done; he announced that he would depart, charging Na Atibu with the task of making a world of men. Not only was Nareau the younger the most active deity, but more Na Atibu allowed his spider son to slay him in order to get a light for the world. The right eye of Na Atibu was flung into the eastern sky as the sun, the left eye into the western sky as the moon; his crumbled brain formed the stars; his flesh and bones sown across the waters became islands and trees. In the construction of the archipelagos the octopus god Na Kika proved very skilful, for his extra arms could pull together vast quantities of sand and stones. When all was ready for construction, the young spider god created the ancestors of mankind, upon whom in due course he played all kinds of tricks.

Ndauthina

Literally, 'torch-bearer'. The Fijian god of seafaring and fishing; he was also the fire god. According to legend, his mother tied lighted reeds upon his head when he was a child, and ever since he has roamed the reefs by night hooded with a flaming brazier. During the hours of darkness Ndauthina was said to cause mischief, being among other things the patron of adulterers.

Ndengei

The serpentine creator deity of Fiji. The shiftings and turnings of Ndengei in his cave were considered to be the cause of earthquakes. This god was chief of the so-called 'root gods', *kalou-vu*, the indigenous pantheon of the Fiji islands. Another serpent deity was Ratu-mai-mbula, who ruled the land of the dead. His other role was that of a god of fertility; he made the sap run in the trees and the crops sprout.

Nei Tituaabine

The Gilbertese vegetation goddess. According to legend, the great chief Auriaria, red-skinned and of a giant's stature, fell in love with Nei Tituaabine, a red-skinned maiden with eyes that flashed like lightning. But their love-making bore no fruit, and soon Nei Tituaabine fell ill and died. From the grave of this beautiful girl, however, three trees grew; out of her head sprouted the coconut palm, out of her navel the almond, and out of her heels the pandanus. Nei Tituaabine thus was transformed into the tree goddess and her memory preserved.

Njirana

According to the Jumu in western Australia, Njirana and Julana were father and son, but the latter could be seen as an extension of Njirana's personality. It is even his phallus, which is compared to a gigantic bull-roarer, the ceremonial stone swung on a string. Julana delights in the pursuit of women, whom he surprises by travelling beneath the sand. This renowned pair travelled the continent in 'dream time', when the ancestral spirits sleeping underground awoke and roved the earth, and their exploits form a cycle of myths. For an unknown reason Njirana is associated with dogs. He is supposed to have killed the bad ones, and favoured the good—the ancestors of present-day dogs. Julana too may have been a killer of rats.

Nu'u

The Hawaiian Noah. Nu'u-pule, 'praying Nu'u', escaped the flood in a large vessel with a house on top of it. Having landed at the summit of a mountain on Hawaii and sacrificed kava, pig, and coconuts to heaven, the god Kane descended on a rainbow and explained 'his mistake'. The tidal wave, a familiar catastrophe in the Pacific Ocean, was connected with the rising of an 'undersea goddess' from the depths. The Banks islanders relate how the Melanesian hero Qat built a canoe on high ground and awaited the coming of the deluge there. The biblical flood story has been entwined with both Melanesian and Polynesian legend, but there is no reason to suppose that independent stories did not exist prior to the arrival of missionaries. In Hawaii there was said to be a certain tree that grew over Ka-wai-o-ulu, 'the waters of generation', and held these waters together with its great roots. Were it not for this tree water would submerge all the valleys.

Oa Rove

A Papuan deity of unlimited life and strength. The Roro-speaking tribes of the south regard him as a changer god, the rove, 'sacred one', who could transform his appearance at will. Once he persuaded all the women in a village to get into a great canoe, which he sailed to the top of a mountain. It was a punishment because the men had taken his game and fish. When the injured husbands climbed up to get back their wives, they found Oa Rove sitting on an inaccessible rock from which he tossed a spear, a bow and arrow, and a club. Then he threw down a stone as well as a corpse. All these weapons were given to them that they might be able to kill each other easily.

Olofat

The Micronesian hero. In the Caroline Islands Olofat, or Olofad, was the son of Lugeilan, a deity identified with the trickster god Luk. His mother was a mortal women who experienced a magical conception.

According to legend, Olafat decided to visit heaven on a column of smoke in order to claim recognition of his celestial relatives. The upshot was a long and eventful war against the sky gods and his own death. But Lugeilan felt sorry for Olofat. He resuscitated the presumptious son and obliged the gods to make room for him in the sky. One tradition suggests that he became the fire god. After this elevation, however, the daring and playful side of Olofat's character was in no way diminished. While he interpreted the commands of his father to men, he could not resist tricking and deceiving them, so that a number of his jokes led to unforeseen consequences. For instance, he outfitted the shark with teeth.

Olofat is a contradictory figure. Throughout the cycle of myths about his exploits there runs a basic theme—the divine inheritance dwelling in the mortal body. Olofat is torn between two worlds: like the Sumerian hero Gilgamesh, he cannot accept the reality of death, though he seems to have been more successful in his personal quest to escape from its toils.

Oro

The Tahitian war god. In time of peace he was called Oro-i-te-tea-moe, 'Oro of the spear laid down'. Son of Hina-tu-a-uta, 'Hina of the land', and Ta'aroa incarnate in a breadfruit branch, Oro was 'the manslayer', the one who took pleasure in bloody fights and human sacrifices. He had three fearsome daughters—Toi-mata, 'axe with eyes', Ai-tupuai, 'eater of summit', and Mahu-fatu-rau, 'frog of many owners'. His only son was Hoa-tapu, 'sworn friend'.

Pahuanuiapitaaiterai

According to the Tahitians, a sea demon, one of the foes of the deep. Personifications of the dangers faced by mariners, Pahuanuiapitaaiterai, 'the great one that opens to the sky', and his kin were greatly feared. Other demons included Puatutahi, 'coral rock standing alone', Ahifatumoana, 'sea serpent', Arematararoa, 'long wave', and Arematapopoto, 'short wave'.

Paka'a

God of wind. Credited with the invention of the sail, Paka'a inherited his authority over the winds and storms from his grandmother Loa. He was one of the lesser Hawaiian gods. In order not to omit any one of the host of lesser deities formed out of the spittle of Kane when he was shaping the earth, it was customary to begin a prayer thus: 'Invoke we now the 40,000 gods, the 400,000 gods, the 4,000 gods. . . .'

Papa

Ancestress of the Hawaiian people. She was the earth goddess, queen of the underworld, and mother of the gods. Papa means 'flat' and may have referred to the submerged foundations on which islands were supposed to rest. She was called Papa-hanau-moku, 'the one from whom lands are born'. A mortal ancestor, as opposed to this divinity, was Wakea, from whom all Hawaiian genealogies stem. Son of Kahiko-lua-mea, 'very ancient and sacred', Wakea ruled as a great chief and married Papa, who bore a daughter Ho'ohoku-ka-lani. It was Wakea's incestuous love for his daughter that aroused Papa's fury and led to the separation of husband and wife, not to mention the coming of death. Ho'ohoku-ka-lani's first child by her father was born in the form not of a human being but of a root, and was thrown away. It grew into a plant and so Wakea named their second child, a human one, Ha-loa, 'long rootstalk'. Vegetable growth was regarded by Hawaiians with more religious awe than animal life because it seemed unrelated to man.

The marriage of Papa and Wakea, probably a sister-brother union, reflects an ancient practice among noble families in Oceania. It seems likely that in Japan a similar custom was set aside through Chinese influence. The dissolution of the original marriage was used to account for the origin of the different classes in traditional Hawaiian society. From one of Papa's children by a second husband it was said the slave class descended. Apart from these legends, there also survives a miniature creation myth in which Papa gave birth to a gourd—a calabash and its cover. Wakea tossed the cover upwards to form the sky, the pulp the sun, the seeds the stars, the white lining the moon, the ripe white meat the clouds, and the juice the rain. Of the calabash itself he made the land and the ocean. The Maori version of creation is quite different: like the Greek Ouranos, Rangi was reluctant to have Papa's children freed from the earth womb.

Pele

A Polynesian fire goddess associated with the flow of lava. Renowned for her beauty—her back was straight as a cliff and her breasts rounded like the moon—Pele wandered widely before she settled on Hawaii. One legend says she was searching for her husband, Wahieloa, who had been enticed away by a rival. With her came the sea, which poured from her head over previously dry land: a tearful inundation. When roused to anger, however, she would turn people and animals to stone. 'Swift retribution is hers.'

Having assumed the form of a beautiful maiden, Pele won the heart of a young chief named Lohiau, 'handsome of body'. She left him on the third night of their marriage and told him to await her messenger to bring him to the house she was making ready for him. Because it took her sisters and attendants a long time to reach the village where Lohiau lived, the young chief died of grief. Undaunted by this set-back, they recalled his spirit and restored it to the body; then, as Pele had instructed, they started back with Lohiau to the divine crater. Once again the journey was long and arduous, so much so that Pele was furious at the long delay and impetuously overwhelmed them all with fire. What annoyed her most was the open admiration of her sisters for the handsome Lohiau. As a result of this quarrel Pele's family dispersed and for a second time Lohiau's spirit wandered abroad. In some versions of the legend the young chief is restored to life again and marries Hiiaka, Pele's favourite sister.

This story of the tempestuous goddess of volcanic fire contains a profound awareness of the unexpected and inexplicable character of divinity. 'Pele has light down in the earth, without heat,' the old Hawaiians said, 'above is fire ever burning. . . . Suddenly, she will burst into lightning flame with roar and tumult.'

Pulotu

Land of the dead. The Tongans formerly believed that it was an unseen island, to which one journeyed in a boat. Almost identical with the world, Pulotu supported many of the gods and the souls of departed chiefs.

Qat

The good-natured spirit hero of Banks Island. Although some people claim him as their ancestor, this Melanesian hero never was a man: he was a vui, 'spirit'. Born of Qatgoro, a stone that burst asunder, Qat grew up and talked at once. Of his eleven brothers the most notable were Tangaro Gilagilala, 'the wise one' who understood all things and could instruct others, and Tangaro Loloqong, 'the fool', who was ignorant of everything and behaved like an idiot.

Qat created things, but not the pre-existent world. He made pigs, trees, men, and night. One myth of the origins of life and death represents a dual creation by Qat and Marawa, a spider vui. For six days Qat carved the bodies of men and women from a tree; next he hid them for three days; then for three days, he brought them forth and, by dancing and beating a drum, 'he beguiled them into life', so that they could stand of themselves. But Marawa, after his wooden people showed signs of life, dug a pit, covered the bottom of it with coconut fronds, and buried them in it for six days. On digging up these people and scraping off the earth, he found them all decomposed. This was the origin of death among men.

Friendly rivals rather than deadly enemies, Qat and Marawa helped each other in times of difficulty. More than once Marawa rescued Qat from a trap prepared by the latter's brothers. Jealous of Ro Lei, Qat's beautiful wife, and his magical powers, the brothers conspired against him. On one occasion they tried to drown Qat, seized Ro Lei, and paddled off to a distant island. Then Qat took a coconut-shell bottle and stowed all his things within it, made himself small and took his seat within it, and told his mother to throw it into the sea. So he floated in the bottle till he passed the canoe of his brothers. Eating one of his bananas, Qat threw the skin into the sea where the canoe would come along. His brothers saw it, but they would not believe Tongaro Gilagilala when he declared: 'It is Qat who has eaten this banana, and has thrown the skin here for us to see, to give us notice that he is not dead, but that he has escaped and is following us.' Only on landfall did they realize that Qat himself awaited them. The wronged brother smashed their canoe with his axe, but he asked them in future to live in harmony together.

The cannibal Qasavara, a monstrous vui, actually ate Qat's brothers when they went in search of fruit. Qat killed Qasavara, and found the bones of his brothers in the monster's food chest. He revived them by blowing through a reed, and bidding them, if they were his brothers, laugh. The Banks islanders say that the best of everything was taken from the island when Qat left them, and they looked forward to his return until comparatively recent times. Shortly after the slaying of Qasavara it is said that Qat, his wife, and his brothers, along with their possessions, left by canoe.

Rakim

Literal meaning: 'rainbow'. On Ponape, an island in the Carolines, he was the carpenter god. Through his aid the people built their houses and canoes. In Micronesian mythology the capability of a well-contructed canoe encompassed flight.

Rangi

The Maori Ouranos. So close did Rangi, 'sky', embrace Papa, 'earth', that their children could not break free from the womb. At last the children, worn out by the continued darkness, consulted among themselves, and fierce Tu-matauenga said: 'It is well, let us slay them.' But Tane-mahuta, father of the forests and of all things that inhabit them, advised otherwise. 'It is better to rend them apart', he said, 'and let the heaven stand far above us, and the earth lie under our feet. Let the sky become a stranger to us, but the earth remain close to us as our nursing mother.'

Several of the brothers vainly tried to rend apart the heavens and the earth. At last it was Tane-mahuta himself who succeeded in this titanic task. He placed his head on Papa and feet on Rangi; then he strained his back and limbs 'with mighty effort'. Slowly but surely his parents were parted.

The storm god Tawhiri-ma-tea, however, sided with Rangi against his rebellious brothers and sisters. He sent forth fierce squalls, whirlwinds, dense clouds, thunderstorms, hurricanes: he uprooted trees in the forest, levelled the open ground of bushes, and lashed the shore with surging waves. Only Tu-matauenga, the god of fierce human beings, withstood the storm god's onslaught. Tu-matauenga then turned on his cowardly brothers, and 'consumed the whole of them, in revenge of their having deserted him and left him to fight alone against Tawhiri-ma-tea and Rangi'. Since he could not vanquish the storm god, 'by eating him as his food', he left him as an enemy of man on land and sea. Their long struggle, the Maoris always claimed, was the cause of the inundation of great areas of land.

The cosmogonic succession appears as follows: from the void, Te Kore, emerged night, day and space; in the latter were evolved two formless existences, a male and a female; from these sprang Rangi and Papa, the divine parents whom Tane-mahuta separated into sky and earth; after this event, and the struggle between Tu-matauenga and Tawhiri-ma-tea, the beings hidden in the earth womb were able to increase and multiply. An alternative creation myth concerns a cosmic egg dropped by a bird into the primeval sea; it broke, not surprisingly, and out came a family, a pig, a dog, and, luckily for them all, a canoe.

Rokola

The Fijian carpenter god. He built the canoes that allowed the Fijians to navigate the seas and settle their groups of islands. During the Tuka heresy Rokola was identified with Noah by the followers of Ndugumoi, an hereditary priest. Although in 1876 the Fijians had all nominally accepted Christianity, this man led a popular syncretic movement that was the forerunner of Melanesian 'cargo cults'. Known as Navosavakandua, 'he who speaks once', Ndugumoi saw clouds full of flying chariots and taught that there were originally two gods, Jehovah and Ndengei, the indigenous snake deity. Jehovah had challenged Ndengei to make men, but the latter failed to do so and was driven away. When Ndugumoi declared the advent of the millennium and directed his followers against the British authorities, he was arrested and sentenced to a term in prison. Legends gathered round the prophet: the authorities tried to kill him without success—by dropping him down the funnel of a steamer and by putting him into the huge rollers of a sugar mill. Both the efforts of civil servants and missionaries against the Tuka heresy foundered, and long after Ndugumoi's death it was his version of Christianity that predominated.

Ro'o

The prayer chanter. On Tahiti Ro'o was a god with plenty of names: he was Ro'o-i-te-hiripoi, 'Ro'o-in-distress; Ro'o-aninia, 'Ro'o-in-dizziness'; Ro'o-tuiaroha, 'Ro'o-in-faintness'; Ro'o-i-te-mohimohi, 'Ro'o-in-dimness'; Ro'o-te-hamama, 'Ro'o-in-gaping'; and many others. Invocations to Ro'o were made to cast out diseases, and he cured the sick and the injured by driving out evil spirits. The prayer-chanter god was the son of the sky god Atea.

Sisimatailaa

In Tongan legend, the son of the sun. A woman bore Sisimatailaa because she 'used to go fishing very often and was in the habit of facing west and stooping with her back to the sun'. When the boy grew up he sailed to Samoa. There he fell in love, and so he returned to tell his parents about the impending marriage. His mother told him to climb a small hill and address the rising sun. This Sisimatailaa did, and received from his celestial father two packages; one he could open to obtain riches, the other he was to keep unopened. The wedding took place, after which Sisimatailaa suggested that they should sail to Tonga. On the voyage his bride importuned him to open the forbidden package too. Such a quantity of things came from it that the boat sank and the pair were drowned.

Ta'aroa

On the island of Tahiti, he was the supreme being and the creator deity. He was the author of life and death; he was called Rua-i-tupra, 'source of growth'; his shadows were the whale and the blue shark. Out of his own body Ta'aroa built the first *fare-atua*, 'god's house', which became the model for all temples. This house was called the bed of the great lord, roi-i-te-fatu-Ta'aroa. In 1769, on a visit to Tahiti, Captain Cook noted that 'the general resemblance between this repository and the Ark of the Lord among Jews is remarkable'.

In ancient times the people were afflicted by a great drought, and they exclaimed: 'Ta'aroa, the world maker, whose curse is death, is angry: he is consuming us!' So their king ordered the priests to pray for deliverance, but they could not please the god. Then the king said that they must tremble and abase themselves by a human sacrifice, because the gods liked human flesh, which was called long-legged fish, *te avae roroa*. It found favour with Ta'aroa and rain fell again. But this seldom happened before the deluge for the reason that the voracious war god Oro had little authority then. Victims were chosen from prisoners-of-war.

The Tahitian creation myth places Ta'aroa within the darkness of the cosmic egg. He 'developed himself in solitude; he was his own parent, having no father or mother. Ta'aroa's natures were beyond count; he was above, below, and in stone; Ta'aroa was a god's house; his backbone was the ridgepole, his ribs were the supporters.' Then the god cracked the shell, came out and stood upon the broken pieces. Peering into the primeval darkness he realized that he was alone: there was no land, nor sky, nor sea. Only a void existed. Weary of the silence and the emptiness, Ta'aroa used one part of the shell as 'the great foundation of the world, for the rocks and the soil'; another part became 'the dome of the sky'; having himself assumed the form a person, the god created everything that is now in the universe. A variant legend says that Ta'aroa made the universe from his own body, except for his head.

Taburimai

In Gilbertese mythology, the son of Bakoa, a semi-divine ancestor. The Gilbert islanders distinguished between three kinds of beings: the gods, *anti*, the demi-god ancestors, *anti-ma aomata*, and men, *aomata*.

The first offspring of Bakoa and his wife, Nei Nguiriki, were all fishes. Later were born the man Taburimai and his brother Teanoi, 'the hammer-headed shark'. Because Taburimai had a different shape, the fish children were ashamed and plotted his death. Teanoi warned Bakoa and he sent Taburimai away on the back of the shark brother. Having landed the threatened man on the island of Samoa, Teanoi gained the sky and became a star. Taburimai stayed on earth, sailed among the islands, and married a woman. Their son was the adventurous Te-ariki-n-tarawa, who claimed *uekera*, the sacred tree that reached to heaven, and took to wife Ne Te-reere, the tree goddess. From their union came Kirata-n-te-rerei, 'the most beautiful of men', the founder ancestor whose handsomeness was enough to beget children without meeting a woman.

Tagaro

In the New Hebrides, the wise and benevolent spirit hero Tagaro is opposed by Suqe-mutua, the spirit who would have all things bad. Tagaro came down from heaven, made men and other things, and went back to heaven again. Fork-headed Seqe-mutua, on the other hand, belonged to the earth, and his malevolent disposition led to his exile in a bottomless chasm, where he rules over the ghosts of the dead.

In this part of Melanesia there are various traditions concerning spirits, vui. On some islands Tagaro and his kind are held to be

The Polynesian god Tangoroa in the act of creating other gods and men

immortal and like men, except that they do not eat or drink. They are, however, only visible to the dead. Other islands have vui for sacred places and stones. One myth relates the profound gulf between Tagaro and Suqe-mutua over the nature of mankind. When they created men, Tagaro said they should walk on two legs, Suqe-mutua that they should go like pigs: happily, the word of Tagaro stood, and people built villages for themselves. The wife of the saviour of mankind was Vinmara, 'web-wing'. One day Tagaro saw winged women fly down from heaven to bathe. He noticed them take off their wings, stole one pair, and hid them in his house. He then returned to the beach and found they had all flown but the wingless one, whom he married. Later the scolding of Tagaro's brothers saddened Vinmara: she went into the house and sat weeping alone, till her tears wore away the earth hiding her wings. With their aid, she flew back to heaven.

Tane-mahuta
In Maori mythology, the father of forests and of all things that inhabit them, or that are constructed from trees. He separated Rangi, the sky father, from Papa, the earth mother, but lost place to Tu-matauenga, the god and father of fierce human beings. His chief enemy, however, was the sea god Tangaroa. In Tahiti, Ave-aitu, 'the tailed god', was the leader of the hosts of Tane-mahuta in time of war. Ave-aitu was probably a sorcerer god, envisaged as a meteor, cone-shaped with a large head and a long fiery tail.

The Hawaiians called Tane-mahuta by the name of Kane and made his antagonist the squid god Kanaloa, who was associated with sorcery and the underworld. The legends place Tane-mahuta and Tangaroa, or Kane and Kanaloa, as the good and evil wishers of mankind. They are the equivalent of the Melanesian myth about To-Kabinana and To-Karvuvu. The curse of Tangaroa, for instance, introduced death into the world.

Tangaroa
The Polynesian god of fish and reptiles. In Hawaii he was known as the squid god Kanaloa. The Maoris say that Tangaroa fled for safety to the ocean when the storm god Tawhiri-ma-tea raged on behalf of Rangi, their father.

A story from the Tuamotu Archipelago, renowned for the archetypal quality of its

legends, relates a struggle between Tangaroa, or Tagaroa, and Rogo-tumu-here, the demon octopus. Once Tagaroa sailed to the island of Faumea, a counterpart of the mysterious Hawaiian goddess Haumea. Faumea was a woman who had eels in her vagina which killed men, but she taught Tagaroa how to entice them outside. He slept with her and she bore Tu-nui-ka-rere and Turi-a-faumea. The latter married Hina-a-rauriki; the newly-weds took pleasure in surfing, but one day the demon octopus Rogo-tumu-here seized Hina-a-rauriki and dragged her down to the bottom of the ocean. So Tagaroa, Tu-nui-ka-rere, and Turi-a-faumea built a canoe. When Tagaroa recited a canoe-launching chant, Faumea withdrew the wind into the sweat of her armpit, and he had to utter a chant for its release. Tagaroa asked Faumea to hold onto Tu-nui-ka-rere, who slipped away into the sky and was lost. Only Turi-a-faumea and Tagaroa, therefore, sailed out to Rogo-tumu-here's lair. On a hook baited with sacred feathers did Tagaroa draw up the demon octopus to the surface. Tentacle after tentacle they hacked off until the monstrous head was within reach. Tagaroa cut that off and Hina-a-rauriki was drawn out from its mouth covered with slime.

According to the Maoris, the antagonism between Tangaroa and Tane-mahuta, father of the forests, dates from the time of the conflict with Tawhiri-ma-tea. Some of Tangaroa's children decided not to follow him to the ocean but, instead, they took refuge inland. Afterwards Tane-mahuta supplied the offspring of Tu-matauenga, the god of fierce human beings, with canoes, with spears, and with fish hooks made from his trees, and with nets woven from his fibrous plants, that they might destroy the offspring of Tangaroa. In revenge, Tangaroa enjoyed sinking canoes, flooding the land, and eating away the shore.

Te Bo ma Te Maki
Literally, 'the darkness and the cleaving together'. The primordial substance in Gilbertese mythology. Over this 'heaven and earth', dark and compact at the beginning of things, walked Nareau, the spider creator.

A variant creation myth has heaven and earth move, like the two hands of a man being rubbed together, so that Tabakea, 'first of all', and Na-Kaa, his brother, appear. In the darkness, called Te-bongi-ro, these gods put the universal process in motion.

To-Kabinana

A Melanesian creator hero. The New Britain islanders tell of a pre-existent spirit, 'the one who was first there', who drew two male figures on the ground, cut open his own skin, and sprinkled the drawings with his own blood. He then shaded the figures with large leaves till they emerged as two men, named To-Kabinana and To-Karvuvu.

Whilst To-Kabinana always did things of benefit to the world, To-Karvuvu never succeeded in avoiding unfortunate actions. One day To-Kabinana climbed a coconut tree, picked two unripe fruit, and threw them to the ground. They split open and released two beautiful women. To-Karvuvu admired them and asked his brother how he had come by them. Having discovered the secret, To-Karvuvu also climbed a coconut tree, picked two unripe fruit, and threw them to the ground. Unhappily, they landed point downward, and the women who came from them had flat ugly noses.

Another day To-Kabinana carved a certain fish out of wood and cast it into the sea, where it might live forever after. This grateful fish used to drive other fishes to the beach, so that To-Kabinana could simply pick them up. Impressed, To-Karvuvu carved a shark and placed it in the waves. When this ungrateful fish did not drive other fishes to the beach but ate them instead, To-Karvuvu was sorry and told his brother what he had done. To-Kabinana said: 'You are despicable. Now our descendants will suffer. That shark of yours will eat both fishes and men.'

The twin brothers represent the antithetical character of Nature. The New Britain islanders explain the unpleasant, disturbing, and fearful aspects of the world in terms of To-Karvuvu's foolishness. They say that although creation is good, and in the actions of To-Kabinana this goodness becomes actual, unfortunately he has a half-witted brother who is always interfering with what he does. To-Karvuvu, in other words, adds to creation the dark side of evil, the blood trailing from the jaws of that archetypal killer, the shark.

Tpereakl

A Micronesian creator deity. Tpereakl and his consort, Latmikaik, who arose from a wave-beaten rock, ruled the universe together. While Tpereakl lived in the sky, Latmikaik took up residence at the bottom of the sea, where she gave birth to two sons as well as shoals of fish. The earth appears to have been built by the fishes, just as the matings of certain gods and fishes produced mankind.

Wati-kutjara

The two totemic ancestors of many legendary cycles. Lizard men. One of them was called Kurukadi and his totem was the iguana; the other's name was Mumba and his totem was the black iguana. The Mandjindja in western Australia believe that the Wati-kutjara descended from the mountains during the 'dream time', the age in which the ancestral spirits sleeping beneath the ground arose and wandered the earth. The Wati-kutjara made ceremonial instruments, like the inma board: the dark patches in the Milky Way, known as *kadri-paruvilpi-ulu* or 'river course sky', are boards they placed in the sky, while those given to men on earth are the means of remaining in contact with the 'dreaming' ancestors.

When the moon man Kulu, or Kidilli, attempted to force the first women, the lizard men struck and wounded him with their magical boomerang. Kulu soon afterwards died in an obscure water hole. This was the first death. A variant states that the conical mound associated with this conflict represents Kidilli's phallus, which the Wati-kutjara cut off. And the molested women, ancestral spirits rather than the first human beings, are said to have fled to the sky and become the Pleiades.

Yalafath

The creator deity of Yap, an island in the Carolines. He was looked upon as a benevolent but indolent being, and sometimes thought of as incarnate in the albatross.

Yurlungur

The great copper python of the Murngin in northern Australia. Once two young women who had slept with men from a forbidden clan arrived at the *auwa*, the sacred place belonging to Yurlungur. It was a water hole called Mirrirmina, 'rock python's back', and in the deep subterranean waters below this water hole dwelt the ancestral snake spirit. When the older girl started to cook the animals they had caught, these creatures leapt out of the fire and ran to the sacred water hole and jumped into it. Next the older girl went out to gather bark for the younger girl's new-born baby. She approached the Mirrirmina well, and it happened that her menstrual blood fell into the water hole and was carried down to the abode of Yurlungur. The head of 'great father snake' was lying quietly on the bottom of the pit, but he opened his nostrils and smelled hard as the polluted blood drifted downwards. Yurlungur then raised his head and slowly crawled upwards. As he rose up from the bottom of the pool the well water rose too, and flooded the land. Yurlungur saw the two young women, his descendants. Although the young women chanted in order to prevent the flood from swallowing them, the ancestral snake spirit pursued and caught them. He licked them, bit their noses, and swallowed the women and the baby. Later there was a conference of snakes, each one standing very straight, and Yurlungur confessed that he had eaten his kin. So it was that he agreed to regurgitate the two young women and the new-born child.

Yurlungur is 'the great father'. His voice is thunder, and the water of the well in which he lives, shines like a rainbow. He is the 'rainbow serpent', a potent deity in aboriginal religion. Association with the weather, especially rain clouds, is found wherever tribes worship the python. Yurlungur is plainly the focus of a fertility cult: the wet season, when the waters rise and snakes come out of the ground like the new shoots of plants. One tradition has a rain chief, Ataintjina, use a serpent for rain-making. On a distant western shore, Ataintjina feeds a 'young rain man' into the jaws of a sea serpent. Inside the belly of this creature the victim lives for two years and gathers into his body 'shining shells', before he is spat out on the beach. Ataintjina then has the 'young rain man' thoroughly smoked by women: as in Murngin initiation rites, this is to make him 'strong'. Preparations are complete when the victim uses the *takula*, 'shining shell', to transform himself into a cloud. Rising into the sky, the 'young rain man' stands on his head and unties his hair, out of which rain pours to the earth. Whenever he drops a takula there is a flash of lightning. A rainbow, the watchful soul of Ataintjina, follows close to the rain-maker, who usually fastens it to his own head. The 'young rain man' having fulfilled his task, returns to the distant western shore and seeks to transform himself back into a human being. Sometimes Ataintjina obstructs this operation, inadvertently causing a drought. Otherwise the rain chief keeps ready for use his 'young rain men' and sends across the Australian continent numerous great clouds.

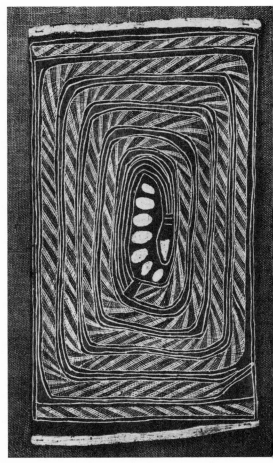

An Australian aborigine bark painting of Yurlungur, the great copper python

Further Reading

Introduction
Barthes, R *Mythologies*, trans. A Lavers, London, 1972
Blaker, C and Loewe, M *Ancient Cosmologies*, London, 1971
Campbell, J *The Hero with a Thousand Faces*, New York, 1949
Campbell, J *The Mask of God: Primitive Mythology*, New York, 1959
Frazer, Sir J *The Golden Bough*, London, 1922
Graves, R *The White Goddess*, London, 1948
James, EO *Prehistoric Religions*, London, 1957
James, EO *The Origin of Religions*, London, 1937
James, EO *The Origin of Sacrifice*, London, 1933
Jung, CG *Man and His Symbols*, London, 1964
Jung, CG *Modern Man in Search of a Soul*, New York, 1923
Jung, CG and Kerényi, C *Introduction to a Science of Mythology. The Myth of the Divine Child and Mysteries of Eleusis*, trans. RFC Hull, London, 1951
Kirk, GS *Myth. Its Meaning and Functions in Ancient and Other Cultures*, Cambridge, 1970
Malinowski, B *Myth in Primitive Psychology*, London, 1926
Malinowski, B *Sex and Repression in a Savage Society*, London, 1927

West Asia
Aldred, C *Akhenaten and Nefertiti*, London, 1973
Budge, Sir EAW *Babylonian Life and History*, London, 1884
Burrows, M *The Dead Sea Scrolls*, New York, 1956
Cerny, J *Ancient Egyptian Religion*, London, 1952
Delaporte, L *Mesopotamia: The Babylonian and Assyrian Civilization*, trans. V Gordon Childe, London, 1925
Dhalla, MN *Zoroastrian Civilization*, New York, 1922
Driver, GR *Canaanite Myths and Legends*, Edinburgh, 1956
Fraser, Sir J *Folk-lore in the New Testament*, London, 1918
Gaster, TH *Thespis. Ritual, Myth and Drama in the Ancient Near East*, New York, 1950
Grant, RM *Gnosticism. An Anthology*, London, 1961
Gurney, OR *The Hittites*, Harmondsworth, 1952
Herm, G *The Phoenicians*, London, 1975
Hooke, SH *Babylonian and Assyrian Religion*, London, 1953
Hooke, SH *Middle Eastern Mythology*, Harmondsworth, 1963
Jacobsen, T *The Treasures of Darkness. A History of Mesopotamian Religion*, New Haven, 1976
James, EO *Myth and Ritual in the Ancient Near East*, London, 1958
James, EO *The Worship of the Sky-God*, London, 1963
James, MR *The Apocryphal New Testament*, Oxford, 1924
Kaster, J *The Literature and Mythology of Ancient Egypt*, London, 1970
Kenyon, K *Amorites and Canaanites*, London, 1966
Kramer, SN *History Begins at Sumer*, London, 1958
Lang, DM *Lives and Legends of the Georgian Saints*, London, 1956
Moret, A *The Nile and Egyptian Civilization*, London, 1927
Moulton, JH *Early Zoroastrianism*, London, 1913
O'Leary, de Lacy *The Saints of Egypt*, London, 1937
Oppenheim, AL *Ancient Mesopotamia*, Chicago, 1964
Pritchard, JB *Ancient Near Eastern Texts Relating to the Old Testament*, Princeton, 1950
Pritchard, JB *Solomon and Sheba*, London, 1974
Ringgren, H *Religions of the Ancient Near East*, trans. J Sturdy, London, 1973
Steindorff, G and Seele, KC *When Egypt Ruled the East*, Chicago, 1942
Zaehner, RC *The Dawn and Twilight of Zoroastrianism*, London, 1961

South and Central Asia
Babbit, I, trans. *The Dhammapada*, New York, 1936
Bhattacharji, S *The Indian Theogony*, Cambridge, 1970
Bouquet, A C *Hinduism*, London, 1947
Coomaraswamy, A K *Elements of Buddhist Iconography*, Cambridge, Mass, 1935
Cowell, E B, trans. *The Jataka, or Stories of the Buddha's Former Births*, Cambridge, 1895–1907
Davids, T W R *Buddhism, Its History and Literature*, London, 1896
Elwin, V *The Tribal Myths of Orissa*, Oxford, 1954
Hoffmann, H *The Religions of Tibe*, trans. E Fitzgerald, London, 1961
Jaini, J *Outlines of Jainism*, Cambridge, 1940
Keith, A B *The Religion and Philosophy of the Veda and Upanisads*, Cambridge, Mass, 1925
Kramrisch, S *The Hindu Temple*, Calcutta, 1946
Lengyel, E *Asoka the Great. India's Royal Missionary*, London and New York, 1969
Levy, P *Buddhism—a 'Mystery Religion?'*, London, 1953
Nikhilananda, S, trans. *The Bhagavad Gita*, New York, 1944
Piggott, S *Prehistoric India*, Harmondsworth, 1950
Renou, L *Religions of Ancient India*, London, 1951
Zaehner, R C *Hindu and Muslim Mysticism*, London, 1959
Zimmer, H *Myths and Symbols in Indian Art and Civilization*, New York, 1946
Zimmer, H *Philosophies of India*, New York, 1951

East Asia
Anesaki, M *History of Japanese Religion*, Tokyo, 1963
Bynner, W, trans. *The Way of Life according to Lao Tzu*, New York, 1962
Cole, F C *The Peoples of Malaysia*, New York, 1945
Coomaraswamy, A K *History of Indian and Indonesian Art*, New York, 1927
Cotterell, Y Y & A B *The Early Civilization of China*, London, 1975
Needham, J *Science and Civilization in China, 2: History of Scientific Thought*, Cambridge, 1959
Sandin, B *The Sea Dayaks of Borneo before White Rajah Rule*, London, 1967
Smith, D H *Confucius*, London, 1971
Steinilber-Oberlin, E *The Buddhist Sects of Japan*, trans. M Loge, London, 1938
Waley, A *The Way and Its Power: a Study of the Tao Teh Ching and its place in Chinese Thought*, London, 1934
Watts, A W *The Way of Zen*, London, 1957

Europe
Branston, B *Gods of the North*, London, 1955
Branston, B *The Lost Gods of England*, London, 1957
Cook, A B *Zeus*, Cambridge, 1914–20
Curtin, J *Myths and Folk Tales of Ireland*, Boston, 1890
Farnell, L R *Greek Hero-Cults and Ideas of Immortality*, Oxford, 1921
Gimbutas, M *The Balts*, London, 1963
Grant, M *Roman Myths*, London, 1971
Guthrie, W K C *Orpheus and Greek Religion*, London, 1935
Kerényi, C *Dionysos. Archetypal Image of Indestructible Life*, trans. R Manheim, London, 1976
Kerényi, C *The Gods of the Greeks*, trans. N Cameron, London, 1951
Kerényi, C *The Heroes of the Greeks*, trans. HJ Rose, London, 1959
Kirk, G S *The Nature of Greek Myths*, Harmondsworth, 1974
Knight, W F C *Cumaean Gates*, Oxford, 1936
Lethbridge, T C *Gagmagog. The Buried Gods*, London, 1957
Lloyd-Jones, H *The Justice of Zeus*, Berkeley, 1971
MacCulloch, J A *Medieval Faith and Fable*, London, 1932
Murray, G G A *Five Stages of Greek Religion*, Oxford, 1925

Pallottino, M *The Etruscans*, trans. J Cremona, Harmondsworth, 1955
Piggott, S *The Druids*, London, 1968
Rees, A and B *Celtic Heritage. Ancient Tradition in Ireland and Wales*, London, 1961
Rose, HJ *Ancient Greek Religion*, London, 1946

America
Boas, OV and Xingu, CV *The Indians, Their Myths*, London, 1974
Burland, CA *The Gods of Mexico*, London, 1967
Burland, CA *Montezuma*, London, 1973
Carpenter, E *Eskimo*, Toronto, 1959
Clark, EE *Indian Legends of the Pacific Northwest*, Berkeley, 1963
Deren, M *Divine Horsemen. Voodoo Gods of Haiti*, London, 1953
Grinnell, GB *Blackfoot Lodge Tales. The Story of a Prairie People*, New York, 1892
Hemming, J *The Conquest of the Incas*, London, 1970
Johnson, EP *Legends of Vancouver*, Toronto, 1922
Kroeber, AL 'The Arapaho', *Bulletin of the American Museum of Natural History*, 1904,
  volume xviii
Matthews, W *Navaho Legend*, Boston, 1897
Morley, SG *The Ancient Maya*, Stanford and London, 1946
Rasmussen, K *The People of the Polar North. A Record*, London, 1908
Reichel-Dolmatoff, G *Amazonian Cosmos. The Sexual and Religious Symbolism of the Tukano
  Indians*, Chicago, 1971
Sahagun, Fray Bernardino de *General History of the Things of New Spain*, Utah, 1960–70
Schmidt, W *High Gods in North America*, Oxford, 1933
Sejourne, L *Burning Water. Thought and Religion in Ancient Mexico*, trans. I Nicholson,
  London, 1956
Spence, L *The Myths of the North American Indians*, London, 1914
Thompson, S *Tales of the North American Indians*, Cambridge, Mass, 1929
Valiant, GC *Aztecs of Mexico. Origin, Rise, and Fall of the Aztec Nation*, New York, 1944

Africa
Abrahamsson, H *The Origin of Death. Studies in African Mythology*, Uppsala, 1951
Brown, JT *Among the Bantu Nomads*, London, 1926
Cronise, FM and Ward, HW *Cunnie Rabbit, Mr Spider and the Other Beef. West African
  Folk Tales*, New York, 1903
Dornan, SS *Pygmies and Bushmen of the Kalahari*, London, 1925
Forde, D *African Worlds. Studies in the Cosmological Ideas and Social Values of African
  Peoples*, Oxford, 1954
Frobenius, L and Fox, DC *African Genesis*, London, 1938
Hollis, AC *The Masai*, Oxford, 1905
Little, KL *The Mende of Sierra Leone*, London, 1951
Lystad, RA *The Ashanti*, New York, 1958
Mbiti, J *Concepts of God in Africa*, London, 1970
Middleton, J *Lugbara Religion. Ritual and Authority among an East African People*, Oxford,
  1960
Parrinder, EG *African Traditional Religion*, London, 1962

Oceania
Beckwith, M *Hawaiian Mythology*, Honolulu, 1970
Christian, FW *Eastern Pacific Lands; Tahiti and the Marquesas Islands*, London, 1910
Christian, FW *The Caroline Islands. Travel in the Sea of the Little Islands*, London, 1899
Codrington, RH *The Melanesians. Studies in their Anthropology and Folk Lore*, Oxford, 1891
Elkin, AP *The Australian Aborigines. How to Understand Them*, Sydney, 1938
Furness, WH *The Island of Stone Money. Uap of the Carolines*, London, 1910
Gifford, EW 'Tongan Myths and Tales', *Bernice Pauahi Bishop Museum, Bulletin 8*,
  Honolulu, 1924

Gill, W W *Myths and Songs from the South Pacific*, London, 1876

Grey, Sir G *Polynesian Mythology and Ancient Traditional History of the Maoris as told by their Priests and Chiefs*, London, 1855

Grimble, Sir A *Migrations, Myth and Magic from the Gilbert Islands. Early Writings arranged by R. Grimble*, London, 1972

Henry, T 'Ancient Tahiti', *Bernice Pauahi Bishop Museum, Bulletin 48*, Honolulu, 1928

Roheim, G *The Eternal Ones of the Dream*, New York, 1945

Seligmann, C G *The Melanesians of British New Guinea*, Cambridge, 1910

Spencer, B and Gillen, F J *The Native Tribes of Central Australia*, London, 1899

Stair, J B *Old Samoa*, London, 1897

Thomson, B *The Fijians. A Study of the Decay of Custom*, London, 1908

Westervelt, W D *Legends of Maui, a Demi-god of Polynesia, and his Mother Hina*, Honolulu, 1910

White, J *The Ancient History of the Maori; His Mythology and Traditions*, Wellington, 1887.

Worsley, P *The Trumpet Shall Sound. A Study of 'Cargo' Cults in Melanesia*, London, 1957

Acknowledgements

The publishers wish to thank the following for granting permission to use their illustrations:

Cincinnati Art Museum: 23, 110. Cooper Bridgeman Library: 220. Robert Harding Associates: 54, 76, 103, 105. Michael Holford: 8, 26, 41, 44, 62, 64, 69, 80, 86, 90, 98, 109, 130, 144, 148, 166, 179, 189, 191, 195, 215, 229. Kansas City, Atkins Museum of Fine Arts: 79, 85. London, British Library: Frontispiece. London, Museum of Mankind: 231, 242. London, Victoria & Albert Museum: 67, 70, 83. Mansell Collection: 12, 21, 33, 34, 37, 118, 131, 139, 142, 164, 183, 196. New York, Museum of the American Indians: 185. New York, Brooklyn Museum: 168. Paris, Musée de l'Homme: 201, 204, 209, 213. Philadelphia, University Museum: 17. Photo Resources: 48, 50, 60, 81, 113, 120, 123, 125, 126, 137, 153, 173, 193, 199, 235. Ronald Sheridan: 14, 29, 31, 72, 133. Stockholm, Topografiska Arkivet: 159, 160. Sydney, Art Gallery of New South Wales: 245. Visual Arts Library: 95.

Picture research by Celestine Dars.

Maps drawn by Harold Bartram.

General Index

Names in bold print are main entries. The pages on which these can be found in the dictionary are also indicated by bold print. Thus the main entry for **Adapa** occurs on page **22**.

Abaluyia, 210, 218, 219
Abassi, 202
Abe Mango *see* Page Abe
Abraham, 20, 39, 47
Abydos, 41
Abzu *see* Tiamat
Achilles, 128, 154
Achimi *see* Itherther
Actaeon *see* Artemis
Adam *see* Satan
Adapa, 22
Aditi *see* Rishis
Adlivum *see* Sedna
Admiralty Islands, 223, 230
Adonis, 23, 130, 131, 134, 152
Adroa, 202–3
Adyok *see* Ajok
Aeneas, 128–9, 131, 157
'Aeneid' *see* Virgil
Aeshma *see* Sraosha
Aesir, 129
Africa, 170, 172, 197–219 *see also* West, East and South Africa
Agamemnon *see* Erinyes
Agbe-Naete *see* Mawu-Liza
Age *see* Mawu-Lisa
Agni, 63, 82
Agwé, 172
Ah Puch, 172, 180
Ahoeitu, 225
Ahriman, 18, **23–4**, 39, 45, 53
Ahura Mazdah, 18, **24**, 38–9, 45, 48, 53, 65
Ai Apaec, 172, 189
Aido Hwedo *see* Mawu-Lisa
Aietes *see* Jason
Aigamuxa, 203
Aisoyimstan *see* Punotsihyo
Ai-tupuai *see* Oro
Aizen-myoo *see* Fudo-myoo
Ajok, 203
Ajysyt, 97
Akamba, 197, 203
Akan, 197, 212
Akhenaton *see* Re
Akhetaton, 43
Alalus *see* Ullikummi
Alchera, 10, 225
Ale *see* Chuku
Alecto *see* Erinyes
Alexander the Great *see* Rishabha
Algonquins, 167, 177, 178, 181, 185, 193
Alilat, 24
Allah, 22
Altjira, 225–6
Aluberi *see* Kururumany
Alur, 206
Amaterasu, 97–9, 112, 114
Amazon River, 170
Amazons *see* Priam
Amenophis IV, 16
America (North, Central and South), 165–95
Amida-nyorai, 99
Amitabha, 63, 99, 110

Amma *see* Nommo
Ammon *see* Amun
Amor *see* Cupid
Amotken, 172
Amphitrite *see* Poseidon
Amrita, 63
Amun, 25, 41, 43
An, 22, **25**, 36, 51
Anansi, 200, **203**
Anana, 63–5
Anat *see* Astarte
Anchises *see* Aphrodite
Andriamahilala *see* Andriambahomanana
Andriamanitra *see* Zanahary
Andriambahomanana, 203
Angakoq, 172–3
Angra Mainya *see* Ahriman
Ankor Wat, 96, 103, 104
Annwfn *see* Pwyll
Anshar *see* Tiamat
Antichrist, 124, 129
Antiope *see* Theseus
Anu *see* An
Anubis *see* Osiris
Apache, 192
Aphrodite, 23, 128, **129–32**, 136, 141, 144, 152
Apis *see* Ptah
Apollo, 85, 124, **132**, 134, 140, 145, 157, 163
Apophis *see* Re
Apoyan Tachi *see* Awonawilona
Apsyrtus *see* Jason
Apuleius, Lucius, 9
Aqhat *see* El
Arabia and the Arabs, 22, 24, 25, 27, 45, 47, 48, 53, 197, 206
Aranda, 224, 225, 233
Arawak, 170, 182, 184
Arawn *see* Pwyll
Ares *see* Aphrodite *and* Mars
Ariadne *see* Theseus
Arjuna *see* Vishnu
Ark, 25, 242
Armenia, 52, 53
Artemis, 132, 134, 143, 163
Arthur, 124, **132–4**, 141, 146, 147, 157, 177, 188
Aruru *see* Gilgamesh
Asa, 203
Asclepius, 119, 132, **134**, 144, 192
Asgaya Gigagei, 173
Ashanti, 212, 214, 216
Ashur, 25
Ashurnasipal *see* Ishtar
Asia *see* East, South and Central *and* South-east Asia
Asia Minor, 22, 128, 132, 143, 144
Asiaq *see* Pinga
Assyria and the Assyrians, 15–53, 130
Astarte, 23, **25–7**
Asuras, 65, 73
Ataintjina *see* Yurlungur
Ataensic, 173, 178
Atai *see* Abassi
Atar *see* Ahura Mazda
Atea, 226
Athena, 132, **134**, 149, 154
Athirat, Athtar *and* Athtart *see* Astarte
Atius Tirawa, 173
Atlas *see* Prometheus
Aton *see* Re
Atrahasis *see* Enlil
Atri *see* Rishis
Atropos *see* Moirai
Attis, **27**, 39, 134, 144
Atum *see* Re
Auca, 178

Audhumla *see* Bor
Auriaria *see* Nei Tituaabine
Australia and the aborigines, 10, 193, 221–45
Auwa, 226
Avalon *see* Arthur
Ave-aitu *see* Tane-mahuta
Avolokitesvara, 61, **65**, 74, 75, 82, *see also* Kuan-yin
˜Awitelin Tsta *see* Awonawilona
Awonawilona, 174
Ayar Auca, Ayar Cachi, Ayar Manco *and* Ayar Oco *see* Manco Capac
Ayida *see* Dumballah
Az *see* Ahriman
Azra'il, 203
Aztecs, 165, 167, 169, 174, 178, 182, 185, 187, 188, 189, 191, 192, 194, 195

Baal, 25, **27–8**, 34
Babel *see* Nimrod
Babylon and the Babylonians, 9, 10, 15–53, 82, 146, 152
Bacchus *see* Dionysus
Bachue *see* Chiminigagua
Bacongo, 214
Bagadjimbiri, 226
Bahubali *see* Gommatesvara
Baiame, 226
Bakoa *see* Taburimai
Balder, 129, **134–5**, 147, 150
Bali, 96, 101, 113
Balts, 127, 156, 163
Bamapana, 226
Bambara, 216
Bamum, 218
Bank Island, 227, 234, 238, 239
Banoi, 226–7
Bantu tribes, 197, 207, 208, 218
Banyarwanda, 205, 207
Baron Samedi *see* Ghede
Baruch, 20
Basilisk *see* Bestiaries
Bastet, 28
Beelzebub *see* Satan
Behemoth *see* Leviathan
Benten, 99
Beowulf *see* Grendel
Berbers, 197, 206
Bercilak de Hautdesert *see* Gawain
Bergelmir *see* Odin
Bestiaries, 135
Bestla *see* Bor
Bhagiratha *see* Shiva
Bharadwaja *see* Rishis
Bharta *see* Gommatesvara
Bhrigu *see* Rishis
Binbinga, 227
Birrahgnooloo *see* Baiame
Bishamon-tenno, 99
Blackfeet, 188, 189
Bobbi-bobbi, 227
Bochica, 174
Bodhidharma, 99–100
Bon, 61, 82
Bonnacon *see* Bestiaries
Bor, 135
Boraro *see* Vai-mahse
Borneo, 97, 108, 112, 113
Borobudur, 96, 102
Brahma, 57, 63, **65–6**, 67, 72, 75, 78, 79, 82, 85, 87, 104
Bran, 135
Brazil, 170, 181, 184, 187, 189, 192
Brekyirihunuade, 197
Bres, 135
Briganta, Brigindo *and* Brigit *see* Dagda